Disabled Mothers

Disabled Mothers

Stories and Scholarship by and about
Mothers with Disabilities

Edited by
Gloria Filax and Dena Taylor

Canada Council **Conseil des Arts**
for the Arts **du Canada**

The publisher gratefully acknowledges the support of the Canada Council for the Arts for its publishing program.

Demeter Press logo based on the sculpture "Demeter" by Maria-Luise Bodirsky <www.keramik-atelier.bodirsky.de>

Printed and Bound in Canada.

Library and Archives Canada Cataloguing in Publication

Disabled mothers : stories and scholarship by and about mothers with disabilities / edited by Gloria Filax and Dena Taylor.

Includes bibliographical references.

ISBN 978-1-927335-29-1 (pbk.)

1. Parents with disabilities. 2. Mothers. 3. Parenting. I. Filax, Gloria, 1951-, editor of compilation II. Taylor, Dena, editor of compilation

HQ759.912.D58 2014   306.874087   C2014-900839-2

Demeter Press
140 Holland Street West
P. O. Box 13022
Bradford, ON L3Z 2Y5
Tel: (905) 775-9089
Email: info@demeterpress.org
Website: www.demeterpress.org

For the two Muriels in my life:

My mother Muriel Alcorn MacIntyre Filax
(November 9, 1921—December 15, 2012)

My sister Muriel June Filax Chimiuk
(June 5, 1949—December 8, 2013)

With love, laughter, and sorrow,
—Gloria

And for Becky and Anna,
who continue to teach and surprise me
—Dena

Table of Contents

Introduction   I
  Gloria Filax and Dena Taylor

Considering Motherhood   19

I "Where Do Babies Come From?": Meeting Joanne and Kyle:
   a Reflection on Mothering, Disability and Identity   21
   Samantha Walsh

2 Scrutinizing and Resisting Oppressive Assumptions about Disabled Parents   31
   Christina Minaki

Mothering with Disabilities   49

3 Mothering in Silence: Historical Perspectives on Deafness, Marriage, and Motherhood   51
   R.A.R. Edwards

4 It's a Miracle   71
   Katharine Hayward

5   Use of Aids and Adaptations in Childcare for Mothers with
     Spinal Cord Injury   87
     Anita Kaiser, Kathryn Boschen and Denise Reid

6   Embodying my Passions: Becoming a Radical Feminist Mother   109
     Michelle Tichy

7   Mothers with Fetal Alcohol Spectrum Disorder: A Need for
     Long Term Sustained Services   121
     Karen Nielsen and Ann Marie Dewhurst

8   Sybil   139
     Meredith Powell

9   Disabling Mothers: Constructing a Postpartum Depression   155
     Lynda R. Ross

10   My Daughter, My Selves? Motherhood, Multiplicity, and the
     Creation of Meaning   177
     Kristina Passman Nielson

11   Ideal Motherhood and Surveillance: Young Mothers with In-
     tellectual Disabilities Share Their Stories   195
     Amanda Malone

Mothers with Multiple Social "Stigmas"   215

12   Centering the Broken, Brown Body: Reflections on Disabil-
     ity, Race and Motherhoods   217
     Seema Bahl

13   Motherhood Experiences of Racialized Disabled Women   233
     Bahja Nassir

14   Non-existent & Struggling for Identity   255
     Vicky D'Aoust

Disabled Mothers and the Judicial System   275

15   Disabled Mothers: Misadventures & Motherhood in the American Courts   277
Ella Callow

16   Unruly Mothers or Unruly Practices? Disabled Mothers Surviving Oppressive State Practices in Australia   295
Carolyn Frohmader, Helen Meekosha and Karen Soldatic

The Child's Perspective   315

17   Disabled Mothers: Perspectives of Their Young Adult Children   317
Paul Preston and Jean Jacob

18   Learning How to Swim: Finding Meaning in Disability from a Daughter's Perspective   339
Gina Blankenship

Resources   349

Author Biographies   353

Introduction

GLORIA FILAX AND DENA TAYLOR

To imagine one's self as a mother, making the decision to become a mother, and acting on this choice is an act of bravery for disabled women. This is because disabled women and girls who desire children are thought to be selfish or unrealistic (Cassiman 291). Dominant discourses about mothers not only feature able-bodied women but women of a certain age who are white, heterosexual, and economically secure with a husband close at hand. Consider, then, a woman who is a mother, and disabled, but also poor, non-white, lesbian, single and/or young, and how these often stigmatized identities pulse along with disability to produce interconnecting oppressions. Continuing to mother when one has a disability or disabling illness or when one is identified as a social Other are acts of bravery in the face of cultural norms that work against disabled people.

For disabled mothers, regardless of when they became disabled, losing custody of children is an omnipresent fear, and for some–those with intellectual disabilities (Reeves) and psychiatric disabilities (Preston)–even more a risk. Rather than see the possibilities for children with disabled mothers, these children are regarded as working overtime to care for their mothers. Oppressive laws, legal practices, policies, and social service agents work in concert to make the lives of disabled mothers and their families difficult. Disabled parents face barriers to adoption and lack sufficient support with childcare, obtaining adaptive parenting equipment, transporting their children, and accessing information, as well as facing attitudinal barriers (Preston). Lack of accessible information and adequate support–medical, social, educational, and otherwise–is a major challenge to disabled mothers whose mothering is an exercise in interdependence and vulnerability (Bost) as opposed to the norm of mothering as an individualizing, independent process. Simply by being themselves, disabled mothers challenge Western society's construction of ideal motherhood and childhood.

This edited collection is rich in representing narratives and research that challenge normalized ideals of mothering and mothers that both enable and disable the daily lives of mothers with disabilities. The following sections introduce you to critical disability theory including the three dominant models of disability followed by an overview of the five sections and eighteen chapters that make up this book.

CRITICAL DISABILITY THEORY

Disability theorist Rosemarie Garland Thomson observes that a presumed correspondence between disability and femaleness has persisted throughout the history of Western thought since Aristotle declared "the female is ... a deformed male" (20). The Aristotelian notion that equates the nondisabled body with the male and the disabled body with the female has contributed to both sexism and ableism.

Thomson notes "many parallels exist between the social meanings attributed to female bodies and those assigned to disabled bodies" (19). Female bodies and disabled bodies are both assumed to be feeble bodies that "must therefore have a feeble mind" (Stone 10). Furthermore, disabled bodies are feminized by the culture and therefore considered to be dependent (Lewiecki-Wilson and Cellio 4).

The association of the female body with disability signals how "the figure of the mother is over-determined and vexed for both feminism and disability studies" (Lewiecki-Wilson and Cellio 3). Disability is invisible and often unspeakable. Those who cannot conceal impairments are shunned because they cannot help drawing attention to their bodily "imperfections" or hide their disability (Stone 11). Girls and women are also expected to stay in the background. Yet it is not possible to conceal the physical evidence of later stage pregnancy, and the presence of babies and children mean that mothers are highly visible. For disabled mothers, because concealing mothering is not an option, often their disability is exposed as well. Having a visible disability makes these mothers vulnerable to increased social surveillance and scrutiny with the concomitant moralizing about the capacity and quality of their mothering.

In her book on mothering, *Of Woman Born,* Adrienne Rich provides a poignant account of the institution of motherhood for western women, an institutional identity which is almost impossible for most women to achieve, including those who conform to social norms. While Rich did not write about disability and mothering directly, her description of motherhood as a "painful, incomprehensible, and ambiguous ground" poignantly applies to disabled mothers (15). Rich wrote about the difficulty of mothering in relation to the harshness of social norms that govern the institution of motherhood. For disabled mothers, these social norms can be even more constraining. This edited collection is about disabled mothers who have taken on the hydra-headed beast of social norms that make up the intersection of gender and disability in contemporary, western cultures. Each disabled mother represented in the stories and research that follow resists these social norms; sometimes they submit to them, often they just disappear and as often they are disappeared only to reappear as an object of another's imagining.

Narratives and stories, theory and research on disability and disabled mothers are important to understanding how disabled mothers are both subject of and subject to dominant ideas about gender roles, motherhood, mothering, and disability. Theory and research can offer ways to inform, think, and understand experiences of disabled mothers in order to disrupt myths about mothers and disability that are disabling. There are many ways of mothering and many kinds of mothers. The chapters in this book point to some of these through the voices of disabled mothers and research on mothers with disabilities.

WHO IS DISABLED?

The question of who is to be counted among the disabled is a recurring theme in discussions of disability. Who is disabled and the meaning of disability are much different when disability is regarded as a problem to be solved rather than as a condition that has been produced by social organizations, or when it is understood as an embodied revelation from which, among other things, it is possible to critique the imperative of normalcy.

Answers to the question of who is disabled influence social policy, self-identity, and possibilities to affect change. These have profound effects on people's lives. While it is useful in some circumstances to distinguish people with disabilities who are ill from those who are disabled but not ill, it is also true that many people who have physical impairments have health problems and many chronically ill people are disabled by their illnesses. Those who are ill present a challenge to the disability movement (Wolfe 253). For example, many disability movement activists reject the impulse to prevent and cure disability, while those who are ill will often look for cures and an end to their suffering. Wolfe wants the disability movement to rethink the scope of its concerns so that it does not leave ill people on the "wrong" side of those who are or are not worthy to benefit from its efforts. As Linton indicates, to count as disabled might be as simple as "you are disabled if you say you are" as long as it is recognized that disability "is mostly a social distinction ... a marginalized status" with this status assigned by a majority culture (Gill 44).

The notion that disability labels should be reserved for the healthy disabled, or at least that they should not be extended to chronically ill people, suggests that there may be a hierarchy of what counts as a disability. Beresford suggests that some illnesses or afflictions are not easily countenanced within disability activism or disability communities for fear of their association with mental illness (167). This suggests that there is a "hierarchy of impairments" that affects how people with and without disabilities regard "impairment groups" (Deal 898).

Often, defining what counts as disability falls to those who are in institutional or professional positions. Definitions are narrow so that fewer people are entitled to benefits. Yet, public recognition of disability may be refused by some who are impaired or disabled by the culture in order to avoid social stigma. In contrast the Deaf community regards itself as a distinct linguistic and cultural community that is only disabled by hearing people's inability to communicate in sign language. High functioning autistic individuals who identify as Autistic regard themselves as a distinct cultural community as well.

Titchkosky suggests another way of understanding disability. She represents disability as a social space that is constituted from disability identity, relations to the disabled body that occur between people, and the ways disability identity and inter-subjective relations to the disabled body are interpreted (48). She argues that neither disability nor non-disability can be understood merely by their objectified physicality. Instead both disability and non-disability must be understood as the lived experiences of people in relation to each other. Since the relationships of disability are further impacted by other axes of difference such as gender, race, ethnicity, class, geographical home, and, as evident in this collection, mothering, the relationships of disability are complex.

Central to identification as disabled is what terms to utilize when communicating about disability. Some writers prefer "people with disabilities" to underline that disablement is not the defining characteristic of a person. Others, including Titchkosky, refer to "disabled people" to emphasize disablement as a social process, and therefore a sociopolitical matter, that prevents certain people from access to resources and goods available to others (48). Those who follow the social model of disability argue that the phrase "people with disabilities" reflects a medical approach to disability (Shakespeare 268) and weakens the idea of disabled people as an oppressed group in society (267). Titchkosky argues that the term "people with disabilities" implies that disability is not part of what it is to be a person, not quite part of personhood thus not quite part of the self, and leaves disability as a problem (24). The phrase "disabled person" points to disability as a form of interrelatedness that shifts focus away from the individual to what Frank describes as the relational way in which bodies are inscribed by culture, how the body projects itself into social space, and the boundary of these reciprocal social relations (209). And yet, "disability is not a thing, an essence, a fixed identity, or a single kind of experience, even though language often leads us to talk about it that way" (Lewiecki-Wilson and Cellio 3).

Differences in approach to using "disabled mothers" or "mothers with disabilities" may reflect national or regional preferences. The conundrum of what words to use for the title of this book rose early in the responses from some chapter writers and made for many email exchanges in our attempts to come up with a book title. We decided that authors should use the language they felt appropriate while in the introduction we would point to some of the debates about labeling and naming including who has the power to name, describe, and analyze experience.

Whether one identifies as a disabled mother or mother with a disability, there is a need for language that can refer to group or individual identity in order to mobilize ethical claims regarding legal rights. Reference to "the disabled" is fraught with a tension between not wanting to reduce differences between people to a singular notion while wanting to take advantage of benefits that might accrue to being identified as a single political entity. "[N]ice words" such as "physically challenged" and "special people ... are often used by agencies [to] control the lives of people with disabilities" (Linton 223).

THE PROBLEM OF NORMALIZING DISCOURSE: DISABLING
THE DISABLED

> [D]isability draws the attention of fields that seek to cure, fix,
> repair, or deny its existence. *Disability is a difference that ex-*
> *ists only to be undone.* (Snyder and Mitchell 190, italics in the
> original)

Prior to the nineteenth century there was no concept of normal and abnormal, nor was there a concept of the disabled in relation to a standard (Davis
4). Davis describes how the field of statistics signified normal to mean what
is typical or most common and, as a consequence, divided populations into
standard and non-standard sub-populations. As Davis indicates, "the idea
of the norm pushes ... variation of the body through a stricter template
guiding the way the body should be" (9). The emergence of a notion of
normalcy, says Davis, creates the "problem" of the disabled person (10).

Titchkosky notes that the most authoritative representations of disability come from medical, therapeutic, and rehabilitative researchers and practitioners, pathologists, and genetic researchers (135). This model known as
the *medical model of disability* includes medical approaches to disability
that regard impairment as sickness or deformity that can and must be altered or cured through medical intervention. Similarly, a rehabilitative approach regards disability as an abnormality or a deficiency that can be altered by professionals. Social science research for the most part has taken
for granted the approach that disability is a problem to be fixed through
expert intervention as well as a form of deviance.

One of the effects of the problem approach to disability, argues Titchkosky, is that it teaches people who are not disabled that their discomfort
in the company of those with disabilities can be attributed to the people
with disabilities and that it is not related to interpretation and interaction
(141). Normalcy, according to Goffman, is a position from which one rec-
ognizes who is stigmatized (5). Stigmatization is a process emanating from
what Goffman refers to as reactions by "the normals" to that which is perceived to be undesirable (13). As Titchkosky indicates, not only do normals
have no differences that are undesirable, it is normal for them to notice those
with undesired differences (142). She notes that disability is an occasion that
consolidates normality through recognition of a problem—the problem of
disability subsumes all of a person's other attributes (144).

Medical model approaches that deal with disability as a problem inform health, education, and social science practices where disability is reduced to the condition of having a body that is a problem that can be cured, improved, or otherwise altered (Titchkosky, see chapter 5). Snyder and Mitchell argue that as long as disabled bodies are regarded as objects of an inexhaustible research, they will be "fodder for any number of invasive approaches" (187). This includes not only the interventions of medicine and therapy, but also social science research that expends the "time, liberty, and energies" of people with disabilities "without concern or adequate citation" (193).

Disciplines such as special education, physical therapy, occupational therapy, communication disorders, nursing, medicine, and adapted physical education and kinesiology often treat disability as insufficiency in need of change or normalization. This leads to an intolerance of difference that in turn leads to organized attempts to remove human differences through cures, rehabilitation, therapies, mainstreaming, or institutionalization if mainstreaming doesn't work.

What does normalization mean for disabled women when gender expectations are that women should reproduce and that motherhood and mothering are a necessary and natural outcome for a happy life? Saxton's research reveals that early "proponents of eugenics portrayed disabled women in particular as unfit for procreation and as incompetent mothers" (122). As Barile writes, "according to the cultural and socially constructed beliefs I was brought up with, it is non-disabled women's responsibility to reproduce, and I, as a woman with disabilities could not, and should not, reproduce" (225).

Compulsory sterilization of the unfit has an intimate, sorry history for disabled people (Snyder and Mitchell 186). While sterilization may be uncommon in the western world in the twenty-first century, there is still a widespread assumption that disabled women have no right to reproduce and/or that there are risks to the health and survival of the foetus and the disabled mother (Thomas 504).

When disabled women consider pregnancy or having children, a discourse of risk tempers their experience because

> [Medical discourse]…has at its core the belief that if there is
> a risk of abnormality, or the risk of worsening an already abnormal bodily condition, then steps must be taken to avoid

> it; [including] genetic counseling outlining the "risks," or the
> option/recommendation of a termination (Thomas 504).

For many of Thomas' research participants there was a sense that passing on or causing impairment in a child was unfair and irresponsible (505). Even if an impairment is not the result of 'bad genes', disabled women are thought to be 'contagious' because they are 'unhealthy' and therefore questionable in terms of their ability to birth a 'healthy' child. The offer to disabled women of genetic counseling and genetic testing serves a eugenics impulse to disappear 'abnormal conditions' through abortion. Wilson writes that genetic research has cast the body as a genetic text with disability a "flawed edition of that text" (53). Hubbard asserts that we would not tolerate tests to identify other stigmatized characteristics, for example skin color.

Children of disabled mothers are often thought to be abnormal or deviant themselves because of close proximity with their disabled parent. Mairs writes about the guilt she experienced as a disabled mother in which she worried that her children were not growing up with a 'normal' mother (qtd. in Titchkosky 212). Filax's experience is that 'poor' behavior of a child, especially school age children exposed to the hidden curriculum of middle class values, is often blamed on a mother who is different from the social norms of 'good' motherhood. And, fears of losing custody of one's children are omnipresent (D'Aoust 292).

What disabled mothers need, like most mothers, is support, nurturance, and care. Institutionalized motherhood demands that most mothers in western societies will mother in isolation. Asking for help is often taken as a fault for disabled mothers yet when 'help' comes it is often "'help' that is not helpful" (Thomas 513).

The chapters of this collection demonstrate that disabled mothers exist. Disabled mothers challenge the idea that they are not "good enough" mothers and good enough at mothering (Thomas 510). The experiences of disabled mothers make clear that "the problem of disability" is produced by social barriers that exclude them as disabled mothers (Thomas 508; Shakespeare 266).

DISABLED MOTHERS AS CULTURAL CRITIQUE: LEARNING FROM DISABLED MOTHERS

> Historically, disabled people have been objects of study but not purveyors of the knowledge base of disability. (Snyder and Mitchell 198)

> The formulation of a cultural model allows us to theorize a political act of renaming that designates disability as a site of resistance and a source of cultural agency previously suppressed— at least to the extent that groups can successfully rewrite their own definition in view of a damaging material and linguistic heritage. (Snyder and Mitchell 10)

Is it possible to think differently about disabled mothers even as disabled mothers navigate a dominant gender discourse about the inferiority of the female body and a model of disability that focuses on disability as a problem? How can we move beyond the 'fantasy' of the good mother/bad mother binary to reveal and revel in the in-betweenness of disabled mothering (Lewiecki-Wilson and Cellio 8)?

The idea of oppression is central to the *social model of disability* and effectively shifts medical and individualizing discourse of intervention and cure to a discourse of citizenship and politics (Hughes and Paterson 325). However, the social model also "proposes an untenable separation between body and culture, impairment and disability" (326) that concedes the body and impairment to the domain of medicine. Disabled people do not experience impairment and disability separately. Rather, disability is experienced from the perspective of impaired bodies that have histories and cultural meanings, including cultural meanings about mothering and being a mother. Oppression is social *and* it is embodied as hurtful. Likewise, impairment is embodied, and this embodiment structures interpersonal relationships including those of disabled mothers.

As Snyder and Mitchell indicate, impairment is "both human variation encountering environmental obstacles and mediated difference that lends groups identity and phenomenological perspective ... [E]nvironment and bodily variation ... inevitably impinge upon one another" (6-7). For example, therapeutic beliefs about disability affect disabled women's experiences, including the internalization of what it means to be a mother and mothering, and the psychic toll of "repetitiously attempting to perform activities beyond one's ability" (8). The norms and expectations of culture favour non-disabled people including non-disabled mothers. Coming to an understanding of this is a source of embodied revelation for disabled people (Snyder and Mitchell 10).

The sociality of impairment is often experienced by disabled people as stigma, prejudice, surveillance, and anxiety, or in the case of resistance strategies, as pride. As Titchkosky shows, the sociality of impairment exposes background expectancies—rules, procedures, and norms—used by people as they engage in ordinary life. She argues that inability to engage rules, procedures, and norms often relegates disability to embodied mistakes, but experiences with these background expectancies can also distinguish disability "as a place from which the culturally constituted boundaries between the expected and the unexpected, the visible and the invisible, and the doing and the non-doing of things, can be considered" (17-18). Disability can become "a way of being in the world from which we can learn" (28). For Lewiecki-Wilson and Cellio

> [n]ew forms of knowledge and values emerge from the constraints and tensions of actual embodied situationality. Disabled bodies [including those of disabled mothers] can be emergent forces of important values and actions. (15)

When it is recognized that disability experience can teach us something about culture, the need to remedy disability physically or structurally is less interesting than how disability experience illuminates the workings of the dominant culture. Snyder and Mitchell describe this as cultural diagnosis: disability functions not as an identification of abnormality but as a way to diagnose culture (12). Disability serves as a critique of the dominant culture and as a "productive locus for identification" (12). In the *cultural model of disability,* disability is a site of resistance and a source of cultural agency previously suppressed as it teaches us about alterity as a third space between normalcy and marginalization in which "words, lives, and bodies are combined in unexpected and extraordinary ways" (Titchkosky 220).

The chapters that follow demonstrate how all the various models of disability inform the research and experiences—disability as a problem, disability as socially produced, and disability as cultural diagnosis—and articulate with the norms of mothering to inform the lives of disabled mothers for better and at times for worse. Yet, there is more to disability than what theory or 'experts' have to say about the disabled. In the words of Titchkosky disability "is lived and performed in the midst of others, within exclusionary and oppressive environments, that adds to or acts upon mainstream life and 'normal' identity" (204). The lives of disabled mothers exceed the confines of the categories assigned through normalizing discourse. Significantly, the voices of disabled mothers within these chapters offer us subjugated forms of knowledge that reveal resistance and agency as well as oppression. Disabled mothers have much to teach us–if we are open to such teachings.

OVERVIEW OF CHAPTERS

In our first section, 'Considering Motherhood,' are two personal stories by women thinking about becoming mothers, one by giving birth, one by adoption. The first, by Samantha Walsh, discusses how disabled women struggle to imagine themselves as mothers in a world that is "not particularly excited" to witness such an event. She explores the writings of several authors to examine this issue, and maintains that society needs to create space for disabled mothers. The second chapter, by Christina Minaki, tells about the negative responses she experiences to her desire to be a mother. She explores how the social and cultural models of disability offer a chance to conceive of mothering differently, and what gifts a disabled mother could give to a child. "Who better to teach a child to plan, strategize, brainstorm and problem-solve than someone with a disability…Who better to teach equality, and what it truly means in real time, than a parent with a disability…."

The next section of the book, 'Mothering with Disabilities', includes nine chapters dealing with specific disabilities. R.A.R. Edwards' paper explores the rough terrain of motherhood and marriage in the Deaf community–from the early 19th century through the rise of the eugenics movement to the 21st century when Heather Whitestone, a former Miss America, announced that she was undergoing cochlear implant surgery "to be a better mother to her two hearing sons," and the controversy that ensued.

Katharine Hayward's story is a personal one about her experiences as a mother with juvenile rheumatoid arthritis, and the importance of community resources, family support, and flexibility. The chapter by Anita Kaiser, Kathryn Boschen, and Denise Reid focuses on mothers with spinal cord injury. Their review of the literature and interviews of mothers with SCI provides insights and recommendations for parents, healthcare providers, and also manufacturers of assistive technology.

The following chapter, a personal story by Michelle Tichy, a diabetic academic mother, centers on the experience of a young woman who was told from early childhood that she "must be very careful not to get pregnant." Tichy engages readers in an exploration of how the dominant paradigm can be transformed to help create a more tolerant society that embraces the diversity of mothers. The chapter by Karen Nielsen and Ann Marie Dewhurst concerns mothers with Fetal Alcohol Spectrum Disorder, and how this group of mothers can best be supported by using a strength-based approach.

Meredith Powell's story examines the ways that mothers with mental illness create self-narratives against the negative stigma surrounding them, and how they function as mothers. Lynda R. Ross' chapter is a literature review on how postpartum depression has been created and how this diagnosis disables mothers. These afflictions, she says, "have their origins, not in unhealthy women, but in unhealthy societies. These disorders would barely exist but for the untenable social, economic, and political climates in which women are forced to live their lives."

Kristina Passman Nielson's analysis brings together personal reflection on the experience of mothering and feminist and disability theory. In her autoethnography, she engages the personal, social, cultural, and political implications of the experience of motherhood from the perspective of mental illness. "If and when disability is seen as an example of human variation, of human diversity," Nielson says, "then a more inclusive view of mothering and a more humane definition of motherhood may emerge." Amanda Malone's chapter provides a qualitative account of the experiences that mothers with intellectual disabilities have with the government and other agencies. Her research project explores the lives of five young mothers, drawing on feminist theory, feminist standpoint theory, and the social model of disability.

Then come three chapters in the section 'Mothers with Multiple Social "Stigmas"' on how stigmas intersect. Seema Bahl provides a personal story and analysis of disabled mothers of color, and discusses the profound effects of racism and ableism on the disabled woman of color. She explores her body's nontraditional journey across the landscape of new motherhood as a disabled woman of color whose body continually seeks honor, dignity and visibility. Bahja Nassir examines the motherhood experiences of four racialized disabled women in a qualitative study; these women sometimes challenge Western society's construction of ideal motherhood and childhood. Vicky D'Aoust's chapter concerns the struggle for identity of lesbian disabled mothers. "We do not exist," she says, in the eyes of other communities–even lesbian communities, disabled communities, disabled mother communities, and lesbian mother communities.

These are followed by 'Disabled Mothers and the Judicial System' with two chapters on disabled mothers' experiences with oppressive legal practices. Ella Callow's research paper draws from a current national study in the United States of disabled parents involved in legal cases regarding custody of their children. Callow says efforts to keep or regain custody are more prevalent with the increasing influence of disability studies programs and Article 23 of the United Nations Convention on the Rights of Persons with Disabilities. But, she says, it is important that "the disability community acknowledge the ongoing subjection of disabled mothers by the legal system…and ensure that disabled mothers do not exist, resist and grieve in silence any longer." Carolyn Frohmader, Helen Meekosha and Karen Soldatic cover the history of and advocacy by disabled women in Australia. "The Australian nation state has long removed the children of disabled women," they say, illustrating that for many disabled women in Australia, fundamental human rights have yet to be realized. Organizations such as Women With Disabilities Australia (WWDA) are actively working to reverse the "stolen children" phenomenon as well as other injustices inflicted upon disabled mothers.

Our final section, 'The Child's Perspective', has two chapters that focus on the experiences of children raised by a disabled mother. Paul Preston and Jean Jacob report on a study of young adult children in the U.S. "Many stories are incredibly uplifting," they say, "while a few stories tell of young adults overwhelmed and vulnerable." Preston and Jacob discuss the reasons for some children being overburdened or deprived, including lack of support and other risk factors in the household. The final chapter, by Gina Blankenship, is a personal story about being raised by a mother with multiple sclerosis, and her journey to find meaning in her life, and in her mother's life. She writes, "…my mother's sacred presence in this world serves as a potent reminder to slow down, to be still, to be present, to observe, to reflect, to cultivate humility, compassion, gratitude. To be with her is to feel a sense of clarity about what really matters…."

A list of resources is included at the end: books, journals, organizations, and websites. Also, the works cited at the end of most chapters provide a great many additional sources for further investigation.

We, the editors, invite readers to think about the ways that the theory and various models of disability inform the narratives and research presented in this book in simultaneous and often intermingling ways. We hope that these writings and resources will help to further spread the attitude—to all of society, including health care workers, the court system, and governments–that disabled women can proudly claim the role of mother, and in fact have much to offer the world.

Through a somewhat convoluted process Gloria Filax was given the opportunity to work with Dena Taylor to co-edit this book. Working with Dena has been a remarkable, pleasurable, and rewarding experience. I, Gloria, was happy to add my voice to other mothers and women who write and think about mothering in different contexts. In writing about our experiences we each take up the call from Sara Ruddick that it is necessary to join "the promise of women down the ages who use writing as a tool of combat against despair, against the brutalizing of vulnerable people, against those who brutalize them" (Ruddick 3). The reality of epistemic and physical violence continues to mark the daily existence of disabled women and the lives of disabled mothers. This book was an opportunity for me to draw on my teaching in critical disability studies and to meditate on my own mothering and hidden disability, asthma, which was often debilitating especially as I mothered a young child.

Dena Taylor is not a disabled mother, but the mother of an adult disabled woman who has chosen not to mother. I, Dena, was asked by Demeter Press to edit this anthology because of my previous writing and editing experience, and involvement with the disability world. When told I would need to find a co-editor who was Canadian, a wonderful connection of friends and sisters led to me Gloria, and our working together couldn't have been nicer or easier. Her expertise was invaluable, and because of this, and also the contributors' writings, I learned a great deal in the process of editing this collection.

A note to grammarians: because this book contains writings from Canada, Australia, and the United States, different spelling and punctuation styles occur throughout. The editors have left them in their original form.

WORKS CITED

Barile, Maria. "New Reproductive Technology: My Personal and Political Dichotomy." *Living the Edges: A Disabled Women's Reader.* Ed. Diane Driedger. Toronto: Inanna Publications and Education Inc., 2006, 171-185. Print.

Bost, Suzanne. "Vulnerable Subjects: Motherhood and Disability in Nancy Mairs and Cherrie Moraga." *Disability and Mothering: Liminal Spaces of Embodied Knowledge.* Ed. Cynthia Lewiecki-Wilson and Jen Cellio. New York: Syracuse Press, 2011, 164-178. Print.

Cassiman, Shawn A. "Mothering, Disability and Poverty: Straddling Borders, Shifting Boundaries, and Everyday Resistance." *Disability and Mothering: Liminal Spaces of Embodied Knowledge.* Ed. Cynthia Lewiecki-Wilson and Jen Cellio. New York: Syracuse Press, 2011, 289-301. Print.

Coleman Brown, Lerita M. "Stigma: An Enigma Demystified." *The Disability Studies Reader.* 3rd Edition. Ed. Lennard J. Davis. New York and London: Routledge, 2010, 179-192. Print.

D'Aoust, Vicky. "Non-existent & Struggling for Identity." *Lesbian Parenting: Living With Pride & Prejudice.* Ed. Katherine Arnup. Charlottetown: Gynergy Books, 1995, 276-296. Print.

Davis, Lennard J. "Constructing Normalcy." *The Disability Studies Reader.* 3rd Edition. Ed. Lennard J. Davis. New York and London: Routledge, 2010. 3-19. Print.

Deal, M. "Disabled People's Attitudes toward Other Impairment Groups: A Hierarchy of Impairments." *Disability and Society* 18.7 (2003): 897-910. Print.

Frank, Arthur. "From Disappearance to Hyperappearance: Sliding Boundaries of Illness and Bodies." *The Body of Psychology.* Ed. Henderickus J. Stam. London: Sage Publications, 1998. 205-32. Print.

Hubbard, Ruth. "Abortion and Disability: Who Should and Should Not Inhabit the World?" *The Disability Studies Reader.* 3rd Edition. Ed. Lennard J. Davis. New York and London: Routledge, 2010. 107-119. Print.

Hughes, Bill and Kevin Paterson. "The Social Model of Disability and the Disappearing Body: Towards a Sociology of Impairment." *Disability and Society* 12.3 (1997): 325-340. Print.

Lewiecki-Wilson, Cynthia and Jen Cellio. Introduction. *Disability and Mothering: Liminal Spaces of Embodied Knowledge.* Ed. Cynthia Lewiecki-Wilson and Jen Cellio. Syracuse: Syracuse University Press, 2011. 1-18. Print.

Linton, Simi. "Reassigning Meaning." *The Disability Studies Reader.* 3rd Edition. Ed. Lennard J. Davis. New York and London: Routledge, 2010.

223-236. Print.

Miller, Toby. *The Well-Tempered Self: Citizenship, Culture and the Post-modern Subject.* Baltimore and London: The Johns Hopkins University Press, 1993. Print.

O'Reilly, Andrea. Foreword: Rocking the Cradle to Change the World. *Rocking the Cradle: Thoughts on Motherhood, Feminism and the Possibility of Empowered Motherhood.* Ed. Andrea O'Reilly. Toronto: Demeter Press, 2006. 7-31. Print.

Preston, Paul. "Parents with Disabilities." International Encyclopedia of Rehabilitation. Ed. J. H. Stone, M. Blouin. 18 Sep 2013. Web. http://cirrie.buffalo.edu/encyclopedia/en/article/36/

Rich, Adrienne. *Of Woman Born: Motherhood as Experience and Institution.* 10th Anniversary Edition. New York & London: W. W. Norton & Company, 1986. Print.

Ruddick, Sara. Preface: Good questions … I'll Be Writing On This. *Rocking the Cradle: Thoughts on Motherhood, Feminism and the Possibility of Empowered Motherhood.* Ed. Andrea O'Reilly. Toronto: Demeter Press, 2006. 1-6. Print.

Saxton, Marsha. "Disability Rights and Selective Abortion." *The Disability Studies Reader.* 3rd Edition. Ed. Lennard J. Davis. New York and London: Routledge, 2010. 120-132. Print.

Shakespeare, Tom. "The Social Model of Disability." *The Disability Studies Reader.* 3rd Edition. Ed. Lennard J. Davis. New York and London: Routledge, 2010. 266-273. Print.

Snyder, Sharon L. and David T. Mitchell. *Cultural Locations of Disability.* Chicago: University of Chicago Press, 2006. Print.

Thomas, Carol. "The Baby and the Bath Water: Disabled Women and Motherhood in Social Context." *Maternal Theory: Essential Readings.* Ed. Andrea O'Reilly. Toronto: Demeter Press, 2007. 500-519. Print.

Thomson, Rosemarie Garland (1997). *Extraordinary Bodies: Figuring Physical Disability in American Culture and Literature.* New York: Columbia University Press. Print.

Titchkosky, Tanya. *Disability, Self, and Society.* Toronto: University of Toronto Press, 2006. Print.

Wilson, James. "Disability and the Human Genome." *The Disability Studies Reader.* 3rd Edition. Ed. Lennard J. Davis. New York and London: Routledge, 2010. 52-62. Print.

Wolfe, P. "Private Tragedy in Social Context? Reflections on Disability, Illness and Suffering." *Disability and Society* 17.3 (2002): 255-67. Print.

Considering Motherhood

1.

"Where Do Babies Come From?"

Meeting Joanne and Kyle: a Reflection on Mothering, Disability and Identity

SAMANTHA WALSH

INTRODUCTION

In thinking about how I would approach the topic of disability and motherhood for the purposes of this chapter, I struggled to find a way to encapsulate how my lived experience was mediated through my culture and shaped my relationship to my disability and my potential as a mother. I open the piece with a narrative reflection on my first experience of consciousness about disability and mothering. I then move through how cultural and social experience would create not only an external social tension around disability and mothering, but that the tension would be so great it would engrain itself on my body. To think about this experience I use the work of Dorothy Smith, Debra Gimlin, Rod Michalko and Tanya Titchkosky. I endeavour to move between the need for a shift in the social position of disability and the importance of allowing disabled women positive archetypes of themselves as mothers.

"WHERE DID SHE GET THE BABY?"

The first woman I met who had children who was also disabled[1] was at a wheelchair basketball training camp. I was fourteen years old. I had never met anyone who was disabled and had children. At that time I didn't make the connection that what I was witnessing was a mother and child. We were sitting in an orientation meeting; I kept wondering why there was a small boy about my age who kept following this woman in a wheelchair. I decided it was likely her nephew and that maybe his mom was late. While this was a plausible story and one that makes sense, my reason for the story was that I did not think someone with a disability could be a mom.

In my imagination the little boy's mom is a walking "able" person.[2] Later I learned that the little boy was the son of the woman I had seen in a wheelchair. His mom's name was Joanne and she had spina bifida. I found this shocking, but kept it to myself because wheelchair basketball training camp is not a place to be social and the other more senior women seemed to be un-phased by the fact that Joanne was raising a young boy. I found myself wondering though, *"Where did she get the baby?"*

This question seems absurd given obvious biological explanations for where babies come from. My confusion about where Joanne got her baby speaks more to my own confusion about disability and motherhood. My curiosity with her experience as a disabled mother came from my own experience as a disabled youth. At the age of fourteen, I hadn't been exposed to any positive representations of mothers who were disabled. Moms on TV who were sick or unable to move were positioned as burdens or the undoing of their children's sanity. While I knew adults who were disabled none of them had children or the ones who did were dads. The only present hint that mothering and disability co-existed was in discussions with my own mother where she would speak about what it would be like when I had kids. I also grew up with a number of toys and dolls that were reflective of "pretending" or "learning" to mother. Today my connection to motherhood and disability is shaped by my experiences as a disabled woman, a scholar, and activist. Further, I reflect on mothering as a woman considering her own fertility and cultural obligations. I feel I am called to enact the intersectionality between my gender and disability; I feel obligated to have children, to be a mother to prove my capacity and prowess as mother. I want to change the social imagination that the woman who uses a wheelchair is by default the aunt or childless friend. I am aggravated by media stereotypes of disabled mothers as inadequate; I want to avenge the ignorance of my fourteen-year-old self and create an image of plausible disabled mothering. There is only one issue with my mothering aspirations; I do not currently understand myself as having a need or desire to have children. It is this disconnect between my lived experience and my frustration/sense of obligation to confront a lack of social space and a lacking common social imagination for disabled mothering that troubles me. This trouble comes from thinking about how it is a young disabled woman such as I could ever be confused about who can mother and why not a disabled mother? Further, if I think of myself as a product of my culture, what has my culture done to instill in me, a disabled woman, the notion that a disabled mother cannot exist? How did I make it 14 years believing the disabled mother was a mythical creature? Moreover, is the world being robbed of amazing potential mothers because we as a collective society do not propagate the social imagination of a disabled mother? What if instead there was a discourse that society could not afford to exclude the disabled mother from the concept of mothering?

RULING RELATIONS: DOROTHY SMITH

To explore these questions and concepts I turn to Dorothy Smith and the notion of ruling relations. She explores this concept in the following way:

> That extraordinary yet ordinary complex of relations that are textually mediated, that connect us across space and time and organize our everyday lives—corporations, government bureaucracies, academic and professional discourses, mass media, and the complex of relations that interconnect them. (Smith, *Institutional Ethnography* 10)

She endeavors to think about dominant power structures of organizations and how they influence specific individuals with various identities. Smith explores the taken-for-granted power dynamics and structural discourse which inform one's lived experience.

Smith's work would suggest I was able to believe that there was no conceivable "Disabled Mother" because of a social atmosphere which did not lend itself to creating one. Early in this piece I reflected that I had not seen a positive or functional representation of disability and mothering within the media, that disabled adults I had met did not have children or were dads. Smith would suggest that this lack of representation or negative representation would be part of the "Ruling Relations" that would impress upon me that motherhood and disability could not exist. Smith would also suggest that this powerful discourse would be re-enforced through various micro-aggressions. Smith describes ruling relations as "forms of conscious-ness and organization that are objectified" (*Institutional Ethnography* 13). What she means is that they are external to consciousnesses; they organize knowledge along ideological lines and produce values to regulate other con-sciousnesses. Relations are arranged to privilege some and subjugate oth-ers through subtle micro-aggressions that teach people how they ought to function within the organizations to which they belong.

This concept suggests that my confusion as a young person over dis-ability and mothering and my sense of obligation to disturb my culture is linked. Prior to gaining an understanding that there was a dominant dis-course permeating my culture I was caught up in it without any knowledge. Now positioned as an academic and with far more lived experience I am able to recognize that there is a social discomfort about disability and mothering within the modern western culture I live in.

WHO GETS TO MOTHER?

In my article "'What Does It Matter?': A Meditation on the Social Position-ing of Disability and Motherhood" (Walsh 87-95), I reflect on the dominant social narrative that motherhood and disability cannot exist. In this writing I explore a discussion I have with an esthetician who is panting my nails. She informs me "There are just some things you can't handle." (She is implying I cannot handle being a mother because I am disabled). She goes on to say "Listen, you don't want kids anyway, so what does it matter?"

I use this conversation as an occasion to explore what dominant narra-tives of disability and mothering are, but also to explore my own position on the matter of mothering and disability. I am struck by the notion that from a common sense perspective mothering and disability only becomes an issue for consideration if one wants children. That without a profound want the notion of reproduction becomes a non-issue. In some cases pro-creation and opportunities for disabled mothers are taken up as emergen-cies or unfortunate events. For example: on May 4, 2012 the *Toronto Sun* reported on a local couple who identifies as having cerebral palsy[3] fighting with the Children's Aid Society to keep their baby shortly after it was born (Rush & Li). The Children's Aid Society's assumption that disability is tan-tamount to a lack in the ability to parent speaks to the "ruling relations" of society — the notion that a discourse exists that positions disability as lack and therefore an unacceptable characteristic for someone shaping another's character. Moreover, the actions of the Children's Aid Society serve as a warning (micro-aggression) to others who are disabled and wish to have a child. You not only have to negotiate a culture that allows you almost no point of reference or validation of your experience, but you may also be shamed by your culture for attempting to Mother.

RE-THINKING MOTHERHOOD

In this writing I seek to explore the same issue but to explore it both from how mothering and disability is positioned within the mainstream, and also how this taken-for-granted assumption writes itself on my own consciousness and how this would impact disabled women imagining themselves as mothers. Am I not a mother because my culture has warned me against taking such action? Would my relationship to mothering be different if I lived within a discourse that celebrated and supported disabled mothers?

In my earlier writing and much of my advocacy work I have sought to change the minds, attitudes and raise the consciousness of a theoretical hegemonic gaze. When I wrote about re-thinking motherhood I imagined those re-thinking it would be from a "temporarily able bodied" community. It has only been when reflecting on what I would write when revisiting the topic of disability and motherhood that I am called to think about meeting Joanne and my own internalized understanding of who and what makes a mother. Disturbed by this intense back and forth between my culture and my body, I think about the work of Debra Gimlin. She illustrates the connection between the body and culture.

> [...] The body is a medium of culture. It is the surface on which prevailing rules of a culture are written. The shared attitudes and practices of social groups are played out at the level of the body, revealing cultural notions of distinctions [...] cultural rules are not only revealed through the body; they also shape the way the body performs and appears (Gimlin 3)

If I am to think along with Gimlin, it makes sense that I as a teenager was confused about a disabled body producing a baby. Her work also illustrates the tension I feel as an adult disabled woman about reproduction. I am in a symbiotic interactional relationship with my culture and my body.

My body is written on by the culture and my body becomes the culture. I think back to the statement of second wave feminists on how the personal becomes the political. The discourse I experience is not only an individual perception; it is not an individual understanding of who or what is a mother. I am the product of a culture. I am the production of a culture that says there is a specific body for mothering and it is not the disabled body.

When I think about the disabled body and why it is that the disabled body is not the body of a mother, I am called to the work of Rod Michalko. Michalko contends that in contemporary culture disability is defined as something that is diminishing to life, stigmatized as unworthy or inferior, positioned as the opposite of "normal," desired or ideal. Disability, he writes, is something that must be silenced as a way of masking the unnatural "nature" of normalcy, a socially constructed concept. Disability becomes something that is kept far away, overcome, or removed. Michalko highlights his point using language and normative description of disability as an example. He writes:

> In fact such people, "normals" [people not identified as disabled] often say, 'I don't even think of you as disabled,' or, 'You know, I sometimes don't even notice her disability.' And visibly disabled people themselves, tacitly acknowledge their disability, often saying things like, 'I am a person, just like you. Treat me as a person.' (Michalko 69)

The discourse that disability somehow negates personhood is conceptualized in the example of the "treat me as a person" remark. Michalko's work allows for insight into why it would be confusing for me at fourteen years old to understand a disabled woman as a mother. The act of mothering encompasses reproducing a human and teaching them the nuances of the culture they now share with their mother. It is evident that if disability calls into question personhood, then disability disrupts motherhood. Michalko's work is further corroborated by the writing of Tanya Titchkosky, who observes that disability is often buried in a common sense perception of something gone wrong.

Titchkosky's point that disability is often understood as restriction due to a biological abnormality further compounds why disability and motherhood would be incompatible in my young mind and within my culture. This is not to say that she and I are not aware that disabled people "do not do some things in the ways that non-disabled people do, or may not do some things at all." However, Titchkosky insists that "disability highlights how things are 'normally' done [and] the background expectancies that order this doing in a culture" (15). To that end, she says, the notion that people with disabilities must point out to others that they are people first "highlights the sorry state of affairs of living in a culture whose conception of people is such that 'disabled people' do not quite fit, and the contrary thus remains something of which others need to be reminded" (24). The work of Michalko and Titchkosky allow for an understanding and a realization of how disruptive the notion of disability can be to the concept of motherhood.

There is a cultural need to remove and separate disability as means to preserve or create personhood. According to this cultural understanding, disability is something that inhibits my personhood, so much so that I cannot model what it is to be a person to another person. This cultural position of disability somehow negating personhood and rendering someone unfit to be a model to another person is in fact so encompassing that it was easily able to permeate my own sense of being at age fourteen. I am reminded of Smith's own experience of negotiating how ruling relations and dominate discourse play a role in her own life. She writes:

> Riding on a train not long ago in Ontario I saw a family of Indians [sic]—woman, man, and three children—standing together on a spur above a river watching the train go by. I realized that I could tell this incident—the grain, those five people seen on the other side of the glass—as it was, but that my description was built on my position and my interpretations. I have called them "Indians" and a family, I have said they were watching the train. My understanding has already subsumed theirs. Everything may have been quite different for them. My description is privileged to stand as what actually happened because theirs is not heard in the contexts in which I may speak. (Smith, *The Conceptual Practices of Power* 25)

In this example, Smith seeks to explicate her own standpoint, knowledge and privilege, which allow her to interpret what she is seeing on the train. She writes down her perspective and then challenges it by highlighting that this perspective is the only one being privileged at the time, and the "standpoint" of the "Indian" "family" may be entirely other to her own interpretation. Further, their vantage point is not allowed to enter the ethos of the knowledge production within Smith's writing; they are invisible. I parallel my own experience with Joanne and her son with Smith's analysis of her own assumptions. I would contend that my assumption that Joanne could not be her son's mother, despite witnessing an interactional performance that might suggest a mother and son, speaks to my internalization of dominant ways of knowing who is a mother and what she looks like. And, as Smith points out, the assumed native family's perspective is not even brought into her thought process. This can be thought of as a parallel to me reflecting on my cultural relationship to motherhood; there are disabled mothers that exist within my culture whose experiences are not privileged and knowledge and crafts not legitimised.

The predominant image of mothering is done by an able bodied woman. Smith's own sense that she is captive to dominant discourses and privileges a specific kind of knowledge despite being a Doctor of Sociology who writes on the position of power provides me with an opportunity to think of my own relationship to dominant discourses around disability and mothering. I reflect back to my claim made earlier to not having a profound need to mother. I wonder how much of my choice is informed by a culture that is not particularly excited for me to be a mother. When there is no space for a social figure such as a disabled mother the very concept becomes unintelligible to all. While it remains true, we as a society need to re-think who mothers and why. We as a society also need to create social space for a fluid notion of mothering. There needs to be conscious imaging in all aspects of society which brings life to the disabled mother. She is not a mythical creature who only appears by fluke. It is not enough to simply allow or tolerate the disabled mother. We need the reaction of a fourteen-year-old girl upon seeing a disabled mother to be "Can I hold your baby?" rather than "Where did she get the baby?"

NOTES

[1] I switch between the two phrases person with a disability and disabled person deliberately. I like disabled person because it speaks to the cultural experience of disability. However, I recognize that person with a disability is preferred in common lexicon.

[2] Joanne and I have remained friends. I briefly consulted her before writing this chapter. My original intention was to try and co-author something with her, but time did not allow. Joanne has been a fantastic example to

me as a disabled woman. She has completely shifted my imagination for what is possible for me as a woman who has a disability. Her son is now a grown adult with a son of his own. Joanne blogs and is an advocate of people with disabilities being supported and accepted as parents. She has written on the topic within her blog: "East Meets West: Sam and Jo's Perspective" (http://eastmeetswexx.blogspot.ca/2013/01.html)

[3]Cerebral palsy is the medical condition I have. I find the reporting on this issue particularly disturbing. The Canadian media focused disproportionately, I feel, on "how the baby was conceived", the financial status of the couple, and that they would have lots of "help" with the baby. I question why any of this had to be highlighted as it is typical of young couples to: have sex, struggle with money, and need help with a new baby.

WORKS CITED

Gimlin, Debra. *Body Work: Beauty and Self-image in American Culture.* California: University of California Press, 2001. 3. Print.

Michalko, Rod. *The Difference that Disability Makes.* Toronto: University Of Toronto Press, 2002. Print.

Rush, Curtis, and Anita Li. "Disabled couple thrilled they'll be able to keep their baby." Toronto Star. 04 may 2012: n. Web. 1 Apr. 2013. <http://www.thestar.com/news/gta/article/1173602>.

Smith, Dorothy. *The Conceptual Practices of Power: A Feminist Sociology of Knowledge.* Toronto: University of Toronto Press, 1995. Print.

Smith, Dorothy. *Institutional Ethnography: A Sociology for People.* Oxford: AltaMira Press, 2005. Print.

Titchkosky, Tanya. *Reading & Writing Disability Differently: The Textured Life of Embodiment.* Toronto: University of Toronto Press, 2007. Print.

Walsh, Samantha. "'What Does It Matter?': A Meditation on the Social Positioning of Disability and Motherhood." *Disability and Mothering: Liminal Spaces of Embodied Knowledge.* Ed. C. Lewiecki-Wilson and Jen Cellio. 1st. New York: Syracuse University Press, 2011. 87-95. Print.

2.

Scrutinizing and Resisting Oppressive Assumptions about Disabled Parents

CHRISTINA MINAKI

INTRODUCTION

I am a disabled woman with future plans to adopt. This article will centre around the extremely ableist reaction of my close relative upon his finding out about this aspect of my future plans, while in conversation with my mother. His explosive questioning of both my mother's motives and mine showed how medical conceptions of disability shape meanings assigned to disabled (would-be) mothers, and the oppressive assumptions that under-pin society's 'normal' notions surrounding disability and the ableist expec-tations of mothering 'independently' instead of interdependently. I make use of one particular personal story in order to unpack cultural assumptions that make it possible for my relative to ask my mother how she could have 'allowed' me to have such a 'ridiculous' plan as to 'traumatize' my adopted child through exposure to my disability and — he assumed — the forced role of caregiver. What cultural beliefs allow for the possibility of my desire to parent to be met with the rejoinder: "Have you thought of who will take this poor child to the mall?" My paper will examine how I am regarded as 'below consideration' for motherhood. Using brief excerpts from two novels, I will also analyze examples of motherhood as portrayed in fiction, and discuss how such portrayals can serve either to reinforce or disturb and reshape ableist misconceptions of motherhood. I will explore how the social and cultural models of disability offer us a chance to conceive of mothering differently, and I will 'talk back' to oppressive assumptions surrounding disability and mothering, in order to counter the assumption that disability will only take away from a child's experience of mothering.

MOTHERHOOD AND ME: THE SHAPE OF MY DREAM

I have always known that, however complex the decision to adopt is for anyone, as a disabled woman, the process would be even more hurdle-ridden for me.

Growing up, I understood that being a mother with cerebral palsy meant that I would require assistance to perform some of the physical tasks of mothering. In our lives together, my child and I would need to live and work with others who would 'be my hands', and in so doing become part of our circle. Waiting for others to 'be your hands' (and feet) is not always a pleasant wait, and instructing others, negotiating styles, approaches, compromises and interdependence is a complex process. But if it is acceptable for an able-bodied mother to hire a nanny, to make juggling parenting, career and domestic responsibilities possible, why is this course of action assumed to be taboo for me?

These challenges and complexities accompany the joy of a full, multi-faceted life, with all its shades of grey. But in our ableist, 'normal' society, I am labelled as 'problem' because I have the nerve to entertain a plan to make the role of mothering real for me. This points to the fact that our society only understands disability as a hindrance that makes parenting truly impossible.

Until quite recently, only my most immediate family members knew about my future plans to adopt. It was after my father's death, however, that a slightly more removed – yet still close – relative discovered these plans.

I can summarize his reaction this way: he was furious. He confronted my mother, asking how she could support such a 'ridiculous' idea, when she knew it would mean 'subjecting' a child to my disability. He was clearly incensed, and — with me absent from the conversation and therefore unable to defend myself and my true intentions — he accused my mother and me of using adoption as our means to hatch a plan wherein my child would become my future caregiver. He was upset by my 'thoughtlessness' in wanting to 'drag a child into' such a 'mess' as life with me as a disabled mother. He wondered if we had ever thought of how 'embarrassed' my adopted child would feel about my disability, and if we had considered who would take the 'poor child' to the mall.

The complex injustice of this incident fueled my analysis and reflections in this chapter, and showed me that my battle to become an adoptive parent begins now—long before any child enters my home as mine.

The battle begins over the *idea* of me as a disabled parent.

DON'T BE SHY, TELL ME HOW YOU REALLY FEEL...

My relative's concept of my disability is completely governed by the medical model, wherein there is an accepted norm for disability and disabled people—a norm for the "abnormal". According to this worldview, disability is a powerless, ineffectual state, indicating only limitation and lack. It is, furthermore, in need only of care, and giving only an occasion for the non-disabled world to act out on it—in pity, ignorance, arrogance, compassion, etc. Note the words of Rosemarie Garland Thomson:

> ...[D]isabled women must...defend against the assessment of their bodies as unfit for motherhood or of themselves as infantilized objects who occasion other people's virtue. Whereas motherhood is often seen as compulsory for women, disabled women are often denied or discouraged from the reproductive role...Making disabled women the objects of care risks casting them as helpless in order to celebrate nurturing as virtuous feminine agency. (26)

Disability, taken this way, is passive. No parenting possible here. In fact, to consider parenting as a disabled woman — or man — according to this perspective, is the neck-breaking height of high hopes. (It is worth noting that according to this faulty logic, *of course* no one could parent with a broken neck.)

It is impossible for me to ignore the fact that, while my relative had a heated conversation with my mother about my parenting plans, he has never spoken directly to me about it, and is not open to doing so. His refusal is one more way in which my voice (a voice of disability) is silenced. He has not given me an opportunity to discuss with him the legitimacy of my plans and intentions, the degree of thought I have put (and am putting) into them, and the detailed structure of support and financial resources I know I will need before I undertake this.

Resistance to disabled women as mothers (or disabled people as parents) is wrapped in the misconceived link between disability and incompetence. There is a super-competence immediately associated with being mothers, and working mothers. Competence itself is assumed to possess, to require, an able body in order to exist. Competence does not assume the presence, viability or vitality of the disabled body. 'Flawless' competence, however, is an illusion. The 'super-competent' body (able to do it all and have it all, all the time, with little to no help) is in fact unreal and unreachable for anyone, yet it is touted as the only way to be.

My disability is misconstrued as suitable grounds for my erasure from the scene of parenthood. Disability is understood as a tragedy, an embarrassment, the culprit blamed for my "reduced life chances" (Goffman 5). My mother and I are blamed for having the nerve to consider 'dragging' a child into my 'mess' — the mess of disability. This demonstrates that our everyday lives with and in disability have much to reveal, upon analysis, of the cultural conceptions and assumptions that organize the ongoing marginalization of disabled people. My relative's question, "Have you thought of who will take this 'poor' child to the mall?" underscores his prejudicial belief that a child entrusted into my disabled hands is to be pitied, and also brings into specific relief his rejection of any understanding that I myself could chaperone such an outing. Taken further, his conceptualization of disability as lack, coupled with his ideas about disability's synonymous relationship with incapacity and shame made him question even whether I *should* make such a trip, with my child in tow. In the face of such oppressively normative assumptions, even going to the mall as a disabled person (in a society where many believe such an everyday act to be impossible and/or embarrassing for disabled people and their 'traumatized' companions) is an act of resistance. There is something else very unsettling or troubling going on here. If it is embarrassing to be with a disabled mother in the mall, what about disabled children? Are they to be shut away at home, kept out of the public?

The mall is an epicentre of consumerism. With its constant barrage of advertising, super-thin models, and a city of clothes and products and confusing, potentially damaging messages about body image, the mall will not be the focal point of my strategy for raising my child. While there is something to be said for bonding during occasional shopping trips, the mall is also the place where 'normal' conceptions of the body are reinforced. If anything, I will be using the mall to teach my child about the many oppressions that come from clinging to 'normal' as an absolute.

Unavoidable too, is the knowledge that it is not only my competence being questioned and denied here. I am disabled and therefore would be a 'bad' mother (because disability is by definition 'bad'), and also my mother is a 'bad' mother for supporting my 'foolish' plan. My relative's anger was palpable as he thundered over the 'threat' of my ambition to overthrow everything he thinks of as 'normal' about parenting. He railed about my 'thoughtless' lack of judgment—thus framing my disability as an 'obvious' reason to question my decision-making and logic, on this topic at least. The link between disability and selfishness was made stunningly quickly by my relative. It did not occur to him that I want to adopt a child in order to care for him or *her*, not because I expect the reverse.

The assumption that life with me would be a life of servitude and caregiving is offensive, but also indicative of the idea of disability as burden, which is so prevalent in society.

DISABLED MOTHERS IN LITERATURE

In my professional roles as librarian, author and book reviewer, it did not take me long to notice that, in the majority of fiction I read within these professional roles, disability was being portrayed in disparaging ways. Disabled characters either died, were cured, or 'beat' their 'tragic' embodiments through overcoming them and doing what disabled people 'should not' be able to do. While reading these books, I often remembered my own painful experiences of exclusion while growing up. This pain was repeated as I read fiction that erased disability either by ignoring it completely or releasing it in oppressive ways that were made to appear 'normal'.

My own experiences have convinced me that instead of being upheld, normalcy as absolute must be deconstructed and toppled, and its oppressive nature exposed. Just as literature can be (and is) so often used to more deeply entrench normalcy's unquestioned position, it can (and must) be used to shake that unquestioned position. To that end, I will now discuss excerpts from two novels: *Chanda's Wars* (Stratton, 2009), and *The Poisonwood Bible* (Kingsolver, 1998). My discussion will illustrate some of the ways in which disability and motherhood can powerfully interact.

"DON'T WISH FOR THAT": DISABILITY PORTRAYAL IN ALLAN STRATTON'S *CHANDA'S WARS*

Chanda's Wars is a young adult novel about child soldiers. While disability is not the focal point of its subject matter, there is a secondary character in the novel, a black African woman named Auntie Lizbet who has a club foot. In the following passages, Auntie Lizbet's difference is written as something to fear, something sinister, which makes her character evil, murderous, and other-than-human. I include it here to illustrate how disability is vilified and divorced from motherhood in literature, a major vehicle in entrenching oppressive attitudes surrounding disability.

> "Then there's Auntie Lizbet and her funny shoe. Her left foot is really a hoof."
> "I remember the hoof," Soly says solemnly.
> "And remember her tail, swishing under her dress? And the sharp little horns under her bonnet? Auntie Lizbet's a witch. If you're not careful, she'll come in the middle of the night and eat you."
> "She will not."
> "Will too. And then she'll throw up." (Stratton 78)

Auntie Lizbet is written above entirely in animalistic terms. Her club foot (referred to as a 'hoof') is tied up with her assumed sinister intentions. She is a witch who eats (and vomits) children – a witch with a hoof, horns and a tail. She is written as perilous. Also, her club foot, which is truly a part of her body, is brought into the space between the two children along with manufactured, fear-inducing embodiments (horns, sharp teeth) which have been fabricated to reinforce the notion that Auntie Lizbet's difference means only trouble. The idea that she does her fearful deeds at night extends the dread of her 'crimes'. She and her embodiments become part of a mythology that conceives of difference as troubling, even horrifying. This is another 'normal' way to perceive of difference as a great danger, signifying great, impending doom. Paul Darke puts it this way:

> [T]he role ... [stereotypical] images have had in the perpetu-
> ation of the disablement of impaired people ... [is] that they
> tap into ...a 'normal' psychological fear of bodily decay and
> death ... [C]ultural images rationalize the social construction
> of marginalized groups as Other, liminal, or abject; they are

not essentialist psychological acts but attempts to rationalize …those social constructions that seem 'true' but which are mere construction. (182, 191)

Auntie Lizbet's portrayal is based on what is termed physiognomy, wherein the following is true:

For cultures that operated upon models of bodily interpretation prior to the development of internal imaging techniques, [p]hysiognomy became a paradigm of access to the ephemeral and intangible workings of the interior body. Speculative qualities such as moral integrity, honesty, trustworthiness, criminality, fortitude, cynicism, sanity, and so forth, suddenly became available for scrutiny by virtue of the "irregularities" of the body that enveloped them. For the physiognomist, the body allowed meaning to be inferred from the outside in; such a speculative prac-tice resulted in the ability to anticipate intangible qualities of one's personhood without having to await the "proof" of actions or the intimacy of a relationship developing over time. By "reasoning from the exterior to the interior," the trained physiognomist extracted the meaning of the soul without the permission or the participation of the interpreted. (Mitchell & Snyder 58-9)

What is most disturbing about the above is that disability is still most often portrayed this way in literature and film. The disabled character has the bad attitude, the bad outcomes, the bad intentions or the tragic history and future. Physiognomy is not in the past, and is not only part of 'foreign' cultures. Physiognomy is part of disability portrayal now and today, and is used in the defacing of real disabled lives. Through the example of Auntie Lizbet's dehumanization and erasure from the arena of motherhood, we notice some of the ways in which her disability is manifest to make this character subhuman and in so doing, delegitimize her (Baynton 36).

In the passage from *Chanda's Wars* below, the bond that grows between Iris and Auntie Lizbet is somewhat encouraging, from a disability studies perspective. Iris, after all, clearly comes to understand and welcome Lizbet's club foot as part of her. Iris talks to her aunt while "doodling" on it – demonstrating her ease with it. The good news ends there, however:

All the while, Iris sits cross-legged on the ground beside Auntie Lizbet. During a lull, she rests her head against Auntie's knee.

"Auntie," she asks into the silence, "do you ever miss not being a mama?"

"Oh, sometimes, I guess," Auntie says simply, staring at the coals of the firepit. "But if I was a mama, all my love would have to go to my children, wouldn't it?"

Iris thinks a bit. "I guess it would."

"Then I wouldn't have any left over, would I?"

"No, I guess you wouldn't."

"So maybe this is best," Auntie says, stroking Iris's hair. "This way I have lots of love, all stored up to give to little girls who don't have mamas."

A pause. "Little girls like me?"

"Little girls like you."

Iris smiles. She doodles a finger on Auntie's club foot. "When I grow up, Auntie, I want to be just like you."

"Hush now, hush. Don't wish for that." (Stratton 120-1)

The traditional life goal of an African village woman is to reach for marriage and a family, yet Lizbet's club foot effectively excludes her from this goal—in her own mind as well as others. Iris says she wants to be just like her aunt, which is encouraging for disability—since she clearly means club foot and all—but Lizbet's response collapses that entirely. She wants to silence such a desire, as if having that wish is unthinkable, unspeakable—as if a life embodying difference is not a life worth wishing for, or having, at all. Lizbet has internalized this, and with her, the readers who take in her words. The message here is unmistakable: disability and motherhood do not mix. Still, however, Lizbet is a good mother (figure) to Iris. This is where resistance comes in.

Like a 'good' disabled character, Lizbet rejects Iris's perception of her disabled life as a desired one. Granted, life in rural Africa with a club foot would be difficult—made so by the fact that Lizbet had to suffer the responses of others to her difference—but the 'fact' of her difficult life only reinforces fear of difference. As well, Lizbet's problems are understood to originate in her body. If she were 'normal,' she would be married and surrounded by her own children. The problem of her singleness and childlessness is understood to be the fault of 'the problem' of her body. No mention at all is made of the real problem here: the attitudes around her that understand her club foot as a misfortune that justifies her exclusion.

This novel takes place in a homogeneous racial environment and its plot—centering on the plight of child soldiers—does not depict a conflict fueled by racism but instead by anti-government extremism. Auntie Lizbet's disqualification from motherhood does not occur on the basis of race, but rather because of her disability and corporeal 'deformity'. *Chanda's Wars* was published in 2009, and as a novel set in Africa but written in present day North America, it depicts current times and is meant to contribute to social justice education for today's young adults. It upholds the standard that racist ideology is "no longer an accepted part of discourse" (Baynton 42). Such transformation has not occurred in terms of representations of disability. The representation of disability put forth in this novel reinforces the fact that: "The expressions of disability, seemingly everywhere in the mass media are provocative... because viable status is not granted to disability" (Titchkosky 6).

Readers of *Chanda's Wars* are taught through this work of fiction that war, cruelty, violence and the exploitation of children is wrong. This same fictional work, however, does nothing to dispel myths about disability and disabled mothers. Lizbet's exclusion from motherhood on the grounds of her disability is made to 'make sense'. Readers are comforted by Lizbet's quiet acceptance of her motherless fate and are not led to question it, but are lulled to accept that her lack of children makes her available to support Iris, and so her childlessness is (mis)understood as meant to be. Once more, Baynton rings true:

> [There is tacit acceptance that] disability is a legitimate reason for inequality, [and this] is...one of the factors responsible for making discrimination against [disabled people] so persistent and the struggle for disability rights so difficult. As Harlan Hahn has noted, "Unlike other disadvantaged groups, such as women and racial or ethnic minorities, [disabled] citizens have not yet...succeeded in refuting the presumption that their subordinate status can be ascribed to innate biological inferiority."...[Such views held on the basis of gender or race] are no longer an accepted part of discourse ... Yet the same [ideas] regarding disability are still espoused widely and openly. (51)

It is written as sad but unavoidable that Lizbet is childless. So a novel meant to bring peace education and social justice to the fore misses the chance to present disability and disabled mothering differently.

DISQUALIFIED!

Carrie Sandahl writes: "[Whether a symbol for] denial of truth …a beacon of evil … [or] …a mark of shame …disability in the dramatic canon always signifies" (255). In turn, Lennard Davis also states: "The loose association between …disability …and …incompetence …established a legacy that people with disabilities are still having trouble living down" (37).

Both of these quotes illustrate what fuels my own disqualification for motherhood—in short, what, in normative terms, makes me 'not mother material'. I do not embody what normalcy dictates a 'real' mother to be. Therefore instead of reaching the conclusion that there is something amiss with the construction of 'normalcy' itself, the accepted conclusion is that I should not and could not pursue parenthood.

My enactment of motherhood will show how 'normal' conceptions of motherhood leave unimagined the possibility of the life of disability as a desired life and of a disabled parent as a desired parent. However, the existence and success of disabled parents and their diverse approaches to and enactments of parenting expose the myriad ways in which effective parenting can materialize, and so matter. The viability of parenting in this multitude of ways proves that having but one accepted model for parenting is a constructed, human-made restriction. Normalcy's idea of its own supremacy does not allow the observation that 'independence' is an oppressive, dangerous fallacy. Thus it excludes a version of mothering not restricted by an (ultimately false) show of solo competency. If normalcy were to 'notice' and acknowledge anti-ableist parenting, which by definition goes against the oppressions of the arbitrary 'normal' standard, it would be noticing what the example of my parenting will have to teach: that the 'normal', 'independent' order of parenting ignores the interconnectedness of people and of life itself. In this way, it is in fact a disorder.

In my experience of being an ambitious disabled woman, I've observed much fear in able-bodied society regarding disability's presence, and disabled people's participation in society. This anxiety reaches a whole new level when it comes to disabled mothers. In a society where the most accepted role for disability is "rolelessness" — a term referred to by Michelle Fine and Adrienne Asch (233)—my expectations of living a full life, including motherhood, are framed as arrogant, delusional and even dangerous. Margrit Shildrick states:

> Where the monstrous other, and more particularly the monstrous mother, has figured an anxiety about the disorganization of the embodied self, the move has been to effect strategies of exclusion and vilification that deny full humanity to those who are ostensibly different (46)...Like other women, mothers, as a highly discursive category, have often represented both the best hopes and the worst fears of societies faced with an intuitive sense of their own instabilities and vulnerabilities(30)...the monstrous as being intrinsically opposed to the familiar course of nature, an affront to the expected that 'throws doubt', as Canguilhem puts it, 'on life's ability to teach us order' (1964:27). (29)

My disabled body, my spastic slow limbs, my wheelchair, all go directly against conceptions of the 'normal' mother. But the 'mess' of my disability is a blessed mess. If the 'picture' of me as mother is disturbing, disorderly, unnatural, abnormal, this is welcome news to me, because the problem here is not my dreams and plans of motherhood, it is the restrictive, oppressive order of normalcy, as it is used to exclude disability—taken for granted as an 'excludable type' (Titchkosky 5). I am pointing to the fact that there is nothing natural about the 'natural' order, which proclaims on one hand that "it takes a village to raise a child," yet opens the gates of the village only to a few, strictly dictating that those in the village who do the raising must appear 'normal enough'. Contrary to popular belief, disability can teach us much about order—mostly, that we need a new one.

FINALLY, THE BRIGHT SIDE: MAMA MWANZA IN BARBARA KINGSOLVER'S *THE POISONWOOD BIBLE*

While the portrayal of Lizbet's disability in *Chanda's Wars* is disheartening, there are also positive representations. Given the power of colonialism and war, it could be fair to say that many of the oppressive understandings of disability that are clearly observable in 'foreign' cultures could be heavily informed by Western influence. Notice the following portrayal of a disabled mother in preindependence Congo, in the novel, *The Poisonwood Bible*:

…Mama Mwanza's legs didn't burn all the way off but it looks like a pillow or just something down there she's sitting on wrapped up in a cloth sack. She has to scoot around on her hands. Her hand bottoms look like feet bottoms, only with fingers.

…[H]er husband and her seven or eight children…don't care one bit about her not having any legs to speak of. To them she's just their mama and where's dinner? To all the other Congo people, too…Nobody bats their eye when she scoots by on her hands and goes on down to her field or the river to wash clothes with the other ladies that work down there every day. She carries all her things in a basket on top of her head. It's as big as Mama's big white laundry hamper back home and seems like she's always got about ten hundred things piled up in there. When she scoots down the road, not a one of them falls out. All the other ladies have big baskets on their heads too, so nobody stares at Mama Mwanza one way or another. (Kingsolver 45-6)

Mama Mwanza's alternative corporeality is understood as a natural part of life in her village. No one questions her ability to care for her children or find alternative ways to accomplish tasks effectively. She "scoots around on her hands [and] her hand bottoms look like feet bottoms," yet her alternative corporeality is understood as natural, as is her competence (Kingsolver 26). While the opposite is often true in Africa and all other parts of the world, the above passage (written by an American author) is encouraging. As I read it, I think of my own potential motherhood. While, to my child, I will not collapse my difference and become 'just Mama and where is dinner?' I will live my disability, and teach it, as part of the fluidity, complexity and richness of our days.

Far from being a tragic mess to be avoided, I would emphatically argue that my disability will have much to teach my child, especially in a North American society governed by such narrow, erroneous conceptions of parenting that disqualify me from motherhood as a matter of course.

WHAT DISABILITY GIVES

I fully intend to live in my disability as a teaching tool. My disability will widen my child's perspectives. It will be between us as I nurture, love, support, instruct, discipline and teach my child, as we learn and grow together. Disability, like racial, ethnic and cultural differences, is not to be written off as an unfortunate burden. They are to be embraced as part of the complex, multi-layered human experience. The most important aspects of parenting are those of leader, teacher and supporter, and these roles can be powerfully undertaken while living in disability — all the better to teach innovation, respect, creativity, love and adaptability.

Who better to teach a child to plan, strategize, brainstorm and problem-solve than someone with a disability, who has had to learn these skills as a matter of course on a daily basis—who has often had to devise not only Plan A, B, or C to accomplish tasks or reach goals, but even Plan X, Y, or Z, to say nothing of recruiting the team necessary to make plans happen! Who better to teach equality, and what it truly means in real time, than a parent with a disability, awakened — through disability—to a world where doing the work of equality, and learning and teaching its lessons is necessary, important, and active.

In this section, I refer to a few disability studies scholars and cultural philosophers whose work helps me make my argument for how disability is a good and useful life within which I can raise a good and useful child.

William Ayers states: "[w]e must [insist] that all human beings matter, even when law or custom or social practice or brutality or invasion or restriction says otherwise" (Feuerverger xi). *Educere*—the Latin word for 'educate' means 'to lead out' or 'to transform', and it is that definition, that calling, to which truly effective parenting (and educating) adheres—instead of honouring the principle of 'survival of the fittest', which oppression holds so dear. I believe it is children who receive and remain true to this kind of education—education toward real equality across differences—who are and will be most likely to survive and thrive in school, work, and life.

The reality is that our economic struggles, unfolding directly before us now with the collapse, rescue and re-emergence of corporation after corporation, are insisting that we learn to do things in new ways. If we keep doing what we've always done, we will keep getting what we have already gotten. The truth is, it is our diversities, our differences, that can teach us to do things differently.

We need people living in anti-ableist perspectives to shake up, question, and re-make the world in new and fresh ways. I am such a person, and I intend to raise such a child. As the literary theorist Terry Eagleton states:

Children make the best theorists, since they have not yet been educated into ac-cepting our routine social practices as 'natural,' and so insist on posing... the most embarrassingly general and fundamental questions regarding [those practices] with a [wonder] which we adults have long forgotten. Since they do not yet grasp our social practices as inevitable, they do not see why we might not do things differently. (qtd. in Feuerverger 40)

Disabled bodies, and thus the experiences of disabled people in those bodies, are so often alienated from life in the mainstream centre of society—on the grounds of their 'inferior' embodiments, their unwelcome difference from 'normalcy'. Rod Michalko has this to say about disability's exclusion:

Suffering here does not refer to the conventional sense of "suffering a disability" but refers instead to the suffering of the multitude of interpretations of disability, the political acts that culturally organize and define disability—the suffering of our society's choices made in regard to the meaning of disability. The animating question I use to understand disability in this way is that raised by Irving Zola (1982, 244): "Why [has] a society been created and perpetuated which has ex-cluded so many of its members?"... [H]e meant to issue a challenge to his society... (15)

The notion that both the disabled and non-disabled communities suffer from attempts to erase, marginalize and oppress disability through the enforcement of normalcy is captivating. Rosemarie Garland Thomson, in turn, brings us to an understanding of the richness of the disability experience, as much more than the oppressive ways it is understood in society—as a legitimate form of "ethnicity and identity" (6) in our social space. This is crucial to rethinking normalcy's (perceived) supremacy.

Framing disability as ugly, weak, inferior, unfortunate, pitiful, tragic, sinister, ad infinitum, both justifies and reinforces the (mis)treatment, discounting and discrediting of disability in the lived experience of disabled people.

Seeing hope in expulsion, in what is termed "casting out" (Razack 5) of disability, or racial difference, or any 'transgressive' embodiment at all, does not come easily. Yet, there is hope, not so much in the fact that one is cast out, but in the fact that one is always cast out to another location, an alternative place, 'another somewhere' that offers another way to be in the world.

Since normalcy, and its supremacy, are entirely false (normalcy is forever stuffing and forcing disability into oppressive confines where it does not belong), and theorizing disability and normalcy's oppression is part of the act of freeing it, the resulting tug-of-war thankfully keeps normalcy on shaky ground. But normalcy has been so entrenched, and is fighting so hard to make its supremacy seem natural, that this uprooting is long, hard, uphill work.

CONCLUSION: WHEN LOVE HAS EVERYTHING TO DO WITH IT

I don't know if my parenting dream will come to pass. This, though, is about far more than me. It is about confronting prejudices, stigmas, and misconceptions surrounding disability and disabled parents. My writing here is not undertaken in anger, but because of the importance of my political convictions.

I love my relative very much—always have, always will. My love is unconditional and therefore not diminished by the hurt his ableist attitude causes me. This points to the strength of love as a decision, not a passing emotion. This is also the type of love essential to the parenting process. That said, when I think about my relative's words to my mother on that day, the obvious ableist prejudice behind them, and his refusal to be open with *me* about his true feelings, I find tears are still very close to the surface. But, I understand that he is a victim. My relative "suffers his society" (Michalko 15). At least to date, he cannot grasp that I can and will be a good mother, that living in disability can be a good life—that disability gives enriched perception and takes away the narrow (mis)conception that there is one 'normal way' to be a mother. Disabled parents point directly to the fact that there is more than one viable strategy available to raise a healthy child. Theorizing on the meaning of marginality, Titchkosky and Michalko state:

> [T]he compelling and seductive character of normalcy conceals the compelling and seductive character of the margin... not only from its "view" but from ours as well.... From the standpoint of the centre, no one desires to inhabit a disabled body, or disabled senses or minds, since to do so is tantamount to barely living at all. The centre conceives of disability as a

devalued life. ...Normalcy imagines—"sees"—no other possibility of human life than itself, and thus, ironically, does not
"see" itself. (7)

[The margins can] show the centre that its margins are not
merely uninhabitable voids, but are instead spaces where it is
possible to reveal... that the centre is not natural, but is human-
made and can be otherwise. (8)

The bottom line here is love—my ability and desire to love and mother
a child, my child's ability and willingness to love me back, my relative's mis-
guided attempt—based in love—to steer me away from a 'mistake', and his
attempt to 'protect' a child from the 'misfortune' of my disability.

Love, however, means allowing my future child to be who he or she is,
without assuming a disastrous reaction to my difference, without assigning
prejudice to a child who may not yet be alive. Love means embracing who
I am—good mother material.

WORKS CITED

Baynton, Douglas C. "Disability and the Justification of Inequality in Amer-
    ican History." *The New Disability History—American Perspec-
    tives.* Ed. Paul K. Longmore and Lauri Umansky. New York: New
    York University Press, 2001. 33-57. Print.

Davis, Lennard. *Enforcing Normalcy.* London: Verso, 1995. Print.

Darke, Paul. "Understanding Cinematic Representations of Disability."
    Ed. T. Shakespeare. *The Disability Reader: Social Sciences Per-
    spectives.* New York: Cassell, 1998. Print.

Feuerverger, Grace. *Teaching, Learning and Other Miracles.* Rotterdam:
    Sense, 2007. Print.

Fine, Michelle and Adrienne Asch. "Disabled Women: Sexism without the
    Pedestal." *Journal of Society & Sociology.* Welfare 8.2 (1981): 233-48.
    Print.

Goffman, Erving. *Stigma: Notes on the Management of Spoiled Identity.*
    New Jersey: Prentice-Hall, 1963. Print.

Kingsolver, Barbara. *The Poisonwood Bible.* New York: HarperPerennial,
    1998. Print.

Michalko, Rod. *The Difference That Disability Makes.* Philadelphia: Temple University Press, 2002. Print.

Mitchell, David & Sharon Snyder. *Narrative Prosthesis: Disability and the Dependencies of Discourse.* Ann Arbor, MI: University of Michigan Press, 2000. Print.

Razack, Sherene. *Casting out: The Eviction of Muslims from Western Law and Politics.* Toronto: University of Toronto Press. 2008. Print.

Sandahl, Carrie. "The Tyranny of the Neutral" Ed. Carrie Sandahl and Philip Auslander. *Bodies in Commotion: Disability and Performance.* Ann Arbor: University of Michigan P, 2005. 255-67. Print.

Shildrick, Margrit. *Embodying the Monster: Encounters with the Vulnerable Self.* London: Sage, 2002. Print.

Stratton, Allan. *Chanda's Wars.* Toronto: HarperCollins Canada, 2009. Print.

Thomson, Rosemarie Garland. *Extraordinary Bodies: Figuring Physical Disability in American Culture and Literature.* New York: Columbia University Press, 1997. Print.

Titchkosky, Tanya. *Reading and Writing Disability Differently: The Textured Life of Embodiment.* Toronto: University of Toronto Press, 2007. Print.

Titchkosky, Tanya and Rod Michalko. *Rethinking Normalcy: A Disability Studies Reader.* Toronto: Canadian Scholars' Press, 2009. Print.

Mothering with Disabilities

3.

Mothering in Silence

Historical Perspectives on Deafness, Marriage, and Motherhood

R.A.R. EDWARDS

INTRODUCTION

History was made at a beauty pageant in 1994. That year, Heather White-stone, a deaf woman, became Miss America. In that instant, she became the first disabled woman to wear the crown. Perhaps we don't often look to Miss America to signal cultural change—what, after all, could be less an agent of change for American women than a yearly contest based on re-inforcing American cultural obsessions with impossibly strict standards of physical appearance for their gender? And yet, seeing a disabled woman snatch the crown from all those able-bodied women was a radical turn of events. A disabled woman, we suddenly learned, could be deemed just as physically beautiful and sexually alluring as an able-bodied woman. A rad-ical statement, indeed, in a culture which typically desexualizes disability, both male and female. It really was a historically gripping moment.

But it was not an uncomplicated victory. From her first steps into the national spotlight, following her crowning as Miss America, Whitestone had a rocky relationship with the Deaf community. The capitalized "Deaf" refers to people with an audiological hearing loss who regard their not as

a medical condition but rather as a linguistic and cultural one, and identify themselves as members of a larger Deaf community of signed language
users. The lower case "deaf" refers strictly to the audiological condition of
hearing loss, and does not imply cultural or community attachments. It is
possible to be deaf, in other words, without being Deaf.

From the Deaf community's point of view, they were pleased, on the
one hand, to see a deaf woman win the venerable pageant, demonstrating
categorically that "deaf is beautiful." In theory, a deaf Miss America, even
more than a Miss Deaf America, as the Deaf community had its own tradition of separate beauty pageants, could serve as a sign of the deaf community's arrival into the mainstream of American life.

On the other hand, in practice, Whitestone turned out to be a most
problematic Miss America from a Deaf point of view. She was raised an
oralist, and knew very little sign language. She preferred to speak, but would
grudgingly use Signing Exact English (SEE), a code for English on the hands,
when she had to interact with other deaf people. She did not know American Sign Language, the separate signed language of the Deaf community,
and, worse yet, denigrated ASL, explaining to her readers of her autobiography that she used SEE because it has "proper English grammar and has
a more advanced vocabulary," while the "vocabulary for ASL is limited,
much smaller than the range of spoken English, and the speakers communicate thoughts instead of complete sentences" (Whitestone 41), a set of linguistic characterizations that are demonstrably false.

Even before she competed in Miss America, there were signs of trouble.
While still competing in Miss Deaf America competitions, Whitestone's
obvious lack of Deaf cultural credentials was held against her. One might
respond that this was only to be expected—you come to a Deaf event, you
have to anticipate Deaf attitudes might prevail. But Whitestone proved entirely oblivious to this basic social reality. Instead, she complained about
it, recalling years later, "Just because I spoke, had a hearing family, danced
ballet, and used Signing Exact English, they had decided that I could not fit
into the deaf culture, that I was not an 'ideal' deaf person" (Whitestone 42).

In point of fact, she was not a culturally Deaf person, ideal or otherwise,
at all. As historian Susan Burch has noted, Whitestone made a point of
both wearing her hearing aids at the Miss America pageant and of revealing
them by wearing her hair up, all the while speaking to communicate. "In
this way," Burch writes, "she specifically acknowledged her physical deafness while distancing herself from cultural Deafness" (Burch, "'Beautiful,
Though Deaf,'" 255).

None of this played well in the Deaf community, which quickly found itself trying to applaud Whitestone politely for her public victory as a deaf woman, while simultaneously keeping a distance from her, quite deliberately rejecting Whitestone's efforts to speak as a deaf woman. (Of course, this in itself was part of the problem: she insisted on speaking, and did not ever seem to understand how her efforts to pass as hearing posed a problem for her initial desire to serve as a Deaf spokeswoman, from a Deaf point of view.) The honeymoon was over in the Deaf community by December 1994, even before Whitestone's year of service as Miss America began; a readers' poll in *Deaf Life* found that 55% of respondents believed that Whitestone did not represent deaf people (28). By the spring of 1995, the mainstream press had caught up with the Deaf press. Headlines like "Beauty and the Battle" appeared in articles detailing the heated argument over Heather that was taking place within the Deaf community.

So by the time Whitestone made the decision to get a cochlear implant in 2002, joining the ranks of the estimated 21,000 Americans with implants, her identity as a deafened hearing woman, and not a Deaf woman, was firmly established. Her bridges to the Deaf world had long been burned. But, by getting an implant, Whitestone opened up another controversy, beyond that of the contested place of implants in the Deaf world, a contentious subject in its own right. Rather, this new controversy centered on Whitestone's explanation of how she came to make this technological choice, to go from passing as hearing by speaking, to trying to becoming physically hearing.

As she described it, the decision to get an implant came after she failed to hear her then two-year-old son John cry out when he fell while playing in the backyard. While her husband had responded to the boy, and his sudden movements had caught Heather's eye, allowing her to soon follow after him, she was nonetheless stricken by the incident. "I didn't hear him crying," she recalled. "I need to be the first one to hear him." Whitestone went on to suggest that her implant would allow her to have "a fuller experience of being a wife and a mother" (Kolchik, 9D). One sees captured in this remark both the technological imperative to cure the disabled body, and the cultural pressure to live up to the increasing demands of intensive mothering, all at once.

It comes as a shock that a deaf woman in 2002 would make that statement. Deaf women have been marrying and mothering in the United States since the nineteenth century. But here in the twenty-first, Whitestone essentially declared that one needed to hear to be a successful wife and mother.

In the hearing press, this declaration about able-bodied mothering captured no attention at all, as far as I can tell. There were no editorials expressing dismay at her belief. Rather, most of the press coverage seemed to take Whitestone's desire to hear her son completely at face value, as a wish beyond criticism or commentary.

Look more closely at Whitestone's explanation of her need for an implant, however, and some other details emerge. Her interviews offered a unique glimpse into the dynamics of a hearing-deaf marriage, from an oralist point of view. Whitestone had always relied upon speech and lipreading to communicate. But as her boys got to be toddlers, she realized the limits of her communication system. "I felt incredibly left out when they understood more than I did of what the people around the dinner table were saying" (Pope). And again, after surgery to receive a second implant in 2006, Whitestone reported that "she was able to hear and understand the conversations better and feel more included in family life than ever before."

Her response to feeling left out and excluded in her own family, as a committed oralist, was not to question her communication system, or even her hearing family's behavior toward its only deaf member. That kind of response would require a culturally Deaf analysis of her situation, asking why her own family should not have to modify its hearing behaviors in order to welcome her, as a deaf person, into her own life. The logic of oralism does not raise such reactions in its proponents. Instead, a flagging oralism demands more oralism. If a deaf person struggles to fit into the hearing world, the problem is not with the hearing world. Besides, oralists know, as Whitestone acknowledged in her own words that "it's not just the hearing world, it's the real world" (Kolchik 9D).

For oralists, then, the problem is always with the deafened body. Whitestone would know well that she is the problem. This, after all, is a woman who spent six years learning how to pronounce her name and who retells that fact in interviews and memoirs as a narrative of valiant personal struggle rather than one of disturbing educational priorities (Anders 5-6). If her body is the problem, modern medicine would provide the solution. She would harness medical technology to pass as hearing even more accurately.

Her second implant apparently succeeded in producing a better, more authentic, hearing performance. Whitestone raved about her implant, remarking, "I have changed far more than I can imagine. My family and friends have noticed the differences and they are very happy as long as I wear them all day long every day. I am very happy too." Even taking into account her protestations of happiness, it is difficult to miss the cultural imperative to hear that this technological innovation imposes on the deaf people who accept this device into their bodies. Her hearing family is really happy, as long as she wears her implants "all day long every day." The performance of passing now has no backstage at all.

Whitestone's eager embrace of the role of hearing woman, as aided by emerging technologies, has deeper ideological precedents. Oralists had long promoted passing as a goal for deaf women. As historian Susan Burch explains, in the early twentieth century, oralists worked hard to link hearing and beauty. The oralist publication, the *Volta Review,* reassured its readers that women could be considered "beautiful, though deaf," and, in the 1920s, argued that oralism encouraged attention to beauty in deaf women because the practice of learning to speak and lipread required the extensive use of watching one's mouth movements in mirrors (Burch 148). There was a widespread belief, Burch argues, "that sexual appeal demanded greater 'normality' for women than for men …Hearing parents particularly encouraged their deaf daughters to practice their oral skills to attract hearing suitors" (Burch 148). Whitestone can be seen as a link in this oralist chain; her hearing parents saw their speaking deaf daughter eventually attract and marry a hearing man.

There is a darker undercurrent here, however, one that makes the equation of hearingness and beauty seem downright innocent. Oralism, as a pedagogical movement, was also deeply committed to and entangled with eugenics. In 1883, oralist and eugenic supporter Alexander Graham Bell issued his *Memoir Upon the Formation of a Deaf Variety of the Human Race.* Here, he worried that deaf-deaf marriages, which he believed were encouraged by the existence of manual residential schools for the deaf which brought together deaf people in large numbers and provided them with a common language, were bringing forth a generation of deaf babies. If this process was left unchallenged, a deaf variety of the human race would surely result.

To thwart that outcome, Bell recommended the twinned solutions of oralism and eugenicism. Deaf people should be taught to speak as hearing people, to encourage them to interact with and marry into the hearing community. And deaf people should be actively discouraged from marrying deaf partners. Ideally, laws would be passed to prohibit such marriages, but Bell recognized that this was unlikely to happen. Active attacks on such marriages, by teachers, doctors, family, and friends, would have to suffice. Bell, together with other oralist allies, would continue to argue against deaf-deaf marriages into the twentieth century.

More deaf people were subjected to these arguments, as oralism gained the pedagogical upper hand in the twentieth century. In 1860, almost no deaf students were taught by oral means. In 1900, nearly 40% of deaf students were taught without the use of the sign language. By the end of the First World War, that number had climbed to nearly 80%.

The worlds of deafness before and after oralism are starkly different. Perhaps in no way is the difference clearer than in the issue of deaf marriage. Whitestone's nineteenth-century foremothers would be shocked to learn that mothering required hearing. They had claimed exactly the opposite, and, one suspects, they assumed the deaf women who came after them would confidently do the same.

The right to marry and mother was claimed early by deaf women. This is rather shocking, in and of itself, for the right of disabled women to marry and mother has historically been challenged. Other essays in this volume make clear how contested the cultural terrain of motherhood has been for disabled women.

Deaf women were early trailblazers down this cultural path. The two most famous deaf wives of the nineteenth century were Eliza Boardman Clerc and Sophia Fowler Gallaudet. Boardman had arrived at the American School for the Deaf in 1817, when she was 23 years old. There, she met Deaf Frenchman Laurent Clerc, co-founder of the school, nine years her senior. They married in 1818. His hearing counterpart at the school, Thomas Hopkins Gallaudet, met his future wife, Sophia Fowler, when she arrived at the school in 1817. She was 19 years old; he was 30. They married in 1821.

In so doing, both women assumed public roles as deaf wives. In both households, the primary language of communication was the sign language. Boardman had lost her hearing as a toddler and still retained some hearing and speech. But her husband did not speak, nor did he read lips, and it was clear that in marrying him, she would live as and claim the identity of a Deaf woman. She would never attempt to use her residual hearing and speech skills to pass as hearing. Similarly, though Fowler had married a hearing man, she was not expected to accommodate herself to his native communication system. Rather, he abandoned his for hers. The household they built together was a signing one.

Both women would raise large families. The Clercs had six children, four of whom, two daughters and two sons, survived to adulthood. All were hearing. The Gallaudets had eight children, four sons and four daughters, all of whom survived to adulthood, all hearing. It did not seem to have occurred to either couple that a disabled woman ought not to bear or raise children. Gallaudet had been of that opinion, when first he embarked upon a career in deaf education, but time with Clerc had changed his views, as had falling in love with a deaf woman himself. It did not seem to occur to either woman that her deafness would interfere with her ability to mother children, whether hearing or deaf, successfully. (I should add for readers that I must write "seem" for, unfortunately, neither woman left behind diaries or letters. Historians must look to their respective life courses, and to things written about them in order to glean insight into their personal histories).

In any event, they were successful women, by the standards of their day. They excelled as wives and mothers, and sent their children out into the world to serve the new republic well. Thomas Gallaudet became an Episcopal priest who founded a church called St. Ann's, which served a mixed deaf-hearing parish in New York City. Edward Gallaudet became the president of the first college for the deaf in the world, named for his father, Gallaudet College, now University. Francis Clerc would also become an Episcopal priest. Sarah Clerc married Henry Deming, a Connecticut state legislator, in 1850. He went on to become mayor of Hartford in 1854. The deaf world of her family in this way aligned with the local power elite of the hearing world. And the hearing world of her husband assumed that the Clerc family was prominent enough in Hartford, though deaf, to be a political asset, rather than a liability, to him. After all, Laurent Clerc was famous and popular in Hartford; after so many years in Connecticut, he had been adopted as a favorite son.

Most importantly, and ironically, by taking on the safest, most culturally sanctioned roles for women, wife and mother, these two deaf women acted as radicals. They demonstrated that disabled women could be wives and mothers, just like able-bodied women, and could fulfill those roles just as well as their able-bodied peers. Upon her death, her eulogists remarked that Sophia Fowler Gallaudet's influence was probably more extensive than she knew: "Who can tell how much of the liberal spirit always manifested by the American public and its legislators towards the deaf and dumb is owing to the spectacle thus early presented of a beautiful woman from that class entering society and presiding over her own household with equal sweetness and tact?"

Establishing that liberal spirit early on was important for the deaf community, for, as we already know, Bell and his eugenic peers were waiting by century's end. What allowed the deaf community to weather the eugenic storm more successfully than some of their disabled peers was precisely this early claim to the roles of wife and mother by these deaf women, the first generation of deaf women to receive education and step into larger cultural possibilities as a result.

But those responsibilities needed to be actively claimed. The prevailing stereotypes of disability of their time largely held that a disabled life would be different, in both possibility and outcome, from an able-bodied life. Deaf women like Eliza Boardman and Sophia Fowler fought back against that stereotype and, in so doing, insisted, in this way, on equality with their hearing peers.

They would claim lives the same as their able-bodied female counterparts, while not denying their essential difference as signing Deaf women. Boardman made the invisible difference of her deafness purposely visible when she posed signing for her 1822 portrait by the painter Charles Wilson Peale. She is pictured with her daughter, Elizabeth, signing /E/. The use of the manual alphabet here marked Eliza as a deaf woman. Though she had an invisible disability and could have chosen to pass as a hearing woman in her portrait, she made her deafness visible. By signing, she revealed herself. By signing, she indicated that her deafness was nothing to hide. She wanted viewers to know they looked upon a proud deaf wife and mother, with a happy child upon her lap.

Marriage was therefore a firmly settled expectation for deaf people of both sexes by the middle of the nineteenth century in the United States. Claiming the right to marry was of crucial importance to the future of the Deaf community. In this way, the historical development of the Deaf community was quite distinct from that of other disabled people. These formative nineteenth-century experiences help to shape the Deaf sense of their difference, not just from the hearing, but also from other disabled Americans. Take the counterexamples of the blind and the developmentally disabled, for instance.

Samuel Gridley Howe, as director of the Perkins Institution for the Blind, articulated a quite different vision of the future for his students. When he began his work with the blind, Howe had believed that they were the equals of the sighted. "But in the mid-1840s," historian Ernest Freeburg notes, "…he had decided that the blind were different, that their sensory deprivation had serious physical, intellectual, and moral consequences." These consequences were understood as overwhelmingly negative. By 1848, Howe had come to believe that the blind were not only physically but also mentally inferior to the sighted (198).

It followed that blind adults ought to be discouraged from both marriage and childrearing. Discussing the evolution of Howe's thinking in this area, literary scholar Mary Klages argues that "the interpretation of blindness and other forms of physical disability as incontrovertibly signifying suffering barred disabled people from reproductive sexuality. Only the most hardhearted could insist on engaging in even the most sanctioned forms of sexuality when those acts might result in the creation of a disabled—that is, a suffering and miserable—child" (52). In order to dissuade the students in his care from even desiring to marry, he moved to segregate the sexes at Perkins. Antipathy toward blind marriage would continue among professionals who worked with the blind, especially with their teachers and administrators, well into the twentieth century.

Interest in educating the developmentally disabled, commonly referred to as "idiots" in this period, also began in the United States in the 1840s, with Samuel Gridley Howe once more playing a part in New England. In 1851, Howe became the director of the first of its kind institution, the Massachusetts School for Idiotic and Feeble Minded Children. While the possibility of educating this population was beginning to be explored, it was not believed that these "idiots" would either marry nor have children. As Walter Fernald, the director of the Massachusetts State School for the Feeble Minded, put it, "They are powerless to resist the physical temptations of adult life, and should be protected from their own weakness… Especially should they be protected from marriage and the reproduction of their kind" (Osgood 52). To ensure that protection, the trend among professionals devoted to the education of the feeble-minded became to recommend that these children be segregated from the general population. A policy of permanent institutionalization of the so-called feeble minded emerged accordingly and prevailed deep into the twentieth century.

The significance of Eliza Boardman and Sophia Fowler is thrown into relief here. Those first two, much heralded deaf marriages, coming so soon after the establishment of deaf education in the United States, allowed the Deaf community to quickly establish both the expectation and practice of marriage as a normative experience for all deaf people. Teachers in the residential schools for the deaf would come to understand that the deaf students in their care would have life patterns identical to those of their hearing peers. They too would graduate, find work, marry, and raise children. In this way, deaf lives could and would look like hearing lives.

A mid-century snapshot of the graduates of the American, New York, and Ohio schools revealed the prevalence of marriage in the Deaf community, and especially the preference for deaf-deaf marriage. While 75 deaf men and 58 deaf women reported hearing spouses, 188 deaf men and 187 deaf women reported deaf spouses. While resistance to deaf marriage, as to all disabled marriages, would increase, as we have seen, with the rise of eugenics in the late nineteenth century, by then, the practice of deaf marriage, at least, was well established. As a result, eugenic leaders would struggle, mostly unsuccessfully, to undo this deeply rooted tradition of deaf-deaf marriage.

Deaf marriage also received ongoing support from the press, at least in Connecticut, the home to the American School for the Deaf. In 1866, another Deaf event occurred in Hartford; the annual meeting of the New England Gallaudet Association of the Deaf was held there in 1866. That meeting also provided, its organizers noted, an opportunity "to celebrate the 50th anniversary of the landing of Gallaudet and Clerc, August 1816." Nearly 400 Deaf people came back to Hartford for that celebration in 1866.

The *Courant* provided its readers with coverage of this 1866 event, noting that some 400 graduates were returning to Hartford "from all parts of the country." They "represent various trades and employments, a large number being farmers. Upon inquiry we were told that probably more than one half of the whole number are married...." (*Courant* 8). The paper reflected positively that this would not remain the case for long, as Cupid was at the convention, "fully armed." Many singles will meet a partner here, the *Courant* predicted confidently. "If this shall prove true, who shall say that the fiftieth anniversary of the Asylum was not a splendid success in more ways than one? And so mote it be" (*Courant* 8).

This public approval of deaf romance grabs attention. The paper applauded the very idea of deaf-deaf marriages, and hoped to see more of them. This sort of easy acceptance of the most commonplace experience of able-bodied adult life as an equally reasonable expectation for a deaf life marks a significant point of departure between the deaf and other disabled communities in the nineteenth century. Here, the deaf are described and understood as being very similar to, and not quite different from, the hearing majority around them.

And yet, crucially, their difference is not denied. The *Courant* also remarked of the conference attendees that "communication by sign is probably as dear to them as our own wordy pronunciations" (8). The paper reminded readers that the communication preference of the Deaf was sign language, and not spoken English. There was no indication that the newspaper reporter expected anything different, no discussion that perhaps it would be better if the deaf would learn to speak like the hearing, rather than sign. Their similarity to hearing people may have been stressed, but their Deafness was equally acknowledged.

It is significant to see this support for Deaf communication preferences in Connecticut in 1866. In that year, there was a movement already underway in neighboring Massachusetts to found an oral school, with the ubiquitous Samuel Gridley Howe leading the charge. Howe would soon confront American School's principal, Collins Stone, with his belief that "speech is essential for human development...there can be no effectual substitute for it." By 1866, Howe was publicly arguing that society should seek "to educate (deaf children) for the society of those who hear...and the earlier we begin the better, "adding that the goal of deaf education ought to be to shape deaf children, through oral education, into the likeness of "persons of sound and normal condition" (Howe 52, 53).

Howe's calls for oralism and normalcy would be joined by Bell's calls for oralism and eugenics. While deaf people continued to marry, these eugenic attacks did provoke fear and controversy within the Deaf community, as the twentieth century went on. The community struggled with how best to resist the rising cultural influence of eugenics. For some, strategic capitulation seemed like the best approach.

In 1920, at its annual convention, the National Association of the Deaf passed a resolution opposing marriages between congenitally deaf partners. The NAD's leaders intended to thwart possible eugenic legislation against them by demonstrating the community's willingness to regulate itself in keeping with good genetic practices. That the NAD's leaders were largely late-deafened and immune from the impact of their own resolutions was not lost on the larger Deaf community, which mostly condemned this wholesale selling out of members of the community. "In the end," historian Susan Burch reports, "Deaf people resisted eugenicists and elite Deaf leaders alike, marrying one another regardless of genetic traits" (Burch 144).

But the question of whether or not deaf people could or should marry, and if so, which kinds of deaf people, had been raised and would dominate the rest of the century. Deaf people had been cast in the same lot as their disabled peers. Their right to marry moved onto shakier ground. The deaf press continued to celebrate deaf-deaf marriages, especially those which produced deaf children, who were known as the "Deaf of Deaf" and seen as the future leaders of the community. But deaf-hearing marriages also received renewed attention, as an indication that the deaf could be integrated, on hearing terms, into the hearing community, by passing as hearing and marrying hearing partners.

The chief example of such a marriage was that of Alexander Graham

Bell himself. He married Mabel Hubbard in 1877. Hubbard had become deaf due to a childhood illness when she was five years old. Her parents were determined to see her speak. They refused to use any gestural communication systems with their daughter. Rather, Mabel was trained by private tutors in the pure oral method. Her mother insisted that family members ignore her home made signs and force her to speak to them (Toward 3). It should be noted that the oral method enabled Mabel to retain her speech, for as a five-year-old she had spoken for years; these teachers did not have to teach her how to speak a language she had never heard.

Nevertheless, her father, Gardiner Greene Hubbard, was deeply impressed with the method's apparent success with his daughter. He determined that all deaf children should be taught orally and so devoted himself to establishing a school for the deaf based on the oral method. Hubbard succeeded in 1867, when the Clarke School for the Deaf opened, becoming one of the first oral schools in the nation. Still, as a result of her early oral training, Mabel grew to have intelligible speech and excellent lipreading skills as an adult (Winefield 74-75).

Mabel and Alexander Bell would raise two hearing daughters, who both survived to adulthood. Two sons, both born prematurely, each died soon after birth. Mabel, unlike Eliza or Sophia, occasionally commented on her experience of being a deaf mother in her letters. Mabel wrote to her husband around 1885, "Your children need you... Why was our wealth given us if not to give you time to make up to your children what they lose by their mother's loss?" (Bruce 319).

"By their mother's loss," Mabel meant to indicate her hearing loss, and, with it, her perception of the negative impact it had on her ability to mother her children. In fact, she would go so far as to confide to her husband in 1899 that her children "suffer from having a deaf mother" (Toward 120). Still, she believed she largely overcame her hearing loss, at least in regards to her role as a mother. She noted in 1906, "From my power of speech reading, I have been able to overcome much of the difficulty and am, I believe, nearly as much the centre of my home as any hearing mother can be" (Bruce 321).

Eliza Boardman Clerc's portrait does not show a woman overcoming her deafness. Rather, it portrays a deaf woman, mothering as a deaf woman. She overcomes not her individual deafness, but rather her society's narrow expectations of what a deaf life would be like. Mabel Hubbard Bell, by contrast, evokes one of the great tropes of able-bodied society's narratives about disability, namely, that it must be "overcome."

As disability rights scholar Simi Linton has noted, in such uses of overcome, "the individual's responsibility for her or his own success is paramount. If we, as a society, place the onus on individuals with disabilities to work harder to 'compensate' for their disabilities or to 'overcome' their condition or the barriers in the environment, we have no need for civil rights legislation or affirmative action." Such overcoming, she continues, is closely related, rhetorically, to urging disabled people to pass. While passing may be done as "a deliberate effort to avoid discrimination or ostracism," it may also be "an almost unconscious, Herculean effort to deny to oneself the reality of one's...bodily state" (Linton 19).

In either vocabulary, the construction of disability as a larger political or cultural reality is denied, and individuals are left to confront the body in isolation. In that social situation, passing becomes a strategic necessity. Both Heather Whitestone and Mabel Bell must pass in their own families. Left alone, isolated in hearing families, whose members recognize only that deafness must be overcome in order for these women to be accommodated in their own households, both women strove to pass as hearing by communicating in a hearing way, Mabel by honing her speech reading skills, and Heather, finally, by accessing medical technology.

But, in addition, both women sought to pass by living solely in the hearing world. Both married hearing men and pointedly distanced themselves from other deaf people, a task surely made easier by their inability to communicate in the deaf world. Heather refers to the hearing world as "the real world," as if the deaf world is somehow ersatz. Mabel wrote of her deliberate choice to disregard even the existence of other deaf people. "I have never been proud of the fact that although totally without hearing I have been able to mix with normal people," she wrote in 1921. "Instead I have striven in every possible way to have that fact forgotten and so to appear so completely normal that I would pass as one. To have anything to do with other deaf people instantly brought the hardly concealed fact into evidence. So I have helped other things and other people...anything and everything but the deaf" (Toward 192).

We can now see the road dividing, in the late nineteenth century. There is no direct path from Eliza Boardman Clerc to Heather Whitestone. The intervening rise of oralism and eugenics diverted that historical development. Heather Whitestone's foremother is not Eliza Boardman Clerc but Mabel Hubbard Bell. It is Boardman Clerc who deserves more attention here as the true radical. She, more so than Sophia Fowler, could have been more like Mabel Hubbard, honing her speech skills, as she retained some residual hearing. Entering a signing school, she walked down a different path. Laurent Clerc was a powerful example of how a deaf person could excel in society without speech. When she married this non-speaking, signing Deaf man, she chose her identity as a Deaf woman.

Other women in the nineteenth-century Deaf world followed in that path. Mary Toles, for instance, was a late-deafened girl; she lost her hearing at the age of 13, an event that rocked her parents, who at first believed that her hearing loss would be "the ruin of her life." They finally sent her to the New York School for the Deaf when she was 15 years old. From their point of view, it seemed like an act of resignation, an admittance that she was really deaf, and would need a specialized education. But, given the late onset of her deafness, it comes as no surprise to discover that she was said to have a beautiful speaking voice. Toles could have easily retained her place in the hearing world, and, indeed, she was always a person who could move comfortably between worlds. But she, like Boardman, identified herself with the Deaf world.

She graduated from the New York School in 1853. In 1854, she married a hearing man, Isaac Lewis Peet, whom she had met at the school. Peet was the vice principal of the New York School for the Deaf. His father, Harvey Prindle Peet, was the school's principal, and a giant in the field of deaf education. The Peets were committed manualists, wedded to the use of sign language for all deaf children. When Isaac took over as principal after his father's retirement, he would become one of the key supporters of manualism, as oralism mounted its challenge to the educational establishment in the late nineteenth century.

By marrying Peet, Toles took her place as an advocate for manualism, for the sign language, and, by extension, for the Deaf community, as a community of manual language users increasingly under pressure to speak. She did not raise her voice; instead, she raised her hands for the deaf. She even taught as a teacher in the New York School for several years after her marriage. As one observer noted of the Peets, "The father, three sons, and a nephew were actively engaged in the work and their hearts were in it. Their wives were interested in it, too. I wonder if we shall see the like again in the profession?" (Jenkins 305).

It would have been relatively easy for Toles, with her beautiful speaking voice, to pass as hearing, but she chose instead to be seen as a Deaf woman. She attached herself to a family deeply invested in the Deaf community, and joined them in their work with deaf children. Unlike Mabel Hubbard, she neither rejected her own deafness nor sought to disassociate herself from the Deaf community she had joined so late in her childhood. To Toles, her deafness "proved a blessing in disguise, giving her opportunities for education she could not otherwise have enjoyed, broadening and elevating her whole future life" (Fay 301).

Her ability to make that series of choices may have had something to do with her luck in being educated in the 1850s. The 1850s marked a crucial decade in the life of the nineteenth-century Deaf community. Scholars have pointed to that decade as the one which an ethnic consciousness had emerged among the deaf, the decade when it became clear that their deafness had been transformed into Deafness. Physical deafness was no longer something that inevitably consigned a person to a limited life on the margins of the hearing world, without a community to call home. Now it could be a ticket into a larger community, the newly emerged community of Deaf people. As Toles would discover, her future was not limited, but broadened, by her deafness, as she went from being a deaf girl to becoming a Deaf woman.

But it would not be as easy a path to follow as the century wore on. The first oral schools opened in 1867, and by century's end, oralism would dominate the entire system of deaf education. A girl like Toles would have been steered by her oralist teachers quite aggressively to pass, by the 1880s, for instance. Her ability to shape her deafness into Deafness would have surely waned.

This was the same problem the Deaf community as a whole faced. As oralism seized control of the educational arena, the traditional place where Deaf culture flourished, the residential school, increasingly became a more hearing place instead. Mabel Hubbard Bell was a role model for young deaf women there, not Eliza Boardman Clerc. The ability to enter the hearing world on hearing terms was prized by educators above all else. The Deaf world was condemned. In fact, oralists like Bell hoped that the oral method over time would succeed in destroying the Deaf world entirely. What need would there be for a Deaf world, when all deaf people spoke, not signed, and moved easily in the hearing world?

Oralists, of course, viewed these outcomes as indications of progress. How could anyone complain about a world without Deafness? But Deaf people, who cherished their history, community, and language, completely disagreed. They fought instead to preserve their world, even as oralist and eugenic attacks increased. They continued to fight into the late twentieth century as the war on the Deaf turned high tech with the introduction of cochlear implants. The following questions arise: who gets to determine the meaning of a deaf life, the Deaf or the hearing? To whose values, Deaf or hearing, do we attend when we debate the future of deafness in our society?

Finally, to whose example do we point, to demonstrate a deaf life well lived? Do we point to Eliza Boardman Clerc? Or do we point to Heather Whitestone? That is, do we understand that a deaf woman can mother as deaf? Or do we insist that the deaf mother must remake herself as hearing, in order to mother in our society? Do we, as a society, have the eyes to see that technology might be limiting our sense of the possible, as well as expanding it? For while Heather Whitestone may think she has gained a world by hearing, Eliza Boardman, Sophia Fowler, and Mary Toles would suggest that she has lost a world, and so have we.

For if we unquestioningly celebrate Heather Whitestone and her example of a deaf mother turned hearing, we might come to believe in turn that one must be hearing to mother well. We risk losing our ability to imagine a social world that includes our disabled sisters and honors them in their disability, believing that they too can marry and mother, and thus take on the major life roles of adult American women generally. And if we cannot even imagine it, will we remain willing to fight for that world? Will we fail to support disabled women as they seek to determine their own futures? Will we instead decide that we, as able-bodied people, know better than they what their future ought to be?

Whose example speaks to us? A nineteenth-century pioneer of disabled women's rights? Or a modern-day pioneer of medical technology? The answers matter, for us, for our sisters, and for our daughters.

WORKS CITED

Anders, Gigi. "Beauty and the Battle," *USA Weekend* (March 3-5, 1995): 4-6. Print.

Baynton, Douglas C. *Forbidden Signs: American Culture and the Campaign Against Sign Language.* Chicago: University of Chicago Press, 1996. Print.

Black, Edwin. *War Against the Weak: Eugenics and America's Campaign to Create a Master Race.* New York: Four Walls Eight Windows, 2003. Print.

Braddock, Guilbert. "Mary Toles Peet." *Notable Deaf Persons.* Ed. Florence Crammatte Washington, D.C.: Gallaudet College Alumni Association, 1973. 12-13. Print.

Bruce, Robert. *Bell: Alexander Graham Bell and the Conquest of Solitude.* Ithaca: Cornell University Press, 1973. Print.

Bruinius, Harry. *Better for All the World: The Secret History of Forced Sterilization and America's Quest for Racial Purity.* New York: Random House, 2006. Print.

Buchanan, Robert. *Illusions of Equality: Deaf Americans in School and Factory, 1850-1950.* Washington, D.C.: Gallaudet University Press, 1999. Print.

Burch, Susan. "'Beautiful, though Deaf': The Deaf American Beauty Pageant." *Women and Deafness: Double Visions.* Eds. Susan Burch and Brenda Brueggemann. Washington, D.C.: Gallaudet University Press, 2006. 255. Print.

—. *Signs of Resistance: American Deaf Cultural History, 1900-1942.* New York: New York University Press, 2002. Print.

Byrom, Brad. "A Pupil and A Patient: Hospital-Schools in Progressive America," *The New Disability History: American Perspectives.* Eds. Paul K. Longmore and Lauri Umansky. New York: New York University Press, 2001. 133-156. Print.

Deaf Life. "Readers' Responses." (December 1994): 28. Print.

Draper, Amos. "Sophia Gallaudet." *American Annals of the Deaf* 22 (July 1877): 177. Print.

Edwards, R.A.R. "Sound and Fury, Or Much Ado About Nothing?: Cochlear Implants in Historical Perspective," *The Journal of American History* 92.3 (1995): 892-920. Print.

—. *Words Made Flesh: Nineteenth-Century Deaf Education and the Growth of Deaf Culture.* New York: New York University Press, 2012. Print.

Fay, E.A. "Mary Toles Peet," *American Annals of the Deaf* 46 (May 1901): 300-305. Print.

Ferguson, Philip. *Abandoned to Their Fate: Social Policy and Practice toward Severely Retarded People in America,* 1820-1920. Philadelphia: Temple University Press, 1994. Print.

Freeburg, Ernest. *The Education of Laura Bridgman: First Deaf and Blind Person to Learn Language.* Cambridge: Harvard University Press,

2001. Print.

Gitter, Elisabeth. *The Imprisoned Guest: Samuel Howe and Laura Bridgman, the Original Deaf-Blind Girl.* New York: Farrar, Straus and Giroux, 2001. Print.

Gray, Daphne with Gregg Lewis. *Yes, You Can, Heather!* Grand Rapids: Zondervan Publishing, 1995. Print.

Hartford Daily Courant. "Convention of Deaf Mutes." August 23, 1866, 8. Print.

Hartford Daily Courant. "The Deaf Mute Convention." August 24, 1866, 8. Print.

Holcomb, Mabs and Sharon Wood. *Deaf Women: A Parade Through the Decades.* Berkeley: Dawn Sign Press, 1989. Print.

Howe, Samuel Gridley. *Second Annual Report of the Board of State Charities; to which are added the reports of the secretary, and the general agent of the Board. January 1866.* Boston: Wright & Potter, 1866. 52. Print.

Jenkins, Isabel Van Dewater. "The Peet Family." *American Annals for the Deaf* 46 (May 1901): 305. Print.

Kevles, Daniel. *In the Name of Eugenics.* Cambridge: Harvard University Press, 1995. Print.

Klages, Mary. *Woeful Afflictions: Disability and Sentimentality in Victorian America.* Philadelphia: University of Pennsylvania Press, 1999. Print.

Kline, Wendy. *Building a Better Race: Gender, Sexuality, and Eugenics from the Turn of the Century to the Baby Boom.* University of California Press, 2005. Print.

Kolchik, Svetlana. "Hearing Repaired," *USA Today* (August 8, 2002): 9D. Print.

Krentz, Christopher, ed. *A Mighty Change: An Anthology of Deaf American Writing, 1816-1864.* Washington, D.C.: Gallaudet University Press, 2000. Print.

Kudlick, Catherine. "The Outlook of *The Problem* and the Problem with the *Outlook*: Two Advocacy Journals Reinvent Blind People in Turn-of-the-Century America." Eds. Paul K. Longmore and Lauri

Umansky. *The New Disability History: American Perspectives.* New York: New York University Press, 2001. 187-213. Print.

Lane, Harlan. *When the Mind Hears.* New York: Random House, 1984. Print.

Linton, Simi. *Claiming Disability: Knowledge and Identity.* New York: New York University Press, 1998. Print.

Milligan, Maureen and Alfred Neufeldt, "The Myth of Asexuality: A Survey of Social and Empirical Evidence," *Sexuality and Disability* 19.2 (2001): 91-109. Print.

Nosek, M.A., C. Howland, D.H. Rintala, M.E. Young, and G.F. Chanpong, "National Study of Women with Physical Disabilities: Final Report," *Sexuality and Disability* 19.1 (2001): 5-40. Print.

"Nucleus Hero: Heather Whitestone McCallum," on Nucleus website, www.cochlearamericas.com Web.

Osgood, Robert. *For "Children Who Vary from the Normal Type": Special Education in Boston, 1838-1930.* Washington, D.C.: Gallaudet University Press, 2000. Print.

Pope, Anne. "Heather Whitestone McCallum: Still Listening with Her Heart," *Hearing Loss: The Journal of Self Help for Hard of Hearing People* January/February (2003). Print.

Selden, Steven. *Inheriting Shame: The Story of Eugenics and Racism in America.* New York: Teachers College Press, 1999. Print.

Supalla, Samuel. *The Book of Name Signs: Naming in American Sign Language.* San Diego: Dawn Sign Press, 1992. Print.

Toward, Lilas. *Mabel Bell: Alexander's Silent Partner.* New York: Methuen, 1984. Print.

Trent, James. *Inventing the Feeble Mind: A History of Mental Retardation in the United States.* Berkeley: University of California Press, 1994. Print.

Whitestone, Heather, with Angela Elwell Hunt, *Listening with My Heart.* New York: Doubleday, 1997. Print.

Winefield, Richard. *Never the Twain Shall Meet: Bell, Gallaudet, and the Communications Debate.* Washington, D.C.: Gallaudet University Press, 1987. Print.

4.

It's a Miracle

KATHARINE HAYWARD

INTRODUCTION

The process of becoming a mother is exciting, exhausting, overwhelming, and deeply rewarding. I use the term *process* deliberately because for me becoming a mother was a planned effort involving negotiations with my husband, health professionals, and my own body. Growing up disabled, I am very familiar with managing my health and the health care system. Yet I didn't know what it meant to be a pregnant disabled woman: where could I find an obstetrician with an accessible exam room, how could I keep my disease under control without harming the baby, how would I advocate for myself with an entirely new set of doctors and specialists, and how would I reconcile the reactions of others while constructing my own identity as a mother?

Throughout my life, I have always had aspirations similar to many others: to go to college, to have a career, to get married, and have a family. Perhaps because of support from my family, friends, and my own self-concept I always felt these goals attainable. Yet I didn't really have any models of disabled women and their lives. I can remember only one instance in my life in which I've seen a mother in a wheelchair with her child. Once on a bus, a young boy of six or seven began talking with me about how he and his mom, who used a wheelchair, got around. He spoke in a matter of fact way about how they could do everything, but that it sometimes meant doing things differently. I remember thinking that if I had a child I hoped he would exhibit such confidence in himself and pride in his mother. I am excited for the opportunity to share my story because I know we disabled mothers exist, and I wish I had someone to help show me the way.

This chapter presents my experiences and reflections throughout my pregnancy and the early months of motherhood through a critical lens utilizing aspects of the medical, social, and ecological models of disability. Models are useful tools for understanding and evaluating phenomena that are abstract in nature (Llewellyn and Hogan 158). The medical model emphasizes the individual, their impairment, and need for treatment while the social model prioritizes societal attitudes, policies, and the physical environment as imposing disability onto individuals (Bickenbach et al. 1174-1176; Hughes and Paterson 330). In my experience, both models offer partial truths. I am not solely my impairment or diagnosis. The way in which I am treated and how I am able to access my community and its resources plays an important part in my everyday life, and the extent to which I feel disabled. However, there are also days that due to pain and limited mobility I am not even able to get out the door. Below I present arguments and critiques of the medical and social models, and recommend the ecological model as an alternative framework for understanding the disabled mother experience.

MODELS OF DISABILITY

Medical vs. Social Model

Several models have been used to understand the disabled experience. Two of the most frequently used models, often in conflict with each other, are the medical model and social model of disability. The medical model took prominence in the 19th century as significant advances were made in medicine. It stresses rationality and science over religious origins in explaining cause of disability (Drum 27; Lupton 36). The medical model views a disabled person as deviating from biomedical norms of physiological or cognitive function resulting from disease or other sources of damage (Bickenbach et al. 1173; Llewellyn and Hogan 158). This places the disabled individual as dependent upon the physician for diagnosis and treatment (Llewellyn and Hogan 158). The goal of the physician is thus to identify any biological abnormalities and "fix" them.

Disabled individuals are viewed as being in a perpetual sick role. As such, disabled individuals are helpless, passive, and dependent upon others. (Fine and Asch 12). Disabled individuals are excused from performing their usual roles and duties, but are expected to respect and follow the orders of medical professionals (Drum 28; Fine and Asch 12; Pfeiffer 98; Waxman 194). For a woman, traditional roles may include wife and mother. A disabled woman may not only be excused from such roles, but perceived as incapable of fulfilling them. Waxman (195) elicited such responses in an exercise of free association with college students who described a woman as "intelligent, leader, soft, lovable, mom, wife," while a disabled woman was described as "crippled, lifeless, someone to feel sorry for, lonely, ugly."

The social model views disability as a social construction shaped by physical characteristics of the environment, cultural attitudes, social behaviors, and the institutionalized rules, policies, and practices of private and public organizations. (Bickenbach et al. 1174). It is used by disability rights advocates to politicize disability by focusing on the relationship between an individual's impairment and the nature of the environment in which the individual functions (Hahn 40). In this model social discrimination is the obstacle to overcome, not the disability (Bickenbach et al. 1174). Under the social model, my disability is not defined by the fact that I use a wheelchair. My disability is created through physical and social barriers such as not being able to take laboratory science courses at my high school because these courses were held in the second story building with no lift. Both the physical accessibility of my high school and the attitude by administrators that this was not their problem created barriers to achieving necessary requirements to attend college, that I was forced to resolve.

The social model of disability has been an important strategy in politicizing disability, and thereby creating legislation and policies that prevent discrimination and ensure access. However, in its politicization of disability the social model has removed the body from discourse. A criticism shared by both those within and outside the disability community is that the social model ignores the real pain, both physical and psychological, that may be associated with impairment (Hughes and Paterson 328; Oliver 38; Swain and French 571; Thomas 577; Williams 135). As a disabled person with a chronic condition characterized primarily by pain, the social model devalues a very real part of my experience. This is not to say that there aren't larger socio-political issues that need to be addressed to advance the rights and participation of disabled individuals in their community. However, the fear of weakening a necessary civil rights movement has restricted an important discourse of the body. The body is a site of meaning, has a history, is fluid and evolving, and is at the core of our lived experience. It is not simply biology as the medical model would propose nor is it inconsequential as the social model may imply through its absence.

Ecological Model

The medical and social models of disability both present important factors in understanding the complexity of the disabled experience, but are both faulted for their singular nature. Some disability scholars have argued for a universalistic approach which posits the entire population is at risk for chronic illness and disability, and that at some point we will all experience some degree of functional limitation (Shakespeare and Watson 25). The universalistic approach argues for policies that would benefit all, acknowledging disability as fluid and continuous (Pfeiffer 98; Turner 264; Williams 138). The ecological model, developed by Bronfenbrenner to help explain the child development process, provides an alternate framework in which to understand the disabled experience in a more universalistic and holistic manner. The ecological model describes the interaction between the individual and the environment under a particular context at different points in time. It begins with the individual and moves outward to acknowledge the multiple systems affecting an individual including the: 1) microsystem consisting of social and physical environments that directly influence an individual including one's home, immediate family and friends, 2) mesosystem, representing the interrelationships between the settings an individual interacts with (system of microsystems), such as work and home, 3) exosystem, or wider organizational policies that indirectly influence an individual such as the health care system, and 4) macrosystem, reflecting the overarching cultural beliefs, norms, and values that set the greater societal context for which disability is constructed. (Bronfenbrenner 39-40; McLeroy et al. 354; Russell 145). An additional dimension spanning each of these subsystems is the chronosystem demonstrating the importance of time in understanding the disabled experience, both in terms of sociohistorical conditions as well as fluidity within one's lifespan (Bronfenbrenner 40).

Throughout this chapter I will discuss the multiple facets of my experience as a disabled mother incorporating aspects of the medical, social, and ecological models of disability. I begin with myself, my body, my mind as the site for negotiating new meaning and as the site for reaction. Several other individuals and environments influenced this process including my husband, my parents, and my home (microsystem). Interactions with doctors (mesosystem) and the health care system (exosystem) became a focal point during my pregnancy and early postpartum months. The attitudes and beliefs about disability (macrosystem) infused themselves into every aspect of my life from the reactions of close friends to medical professionals to strangers on the street. My experience is also affected by variations in my impairment over time and their interaction with my son's transition to different stages of development (chronosystem).

MY IMPAIRMENT: JUVENILE RHEUMATOID ARTHRITIS

Although not the focus of this chapter, I think it is necessary to understand my experiences in the context of my impairment, disability, chronic health condition or whatever you want to call it. The formal diagnosis is juvenile rheumatoid arthritis (JRA), an autoimmune disease that I have had since eighteen months of age. JRA is defined as occurring before the age of 16 with symptoms that include joint stiffness and pain, limited range of motion, warm, swollen, or red joints, fever, rash, and other symptoms that are specific to the various types of JRA (A.D.A.M. Medical Encyclopedia). Tiffany Westrich, a woman with rheumatoid arthritis and founder of the International Autoimmune Arthritis Movement, describes the feeling of rheumatoid arthritis as: pain similar to that after an accident or injury, flu-like symptoms such as nausea, fatigue, and weakness, and physical exhaustion as if just finishing a marathon. She goes on to explain in her article "What does rheumatoid arthritis feel like?" that the flu, injury, and exhaustion are occurring simultaneously, and unlike an illness or injury persists beyond a few days. (Westrich). This description resonates with my experience. JRA is a painful, constant ache in nearly all parts of my body that at times disrupts even the simplest tasks such as getting dressed. One of the most annoying characteristics is its unpredictability. I have had periods in my life where I have felt almost athletic and other times where I have used my wheelchair exclusively. As Westrich states, "Having Rheumatoid Arthritis is not the end of the world it's just another way of living in it." Adapting and readapting are common themes in managing my health, and in turn how I perform my role as "mom." My planning for pregnancy represents the first of many areas where I would need to do things a bit differently.

PREPARING FOR PREGNANCY

At age 12, I started a clinical trial of what at the time seemed a radical medication, methotrexate, which would modify juvenile rheumatoid arthritis itself. All medications come with various risks and side effects. This particular medication causes miscarriages and birth defects, a fact I came across myself when trying to better understand how it affected my disease. At no point during my adolescence while taking this medication did any physician explain this risk to me or advise me to consider birth control when I became sexually active. At some point in my twenties after moving through the health care system, I remember my rheumatologist discussing the serious risks of methotrexate and the steps I would need to take if I ever wanted to become pregnant. This discussion came more than a decade after I had educated myself on the toxicity of this drug and become more proactive in asking questions about my medications and hypothetical pregnancy. The next steps seemed a bit daunting since they required me to stop taking the medication for three months before even trying to become pregnant. At the time my husband and I were discussing this next step I had been taking this medication for 22 years.

There is some literature that pregnancy has a positive effect on rheumatoid arthritis, although there is very little known about what the protective properties of pregnancy are or who will benefit from them. There is also very little that is specific to women with a history of JRA as opposed to adult onset rheumatoid arthritis. Prior to her 1991 study, Ostensen (881) reported only two true studies of pregnancy and JRA in the literature. While there is possibility of remission during pregnancy, there is also potential for a significant flare postpartum. For me, there was also anxiety about the length of time I would be without specific medications while trying to conceive and the theoretical benefits that would occur during pregnancy. My husband and I knew that becoming pregnant would require deliberate planning, but had slightly different time frames for when to start the process. There had been ideas we would start quickly after our wedding, requiring me to stop taking a core medication for managing my arthritis three months ahead of time. However, I did not want the possibility of being in great pain on what was to be a happy day. We compromised that I would stop taking the medication right after the wedding and in three months we could get to the serious act of trying.

SPREADING THE GOOD NEWS

After about six months of trying to become pregnant, nine months including the three months of ridding myself of the methotrexate, I saw in print the word Pregnant on a home kit. You hear about the various people the new mom-to-be calls when she first realizes this exciting and life altering news: her husband/partner, her mom, a close friend. In addition to my husband, my doctors were among the first to know. My husband's reaction was that of relief, which I found humorous since relief is often the reaction people exhibit when hoping they're not pregnant. I expected shock and excitement. He said he was relieved because he felt I wasn't going to be able to make it much longer off my medication and not pregnant. I suppose in his eye we were nearing an unspoken deadline.

I experienced an array of different reactions upon sharing the good news that we were pregnant, some expected and some surprising. I received the usual congratulations and excitement, but also incredulity and concern. More than a few times my pregnancy was described as "miraculous." There were the rare reactions from acquaintances of, "they let you get pregnant," referring to genuine, although not malicious surprise that doctors would allow such an occurrence, as if I needed permission. It was not the variety of responses that was difficult at times, but from where the reactions came. We had not been widely announcing our attempts, so shock seemed appropriate. There were some generational differences on both sides of our families where there was an assumption that for whatever reason I would not be able to have a baby. However, there were a couple of instances when someone close to me reacted with deep concern at my happy announcement. This, for me, was one of the more difficult reactions for me to contend. As a first time mom I had my own concerns, some related to my disability, some related to being a first time mother. It is one thing to feel you have to defend yourself with strangers, but another with those who are in your inner circle. I knew with my rational mind that the concern for me was rooted in love. But my hopeful heart felt deflated. I took a stance that people could have their concerns, but they weren't allowed to dump them on me. I had my own anxious mind to calm late at night, and I was certain any doubts anyone else had were already in my repertoire of "what am I doing."

NAVIGATING PRENATAL CARE

Doctors play an important role for anyone with a chronic condition. Their knowledge and understanding of current treatments, attitudes towards the patient, and how they view health all affect how they interact with their patients. This in turn affects, although partially, the way the patient begins to see herself or at least the way she feels she is being perceived. My husband and I felt very fortunate that my rheumatologist at the time we were planning to get pregnant was our cheerleader from the start. She saw no reason for me not to be a mom. Although I wouldn't have let a doctor who wasn't as supportive deter me from trying to start a family, it made for a very different and less stressful experience for someone knowing the complexity of my body to say you can do it and you deserve it. During my pregnancy I interacted with several new physicians who exhibited various reactions from a purely medical, matter of fact philosophy to inquisitive, genuine interest at how this was really going to work.

The initial planning for pregnancy was nothing compared to the vast coordination and management that occurred during my pregnancy. It had to be managed from so many angles. I've mentioned that JRA is my primary disability, but I also have hypertension and anxiety. This meant there were additional medications that needed to be reviewed and modified. Getting into the ob/gyn's office, quite literally, was the first order of business. At the time of my pregnancy I was walking and intent on maintaining that as long as possible. However, I had to be forward thinking and plan for the possibility of becoming less mobile as I gained weight. For this reason I needed to find a physically accessible gynecologist's office which meant an adjustable exam table. I was fortunate to live in an area where this was attainable.

My first visit to the ob/gyn, the doctor took one look at my list of medications and wasn't sure she had the knowledge base to handle the complexity of my situation. I hadn't been there more than a few minutes when I was already being referred to a perinatologist. Again I was in search of a physically accessible exam table. I found an office that maintained a room with an accessible exam table, but prior to my arrival appeared to be functioning as a storage room. My first visit required the rearranging of boxes and defunct equipment for me to enter with my wheelchair. Despite my multiple visits this became a pattern of moving objects around and searching for a properly working portable sonogram.

However, the attitude of the perinatologist was quite different from the obstetrician. The perinatologist felt my pregnancy could be monitored by my ob/gyn, and that the perinatology staff would handle the management of my blood pressure. One thing I love about specialists is that I am not that interesting to them. To a primary care doctor or an ob/gyn I am complex and demanding. However, in the realm of complicated, high risk pregnancies I was barely a dot on their radar. It was a wonderful experience, for once, to not be that special.

My pregnancy team was expanding. I had my usual primary care physician, rheumatologist, ob/gyn, and perinatologist. I took the title of pregnancy coordinator, making sure that each doctor was monitoring the various tests and that each physician was aware of the various prenatal treatment plans. Between working and all of my medical tests and doctor visits, my weeks were booked. In a way my pregnancy had become another condition. In fact, I was in multiple pregnancy studies as simply being pregnant with JRA was cause for additional scrutiny. Others were often amazed at how well I was doing with my pregnancy. I did have many symptoms of pregnancy, but I was used to dealing with side effects from my arthritis and my medications. Nausea, fatigue, and swelling were already regular occurrences. It is not that I didn't enjoy being pregnant, but much of my time was spent in the hospital and meeting with doctors. Due to the hypertension, I started non stress tests at 32 weeks. In the last couple of months, I was in a doctor's office or at the hospital routinely three times a week and at times almost on a daily basis. The constant interaction with the medical system and the demands it put on my time made it difficult to feel fully present in every moment.

SURVIVING MOTHERHOOD

Breastfeeding

Prior to my son being born I was asked by various women whether I planned to breastfeed. My answer was that I was going to try. Having a background in public health, I am aware and believe in the importance of breastfeeding for its nutritive and protective properties as well as the bond that it nurtures. Within hours after my son was born I was giving it a try. At first the breastfeeding appeared to be going well. While in the hospital, I mostly breastfed while lying down. After a couple days, this method didn't seem to be working as the best position nor did my son seem to be getting enough to eat. After a mild breakdown, no doubt fed by lack of sleep and exhaustion, I recommitted myself to trying as long as I could. At home I continued breastfeeding with the addition of a supplemental nursing system (SNS) to ensure my son got enough nutrition. The SNS while simple in design was a project in itself. A small container of formula was clipped to my shirt while the feeding tube was attached to my nipple with surgical tape so that my son would get the additional needed nutrition while breastfeeding. The process required an extra pair of hands which led to uncomfortable closeness with some family members. Use of the SNS also lengthened the time of each breastfeeding session, and consequently the amount of energy I expended. Even with the wonders of the "boppy" and other breastfeeding accompaniments, the breastfeeding position was becoming more difficult to sustain. In those early months I was breastfeeding every couple of hours which included 30-40 minutes of actual breastfeeding time. My posture became compromised and my arms would remain stiff and sore for the length of time in between feedings.

It was also becoming increasingly apparent that I was not dealing well with the sleep deprivation. Sleep is important for all of us to function, but is also an instrumental component in managing a chronic condition. In truth I can't remember much of that time except feeding and holding my son. My short term memory disappeared and the only thoughts I could really hold on to were my son. Again my husband and I were fortunate to have doctors who supported us and looked out for my well-being. This time it was my son's pediatrician who after seeing me at one of his routine visits reminded me that taking care of myself was an important part of caring for my son. I must have looked as tired as I felt because much to my husband's relief, we were encouraged by the pediatrician at six weeks to use a bottle twice a day. I reserved this reprieve for the night shift and after a few days of six to seven hours of consistent sleep I was a new person or at least more myself.

Adapting Environments

In addition to breastfeeding, there were many other everyday tasks to figure out how to perform. In the first few months, my son slept in a bassinet which was at a good height and small enough for me to easily place my son. But soon we would need to move to a crib and he would grow bigger and still need to be carried. In addition to my disability, I am short and many of the traditional cribs being sold did not work for me to place my son onto even the highest level. Fortunately, we had a hand-me-down drop side crib that would work better, but I still needed to be able to find a way to access the crib when we had to lower the mattress. Through some of my work in the local disability community I was connected with Through the Looking Glass,[1] a nonprofit organization that serves disabled parents as well as parents of disabled children through information, referral, and training. At the time I was living in Berkeley, California, where the center is located, and was able to take advantage of in-home training and the design of adaptive baby care equipment. To date I still use my three prized pieces of adapted baby furniture: adapted crib, high chair seat on a walker, and bike seat attached to my mobility scooter. Our crib was modified to include sliding crib doors so that I could place my son directly onto the mattress without bending over the rails. As he started becoming more mobile, he quickly took to crawling into the crib himself. The high chair on a walker base serves the same function as a high chair, and when my son was younger allowed me to move him from room to room without carrying him. And what became my favorite was the bike seat that through creative testing and handiwork was connected to the base of my mobility scooter.

During the first few months before we had the seat added to my scooter, I could not take my son out with me. During my early outings, without my son, I would recognize every mother with a stroller and think I should have my son with me. Not only would it be easier to run my errands having him with me rather than waiting for someone to be available to watch him, but I loved my new identity as a mom and wanted to show it to everyone by having him with me. Once I had the child seat on my scooter, my world opened up. We went to the grocery store, the drugstore, and out for walks. Nearly every time we go out together, I hear other people comment on how "cool" the seat is. From these different comments I realized that this piece of adaptive equipment is more than a way to increase my mobility and flexibility in having my son with me as I take care of daily tasks such as getting more diapers or milk. Simply by being out and about in the community we are sending the message that disabled women can be and are moms.

Negotiating the physical environment and learning to adapt to my new parental tasks was one part of being a disabled mom, but there were also the emotional and psychological aspects. I was confronted with some of my own insecurities as a mom while attending the 2011 Superfest International Disability Film Festival. Superfest is an annual showcase of juried films that features the work of disabled performers, disabled filmmakers, and all facets of the disability community in general. I have been involved with Superfest for several years as one of the judges and supporters. This time as I sat in the audience I had a new identity shaping my perceptions of the films, one as a disabled mom. With this new identity, the film "Mothersbane" had a strong effect. Culture!Disability!Talent! describes Mothersbane on their website as: "a personal documentary that explores the filmmaker's ambivalent relationship to his mother's physical disabilities and frequent surgeries. It is a mixed-media portrait, alternating between the present–in which his mother ... prepares for a major surgery–and recollections of the filmmaker's past. The film uses 'Super 8 recreations of childhood memories to express the love and anxiety, and protectiveness and dread that has defined his [the filmmaker's] relationship with his mother.'"

As a new disabled mom, I began to worry about how my son would perceive me as he grew older. Would he express anger at times at my inevitable falls, injuries, and bad days? Would he be frustrated that he has to help his mother to perform seemingly simple tasks? How would having a disabled mom shape his view of the world?

Adaptive Parenting

Soon the predictable unpredictability of my disease would present itself. As if to test my worst fears, I experienced several injuries before my son turned one. When my son was seven months old while sitting on the couch with him, I heard a pop. My fears were confirmed when I realized I couldn't put weight on my leg. I was hoping that this was a temporary issue, but in the back of my head I was worried that the thing I had avoided for twenty years was occurring; my hip replacement had dislocated. At this point in time I lived an hour away from the closest extended family so this trip was going to involve all three of us. It took an hour to get myself, my son, and my husband into the van to start our short ride to the emergency room. After scans and several attempts at hip reduction, it was deemed that I had in fact dislocated my hip and would be staying overnight. Once my hip was successfully reduced I felt much better, but now I had a six-week recovery process and full leg brace to input into the parenting equation. I could take care of myself and manage my daily activities, except now my daily activities included caring for an infant who was crawling and cruising. As my son's mobility increased, my mobility decreased temporarily, creating a need for additional support. My mom excused herself from teaching summer school, and would stay with us for the next six weeks for half of every week to help in caring for our son.

Three months later while running errands on my scooter with my son, part of my jacket got stuck on a door while leaving a restaurant, pulling my arm back while my scooter continued forward. Another cracking sound and all I focused on was getting us home safely. By this point our son had started walking, but he still needed to be picked up to transfer to his high chair, bike seat on the back of the scooter, and changing table. We arrived home and by chance someone was doing work on our house so I was able to get my son in the house with some assistance. A trip to urgent care was imminent, but I now lived in the same city as my parents, my brother and his wife. With the greater source of available supports our son remained at home while my husband took me to urgent care. While it took five weeks of various doctors, surgeons, x-rays, and scans to finally pronounce my elbow as broken, I knew that day I was again going to negotiate a new plan for maintaining a daily routine that included at least some lifting.

These incidences point to the need for social support as well as adaptability. Adaptability is an interactional process of constructing and reconstructing routines based not only on my physical abilities, but also my son's developmental stage and access to sources of support. Each of these variables changes over time. Being a mother is a kind of relationship. On my own, a dislocated hip or broken elbow is a nuisance, but does not necessarily change the core of my activities. As a mother, these limitations have a different meaning both practically and emotionally. That being said, my impairment and disability is only one factor in the mother-son relationship. My son is an active agent in determining what will work for both of us and what support we might need. One example is I was trying to discover alternate ways of changing my son as it was getting harder to lift him onto the changing table. An occupational therapist had a great idea about using steps so he could climb up to the changing table. It was a good idea, except my son greatly disliked being changed, and instead of using the steps to climb up to the changing table he created a new plaything. Despite having a plan, I did not have cooperation. The dance of adapting involves finding alternative ways of performing tasks that work for me and my son.

CONCLUSION

In this chapter I presented various models in which to examine disability, providing examples from my experiences as a disabled mom. My experience is a product of many factors, not solely explained through my impairment nor my physical and social environment. These factors are not distinct compartments, but rather interdependent. For this reason, the ecological model provides a useful framework for examining the disabled mom's experience. The ecological model accounts for the fluidity inherent to disability through its focus on interacting environments over time. At the core of the ecological model is the physical, intellectual, and emotional self. I experienced many emotions during my pregnancy and as a new mother related to managing my impairment, taking care of my son, and constructing a new identity. My mental and physical health was affected by the supports I received from my husband and immediate family (microsystem) and varied over time (chronosystem) depending on my level of mobility as well as my son's.

My interactions with doctors (mesosystem) affected my construction of the mother role and how I acted at home. Having doctors, both mine and our pediatrician, support me through my pregnancy and postpartum period gave me the freedom I needed to take care of myself and adjust my daily activities to what worked best for me. I was also fortunate to find physician offices with accessible exam rooms and an organization that supported disabled parents (exosystem). These community resources ensured quality prenatal care and enhanced my ability to fully engage as a mom while easing physical stress.

Beliefs about disability (macrosystem) ranging from tragedy to disability as simply a part of life were reflected in the reactions of others: incredulity, worry, and excitement. These reactions, in turn, affected my own sense of self. At times, the attitudes of others served to compound my own fears and insecurities, and other times reminded me of changing perceptions of disabled individuals as active community members. My identity as a disabled woman has been transformed by becoming a mother. Each day poses new challenges, necessitates novel approaches, and rewards me with unknown joys. And I wouldn't trade it for anything.

NOTES

[1] See http://www.lookingglass.org/home

WORKS CITED

A.D.A.M. Medical Encyclopedia. "Juvenile Rheumatoid Arthritis." *PubMed Health*. U.S. National Library of Medicine, last reviewed June 28, 2011. Web. 3 Aug. 2012

Bickenbach, Jerome E., Somnath Chatterji, E.M. Badley, and T.B. Uestuen. "Models of Disablement, Universalism and the International Classification of Impairments, Disabilities and Handicaps." *Social Science & Medicine* 48.9 (1999): 1173-1187. Print.

Bronfenbrenner, Urie. "Ecological Models of Human Development." *Readings on the Development of Children*. Eds. Mary Gauvain and Michael Cole. New York: Freeman, 1993. 37-48. Web. 28 July 2010.

Culture!Disability!Talent! "Superfest 2011 Winners." *Culture! Disability! Talent!*, n.d. Web. 8 May 2012.

Drum, Charles E. "Models and Approaches to Disability." *Disability and Public Health*. Eds. Charles E. Drum, Gloria L. Krahn, and Hank Bersani, Jr. Washington, DC: American Public Health Association, 2009. 27-44. Print.

Fine, Michelle and Adrienne Asch. "Disability Beyond Stigma: Social Interaction, Discrimination, and Activism." *Journal of Social Issues* 44.1 (1988): 3-21. Print.

Hahn, Harlan. "The Politics of Physical Differences: Disability and Discrimination." *Journal of Social Issues* 44.1 (1988): 39-47. Print.

Hughes, Bill and Kevin Paterson. "The Social Model of Disability and the Disappearing Body: Toward Sociology of Impairment." *Disability & Society* 12.3 (1997): 325-340. Print.

Llewellyn, A. and K. Hogan. "The Use and Abuse of Models of Disability." *Disability & Society* 15.1 (2000): 157-165. Web. 21 Feb. 2007.

Lupton, Deborah. *The Imperative of Health: Public Health and the Regulated Body*. Thousand Oaks, CA: Sage Publications, Inc., 1995. Print.

McLeroy, Kenneth R., Daniel Bibeau, Allan Steckler, and Karen Glanz. "An Ecological Perspective on Health Promotion Programs." *Health Education and Behavior* 15 (1988): 351-377. Web. 19 April 2007.

Oliver, Michael. *Understanding Disability: From Theory to Practice*. New York, NY: St Martin's Press, Inc., 1996. Print.

Ostensen, Monika. "Pregnancy in Patients with a History of Juvenile Rheumatoid Arthritis." *Arthritis and Rheumatism* 34.7 (1991): 881-887. Web. 24 July 2012.

Pfeiffer, David. "The Disability Paradigm." *Journal of Disability Policy Studies* 11.2 (2000): 98-99. Print.

Russell, Fran. "The Expectations of Parents of Disabled Children." *British Journal of Special Education* 30.3 (2003): 144-149. Print.

Shakespeare, Tom and Nicholas Watson. "The Social Model of Disability: An Outdated Ideology?" *Research in Social Science & Disability Volume 2: Exploring Theories and Expanding Methodologies.* Eds. Sharon N. Barnartt and Barbara M. Altman. Oxford: Elsevier Science, 2001. 9-29. Print.

Swain, John and Sally French. "Towards an Affirmation Model of Disability." *Disability & Society* 15.4 (2000): 569-582. Web. 23 Oct. 2006.

Thomas, Carol. "How Is Disability Understood? An Examination of Sociological Approaches." *Disability & Society* 19.6 (2004). 569-583. Print.

Turner, Bryan S. "Disability and the Sociology of the Body." *Handbook of Disability Studies.* Eds. Gary L. Albrecht, Katherine D. Seelman and Michael Bury. Thousand Oaks: Sage Publications, 2001. 252-266. Print.

Waxman, Barbara F. (1991). "Hatred: The Unacknowledged Dimension in Violence against Disabled People." *Sexuality & Disability* 9.3 (1991): 185-199. Print.

Westrich, Tiffany. "What Does Rheumatoid Arthritis Feel Like?" *Healthcentral.* Healthcentral, 14 Dec. 2011. Web. 5 Mar. 2012.

Williams, Gareth. "Theorizing Disability." *Handbook of Disability Studies.* Eds. Gary L. Albrecht, Katherine D. Seelman and Michael Bury. Thousand Oaks: Sage Publications, 2001. 123-144. Print.

5.

Use of Aids and Adaptations in Childcare for Mothers with Spinal Cord Injury

ANITA KAISER, KATHRYN BOSCHEN AND DENISE REID

INTRODUCTION

The generalized life course of finding a mate and having children remains consistent for women following a spinal cord injury (SCI). Childcare requires a great amount of physical endurance for most people, particularly mothers with SCI who have reduced strength and mobility. Utilizing childcare aids and adaptive techniques is essential for mothers with SCI to perform their childcare tasks.

Adaptive techniques have been described in the literature as a learned behaviour between parent and child that enables the successful execution of a childcare task, while taking into consideration the parent's abilities and limitations. The adaptive technique may be applied by the parent with SCI, the child, or both and has been seen in infants from as young as one month old. Typically, adapted techniques have been utilized in areas such as diaper changing, lifting, transferring, and transporting the child.

Previous works have classified childcare tasks into activity groups such as feeding, dressing, diaper changing, bathing, transporting (including lifting and transfers), sleeping, and playtime. Likewise, childcare aids can be categorized according to childcare activity, such as an adapted highchair for feeding or an adapted crib for sleeping.

The benefits and main purpose of childcare aids are to reduce environmental barriers, thereby increasing the parents' involvement in childcare and facilitating the relationship between the disabled parent and the child. Unfortunately, not many commercial childcare products are suitable for parents with SCI, and few adapted childcare aids exist. In many cases, parents modify commercial childcare products or individually customize childcare equipment to suit their needs. The main concern is that modified commercial products invalidate warranties and jeopardize safety standards.

Additional barriers to effective parenting include a lack of adequate education, financial support, social support, accessibility in and outside the home, and information resources.

The disability culture perspective, described in the works of researchers at Through the Looking Glass (TLG), embodies the social model of disability and provides the framework for this study. This paper presents part of the findings of a larger study on mothers and fathers with SCI. The purpose of this study was to understand the use of aids and adaptive techniques in the caregiver role of mothers with SCI. The disability culture perspective facilitated identification of the barriers within society that limited the mothers' autonomy in childcare and enabled the generation of recommendations for future policy change[1].

METHOD

Approach

The value and diversity of ways of combining quantitative and qualitative methods has been well documented (Goering and Streiner, 1996; Pope and Mays, 1995; Strauss and Corbin, 1998; Tashakkori and Teddlie, 1998). A thorough search of the literature produced no suitable assessment tool for recording type and utility of childcare aids. Therefore, a study-specific questionnaire to gather quantitative data was developed for this project to highlight the mothers' use of childcare aids and their involvement in childcare activities. As well, one-on-one interviews with each mother provided detailed qualitative information on how the mothers care for their child.[2] Ethics approval for this study was obtained from the Toronto Rehab and University of Toronto Research Ethics Boards.

Sample

Participants were recruited through a poster and advertising campaign at the Lyndhurst Centre of Toronto Rehab (now UHN/ Toronto Rehab) and the Canadian Paraplegic Association Ontario (now Spinal Cord Injury Ontario (SCIO)). A convenience sampling method was used where eligible individuals were contacted via phone or word of mouth and recruited on a first-come first-serve basis. Participants were six mothers with either traumatic or non-traumatic SCI, living within the Greater Toronto Area, who had had a child post-injury under the age of six at the time of the mother's consent to participate in the study.

Procedures

A pilot study was conducted first to test the clarity and validity of the interview guide. Participants recruited through SCIO were two women with SCI who had had a child post-injury currently six years of age or older. These mothers would not have been eligible for the actual study. Revisions were made to the interview guide and the pilot study was terminated.

Potential participants were screened over the telephone to determine their eligibility to participate in the full study. A demographic form was filled out for individuals who met the inclusion criteria and verbal consent was obtained over the phone. The information collected on the demographic form included the participant's contact information, SCI etiology, hand function, ages of child/children, and willingness to participate. All eligible participants were invited for an interview that subsequently took place either at the participant's home or in a private room at Toronto Rehab.

On the day of the interview, participants signed a consent form and filled out a questionnaire. The questionnaire was divided into three sections. The first section required participants to rate a set of six childcare activities (feeding, dressing and changing, bathing, transporting, leisure, and bedtime) in order of importance to them. The second section asked participants to indicate which childcare aids they used within each of the six childcare activity groups, how they were acquired (standard commercial product, modified standard, adapted aid, or custom-made), and whether the childcare aids met their needs (yes, partially, no). The final section required participants to indicate their three most essential childcare aids.

Immediately following the questionnaire, in-depth, one-on-one interviews were held with each participant. During the interview, participants were asked to elaborate on their responses to the questionnaire in addition to answering questions regarding their involvement in childcare, their use of childcare aids, and their access to resources and services. The interviews lasted 1-1½hours in duration. They were audio-taped for quality assurance and transcribed verbatim.

Data Analysis

Data from the six demographic forms and questionnaires were entered into an Excel spreadsheet. Descriptive statistics were used to analyze the information collected from the demographic form. The questionnaire was analyzed in conjunction with corresponding responses provided through the interview transcripts. The information was presented as percentages and frequency counts both graphically and in table format, and supplemented with data drawn from the interview transcripts.

Transcribed interviews were verified for accuracy and completeness and then the data were coded into categories of information using a conventional content analysis approach (Hsieh and Shannon, 2005; Elo and Kyngas, 2007). The constant comparative process was used to compare newly coded transcripts with previously coded transcripts, and any new information that arose was coded into new categories. Participants were continually recruited and interviewed until no new information arose and saturation of categories was achieved. Once all transcripts were fully coded, an inductive process was used to relate and connect categories together. Categories of information were continuously regrouped until several main themes emerged from the data.

Dependability, credibility, and transferability were achieved through the use of verbatim accounts from participant interviews, inter-analyst comparisons of coded transcripts, triangulation, and saturation of categories (Burla et al., 2008; Elo and Kyngas, 2007; Graneheim and Lundman, 2004; Hsieh and Shannon, 2005; Tashakkori and Teddlie, 1998). Sources of triangulation included mixed methods design, multiple raters, questionnaires, and interview transcripts.

The following terminology was used for reporting the qualitative interview findings in relation to the number of participants in the study:

All   = all 6 participants
Most = 4-5 participants
Some = 3 participants
A few = 1-2 participants

FINDINGS

Participants

Six mothers with SCI participated in this study. Five mothers were Caucasian, had sustained a traumatic SCI, had full hand function, and were primary caregivers of their children. Four mothers were married and financially independent, while the remaining two mothers were single and lived on social assistance.

Involvement in Childcare Activities

In the first section of the questionnaire, participants ranked six childcare activities in order of importance to them. Mean scores indicated that feeding the child was ranked as the most important activity, followed by leisure, dressing and changing, transporting, bathing, and bedtime. Participants reported that the non-physical aspects of parenting (emotional engagement, bonding, and communication) were much more important to them than the physical aspects, and were something they were all capable of doing independently. Feeding, particularly breastfeeding, was considered by the mothers to be a necessity, as well as an important opportunity for them to bond and interact with their child. Bedtime was ranked as the least important activity to be involved in because of the challenge of lowering the rail of the crib and transferring the child to bed without waking up the child.

Participants said that their degree of involvement in childcare activities depended on a number of factors including their physical capabilities and adaptive techniques, their child's level of independence and adaptation to their abilities, the availability of suitable childcare aids, and accessibility of the environment. They said that in most instances they combined aids with adaptive techniques to perform their childcare tasks.

Every participant found at least one of the childcare activities challenging in some way. Most mothers however negotiated their role by participating in tasks or activities with their child based on their own abilities. In situations where a task was too difficult or unsafe to perform, participants would forego the task to their spouse, family member, or support provider. This often occurred with outings to the playground which most mothers complained about being inaccessible. Accessibility both in and outside the home was described as a barrier to childcare.

At other times, participants reported engaging in difficult tasks by assisting their spouse or other family member in a supportive role while the family member performed the bulk of the task. For example, one mother who was unable to bathe her child would assist her parents by passing them items, or taking her child after the bath to wrap her in a towel and dry her.

Some participants stated that they were able to complete the majority of a childcare task, yet required an able-bodied person to assist with difficult aspects of the task or simply play a supervisory role in the chance of an unforeseen circumstance that they may not have been able to handle. Often, participants stated they would restrict their leisure activities or outings to when a support person was available.

All participants reported that they were independent with some of their childcare tasks. Even then they had to contend with various issues, like the level of difficulty and energy required to execute the task, which often affected the frequency with which the task was performed. In instances where the difficulty and required energy level were high, participants would only perform the specific task on rare occasions when it was a necessity and no other individuals were around to assist. A prime example is bedtime routines, which most mothers were able to perform independently but with great difficulty.

Table 1 presents participants' current level of involvement in each of the six childcare activities, which were further divided into more specific tasks based on what participants described during their interviews.

All participants were independent with dressing and changing their child and had the most difficulty with bathing their child, with half of them not being involved at all. Accessibility within the bathroom, limited strength and balance, and fears and safety concerns over handling their child when they were wet and slippery were the key issues stressed by the mothers. Most mothers were independent with feeding, leisure, and bedtime activities. They were also able to transfer and transport their child indoors, but had great difficulty transporting their child outdoors due to a lack of suitable aid, such as an adapted stroller.

Some participants recognized that their level of involvement with each

Childcare Activity		Mothers $(N = 6)$
Feeding		1 primary with support 5 independent
Dressing and Changing	Dressing	6 independent
	Changing	1 not applicable 5 independent
Bathing		3 not involved 1 assistant 2 independent
Transporting	Indoors	1 not involved 5 independent
	Outdoors	2 not involved 4 independent
	Transferring	1 not involved 5 independent
	Lifting	2 not involved 4 independent
Leisure		1 primary with support 1 independent 2 independent
Bedtime	Naptime	1 not applicable 5 independent
	Bedtime	1 not involved 5 independent

Table 1: Current level of involvement in childcare activities.

Note: Not Applicable represents situations where the child is older and independent in that particular activity. Not Involved represents situations where the participant is not involved in that particular activity. Assistant represents situations where the participant acts as an assistant to the primary caregiver when performing the task. Primary with Support represents situations where the participant is the primary caregiver for that particular activity, but requires some assistance either directly or indirectly through supervision in order to complete the task. Independent represents situations where the participant is independent in that particular activity either with or without the use of childcare aids.

childcare activity increased in relation to their child's growth and development. For example, a few participants reported being unable to bathe their child as an infant due to their lack of strength and balance, yet when the child learned to sit up independently the mothers were able to perform the task. Most mothers reported relying heavily on their spouse, other family members, or support providers to aid with childcare and they spoke of this reliance as being a necessity. A lack of support was described as a huge barrier to parenting and a few mothers spoke about their worries over the unbalanced parental roles and the burden they were placing on their spouse and other family members. This mother described it best, "I want to be independent. I can't ask my husband to do everything. You bathe the baby, you transfer the baby. You hold the baby. No I can't do that. I'm her mother."

Most mothers stated that planning was a crucial aspect of parenting. Participants maintained that planning ahead was essential in order to make sure they had support providers available to assist them with difficult childcare tasks, as well as to enable them to find time for self-care needs and to get relief from childcare.

Type and Utility of Childcare Aids and Adaptations

Participants were very resourceful when it came to figuring out how to be involved in childcare. In some cases, they were able to purchase adapted aids like a reaching aid that allowed them to pick up toys off the floor or other objects that were beyond their reach. In most instances childcare aids were unavailable for purchase or simply did not exist, in which case the mothers had to make do with standard childcare equipment purchased at regular department stores.

A few participants described how they modified some of their standard childcare equipment to better meet their needs, such as cutting the legs off a change table to make it lower for them to use. Some participants were able to find specific brands of standard childcare equipment that were suitable for them such as breastfeeding cushions with belts that they could strap around themselves and their wheelchair. For the most part, participants reported substituting useless standard childcare equipment with items in their home to meet their needs. For example, some participants used a desk as a substitute for a change table.

The second section of the questionnaire asked participants to indicate all childcare aids they used for each childcare activity, how they were acquired, and whether the aid met their needs. Utility of the aids were calculated using the need ratings as follows: $yes = 1, partial = 0.5, no = 0$. The following formula was then used to calculate utility:

$$\frac{X_{1(yes)}+X_{1(partial)}+X_{1(no)}+\cdots+X_{n(yes)}+X_{n(partial)}+X_{n(no)}}{Y_1+\cdots+Y_n} \times 100$$

where X represents the number of responses for that need rating, Y represents the number of participants who used the aid for that particular childcare activity and n represents the childcare activity the aid was used for.

In total, 120 childcare aids or combination of aids were used by participants to perform their childcare tasks. The majority of aids (77.5%) were standard commercial products, many of them being substituted household items. Only 5% of aids were standard commercial products that were modified after purchase, and no aids were custom-made. The remaining 17.5% of aids were adapted equipment purchased at a healthcare store. Of the 120 childcare aids owned by participants in this study, 61.4% completely met participants' needs, 17.0% partially met participants' needs, and 21.6% of aids did not enable participants to perform the designated childcare task.

Participants used 24 different types of childcare aids to perform their childcare tasks (see figure 1).

Over 40% of childcare aids were used for leisure activities. Only two types of aids were used for dressing and changing the child: the change table and the parent's bed. Participants used several interesting combinations of aids in order to feed and transport their child, such as a bouncy chair on the couch for feeding and the child's clothes (mainly overalls) for lifting them up off the floor. Participants reported that as their child grew older they had to change aids in order to accommodate the growth of their child, such as switching from a baby carrier to a lap belt when transporting their child.

Seven of the 24 types of childcare aids served multiple functions for some of the mothers in this study (see table 2).

The two types of aids that supported participants the most in performing their childcare tasks were the change table and their bed with or without the aid of pillows, which served four functions each. All aids which served multiple functions were used for feeding and leisure activities. Four of the multi-functional aids were used by only one participant, and none of the aids that served multiple functions were used to bathe the child.

Popularity of childcare aids, as shown in Figure 1, did not reflect utility (see figure 2). For example, the crib was used by five participants but had a utility score of only 50%. One-third of childcare aids had 100% utility, half of which were used for leisure. Nearly one-third of childcare aids

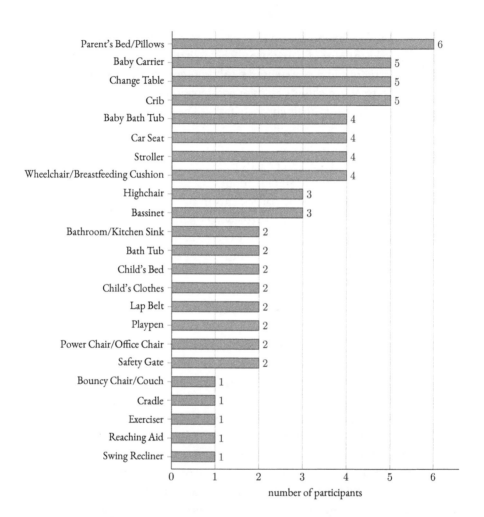

Figure 1: Types of childcare aids used by participants in order of popularity.

Childcare Aid	Childcare Activity					
	Feeding	Dressing	Bathing	Transport	Leisure	Bedtime
change table	✓	✓			✓	✓
parent's bed with/without pillows	✓	✓			✓	✓
swing	✓				✓	✓
wheelchair with/without cushion	✓			✓	✓	✓
bassinet					✓	✓
bouncy chair on couch	✓				✓	
recliner	✓				✓	

Table 2: Childcare aids with multiple functions.

had less than 40% utility. In the interviews, items participants most complained about being poorly designed and impeding their involvement in childcare were the stroller, car seat, bath tub, and crib. The childcare activities with the highest average percent utility of childcare aids were feeding (82%), leisure (77%) and bedtime (75%). Bathing had the lowest average percent utility with a score of 50%.

In the final part of the questionnaire, participants had to indicate their three most essential childcare aids. Overall, there was minimal agreement, but the four aids selected by more than one participant were the baby carrier, breastfeeding cushion, change table, and crib, two of which served multiple functions. None of the essential aids were used for dressing or bathing the child. In the interviews, participants described essential aids as being handy, functional, convenient, multi-functional, and safe to both the parent and the child. Participants stated that essential aids made the task faster and easier to perform, and reduced the hassle, energy, and pain when performing the task. Essential aids also enabled some participants to be independent and mobile with their child.

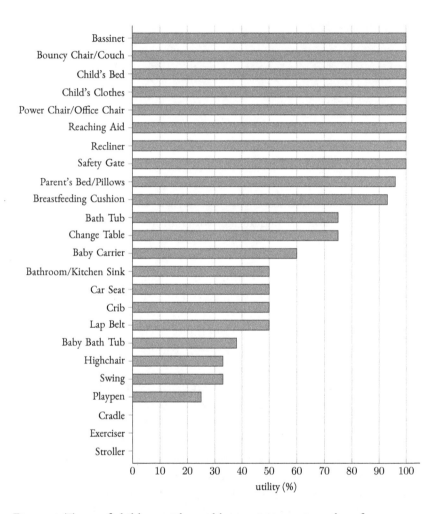

Figure 2: Types of childcare aids used by participants in order of greatest utility.

Adaptive Techniques

A unique insight some participants spoke of was the adaptation of their child to their disability. In some instances the adaptation was positive and aided the participants in performing their childcare tasks, such as when their children would learn to lift their hands and feet up or roll from side to side to assist the mothers with dressing and changing them. At other times, the child's adaptation to the mother's disability was negative and impeded their ability to care for their child, such as when the child would purposely hide behind furniture where their mother couldn't reach them. In addition, participants spoke about how they adapted their technique in order to perform their childcare tasks, such as using a table to lean on and support their upper body as they transferred their child on and off their lap. Often, the mothers and children adapted to one another during a childcare task, such as when the child would learn how to climb up onto the mother's lap in the wheelchair by stepping on her feet and grabbing her thighs as the mother would grab the child and pull him or her up.

Quality and Availability of Information Resources and Services

Most participants found they had to be self-directed learners and found the internet to be the most effective tool for gathering information on parenting for people with disabilities. On the whole though, most participants stated that there was a lack of information available and a limited number of resources. A few mothers felt they had been misinformed regarding available services, childcare aids, and capabilities of people with SCI to become parents.

Most participants had minimal success in finding adapted childcare aids. Products that were discovered online, such as adapted cribs, were all custom-made or not available in Canada and were considered to be costly and unaffordable, particularly for the mothers on a fixed income. These mothers were unaware of funding sources to acquire the necessary aids and ultimately had to settle with purchasing standard childcare equipment that they were unable to use, which limited their involvement in those specific childcare tasks.

Most participants described peer support as being an invaluable resource for learning about available services, resource information, and childcare aids, yet only a few of them knew of or spoke to other parents with SCI. Of greatest worth were the experiences that other SCI parents were able to share with the participants on how they performed specific childcare tasks.

With regards to available services, participants mentioned a few organizations and hospital programs in their community that were helpful in providing some general information on infant care, such as breastfeeding and diaper changing. But overall they felt that information specific to parenting with a disability was limited and that there was a shortage of knowledgeable experts.

Some participants were critical of the lack of support and assistance they received from government organizations. Participants who utilized homecare services had difficulty increasing the number of hours of assistance they required during pregnancy and afterwards. These mothers were also surprised that homecare did not provide them with any assistance in child care.

Discussion

For the mothers in this study, motherhood meant engaging in meaningful childcare activities which focused more on the non-physical as opposed to the physical aspects of parenting. Similar findings were reported by Kirshbaum and Olkin (2002) who described how feeding and leisure activities allowed mothers to nurture, interact, and bond with their child.

In spite of their disability, most of the mothers in this study maintained a primary caregiver status within their home, a role that was stressed in other works as well (Alexander, Hwang, and Sipski, 2001; Cowley, 2007; Reid et al., 2003). The type and degree of involvement in childcare activities was often carried out in a strategic manner based on the mother's capabilities. Previous studies also reported how husbands or other support persons performed childcare and household activities that the mothers with a physical disability were unable to carry out (Alexander, Hwang, and Sipski, 2001; Kirshbaum and Olkin, 2002; Prilleltensky, 2003). Tulega and Demoss (1999) described the execution of childcare activities in terms of the concept of task demand, which combines two elements: difficulty and effort. Similarly to how we reported difficulty and energy expenditure affecting the frequency at which a task is performed, they explained that certain tasks, such as bathing the child, may require a great deal of effort by the parent to set up but the task itself is not difficult for the parent to do.

Overall, this study and previous works found bathing and bedtime to be the most challenging activities (Alexander, Hwang, and Sipski, 2001; Cowley, 2007). Alexander and colleagues likewise reported mothers struggling with outdoor activities such as taking their child shopping or to a playground. Tulega and Demoss (1999) reported transitional tasks, such as transferring the child to bed, as being the most challenging aspect of childcare, which was also stated by mothers in this study.

Tulega and Demoss (1999) reported how the absence of childcare aids limited parents' role in childcare and increased their need for formal and informal supports. Childcare aids increased the balance in division of labour between couples (Kirshbaum, 2000), and mothers with physical disabilities stated that their satisfaction with their role in the family would be improved with the provision of childcare aids and better accessibility and services (Cowley, 2007; Kirshbaum and Olkin, 2002).

Use of childcare aids and adaptive techniques, although varied among participants in this study, was central to their successful involvement in childcare. Most intriguing are the adaptive techniques children develop to compensate for their mother's limitations during a childcare task. Although previous studies failed to identify negative adaptations that hindered parents in their caregiver role, as was expressed in this study, they did describe the reciprocal adaptation between parent and child (Cowley, 2007; Kirschner et al., 2010; Kirshbaum 2000; Kirshbaum and Olkin, 2002; Tulega and Demoss, 1999).

Lack of appropriate childcare aids can severely hinder involvement in childcare, especially in SCI. What literature exists in this area notes that most standard childcare aids fail to meet the needs of parents with disabilities, and adapted aids are unavailable on the market (Kirshbaum and Olkin, 2002; Reid et al., 2003; Stonehouse, 1999; Tulega and Demoss, 1999). Often, childcare aids are either individually customized or are commercial products that have been modified after purchase (Demoss et al., 1995; Kirshbaum and Olkin, 2002; Shein, Nantais, and Tonack, 2003; Stonehouse, 1999; Tulega and Demoss, 1999). Several other studies, in addition to this one, report on the various types of aids that parents with physical disabilities use to care for their children.[3]

Mothers in this study tended to use mainly standard commercial products, many of them being substituted household items. Although the findings here indicated no relationship between utility and popularity of childcare aids, a strong relationship does exist between utility of childcare aids and involvement in childcare. In fact, childcare activities that participants considered to be the most important to be involved in (feeding and leisure), were the activities that they were actually most involved in, as well as the activities with the greatest utility of childcare aids (feeding 82% and leisure

77%).

Alexander and colleagues' (2001) study of 88 mothers with SCI reported similar use of childcare aids with the five most common being the reaching aid, adapted baby carrier, adapted change table, adapted crib, and harness or straps. As well, aids that mothers in Alexander's study reported the greatest need for, such as the baby bathtub and stroller, were aids that had less than 40% utility in this study. The lack of appropriate aid for these childcare tasks is reflective of the mothers' limited involvement in these activities.

Poor accessibility, both in and outside the home, decreased independence in childcare. Tulega and Demoss (1999) described how the physical layout of the home and space restrictions affected the number and types of childcare aids parents could obtain. Further obstacles including poor transportation, inaccessible home environments, inaccessible parks and buildings, poorly designed sidewalks, and winter conditions hindered parents' autonomy and participation in childcare (Kirschner et al., 2010; Kirshbaum 2000; McKeever et al., 2003; Paltiel, 1997; Reid et al., 2003; Stark, 2001).

Although the preferred format of receiving information was not discussed in other works, a few did mention the importance and value of formulating a peer network (Kirschner et al., 2010; Prilleltensky, 2003; Stonehouse, 1999). Nevertheless, the lack of resource information and services hindered parents in their caregiver role and can be directly correlated with poor ability to plan. In effect, parents in this study implied that knowledge leads to planning, which leads to independence in childcare. In other words, with the appropriate knowledge mothers could have better prepared themselves by organizing a support system and acquiring childcare aids in order to optimally care for their child (Kirschner et al., 2010; McKeever et al., 2003).

Other studies reported similar findings of poor resources and services, conflicting resource information from service providers, and lack of professional expertise (Cowley, 2007; Kirshbaum and Olkin, 2002; Paltiel, 1997; Prilleltensky, 2003; Reid et al., 2003). A 1993 survey of 49 Toronto community health centres found only 13% had staff with special training in dealing with women with disabilities. They also identified numerous barriers to health care, including inaccessible facilities, stereotyped attitudes of health care providers, judgmental attitudes towards pregnant women, and lack of funding for women-centered counselling services (Paltiel, 1997).

Moreover, reliance on informal supports seems to be commonplace since formal supports are inadequate or non-existent, creating an imbalance in division of labour within the family and hindering the mothers' autonomy in their parental role. Prilleltensky (2003) described a nurturing assistance program that enabled mothers to bond and interact with their child, and perform childcare tasks they were otherwise unable to do. However, in general, access to attendant services for personal care was readily available, yet support for the mothering role was not (Kirschner et al., 2010; Prilleltensky, 2003; Reid et al., 2003).

The absence of funding assistance for childcare aids and infant care was prevalent in the literature and a particular hardship for parents relying on social assistance (Kirschner et al., 2010; Kirshbaum 2000; Prilleltensky, 2003; Stonehouse, 1999). Kirshbaum and Olkin (2002) found that childcare aids were seldom reimbursed by public or private health or disability funding systems. Moreover, they stated that 48% of parents were unaware of how to acquire adapted aids.

Based on insights provided by mothers in this study, several recommendations are proposed to manufacturers of assistive devices, health care providers, and policy makers. These recommendations coincide with the priorities established by the National Task Force on Parents with Disabilities and their Families (Preston and Jakobson, 1997).

First, mothers with SCI have the potential to be more involved in childcare if they had the appropriate aid. Manufacturers of assistive devices need to develop adapted childcare products that are commercially available, multifunctional, and have a universal design to enable parents with or without disabilities to perform their child care tasks. Funding support is needed for individuals living on social assistance.

Secondly, due to the scarcity in resource information and poor quality of services reported by participants, an online information service needs to be provided that would allow access to vital information to all mothers with SCI. A practical resource guide would also enable new mothers to learn from the experience of other parents with SCI. Creating a peer support network of mothers with SCI would be an invaluable educational tool for new parents.

In addition, more knowledgeable service providers are needed to assist mothers with SCI in accessing information resources and acquiring childcare aids. Nurturing assistance and temporary increases in attendant care hours for women during their pregnancy and afterwards is also needed. Finally, a system of service needs to be developed where hospital-based programs can be linked with community services to ensure that information and support is provided to parents with SCI from the time they are thinking about having children until after the child is born and gains independence in his/her activities of daily living.

CONCLUSION

Many issues and struggles of parenting are common to all mothers; however, compromised strength, balance, and mobility restrictions pose an additional challenge to mothers with SCI that able-bodied parents do not have to contend with. Use of childcare aids and adaptive techniques is central to the mothers' successful involvement in childcare. Information resources and services are essential to support mothers with SCI in their parenting role. Future research directions could aim to develop childcare aids and a health service delivery model to address the needs of parents with SCI.

NOTES

[1] Information for this section has been obtained through the following sources: Albright, Duggan, and Rahman, 2009; Collins, 1999; Conyers, 2003; Cowley, 2007; Demoss et al., 1995; Kirschner et al., 2010; Kirshbaum, 2000; Kirshbaum and Olkin, 2002; Prilleltensky, 2003; Reid et al., 2003; Stonehouse, 1999; Tulega and Demoss, 1999.

[2] Since the strength of the study came more from a qualitative than a quantitative analysis, a dominant/less dominant sequential design explained by Tashakkori and Teddlie (1998) was selected. For this design, data collected from the study's less dominant quantitative phase were used to help guide and focus the dominant qualitative phase of the study, as well as to provide a meaningful way to work with the data.

[3] See Alexander, Hwang, and Sipski, 2001; Carty, 1998; Cowley, 2007; Demoss et al., 1995; Hunter and Coventry, 2003; Kirshbaum and Olkin, 2002; Shein, Nantais, and Tonack, 2003; Stonehouse, 1999.

WORKS CITED

Albright, Kathie J., Colette H. Duggan, and Reece O. Rahman. "Motherhood in the Context of Spinal Cord Injury." *Topics in Spinal Cord Injury Rehabilitation* 15.1 (2009): 43-58. Print.

Alexander, Craig J., Karen Hwang, and Marcalee Sipski. "Mothers with Spinal Cord Injuries: Impact on Family Division of Labor, Family Decision Making, and Rearing of Children." *Topics in Spinal Cord Injury Rehabilitation* 7.1 (2001): 25-36. Print.

Burla, Laila, Birte Knierim, Jurgen Barth, Katharina Liewald, Margreet Duetz, and Thomas Abel. "From Text to Codings." *Nursing Research* 57.2 (2008): 113-7. Print.

Carty, Elaine M. "Disability and Childbirth: Meeting the Challenges." *Canadian Medical Association Journal* 159.4 (1998): 363-9. Print.

Collins, Carol. "Reproductive Technologies for Women with Physical Disabilities." *Sexuality and Disability* 17.4 (1999): 299-307. Print.

Conyers, Liza M. "Disability Culture: A Cultural Model of Disability." *Rehabilitation Education* 17.3 (2003): 139-54. Print.

Cowley, Kristine C. "Equipment and Modifications that Enabled Infant Child-Care by a Mother with C8 Tetraplegia: A Case Report." *Disability and Rehabilitation: Assistive Technology* 2.1 (2007): 59-65. Print.

Demoss, Anitra, Judith Rogers, Christi Tulega, and Megan Kirshbaum. *Adaptive Parenting Equipment: Idea Book I.* Berkeley, CA: Through the Looking Glass. 1995. NCDDR Hosted Registry Resources. 28 Nov. 2003. Print.

Elo, Satu, and Helvi Kyngas. "The Qualitative Content Analysis Process." *Journal of Advanced Nursing* 62.1 (2008): 107-15. Print.

Goering, Paula N., and David L. Streiner. "Reconcilable Differences: The Marriage of Qualitative and Quantitative Methods." *The Canadian Journal of Psychiatry* 41.8 (1996): 491-7. Print.

Graneheim, U.H., and B. Lundman. "Qualitative Content Analysis in Nursing Research: Concepts, Procedures and Measures to Achieve Trustworthiness." *Nurse Education Today* 24.2 (2004): 105-12. Print.

Hsieh, Hsiu-Fang, and Sarah E. Shannon. "Three Approaches to Qualitative Content Analysis." *Qualitative Health Research* 15.9 (2005): 1277-88. Print.

Hunter, Nicole, and Anna Coventry. "A Part of Life's Tapestry: Early Parenting with a Spinal Cord Injury." *British Journal of Occupational Therapy* 66.10 (2003): 479-81. Print.

Kirschner, Kristi L., Judy Panko Reis, Debjani Mukherjee, and Cassing Hammond. "Empowering Women with Disabilities to be Self-Determining in Their Health Care." *Delisa's Physical Medicine & Rehabilitation: Principles and Practice* (5th Edition). Ed. Walter R. Frontera. Philadelphia, PA: Lippincott Williams & Wilkins, 2010. 1524-44. Print.

Kirshbaum, Megan. "A Disability Culture Perspective on Early Intervention with Parents with Physical or Cognitive Disabilities and Their Infants." *Infants and Young Children* 13.2 (2000): 9-20. Print.

Kirshbaum, Megan, and Rhoda Olkin. "Parents with Physical, Systemic, or Visual Disabilities." *Sexuality and Disability* 20.1 (2002): 65-80. Print.

McKeever, Patricia, Jan Angus, Karen-Lee Miller, and Denise Reid. "It's More of a Production: Accomplishing Mothering Using a Mobility Device." *Disability and Society* 18.2 (2003): 179-97. Print.

Paltiel, Freda L. "The Disabled Women's Network in Canada." *Sexuality and Disability* 15.1 (1997): 47-50. Print.

Pope, Catherine, and Nick Mays. "Reaching the Parts Other Methods Cannot Reach: An Introduction to Qualitative Methods in Health and Health Services Research." *British Medical Journal* 311 (1995): 42-5. Print.

Preston, Paul, and Margaret Jakobson. *Keeping our Families Together: A Report of the National Task Force on Parents with Disabilities and Their Families*. Oakland, CA: Through the Looking Glass, 1997. Print.

Prilleltensky, Ora. "A Ramp to Motherhood: The Experiences of Mothers with Physical Disabilities." *Sexuality and Disability* 21.1 (2003): 21-47. Print.

Reid, Denise, Jan Angus, Pat McKeever, and Karen-Lee Miller. "Home is Where Their Wheels Are: Experiences of Women Wheelchair Users." *The American Journal of Occupational Therapy* 57.2 (2003): 186-95. Print.

Shein, Fraser, Tom Nantais, and Mark Tonack. *An Information Resource Describing Consumer Experiences with Assistive Technology: Spinal Cord Injury Peer Information Library on Technology*. Toronto, ON, Canada: Toronto Rehabilitation Institute, 2003. Print.

Stark, S. "Creating Disability in the Home: The Role of Environmental Barriers in the United States." *Disability & Society* 16.1 (2001): 37-49. Print.

Stonehouse, Heather. "Bringing the Baby Home." *The Parenting Book: For Persons with a Disability*. Ed. Judith O'Leary. Toronto, ON, Canada: Canadian Cataloguing in Publication Data, 1999. 65-79. Print.

Strauss, Anselm, and Juliet Corbin. "The Interplay between Qualitative and Quantitative in Theorizing." *Basics of Qualitative Research: Techniques and Procedures for Developing Grounded Theory*. Thousand Oaks, CA: Sage Publications, 1998. 27-34. Print.

Tashakkori, Abbas, and Charles Teddlie. "Research Design Issues for Mixed Method and Mixed Model Studies." *Mixed Methodology: Combining Qualitative and Quantitative Approaches.* Thousand Oaks, CA: Sage Publications, Inc., 1998. 40-58. Print.

Tulega, Christi, and Anitra Demoss. "Babycare Assistive Technology." *Technology and Disability* 11 (1999): 71-8. Print.

6.

Embodying my Passions

Becoming a Radical Feminist Mother

MICHELLE TICHY

INTRODUCTION

My story is deeply personal and deeply political. It is the authentic journey of one coming of age in several ways through transformative experiences that ground the personal in the political. This chapter begins several years ago at the beginning of my now completed graduate program at a large Research One University in the Midwest. It takes my journey to this point in my life as an ethno-autobiographical reflection of broader issues facing young professional women, especially in academe, who become mothers–particularly those living with hidden disabilities and chronic illnesses. My story is one of idealism, empowerment, and personal choice; the road I have taken has often challenged the status quo and made those who are comfortable feel uneasy. This paper integrates my knowledge as a social scientist, an educator, a mother, and as a self-proclaimed feminist mother. It will highlight who I am and where I am going; starting with my abbreviated childhood story to who I was in 2000 and moving through to the present time, this paper uses my story to open the dialogue reflecting on how my experiences echo the broader experiences of professional women in the early twenty-first century. The paper ends where it begins with reflections on how to apply idealism to subverting the dominant paradigm and creating an honest more equitable place for all people, regardless of gender, disability, marital status, parenting status, race, ethnicity, country of origin, sexual orientation, religious orientation, or any other difference.

WHERE I CAME FROM

I was born December 3, 1974 in New York City. I was my parent's first child, the first of three girls, and I was relatively healthy and happy. I was born with a pinhole cleft in my palate that meant that my mother had to pump breast milk in order to feed me, since directly suckling at her breast would lead to breast milk in my sinuses. My cleft palate was surgically repaired when I was eighteen months old. I was put into speech therapy to help me to fully articulate my words and to overcome the early speech challenges presented by having a pinhole cleft in my palate. None of these early challenges seemed to impact my positive self-concept as I entered preschool. By the time I was in preschool I was a big sister to the first of my two younger sisters and by the time I began second grade I was expecting the arrival of my second sister.

My youngest sister arrived six weeks early and was hospitalized for two weeks; luckily she came home healthy by Christmas that year. The day that she was due to be born I was rushed to the emergency room and was diagnosed with type 1 diabetes, otherwise known as juvenile diabetes. Amongst the shock and the lessons in doing shots into an orange, I was also warned about how dangerous it would be to ever become pregnant. Now, I was only seven years old and I am not sure why the resident thought that it was appropriate to go on and on about all the potential complications of uncontrolled diabetes to a little girl, but he did. I was in the hospital for two weeks and I heard about every possible complication and how careful I would have to be when I went through puberty to protect myself from ever accidentally becoming pregnant. This particular medical resident left a lasting impression on my psyche in all the wrong ways; I left the hospital a seven-year-old that had suddenly become highly anxious and insecure.

Over the next four years I went from being a carefree and vivacious little girl to being an anxious perfectionist who had begun to hate my body. By the age of eleven I had become anorexic with daily bouts of purging and severe restriction. No one seemed to notice that I was barely eating, making myself sick when I did, and working out hours every day. My parents' marriage was slowly falling apart and my severe eating disorder got lost in the shuffle of their constant fighting. By the age of fourteen my parents were on the path to divorce and I was passing out regularly from lack of food and low blood sugar. I was scared and asked my parents if we could get a family therapist, which was my first attempt to get help for my eating disorder and to save my parents' marriage.

I did not save my parents' marriage, but shortly before my seventeenth birthday and a few months before my high school graduation I made the decision with my therapist that I would go inpatient for treatment of my eating disorder the week after graduation. As my parents sold the home I grew up in and moved to separate corners of the world I drove off to a world-class eating disorder clinic with my abusive boyfriend who was two years older (and a story for another time). The boyfriend and I split two months after I started college and three months after I had left the eating disorder clinic. I was supposed to be at this clinic for sixty to ninety days. I lasted for fourteen days because they had never had a diabetic patient and were keeping me on lock-down, out of fear. When I left I was once again reminded that I was broken in the eyes of the medical community; not only was I diabetic, but I would never fully recover from anorexia if I left that clinic. I was reminded once again of the brainwashing I had received regarding complications and being careful not to become pregnant. I was careful, always careful; even when I was sexually assaulted I managed to make sure that no matter how badly I was being hurt I would not get pregnant. As I left the treatment center and moved to the small liberal arts college where I was due to start my first year in college I transitioned from a therapeutic environment to being an autonomous agent in my own journey.

I was actively trying to fully recover and stay on top of my diabetes; this led to more episodes of severe low blood sugar that sent me to the emergency room. Several times I heard the old mantra about being careful not to get pregnant and that this would be very dangerous for the potential baby and me. I even heard once from an eating disorder psychologist that I would be lucky to make it to my thirtieth birthday, that I would never be able to have children safely, and if I did not immediately recover I would certainly be dead before I was fifty. By the age of twenty-two I had graduated with a double major from an elite small private liberal arts college and had started graduate school. Somehow I was beating the odds at least based on what I believed all those doctors had forecast, and I was beginning to reclaim the passion and the spark of the little girl I had been before my diagnosis. In fact that strong inner child of mine encouraged me to seek out the newest technology and get myself an insulin pump and the newest glucose monitor. These two decisions have permanently changed my life for the better.

Before my insulin pump I would brown or black out from low blood sugar once a month and end up in the emergency room at least a couple times a year. Since getting an insulin pump I have not had to go to the hospital for any reason and have not had any emergency room visits for low blood sugar. I credit the insulin pump with allowing me to be brave and empowered in the next stages of my journey. An empowered decision to advocate for my healing and my self opened the door for me to transform myself into a strong agent of change in my own life. In claiming my own power and agency I also claimed my ability to be a change agent in the world, to advocate for those who need a helping hand in finding their voice.

In 2000 I was a recently engaged 20-something young woman with a BA from Oberlin College with a double major in Sociology and Religion. I had spent the previous few years working as a Program Manager for Head Start and taking graduate classes part-time in Educational Leadership. I had obtained my life-changing insulin pump and an updated blood glucose monitor two years earlier, freeing me from dangerous visits to the emergency room for severe low blood glucose. In June of 2000 I began graduate school as a doctoral student at a large Research One University. I was studying Educational Psychology with an emphasis on the Social Psychology of Education and working with world-class scholars in the field on research. Within eighteen months I was married and completing my Masters thesis; I was learning to balance work and life in a meaningful fashion. I felt a strong drive to become a mother at this point in my life. This was something that meant a great deal to me as I entered my late 20s; I wanted to experience the metaphoric and real transformation from a Warrior Maiden to becoming the archetypal and realized Mother. It was a deeply spiritual and personal desire for me as a highly educated woman; I wanted to become a mother while it was still a gentle process and prior to risking high rates of infertility or medical complications. Since I am a woman who was diagnosed at the age of seven with juvenile diabetes and who was warned from the time of my diagnosis that I "probably should not plan on having biological children," safely becoming a mother through my own physical pregnancy was a major symbol of my mastery of my own life and my capacity to beat the odds. So with this loaded backdrop I raced through my doctoral course work and successfully completed my preliminary exams, all of which I did by February 2003.

Literally the day that I successfully passed my final preliminary oral exam I decided that I wanted to become pregnant and began trying with my husband of two years. Being relatively young and healthy despite my chronic illness, I become pregnant quickly. By the end of April I had confirmed that my baby would be due in December. This success was just as deeply gratifying to me personally as my professional completion of my doctoral preliminary examinations. The messages I had received as a young woman coming of age with this chronic condition, juvenile diabetes, were very stern patronizing messages telling me to listen to the medical establishment for "my own well being." These patronizing messages were so powerful that I had deeply internalized them, as had both of my now divorced parents and my two younger sisters; I was receiving messages of "protection" and "risk avoidance" from multiple levels and my inner voice was telling me to claim my own power. So in this simple and primal act of becoming pregnant I had claimed my power as an adult woman in a way that I was unable to do through any of my intellectual accomplishments. I had claimed my right to create my own destiny and to assert my will as a healthy competent adult woman; this was something I had struggled to do for the entirety of my young adulthood. So for me the ability to successfully conceive a child was a major step towards my transformation into empowerment.

Throughout my pregnancy I received a great deal of support from my peers and colleagues, regardless of gender. At the time I perceived the positive support as a sign that academe was prepared for young mothers who made a variety of choices regarding their lives. In hindsight I see the positive attention I received as an outcome of the novelty of my being a pregnant graduate student; most of the other graduate students at my university with children had teenagers or young adult children. I was one of very few graduate students in my program that had ever been pregnant during their graduate career and most of the previous ones had taken leaves of absence. I was not taking any form of leave due to being pregnant; in fact I continued to teach throughout my pregnancy. My students were very supportive and understanding through my first and second trimester; again enforcing my contention that academe was prepared for fully empowered women who choose to become mothers.

The medical establishment, now a bit more enlightened, was supporting my journey into motherhood, with weekly visits to both my endocrinologist and a high risk OB/GYN. I had, out of internalized fear, opted for the status quo medical care for a type 1 diabetic and agreed to see a high risk OB, despite the fact that I wanted a completely natural midwife-assisted delivery. Twenty-some years of warning about the need to be hyper-cautious and to seriously consider the decision to become a mother biologically left me being abnormally conservative and compliant with medical suggestions that did not even fit. In spite of all that I had accomplished and overcome in my life, including being in recovery for a serious eating disorder, I gave much of my power over to the medical establishment during my pregnancy. I proactively sought therapy to prevent an eating disorder relapse during pregnancy, did yoga and other gentle exercise throughout my pregnancy in order to stay as healthy as possible. By giving over so much of my power to the doctors I lost some of my voice during the later part of my pregnancy, leading to me ignoring my gut instinct that I should switch to a nurse midwife. I was having an exceptionally easy and healthy pregnancy, so much so that it was not medically necessary to stay with a high risk OB. Instead of passionately fighting for my right to switch to a nurse midwife (this would have been an exception to the medical and insurance guidelines for people with IDDM) I internalized the battle. Although I do not have regrets, I am very aware that I lost some of my normal spunky and powerful self out of ingrained fear and a lack of outside support to take the alternate path during my pregnancy.

During my pregnancy, I made mindful decisions regarding transitioning into a role that would be more flexible as a graduate assistant for the end of my pregnancy and the birth of my baby. I had taken a job as a Multicultural Counselor at the university's Office of Multicultural Affairs; this allowed me to keep my health insurance while giving me a flexible schedule. During my third trimester I gave up my teaching responsibilities so that I would be prepared for the birth of my baby without having to worry about finding a replacement at the last minute. The multicultural center seemed like a very supportive and caring place to work, even as a doctoral candidate with multiple varied responsibilities. In fact a full time staff member at the center was pregnant at the same time as me and was honored for her role as a working mother.

My daughter was due December 17th, 2003 and I thought this was a perfect time to give birth since the university was closed and no one expected to see me for a month. After a thirty-two hour natural labor, I was exhausted and my baby girl was stuck in the birth canal; I tried everything that my doula and I could think of to help her move into the proper position. Four hours of pushing later and forty-five minutes of allowing the use of a vacuum extractor and I was able to touch the crown of my baby girl, but she was not coming out that way. So finally I consented to allow them to give me a cesarean section if for no other reason than that I was delirious and I just wanted to hold my baby girl. A couple more bumps in the birthing road, mostly the delay between my consenting and the anesthesiologist actually attending to putting in the spinal block into my spine, and my baby girl was finally welcomed into the world. At 9:45am on Friday December 19th, 2003 Alexisandria Kelly Tichy-Reese was born; I was finally able to hold her at 11am after I awoke to find my baby was with the nurses. Having a cesarean section was not in my plans for becoming a mother; I had envisioned a peaceful natural birth with my husband, sisters, and mother in attendance. I did have my mother, both of my sisters, and my husband all in attendance, but it had been a natural delivery that ended in surgery.

Alexisandria developed jaundice within the first two days and I was working night and day to increase my milk supply to help counteract her jaundice with more milk. Between my exhaustion and the medical model that wanted me to leave her in the hospital a few more days I felt beside myself with grief and desperation. Finally on the fourth day I asserted myself as a mother and demanded that they let Alexisandria come home with us. They agreed, allowing Alexisandria to come home with us, along with a blanket of lights that were going to help her little body break down the bilirubin that was causing her to be jaundiced. By Christmas Day Alexisandria was getting better, a home nurse who tested her bilirubin levels and her growth had visited her daily. My surgical wound was not healing well so I went to urgent care on Christmas Day and was told that my incision was becoming irritated and infected; I spent the next three weeks treating my infection with the help of my partner and his mother.

Due to all of the unexpected complications I was unable to return to work on January 18 as I had initially planned. I returned after eight weeks on February 1, 2004, having taken the extra time to heal and to establish Alexisandria's and my nursing relationship. I returned to the university with my newborn baby in tow; I was a quarter time graduate assistant and a full time student so even thinking about paying for childcare was not an option. I was confident in my ability to balance full time attachment parenting with being a full time doctoral candidate and a part time multicultural counselor. During those first few days I had my ups and downs learning to juggle an infant while typing on the computer or answering the telephone. I was blessed with some wonderful undergraduate students who loved babies and enjoyed taking Alexisandria on walks and on brief breaks from my office. I found a smooth flow in my day-to-day work; I enjoyed having my baby in my arms while I was working on projects. I was able to compile all my dissertation data that I had collected just prior to Alexisandria's birth and to begin outlining the first draft of my dissertation document while nursing my little girl. At no point during the first few weeks back to work did I question my decision to try to be an active attachment parent while returning to my roles and responsibilities at the university.

Most of my colleagues and peers seemed excited to have a newborn around campus; all my students embraced my role as a mother and offered to care for Alexisandria for short periods of time. Interestingly with this backdrop of support and understanding I faced the first incidence of female-to-female hostility related to becoming a mother within the first week of returning to campus. I had been planning on taking an interdisciplinary workshop on doing cross-disciplinary research with a female professor that I had never met. Walking into the workshop the first night I was excited and anticipating the wonderful workshop that this was going to be; little did I know what an abbreviated experience this would be for me. At the break the professor asked me to leave because as she put it "nursing is distracting and disrespectful to my other students and thus you need to leave my classroom." I had come to get the syllabus and let the professor know that I was still recovering from surgery, with a sleeping baby on a cold winter night. I had left with tears in my eyes and a sense that I needed to examine the way that this situation reflected larger societal issues that were often cloaked in the "progressive intellectualism" of the graduate school environment. I dropped this professor's workshop without a fight; her email she sent me later that night had been painfully scathing and made me lose any respect I had for her. She had gone on through several pages of email ranting about her experience in the 1980s when she had "put her academic career on hold in order to devote herself to being a stay-at-home mother." She had never obtained tenure due to this break in her process and clearly held hostility towards young women making other choices, such as myself. She was painfully clear about her belief that bringing a newborn to her classroom was disrespectful to her and the other adults in the classroom who deserved the best classroom environment possible. The implication here was that a mother with a newborn baby would undermine the serious nature of the workshop and thus I was unwelcome in that intellectual environment.

Interestingly to me at the time, I did not face any form of overt prejudice from any of my male faculty, all of whom were very supportive of me as a nursing mother, welcoming me into their classrooms and meetings. That same semester that I returned to campus as a mother I took two interdisciplinary workshops with male faculty and one class in my graduate minor of Spirituality and Healing with a male faculty member. I spoke to the other students to make sure that our presence would not be disruptive to any of them and was pleasantly surprised by the positive response I received from my peers. Alexisandria nursed and slept a lot during the workshops and classes that I took; she very rarely cried and as long as I was holding her we had amazingly smooth sailing during the six hours a week we spent in class. Meetings in my department were similarly affirming experiences, with my advisor and peers being supportive and caring to Alexisandria and myself.

My work world was a more complicated situation. Prior to Alexisandria's birth I had perceived the Office of Multicultural Affairs to be a very friendly and supportive work environment. Initially, I had felt that my assumptions had been correct; my immediate colleagues and the students with whom I interacted were all very enthusiastic about Alexisandria's presence. My whole perception shifted when we had a full office meeting with all the managers and bureaucrats involved in Multicultural Affairs; as I always did at that time I brought my baby girl with me to this meeting. During the meeting one senior colleague, who happened to be on phased retirement, began making comments under her breath regarding her inability to concentrate with "those horrible little noises." Finally she asked me to leave, because she could not "concentrate with the sounds of cooing and gurgling" going on during our meeting. I found this event to be spirit crushing and very ironic considering that several people at this meeting were having side conversations and that students kept walking by having loud conversations. I concluded that she had bigger issues with me, because there was no logical explanation for how my baby was bothering her more then the other conversations and noises that were occurring.

By the time my daughter was six months old I had awakened to the fact that my being an empowered mother and a doctoral candidate was highly threatening to the status quo of the university system. This is the point in my journey that I claimed my presence as a "radical feminist mother." I was a mother and I was on a mission to create change! I spent a great deal of time trying to find like-minded women; this was a bigger challenge than I had initially expected. I found support for my attachment parenting and extended nursing through the obvious organizations, La Leche League and Attachment Parenting groups, where I found passionate progressive women who primarily had the ability to be stay-at-home mothers. I continued to seek out support for my overall philosophy and the concrete choices that I was making as a woman and a mother. I found validation through two wonderful magazines, *Brain Child* and *Mothering*. The fact that two magazines were the closest things to a community that I was able to find was disheartening on many levels, yet I was and still am extremely grateful that these resources exist. With no easy entry organizations to connect with I began doing extensive soul searching and personal journaling. I spoke to a full spectrum of women from the very young to the very old about their experiences and insights regarding mothering in all of its forms. These conversations helped to shape my personal vision of being a mother and in claiming my voice as a woman who has chosen to become a mother while continuing my active presence in the broader world. I choose not to be the "hip urban mama" who spends my time dedicated to my work while my daughter is in the care of others. This is a valid and important choice for women to have; it is just not the role for me. I choose not to be the "stay-at-home" or "sequencing" mother, also valid and important options for every woman, just not the right choice for me. I am finding my balance on a daily basis and striving to be the best woman and mother that I can be in the present moment.

NEXT STEPS ALONG LIFE'S JOURNEY

My personal mission statement as a self-described "radical feminist mother":

I am a feminist mother

I practice attachment parenting

I practice co-sleeping and extended nursing

I am a scholar

I am an educator

I seek to balance body, emotion, intellect, and spirit in all that I do

I am a social change agent

I seek to educate those around me through example and open-minded discussion about being a mother who chooses to practice attachment parenting

EPILOGUE

Over the past few years I have continued to make regular choices regarding my life and my role as an empowered mother. I have completed and defended my dissertation; I was granted my PhD in June of 2006. I successfully obtained a tenure track job as a professor; I initially opted for a position at a small liberal arts college in order to maintain balance in my life.

After five years at the small liberal arts college I obtained a job at a state university known for its undergraduate teacher preparation programs. Both of the positions I took came with the perk of having an onsite lab school for my daughter to attend, increasing my contentment with this position and my ability to live authentically. I have ended an abusive partnership and decided mindfully to be a single mother to my daughter for five years before choosing to get remarried to my life partner, further reinforcing my empowerment as a woman. Since starting my journey as both a mother and a scholar I have re-discovered myself as an empowered woman and learned a great deal about living authentically in academe. I continue to bring my daughter with me to all of my conference presentations although now she spends her time playing with a babysitter or other children. I have become a member of the Association for Research on Mothering, which took me two years of searching to find, and now that I have I feel very affirmed in the journey that I am on. I have had the opportunity to present on two panels on Mothering in the Academe at the National Women's Studies Association and continue my intellectual exploration of my personal journey. It is my great hope that all women are offered the options to become the people that they choose to be, whether this includes motherhood or not. We are each on our own journeys and I firmly believe that it is not the role of society, the medical establishment, or even one's family to dictate the choices anyone makes about becoming a parent or not.

7.

Mothers with Fetal Alcohol Spectrum Disorder

A Need for Long Term Sustained Services

KAREN NIELSEN AND ANN MARIE DEWHURST

Karen is a Registered Clinical Social Worker. Ann Marie is a Registered Psychologist. They work together in a collaborative private practice in Edmonton, Alberta.

Parents with disabilities often face greater scrutiny and are more harshly criticized than non-disabled parents (Swain 167). Fetal Alcohol Spectrum Disorder (FASD) is a unique disability. FASD is the term used to describe various conditions that result from prenatal exposure to alcohol (Streissguth, et al 26). It is the leading known preventable cause of developmental disability in North America (Masotti, George and Szala-Meneok 24). It is estimated that nine in every 1000 babies born in Canada have FASD (Motz, et al 15: Tough. Ihe.ca). In this chapter we will explore issues and concerns that arise when FASD affected women become parents.

People affected by prenatal alcohol consumption can present with a broad range of symptoms with varying degrees of impairment (Streissguth, et al 33). The damage done to an FASD affected person is due, in large part, to the amount and timing of parental alcohol consumption. For example, if a mother was drinking heavily during the time her child's facial features were developing, her child will have some of the facial features typically associated with FASD. If she was not drinking then, her child might appear "normal" but may have other cognitive impairments (Chudley, et al 262; Mattson, et al 720). Some of the impairments are evident at birth, but some symptoms are subtle and do not become identified until an FASD affected child enters puberty and starts to struggle with more advanced aspects of development. The reality for many women dealing with FASD is that they may struggle with primary physical and health concerns, cognitive or developmental delays, learning disabilities, and executive functioning difficulties (Gibbard, Wass, and Clarke 73).

Executive functions are cognitive control processes that enable us to monitor ongoing performance in a dynamically changing environment (Barkley, Murphy and Fischer 401; Ridderinkhof, et al 132). Impaired judgment, impulsivity and other executive functioning problems typically experienced by those impacted by FASD become more obvious throughout adolescence and young adulthood and make it even more challenging when attempting to parent. (Rasmussen, et al 187). Having poor impulse control, low tolerance for boredom or frustration and the inability to anticipate the natural consequences of their actions leave women impacted by FASD at risk of becoming pregnant, having a child and having to manage the demands of parenting while still struggling to manage their own lives.

The lack of executive functioning skills is directly connected to the commonly expressed secondary features of FASD. These include indiscriminant or impulsive sexual behavior, substance abuse, violence, and crime (Streissguth, Barr and Kogan 36). As a result of their engagement in these activities, parents who are affected by Fetal Alcohol Spectrum Disorder (FASD) often come to the attention of police and child protection services (Badry 50). As these agencies engage with the woman, her parenting ability comes under scrutiny, as does her ability to juggle maintaining a proper home, attend a myriad of appointments with various authorities and maintain sobriety. It is also a time of high stress and distress for the FASD affected mother especially as she may lack sufficient natural, pro-social supports in her life to help her cope. Apprehension by child protection services of her child is a common response.

International studies have shown that parents with intellectual disabilities have child apprehension rates as high as 40–60% (Llewellyn, et al 406). Given that FASD is one of the leading causes of mental disability it is likely that the children of FASD impacted adults make up a large percentage of those who are apprehended. Curtis (3) describes that there are two basic reasons why parents are involved with child protection systems. The first reason is because of the parent's active behavior choices and patterns, i.e., they have done something specific to put the well-being of their children at risk. Such behavior includes involvement in criminal activities, substance abuse, family violence, etc. Assessments related to active behaviours often involve risk assessments related to the recurrence of specific problem behaviours. Curtis also identifies that parents can be involved with child-protection services due to their passive behavior. Passive behaviours are defined as those parental actions necessary for normal child development that the parent is either unable or unwilling to perform. These passive behaviours are typically considered neglect and are often connected to a parent's lack of capacity to complete parenting tasks due to the parent's level of relevant knowledge or general cognitive functioning ability. A woman impacted by FASD must demonstrate that she is capable of meeting an acceptable standard for being a "good enough" parent who can actively nurture her child while minimizing her child's exposure to harm. To demonstrate this she must prove that she can be a competent parent throughout her child's development.

The Centre for Parenting and Research (14) in Australia defines competent parenting as having three dimensions: perceptiveness, responsiveness and flexibility. Perceptiveness refers to the parents' awareness of their child and what is happening in the child's environment, and the effects of their own behavior on a situation and on their child. Responsiveness refers to the degree to which the parent connects with their child. Flexibility is the parent's ability to respond in different ways according to the needs or demands of specific situations. Parental competency is directly linked to the parent's capacity to parent.

Parenting capacity is the ability to parent in a "good enough" manner in the long term. Parenting ability is the capacity of the individual parent to perform specific parenting tasks under specific circumstances. The parent may or may not be able to maintain the task performance effectively in the long term. The Centre for Parenting and Research (15) maintains that the capacity of a parent to meet the basic criteria for "good enough" parenting can be influenced by a number of factors including substance abuse, marital conflict, stress, mental health problems and learning difficulties. A particularly important issue within this discussion is the parent's ability to empathize with their child and put the needs of their child ahead of their own. Parents impacted by FASD have difficulties consistently providing "good enough" parental care and as a result often become involved with child protection services.

Our experience with FASD affected parents arises from our counselling and assessment work with clients referred by our local child protection organization, an inner city youth support program and the federal government health services program for First Nations and Inuit peoples. Malacrida (100) describes that the social constructions of disability as synonymous with incompetence result in disabled women being disadvantaged in many ways. In our practice, the women we meet have multiple disadvantages. They have thin or non-existent support systems in part because they themselves were raised in the care of child protection agencies. Their own parents were unable to care for them for a variety of reasons. The typical reasons for them going into care included: being abused in one or more ways (i.e., physically, sexually, and emotionally); being exposed to inappropriate behaviours (e.g., prostitution, drug abuse, violence, etc.); being neglected (e.g., physical, emotional, medical or academic needs) or abandonment by their previous caregivers. These experiences often lead to disruptions in their own developmental processes that, in turn, exacerbate their FASD symptoms.

We are often introduced to our clients after a crisis has occurred and child protection services have intervened. Our clients have typically had their children apprehended and are working with us to regain custody of, or access to, their children.

As we discuss the issues that arise for FASD affected mothers we would like to introduce you to Rita. Rita is the name we have created to represent a composite of two clients. We did this to ensure the anonymity of our clients; both gave permission for us to use their life experiences in this paper. She is a thirty-year-old mother of four children who was pregnant with her fifth child when she came into the first counselling session. She has a grade eight education and no work history because of her frequent pregnancies and her limited education. Each of her children had a different father and none of the fathers are involved in the care or support of her children. However, two of her former partners continue to visit with her on an irregular basis. At least four of her former partners have been physically abusive to Rita, including the two who have maintained contact with her.

Rita has excellent verbal skills and demonstrates some insight into the sources of the difficulties in her life. She requested counselling to deal with her ongoing feelings of depression and anxiety. She reported having panic attacks on a regular basis, particularly when she was out in public, on buses or when meeting people she didn't know. She described that it was difficult for her to open her door when she was feeling down and she would often not answer her phone. This behavior was causing serious problems for her because she would not answer the calls of the child protection workers trying to connect with her.

Child protection workers became involved with Rita after police responded to an incident of domestic violence perpetrated by one of Rita's ex-partners. The police contacted child protection services because: a) they noted that Rita's children were witness to the assault against her; b) Rita was abused while pregnant; c) Rita's home was extremely cluttered and filthy; and, d) there was a lack of food in the home. The child protection workers investigating Rita's situation noted her emotional difficulties and referred her for counselling and Rita complied in order to get her children back in her care. They did not know she was FASD affected at the time and the reality of her diagnosis unfolded as we worked with Rita. Rita knew that she had difficulties learning sometimes, but did not understand the nature of her cognitive impairments or why she acted or struggled as she did. Rita's view was that she loved her children and worked as hard as she could to provide for them. She also knew that while she didn't always succeed, her children at least knew that she loved them and she believed that what was best for her children was for them to be in her care.

People who have intact brains and have effective executive functioning skills often find parenting to be a challenging endeavor and know that loving a child is a necessary but insufficient standard for effective parenting (Hoghughi 293-294). Barrett and Fleming (368) suggest that some of the brain mechanisms that are regularly recruited in the mothering process systems lay within the hypothalamus, the limbic system and the cortex (which includes executive functioning). To mother effectively requires the action of systems that regulate sensation, perception, affect, reward, executive function, motor output and learning. These systems are interrelated and are sensitive to the influence of experiences in the mother's life and her day-to-day moods and behaviours. These systems are the ones typically affected by prenatal consumption of alcohol (SAMHSA FASD Center for Excellence) and make it difficult for our clients to consistently demonstrate perceptiveness regarding their children's needs, responsiveness in responding to those needs, and to employ cognitive flexibility in generating solutions to problems and issues that arise while parenting.

The mother-infant relationship has been likened to a complex dance that relies on the integrity and function of numerous physiological and behavioral systems in the domains noted above (Barrett and Fleming 368).

The "dance" is influenced by many factors, including the mother's physiology, cultural experiences, the family context that influenced her own experiences of being a child and being parented, her current thoughts and feelings about being a mother, and the stress she experiences while parenting (Barrett and Fleming 368). As noted previously, appropriate mothering behavior requires being sensitive to infant cues and selecting those cues for processing. For example, Landry, Miller-Loncar, Smith and Swan, (18) identified that it is important for parents to recognize and respond verbally when their children are rapidly developing language. This responding appears to support the development of a set of basic skills necessary for later executive processing. Mothers with FASD may not recognize that their child's vocalizations require them to respond on a consistent basis.

FASD impacted adults often have difficulty with working memory and having an accurate, felt sense of time. (Chudley, Kilgour and Cranston 262; FAS/E Support Network). Impacted adults may not notice time passing and miss opportunities to engage with their child. Our client, Rita, knew that she needed to focus on her children, listen to them and engage with them in their play. However, she would frequently get caught up in online conversations she was having and she would lose track of time, only noticing her children when they did something extreme to get her attention. One of the executive functioning skills she struggled with is the ability to be flexible in her focus and shift easily between ideas or topics. Once engaged in an activity, like interacting on Facebook, Rita could not shift her focus until her task was complete. She could not consistently act on parenting knowledge without prompting and help in redirecting her own attention.

It is also common for FASD affected people to experience a disconnection between what they know and what they do. For example, they may take parenting courses and may absorb information and be able to talk about what they have learned. They may believe that what they have learned is good information and intend to apply their new knowledge. However, in a practical situation, they may fail to act accordingly. They do not necessarily link what they know to what they do in the face of situational influences or pressures. FASD affected mothers frequently repeat parenting "errors", even when they "know" better.

Gelb and Rutman (14) explain that one of the implications of deficits in cognitive processing means that someone with FASD can seem to know something one day but forget it the next day. Another common issue that arises is that women may be inconsistent in what they tell various support people or they may know that they need to provide information but do not know what the "right" answer might be, so they make one up, i.e., they confabulate. FASD affected women may make up pieces of information in order to fill in holes in their memory or gaps in their understanding, or simply in an effort to please others. This type of behavior, i.e., confabulation, is frequently mistaken for lying (Gelb and Rutman 7); see also (Dubovsky.com). This can interfere with developing relationships; it is hard to feel close to someone whom you can't trust or believe. It also leads to many problems with people in authority, e.g., the legal system, Child Protection Services, etc., especially if the authority figure does not understand why the person is confabulating.

Not only must mothers be emotionally prepared and positively motivated to engage socially with their infant, they must be able to selectively attend to the infant in the context of competing stimuli, and they must be consistent in their responsiveness (Barrett and Fleming 369). The immediacy of the demands of others for their attention may leave the FASD impacted mother in a situation where she has to choose between the immediate gratification of a perceived need (e.g., social connection with a partner or friends, an opportunity to earn money, an opportunity to use drugs or consume alcohol) and the adherence to her original plan of focusing on her child. The mother's motivation to parent properly may not be supported in the face of competing demands and she may respond impulsively to the more pressing demands. Having a working knowledge of the woman's executive functioning skills helps us prepare reasonable parenting strategies that support the mother in realistically managing her potential for competing demands and have rescue strategies established in advance.

Like Rita, many of our clients have not been formally diagnosed with FASD and their level of cognitive functioning or executive functioning skills is not fully understood. We find that having a formal diagnosis is helpful to our clients because it opens up avenues to support and resources. However, in the absence of a formal FASD diagnosis, we find it helpful to assess our client's ability to process information and make decisions. Poor executive functioning is a common symptom associated with FASD (Anderson, Damasio, Tranel, Damasio, 289). An efficient manner of doing this is to assess the woman's executive functioning skills (i.e., the set of skills that help people manage new or difficult situations or tasks). They include the ability to engage in deliberate planning, set goals, and use feedback constructively. Put briefly, they refer to emotional control, self-regulation, organization and planning (Barkley 69). Barkley (30) also encourages us to consider executive functioning skills within the context of the individual's life and the demands placed upon them. When our clients arrive without a diagnosis, one way that we assess executive functioning skills is with the Behavior Rating Inventory of Executive Function - Adult Version (BRIEF-A) (Roth, Isquith and Gioia 1). The BRIEF is a self-report instrument that measures different aspects of a person's behavior related to emotional control and ability to plan and organize. The BRIEF gives us a picture of how the woman considers her executive functioning skills to be working and allows us to begin the explanation of how her brain works and also how we can focus our help. There are forms of the BRIEF that allow other informants who know her well to provide feedback on their perceptions of her skills. Comparing the various perspectives with our client allows us to engage her in discussion of her competency and capacity with the view to building upon her strengths and supporting her in planning to deal with her vulnerabilities.

Rita's working memory was poor. She would frequently forget her counselling appointment times and would often show up at the wrong time or not at all. She would then worry that she was in trouble and would provide explanations for her absences that were inconsistent with other information we had received from her child protection workers. Rita also missed appointments with her workers and sometimes was not home when her children were brought for visits. Initially, no one thought to remind Rita, or help her develop an appropriate strategy for remembering. Rita's behavior was initially interpreted as her "not caring" for her children's well-being or her abandoning them. Some of her workers were angry and impatient with her. Simple strategies such as reminder calls or text messages and helping Rita maintain a visually prominent calendar of her schedule greatly increased her attendance at important events and decreased the tension in her working relationships.

Another area where our clients experience significant vulnerability is with the use of intoxicants. Our clients use alcohol and various drugs (e.g., marijuana, ecstasy, crack, etc.) to self-medicate some of their psychological symptoms (anxiety, depression, etc.); to escape from the negative aspects of their lives; or as part of their social interactions. The literature points to the fact that a disproportionate number of people with FASD have substance use problems (Streissguth, Barr and Kogan 34). There is also a high likelihood that women with FASD will become pregnant due to difficulties around planning (e.g., to have condoms, to take the pill at the same time every day or to have their pills or condoms with them when they are away from home) and being assertive (e.g., saying no to exciting activities, resisting the influence of others to have unprotected sex). Given the very real possibility of substance use for women with FASD, in conjunction with likely sexual activity, these women are a high-risk group for giving birth to a baby who is prenatally exposed to alcohol.

Fatigue is another factor that can have a significantly negative impact on executive functioning. Fatigue can be defined as the perception of extreme tiredness or exhaustion that is not associated with prolonged activity and is relieved by rest (Cahill 83). According to McQueen and Mander (467), tiredness and fatigue are common problems for all parents. It has been documented that fatigue increases the risk for depression (Bozoky and Corwin 439; Corwin, Brownstead and Barton 583), a known predictor of poor parenting and child outcomes (e.g., Cohn, Campbell, Matias and Hopkins 21). Adults with fetal alcohol spectrum disorder (FASD) already have elevated rates of depression and anxiety disorders compared to control populations. Barkley, Murphy and Fischer (15) suggest that people who have executive functioning difficulties, like most of the FASD impacted mothers we work with, have brains that are like "gas guzzlers." They describe the brain as a "high energy" organ that uses one-fifth of all the calories an individual consumes. Each decision made consumes some of the brain's available energy. Our clients are "inefficient" thinkers who must actively avoid distractions while they try to focus on completing the original task or decision. They are effectively engaging in two tasks while a woman who is not dealing with these cognitive limitations might only have to engage in one (Hockey, Maule, Clough and Bdzola 849).

The women we work with know that they have disabilities but don't always have a clear picture of how to understand or conceptualize the disability. Part of our work with clients is to support them in making sense of their disability in ways that they can work with to build solutions. We borrow the metaphor of the inefficient car engine to provide our clients with a way of understanding how they might be processing information. This also explains some of the depression, anxiety and fatigue that they might experience. The women we have discussed this metaphor with like it because it explains one reason why their experience of parenting is so challenging. It also allows us to join with them in finding ways to maximize their potential by figuring out how their brain works and ways to improve its functioning. For example, we discuss the importance of sleep, nutrition and exercise in improving brain efficiency. They are then able to have more control over their body and this in turn reduces the negative stress that leaves them feeling so tired.

Fatigue has also been linked to problems with concentration and planning (Hockey, Maule and Clough 849; Van der Linden, Frese and Meijman 46; Keinhuis, et al 394); however, little is known about the relationship between parental fatigue, parenting practices, and child outcomes (Keinhuis, et al 349). As early as 1943, Bartlett (250) noted deficits in higher order cognitive abilities, or executive functioning, under conditions of fatigue. Van der Linden, Frese and Meijman (59) also found that college students who completed tasks to induce fatigue demonstrated significant deficits in executive functioning compared to those not experiencing fatigue. Hockey, Maule and Clough (849) observed the negative impact of fatigue effects on selection of risky choices in decision-making scenarios in another student sample. Research from other fields does however suggest that a parent's ability to manage fatigue requires self-regulation and self-care skills, both of which are already problem areas for people impacted by FASD.

Social supports make a difference in helping women manage their fatigue and stress. Professional interventions such as training and mentoring are very important in simplifying the lives of FASD affected women and supporting their parenting efforts. However, these supports are insufficient to meet all the woman's needs. We have found that most support services available to mothers close just when they are needed most. During the day our clients can access a number of supports. But at 5 p.m., almost all non-crisis oriented services are closed and mentors are not available until the next day. This leaves women who tend to be impulsive with limited tolerance for boredom and loneliness on their own to make decisions. When faced with the prospect of staying alone with their child or going out with friends, especially friends who are suggesting exciting activities such as dancing, drinking or drug use, it is not difficult to predict what choice will win. However, if there are other options that are available to the women that are fun, child-inclusive and age appropriate, the mother may choose differently.

Our clients need help with establishing and maintaining child-friendly lifestyles. They need support in proactively gaining knowledge and skills related to both their own self-care and their parenting. They also need support in anticipating lifestyle problems that might arise and in creating solutions that will work for them given their personal style and resources. Mothers parenting while impacted by FASD need easily accessible consultants available twenty-four hours per day. Should they have access to people they can trust to help them, in the moment, make good choices about how to handle emergent situations, they are likely to make more appropriate parenting choices.

Many of the FASD affected women we encounter are expected to establish their own homes and live alone with their children. This is done with the realization that the partners our clients tend to choose often have their own issues that interfere with our clients' parenting efforts. So, while living alone might work on some levels, it also means that the woman experiences loneliness and fears or anxieties about being alone in her own home. Phobias and anxieties are common in people who are affected by FASD (fasdcenter.samhsa.gov; Pei. Denys, Hughes, and Rasmussen 440). Rita often talked about her phobic responses and anxiety issues during our counselling sessions but limited the discussion to her experiences in public. It wasn't until our working alliance was strong that Rita started to talk about how she struggled with loneliness and her fears of being alone. Rita had a vivid imagination. She had a tendency to notice noises and changes in her environment without understanding what caused them and, in her efforts to figure out what was happening, she imagined the worst. She would then call her former partners to come over. The problems arose when they wouldn't leave after she felt better.

Another important issue that impacts a woman's "after-hours" life and ability to manage stress are her leisure skills. The women we work with have had little exposure to leisure activities that are: a) pro-social; b) family oriented; c) affordable; and, d) interesting and engaging. Having the resources to access family-oriented community leisure programs is one barrier. Perhaps a greater barrier is that the mothers don't have people to accompany them or "introduce" them to the new activity. Arranging for a mother to take her children to the "mother-child swim" at the local pool requires a significant amount of planning, e.g., organizing bathing suits and towels, having a locker or money for the locker, having bus tickets/pass to get to the pool, knowing which bus to take and where to get off, determining the right time to arrive and ensuring that she knows the appropriate bus schedules, managing children changing in adult oriented change rooms, and signing up for the program in the first place. After all this effort, the mother may still be anxious about going to a new place, being outdoors at night, or interacting with new people. This fear may actually be the most impermeable barrier, especially if she doesn't have anyone in her natural support system that will go with her and provide support.

It would be simple, given all the challenges they face, to assume that women affected with FASD should not be mothers. However, there is a growing awareness that women impacted by FASD also have a number of strengths that can be recruited to support effective parenting. These key strengths may include the woman's capacity to be creative, athletic, good at using computers, and to have good expressive language skills. Other strengths identified in the literature about people with FASD include being experiential/kinesthetic learners, having determination, and engaging interpersonal skills such as being friendly and outgoing (FASCETS; Saskatchewan FASD; Rasmussen, and Witol 466). Other reported themes relating to participants' self-identified accomplishments included: raising children and/or getting them back from foster care, graduating from school, maintaining a job, dealing with anger issues, and quitting or reducing substance use.

Rita expressed many strengths and demonstrated her resiliency in many ways. The first asset she demonstrated was her resolve to regain custody of her children and maintain custody of her newborn. She committed herself to working with an in-home support person to help her integrate knowledge she gained from parenting classes to the hands-on parenting she was doing in her own home. She worked effectively with a support worker from the First Steps[1] program to resolve many of the life-skills related problems she was experiencing that made her life more complicated (e.g., banking, budgeting, shopping effectively, debt management, meal planning, interpersonal boundary setting, etc.). In counselling she demonstrated her commitment to gaining and applying new skills to manage her anxiety and depression symptoms. She agreed to a "harm reduction" approach to addressing her addiction issues so that it became possible for her to discuss her drug use (primarily marijuana and alcohol) within the counselling environment.

In addition to Rita making changes in her ways of coping, so did the support people working with her. We learned that in order to be successful we needed to work with her vulnerabilities. For example, at the first "service team meeting" we had with Rita, all the professionals working with Rita and her children were present. There were seventeen "authority" figures present and Rita. We met downtown on the 20th floor of an office tower in a room without windows filled with an oversized table that sat 20 people. Rita had been the first to arrive at the meeting and took a chair near the back of the room. As people came in, she became buried in the crowd and essentially trapped. Needless to say, the meeting did not go well. Rita experienced a panic attack and became defensive throughout the meeting. However, she stayed. After that, we recognized our error. We resolved to only meet in places where Rita felt comfortable and that we would limit the number of people attending meetings. The next team meeting was at the office where Rita attended counselling. She knew where her "escape" routes were and she sat near the door. She was given permission to "have a smoke" whenever she needed to during meetings which provided her with the opportunity to refocus and calm herself during discussions. Rita started to request meetings when she felt she needed help communicating her feelings or needs to her case managers. She completed the tasks required of her, demonstrated that with support she could be a "good enough" parent and her children were returned to her care. After a six-month follow-up process the child protection agency was satisfied with Rita's parenting and closed their file, removing most of her supports.

Approximately four months later, new problems started to arise for Rita and old problems started to return. A new incident of domestic violence brought the police back into Rita's home and her children were again apprehended. The reality for Rita was that the only way that she could be successful as a parent was if the supports that were put in place to help her regain custody were maintained over time, until her children were old enough to care for themselves. The supports she needed had to adjust to the developmental needs of Rita and her children. We, as a support team, needed to learn that because of the nature of FASD, Rita would always need a supportive community to help her parent. When she had the right supports she could parent well.

There is an old saying that "it takes a village to raise a child." There is no consensus on where the adage comes from. However, the statement seems to have strong face validity. We believe that a village is needed to raise the children of mothers impacted by FASD. The village needed is one that is designed to meet the holistic needs of these women. Starting from a place of acceptance is important. Women impacted by FASD need help to learn, in ways that are not punitive or derogatory, about how their brain works. Learning about their own brain development in the context of understanding their child's brain development is a helpful start. The teaching needs to be personalized and must be offered within a relational context where the FASD impacted woman feels supported and cared for, while gaining information about the brain or learning new skills.

The therapeutic alliance is critical in building an effective intervention process (Duncan, Miller and Sparks 59). Engaging mothers impacted with FASD in a legitimate, long-term relationship is essential to support their parenting potential. We need to design support systems that work with the women's realities. They need support providers who can respond in nonpunitive ways to impulsive, inappropriate reactions the women have to environmental demands. The responses need to be immediate, appropriate and child focused without taking control away from the mother. Strategies such as regularly planned respite care, and immediately available crisis care, are ones that work with the limited executive functioning skills with which these women struggle. Collaborative or cooperative living environments are critical to limit the need for crisis responding for children.

There is a paucity of research available about how to support parents with FASD in their parenting efforts and yet in spite of this, women with FASD who are trying to parent their children face great scrutiny, harsh criticism and are offered few resources. We know from our work with woman who are struggling with FASD that intervention improves their ability to parent more effectively, and yet few appropriate services are available. There is a need for new methods and models for service delivery that provide for long-term services and support to these woman and their children. Unless change happens, women and children like Rita and her family will continue to struggle.

NOTES

[1]http://fasd.typepad.com/fasd_support_in_alberta/2006/11/first-steps-fas.html

WORKS CITED

Anderson, S. W., H. Damasio, D. Tranel and A. R. Damasio (2000). "Long-Term Sequelae of Prefrontal Cortex Damage Acquired in Early Childhood." *Developmental Neuropsychology,* 18(3), 281-296. Print.

Badry, D. "Fetal Alcohol Spectrum Disorder Standards: Supporting Children in the Care of Children's Services." *First Peoples Child & Family Review* 4.1 (2009): 47-56. Print

Barkley, R. A. *Taking Charge of Adult ADHD.* New York: The Guilford Press, 2011. Print

Barkley, R. A., K. R. Murphy and M. Fischer. *ADHD in Adults: What the Science Says.* New York: The Guilford Press, 2008. Print

Barrett, J. and A. S. Fleming. "Annual Research Review: All Mothers Are Not Created Equal: Neural and Psychobiological Perspectives on Mothering and the Importance of Individual Differences." *Journal of Child Psychology and Psychiatry* 52.2 (2011): 368-397. Print

Bartlett, F. C. "Fatigue Following Highly Skilled Work." *Proceedings of the Royal Society* B 131 (1943): 247-257. Print

Bozoky, I. and E. J. Corwin. "Fatigue as a Predictor of Postpartum Depression." *Journal of Obstetric, Gynecologic, and Neonatal Nursing* 31.4 (2002): 436-443. Print

Cahill, C. A. "Differential Diagnosis of Fatigue in Women." *Journal of Obstetric, Gynecologic, and Neonatal Nursing* 28.1 (1999): 81-86. Print

Chudley, A. E, A. R. Kilgour, M. Cranston and M. Edwards. "Challenges of Diagnosis in Fetal Alcohol Syndrome and Fetal Alcohol Spectrum Disorder in the Adult." *American Journal of Medical Genetics* 145C (2007): 261-272. Print

Classen, C., D. Smylie and E. Hapke. "Screening for FASD in Women Seeking Treatment for Substance Abuse." *Gender Matters Conference.* Toronto, 2008. Print

Cohn, J. E., S. B. Campbell, R. Matias and J. Hopkins. "Face-to-Face Interaction of Postpartum Depressed and Non-Depressed Mother-Infant Pairs at 2 Months." Developmental Psychology 26.15-23 (1990). Print

Corwin, E. J., Brownstead, and Barton. "The Impact of Fatigue on the Development of Postpartum Depression." *Journal of Obstetric, Gynecologic and Neonatal Nursing* 34.5 (2005): 577-586. Print

Curtis, C. "Limits of Parenting Capacity Assessmnets in Child Protection Cases." *Canadian Family Law Quarterly* 28 (2009): 1-22. Print

Dubovsky, D. "Building a Circle of Support for Families Affected by Addictions and FASD: Behavioral Aspects of Women Across the Life Span." *Women Across the Life Span: A National Conference on Women, Addiction and Recovery.* 2004. Web. 9/June/2013. http://womenandchildren.treatment.org/conference-2004.asp

Duncan, B. L., S. D. Miller and J. A. Sparks (2004). *The Heroic Client: A Revolutionary Way to Improve Effectiveness Through Client-Directed, Outcome-Informed Therapy.* San Francisco, CA: Jossey-Bass. 2004. 59. Print

FASCETS. Understanding FASD (Fetal Alcohol Spectrum Disorders). Web. 9 June 2013. http://www.fascets.org/info.html

Fasdcenter.samhsa.gov. *How Fetal Alcohol Spectrum Disorders Co-occur with Mental Illness.* Web.09/June/2013 www.stopalcoholabuse.gov

FAS/E Support Network. *Neurobehavior in Adolescents and Adults.* Web. 8 June 2013 http://come-over.to/FAS/Neurobehavior.htm.

Gelb, K. and D. Rutman. "A Literature Review on Promising Approaches in Substance Use Treatment and Care for Women with FASD." *Literature Review.* School of Social Work, University of Victoria. Victoria: University of Victoria, (2011). Print

Gibbard, W. B., P. Wass and M. Clarke. "The Neuropsychological Implications of Prenatal Alcohol Exposure". *The Canadian Child and Adolescent Psychiatry Review.* 12:3. (2003). 72-76. Print

Hockey, R. J., J. A. Maule, P. J. Clough and L. Bdzola."Effects of Negative Mood States on Risk in Everyday Decision Making." *Cognition and Emotion* 14.6 (2000): 823-855. Print

Hoghughi, M. "Good Enough Parenting for all Children: A Stragtegy for a Safer Society." *Archive of Disease in Children* 78 (1998): 293-300. Print.

Kienhuis, M., S. Rogers, R. Giallo, J. Matthews and Treyvaud. "A Proposed Model for the Impact of Parental Fatigue on Parenting Adaptability and Child Development." *Journal of Reproductive and Infant Psychology* 28.4 (2010): 392-402. Print.

Landry, S. H, Miller-Loncar, K. E. Smith, and P. R. Swank. "The Role of Early Parenting in Children's Development of Executive Processes." *Developmental Neuropsychology* 21.1 (2002): 15-41. Print.

Llewellyn, G, D. McConnell, A. Honey, R. Mayes and D. Russo. "Promoting Health and Home Safety for Children of Parents with Intellectual Disabilities: A Randomized Controlled Trial." *Research in Developmental Disabilities* 24 (2003): 405-431. Print.

Malacrida, Claudia. "Performing Motherhood in a Disablist World: Dilemmas of Motherhood, Femininity and Disability." *International Journal of Qualitative Studies in Education* (QSE) 22.1 (2009): 99-117. Print.

Masotti, P, M. A. George, K. Szala-Meneok, A. Michel Morton, C. Loock, M. Van Bibber, J. Ranford, M. Fleming and S. MacLeod. "Preventing Fetal Alcohol Spectrum Disorder in Aboriginal Communities: A Methods Development Project." *PLoS Medicine* 3.1 e8 (2006): 0024-0029. Print.

Mattson, S. N., E. P. Riley, L. Gramling, D. C. Delis and K. L. Jones. "Heavy Prenatal Alcohol Exposure with or without Physical Features of Fetal Alcohol Syndrome Leads to IQ Deficits." *Journal of Pediatrics* 131.5 (1997): 718-721. Print.

McQueen, A. and R. Mander. "Tiredness and Fatigue in the Postnatal Period." *Journal of Advanced Nursing* 42.5 (2003): 463-469. Print.

Motz, M., M. Leslie, D. J. Pepler, T. E. Moore and P. A. Freeman. "Breaking the Cycle: Measures of Progress. 1995 – 2005" *J.FAS Int.* 4 (2006). 1-134. Print.

Pei, J., K. Denys, J. Hughes and C. Rasmussen. Mental Health Issues in Fetal Alcohol Spectrum Disorder. *Journal of Mental Health*, 20(5), Print. 473-483. 2011. doi:10.3109/09638237.2011.577113

Poole, N., K. Gelb, and J. Trainor. Substance Use Treatment and Support for First Nations and Inuit Women at Risk of Having a Child Affected by FASD. Conference Presentation. *British Columbia Centre of Excellence for Women's Health*. Vancouver: British Columbia Centre of Excellence for Women's Health, 2008.

Rasmussen, C., G. Andrew, L. Zwaigenbaum and S. Tough. "Neurobehavioural Outcomes of Children with Fetal Alcohol Spectrum Disorders: A Canadian Perspective." *Paediatric & Child Health* 13.3 (2008). Print.

Rasmussen, C., K. Horne and A. Witol. "Neurobehavioral Functioning in Children with Fetal Alcohol Spectrum Disorder." *Child Neuropsychology,* 12(6), 453-468. 2006 doi:10. 1080/09297040600646854. Print.

Ridderinkhof, K. R., W. P. van den Wildenberg, S. J. Segalowitz, and C. S. Carter. "Neurocognitive Mechanisms of Cognitive Control: The role of Prefrontal Cortex in Action Selection, Response Inhibition, Performance Monitoring, and Reward-Based Learning." *Brain and Cognition* 56 (2004): 129-140. Print.

Roth, R. M., P. K. Isquith and G. A. Gioia. *Behavior Rating Inventory of Executive Function - Adult Version.* Lutz: Psychological Assessment Resources Inc, 2005. Print.

Rutman, D., C. La Berge and D. Wheway. *Parenting with FASD. Challenges, Strategies and Supports: A Research and Video Production Project.* Research Report. University of Victoria. Victoria BC, 2005. Print.

SAMHSA FASD Center for Excellence. *Fetal Alcohol Spectrum Disorders: Curriculum for Addiction Professionals - Level 2.* U.S. Department of Health and Human Services, 2007. http://www.skfasnetwork.ca/main

Streissguth, A. P., H. M. Barr, J. Kogan and F. L. Bookstein. *Understanding the Occurrence of Secondary Disabilities in Clients with Fetal Alcohol Syndrome (FAS) and Fetal Alcohol Effects (FAE).* Seattle, WA: University of Washington School of Medicines, Department of Psychiatry and

Behavioral Sciences. 1996. Print.

Swain, P. A. "Good Enough Parenting: Parental Disability and Child Protection." *Disability & Society* 18.2 (2003): 165-177. Print.

The Centre for Parenting and Research. "Assessment of Parenting Capacity." *Research Report.* NSW Department of Community Services, 2005. Print.

Tough, S. "Incidence and Prevalence of FASD in Alberta and Canada." 2009. *Institute of Health Economics.* Web. 08 June 2013. www.ihe.ca/documents/002-Tough.pdf

Van der Linden, D., M. Frese and T. Meijman. "Mental Fatigue and the Control of Cognitive Processes: Effects on Perserveration and Planning." *Acta Psychologica* 113 (2003): 45-65. Print.

8.

Sybil

MEREDITH POWELL

INTRODUCTION

This is a true story. On the surface, the woman I call Sybil charms all she meets. My Sybil is a beauty. She is educated. I love her, as she is my sister, my soul-mate, and my best friend. Anyone who knows the woman I call Sybil in this narrative would be shocked to the point of rejecting the truth of this narrative. But, dear reader, my intent was to create a narrative from beginning to end–to illuminate mothering with disability in academic essay form. My apologies, you must forgive me for abandoning a thesis, proper essay form, respectable quotations from critics and experts and such.

APOLOGIES

I have failed in this regard. There is really nowhere to start, and nowhere to end. I love a woman, and this is her story. She is 30 years old. She is nervous and shy. She tries to hide it under the veneer of an academic. She is a single mother. She has two children, a girl and a boy. They are happy. They excel in daycare. The daughter is very advanced and the son is writing his own name at four. Despite her best attempts, they are doing fine today. That is today.

What I compiled are excerpts from a diary Sybil kept during a mania fuelled by prescription medication and a divorce during the summer of 2012. Sybil's actual medical documents pepper her manic narrative. When I examined these documents, my vision of an academic paper dissolved, and what I have created is simply a compilation of snapshots. Please forgive me if I fail to name this woman I love, instead using Sybil, the first documented split-personality disorder case in literature. While this narrative is her truth, she cannot publicly own it. As such, I have pieced together a narrative for her who is afraid to speak. As such, I have refused transitions and proper grammatical structure. This is simply her truth. How her brain operates on paper. In the words of my love, "I spiral and spiral and spiral when I give in to my streak."

In mental disabilities, disabilities that cannot always be seen, there is a tendency to deny the disability especially within a society that prizes able-bodiness, attractiveness, and assertive nature. The process of "deviance disavowal" (Davis 1977) is the attempt to deny the handicap and maintain a 'normalcy' of life unacknowledging of the disability. (Safilios-Rothschild 1970). Alternately, some people might create a narrative or self-define in opposition to the label a psychiatrist might give (Frank, 88; Goffman, 1963b; Levitin, 1975; Voysey, 1972).

This, dear reader, is my narrative.

Sybil is a pleasant young woman who has a psychiatric history dating back to at least 1999. She has a number of past diagnoses including polydrug abuse, cyclothymic disorder, intermittent explosive disorder, panic disorder, borderline personality traits, bipolar type II, mixed person disorder with antisocial and borderline traits present, and borderline personality disorder.

—*Diagnosis from 1999-2001, summarized on November 28, 2011 in a Psychiatric and Mental Health Consultation for recurring anxiety and panic disorder.*

February 2012

Today I had to call emergency childcare for my children. I am too ill to care for them. My medication is unbalanced and I have been playing with doses all day to try to find some balance before I see my doctor next week. The pharmacists know my voice without me speaking my name. I am on the phone with my doctor almost daily. I feel ashamed, worthless, sick, needy. My self-narrative of a strong woman building a career, marking with confidence, building a home and a future has broken down completely. I sit at home, alone, windows drawn on a sunny day while my children are entertained by happy people, whole people on their fathers side who no longer speak to me. I feel an outcast, a mentally ill pariah who no one wants to be around. I get sudden dumps of deep depression. I chase the highs that usually surround material goods and projects and the even normal line that it appears the majority of people I know completely eludes me. I wonder if I will ever be able to go out without taking a bag containing 4 pill bottles in it in case of emergency. I wonder if the 3 years I spent off medication while having my children, breastfeeding my children drug free was better than living on medication. What is mental stability? What do I even have? A psychiatric report spanning over 17 years cant even tell me exactly who I am, what is wrong with my brain, where the imbalance, if one, is. What if Im fine and my environment is imbalanced? What if I'm in the wrong place and time? What if I cant hide my emptiness, my gap, my hole and everyone else can? Last week a friend from high school hung himself and I am dreaming of him nightly. Does everyone have an empty hole? An inability to cope at times? Im sure most people don't spend days trying to self-analyze why reading Kristeva makes them crazy. Today, I will cry myself to sleep after marking and feel like a failure as a mother.

There is a very long history of distractibility, sensitivity, under-achievement , daydreaming, and inconsistency. She describes herself as easily bored and at times quite impulsive. She tends to feel very anxious and restless in boring situations, but is quite calm in high stress situations.

—*November 29 2011; notes from Hollywood Psychiatrist*

February 2012

Because lets be honest. When you are a mother, no one will treat you with kid gloves. A mother is supposed to be strong, loving, caring, protective. When a mother says she is too ill to take care of her children no one cares. She is a burden, a failure, a liability, an eye-roll. Reaching out for help is very difficult. My mother told me to call my children's father, who is at work and school all night. My children's father barely spoke to me all day, picked up the kids and didn't tell me when he did, and when I phoned to see if the kids were ok he promised to call me back and didn't. My children's extended family didn't call at all to say the kids were ok, and Im afraid to call back because when I call their house they tell me not to call, or simply don't answer the phone. I am an outcast. Not a swimmer. A failure because I cant perform and when I ask for help I am shunned. I wonder if the multiple women and men suffering from severe mental illness such as schizophrenia I read about in the news reached out for help. I wonder what services they received. I wonder what responses came back to them. The message that they had to pretend to be healthy or shunned? Simply ignored?

The idea the head or the brain is the entire governing body of a person is particularly central to the increased stigma with men-tal illness. The majority react with fear, distance, and particular distaste for mental disorders. A Leyser and Abrahams study in 1982 predicts that people have the most aversion to disabilities that could result in the most unpredictable or possibly dangerous behaviour.

March 2012

I love it, this feeling of being lighter than air. my clothes are falling off me, i glide the floors, i am floating…finally my body is starting to mirror my mind state, slipping away, I'm channelling Sylvia Plath. i cannot consume food. my body refuses to eat. i can see my parents whispering about me at easter. my 20 month old grabs me for 10 minutes and doesn't let go. she looks at me, presses my chest, and says "mommy hurt". how does she know thats where the constant pressure congregates? i take laxatives if i do eat. i cant stand being full. i go days without eating a meal. i buy sandwiches only to throw them away. my food rots. my brain rots. i call my children's father and ask him to take the children. i am past the point. i cannot mother. sometimes i have unspeakable thoughts. they flash in my mind and i cant figure out if they come from me, or something i read on the news. i scare myself. i scare others. i feel my children slipping away from me and reattaching to their father. it hurts, and i tell myself that if i was a better mother i would just climb out of my own head, put them first and be the loving mother they need. I'm selfish. I'm alone. I'm a bad mother. i am not alone, I have many voices in my head and they are all arguing with each other. I'm hard on myself, but knowing that doesn't let me ease up. i agree to pick them up from school only to have anxiety for hours upon hours…i cut my meds, i increase my meds, i want to stop my meds, i cant stop my meds. i have forgotten what exactly is wrong with me. all i know is something is very wrong. i tell myself that being alone for a month will allow me to fix myself, but I'm not exactly sure if I'm a reliable source.

Sybil continued to have difficulty stabilizing on medication and her compliance with medication was limited ...Sybil's mood continued to be more depressed ...she agreed to continue on Wellbutrin XR 300mg and Clonazopam 2x day

—Psychiatrist who peered at me through the triangle he made with his hands while slouching in his chair.

Additional Diagnoses: AXIS 1: Attention-Deficit/ Hyperactivity Disorder—Combined Type; Polysubstance Abuse—in sustained full remission.
Recommendation: Clonazopam and Ritalin.

May 2012

its 12:40 and its been about 2 months since I've written. I just left my relationship and I'm spiralling out of control. Im completely addicted to being high. I befriend the girl across the hall whose baby daddy is in jail for murder. I vow to help her get her GED and get to university to raise her status. She's a smart girl, crack head mother, life in foster care. I look into her eyes and see myself, in another circumstance. Im going to teach her how to get to a better place on her own. I love women. I see myself.

Sybil is a very pleasant and engaging woman. She is dressed in stylish clothing. Her hygiene and grooming are both excellent. She manifests good eye contact. There is no psychomotor agitation or retardation noted. There are themes of guilt and poor self-esteem.

—Hollywood Psychiatrist

May 2012

The children are gone. I cant stop spending and getting high. Where are the boundaries if you cant make your own boundaries? Why am I more magnetic than any other person? 3 people fell in love with me this week. What is it that people actually fall in love with. I cannot be around my children and I am batshit crazy. The best place for my children is to not be around me. I. AM. NOT. A. GOOD. MOTHER. Tomorrow I shall read Melanie Klein and assuage my guilt. I told a drunk guy I didn't want full custody of my children. I need half my life to succeed, and they are half their fathers. He equated me to the woman in England who killed her children. I cried. Academically, I wish I could work on in my head emotions that overcome the reality of the stupidity of everyday life. classical rationalism: from the 16thc to the 17c we attempted to mathamaticize and make nature calculable. where are the natural resources of the non-rationalizatable? medicine is not helping. it is not working. where is the nature fix? what are we missing? the medical model of analysis is lacking. My mania is spurned by and cycling by pharmaceutical drugs. Why am I broken?

To write. An act which will not only "realize" the decensored relation of woman to her sexuality, to her womanly being, giving her access to her native strength; it will give her back her goods, her pleasures, her organs, her immense bodily territories which have been kept under seal; it will tear her away from the superegoized structure in which she has always occupied the place reserved for the guilty (guilty of everything, guilty at every turn: for having desires, for not having any; for being frigid, for being "too hot"; for not being both at once; for being too motherly and not enough; for having children and for not having any; for nursing and for not nursing ...) – tear her away by means of this research, this job of analysis and illumination, this emancipation of the marvellous text of her self that she must urgently learn to speak. A woman without a body, dumb, blind, can't possibly be a good fighter. She is reduced to being the servant of the militant male, his shadow. We must kill the false woman who is preventing the live one from breathing. Inscribe the breath of the whole woman.

—*Irigaray*

July 2012

I am enough. My sisters cook me food, feed me, ignore the fact I snort my medicine in secret, speak to me, hug me, cry with me, speak of their children but stop speaking when they see my pain, encourage me, never diminish me. They speak to me about theory, about love, about my worth, about the impossible: the energy connection, what lies outside, variances in the time space continuum, our psychical drives, the Chora. Most of my time is spent smoking under the power lines, tapping into their hum, passing through the thetic and into that space without language, I access forms and stand both at what is the end of time and the limitless space of beginning. Giving myself cancer, messing with my brain waves as has been suggested, but freeing me like water. I am in love. I am in love with life, I am born again, I am beautiful, I am free from tyranny of an abusive relationship, I am back. I am me. I sleep for 3 hours a night. I am wild. I run without shoes into the field and meditate under those lines, sucking up my wild space greedily. I had children. I try not to think of it. A pain comes when they cross my mind. If I'm honest, I need to be alone. I cannot parent them right now. But when I ignore the pain it feels so good to be me. I don't want to parent. Is it because I'm ill or is it because I need to be free of the self imposed prison sentence I lived alone, bred alone, bore alone, spent alone, cried alone, lost my desire, believed I was undesirable, hated desire, sensuality, sexuality, looked into a mirror and saw ugliness, unwantedness, neediness, clingyness, child sucking breast sucking out my brains and my power and my life, leaving saggy breasts saggy skin saggy brain saggy old woman turned thin. Sick? Alive. I'm finally alive. I am back. I'm back in a way I have never been before. I have connections to my girlfriends stronger than I ever thought possible. We bleed together. We think the same thoughts. I note the lines allow me to transgress into the Chora and my girlfriend tells me she knows the same thing. I sense things before they happen. I am magic.

Woman for women. There always remains in woman that force which produces/is produced by the other – in particular, the other woman. In her, matrix, cradler; herself giver as her mother and child; she is her own sister-daughter. You might object, "What about she who is the hysterical offspring of a bad mother?" Everything will be changed once woman gives woman to the other woman. There is hidden and always ready in woman the source; the locus for the other. The mother, too, is a metaphor. It is necessary and sufficient that the best of herself be given to woman by another woman for her to be able to love herself and return in love the body that was "born" to her. Touch me, caress me, you the living no-name, give me my self as myself. The relation to the "mother," in terms of intense pleasure and violence, is curtailed no more than the relation to childhood (the child that she was, that she is, that she makes, remakes, undoes, there at the point where, the same, she others herself)…don't denigrate woman, don't make of her what men have made of you.

—*Helene Cixous, The Laugh of the Medusa*

August 2012

Day 5 detox. I slept for 3 days. My mother came to pick up my children as I couldn't get out of bed. My daughter stays by my side, "mommy broken. are you tired mommy? lie down. go to sleep". She pats my back like her brother taught her from daycare (slap, slap) and sings "you are my sunshine". the song I used to sing, pregnant and alone, every night to my unborn son while crying hysterically in the shower. 300 dollar water bill. My own mother looks at me and tells me she's proud of me. Drugged out daughter in detox. Yet again. I miss the mania. Look around and see what Ive bought, what Ive done, what Ive accomplished, what Ive ruined. who I've ruined. For the first time in months I miss my children. Their fathers week. I sit alone and plan activities for our week together: the museum, the park, the butterfly conservatory, visit with nanny and poppa, visit with cousins, the pool, soccer...neither his father nor I took my son to soccer. For the first time in months, I see the world through my children's eyes and the pain stops me. I have failed him so badly. Im going to talk to him on his level all week. The mania is gone, but the mother is back.

From 2000-2008 medications used:

- Effexor 75mg

- Serzone

- Wellbutrin 150mg 2x day

- Valproate 750mg

- restarted Wellbutrin 150mg and Lithium Carbonate 900

2011-2013:

- Ritalin 60-100 mg day

- Ciprolax 20mg day
- Clonazopam 2xday

August 2012

10 years. for 10 years I slept with the same man. Had his children. Paid his bills. Supported the family. Begged him to love me, to cherish our family. He never loved me, my mother says. he manipulated me. left for days, weeks, months. years. he left me 9 years ago. he mostly manipulated me. Squished me. Why? why did I stay? I met a man online and drove to his house at midnight to have sex. To feel like a woman again, and not a mother living in public housing. I wore a dress, heels, and popped pills all the way to toronto. I was blazing high. The sex was amazing. I felt single, new, alone, free. Then I went crazy. demanded things, sent endless manic texts, became the worst of myself, pushed him away, pulled him back, pushed him away, pulled him back. wrote the worst into him, wrote the worst of myself. lost all control. had amazing sex again, this time as the booty call. I miss him as I first met him. I miss myself. that in control version that i imagine, but in reality never is, never was, but will i be? I said goodbye. to him, not to me.

September 9, 2010. Marital Counselling notes:

Sybil and Branson have returned to counselling [after numerous attempts] to stabilize relationship conflict. They have experienced conflict over the past 7 years and have ended and reunited many times. They feel counselling is the final attempt to repair the relationship.

—Girl Next Door Counsellor

February 15th, 2011

Sybil and Branson returned to counselling following earlier counselling support in August and September 2010. They attended 3 sessions, however, Branson left early during the last session. They did not request further support.

—*Girl Next Door Counsellor*

August 2012

I had sex with a 35 year old man, who, after drinking half a bottle of tequila with, slowly reveals himself as a possible sociopath who rejects women and then pays hackers to open their email, finds out who they are dating after him, and creates fake women through email who he then seduces through email and forwards this to the women he rejected (for wanting to meet his friends, or marry him, or have his children). Funny, the only guy I see in front of me is a little boy I could boss around. Then again, Im on 4 Clonazopam, half a bottle of wine, a 1/4 of a 40 of tequila, and 200mg of Ritalin. Im clearly not in a position to judge anyone, and I feel like he understands me, even though I realize I actually don't know his last name. To be truthful, I really don't care. I don't feel an ounce of love or sexual desire, but I'm interested in his symptom. Its the second day I have not had my children. I kept them for 2 weeks before their father intervenes, keeping them for 10 days on the lie he is taking them to the cottage. For those 2 weeks, I was the perfect mother. I went on school trips, I have a lawyer now, I have affidavits in support of my custody because, in their fathers words, "I am a suicidal anorexic who had a complete mental breakdown who is verbally abusive, emotionally manipulative, and dishonest". Id agree with the complete mental breakdown part. Ive been working for the past 2 weeks with the kids from 8am-4am. Ritalin seems, to me, the least of my worries when Im taking loans to support myself and my ex is denying support and refusing to repay loans. These replies come peppered with constant insults on my sanity. He loves to demean me. He always has. 10 years. Tomorrow I will see my lawyer. Im smoking a pack a day. I sleep at 5am-11. Im so depressed, but the last two weeks with my children were the most heartbreaking of my life. Everyday I played the perfect mother, and I was happy. but numb. Im still numb.

Dear Reader:

i wanted to write an academic paper. i was to have a thesis, an argument, a respected piece of self-analysis that gave bipolar illness a good name, proving to society that integration and respect is necessary. bipolar but not a victim. a strong woman. i would integrate words of my psychiatrist around my own narrative, creating a disjuncture that would prove seemingly ill minds are able to self-narrate and sickness is but a scientific division.

sickness is a scientific division. where it comes from science cannot define with division. symptoms meld into one another, dual-diagnosis, tri-diagnosis: then your fucked. my file claims I'm a sociopath, an addict, bipolar, ADD. what are those things really? I wanted to fit within society, but as i was walking today to my car in public housing, dressed for a meeting with my advisor, i heard men drinking beer asking each other what i do, and one responds "crack whore." am i the problem? i must be a crack whore if they say i am. social discourse is construction of divided symptomatic marks, creating an entire organism out of fluid, changing identities. I am a mother. I am very, very intelligent, I love life so much that sometimes I cant stand it and I cant sleep, everything is amazing, I want to move, move, move. should i slow down? ill be dead in 60 years or less I assume. Should i spend my life feeling sick, feeling less, when I know I feel truly myself while in mania? because i want it all. I'm never satisfied. I'm a hunter, always learning, always moving, always ready for fight, for prey, and i protect what i love, but sometimes i have to leave as is my nature. what am i really? my obsession with julia kristeva is highly personal. i think of her writing often, her theories, and i see them, feel them, try to reach them in my life. some call her a genius, and some call her too complex, second-wave (and thus out of vogue), but i find her real. i told my friends about the sociopath date, and they were frightened. all of them. yet the entire time i wasn't scared at all, but fascinated. he was being real, opening up what he really experiences in his head. is he missing part of his frontal lobe? was it childhood trauma being pushed around as a younger child? who the fuck knows. but talking to him was real. i learned something about humanity, about people, about our nature. im not sure what it is, but i suspect we are all pretty fucked up. the person that scared me the most was the one i loved, the one who identified as normal. but maybe i only liked him because adhering to his stability, his lie, would mask the fact that i am unable to lie to myself anymore.

every story has a climax, but life runs more like a joycean novel: a series of climax and anti-climactic events that appear confusing to most, boring to some, but your own set of stories, or anti-stories will attract more than a few dedicated and/or critical readers. readers who pick us up, discard us if they read a distasteful event. these are my words.

I lie next to my daughter and listen to hear breathe. She is the one I miss most when she is gone. Ever since she was born, she just belonged to me. in my arms. my mother says she is exactly like me as a child. i see it. she's funny. charming. loves life. looking to have fun. 'all for fun'. yesterday she was awake all night and i wondered if a 2 year old can be manic.

fuck. for all i know i could be descended from marie de france. just my luck. 10, 12 kids? and still telling crazy stories and lovin her some sexy jesus. yes, I'm that woman. am i wrong to think marie had a sense of humour about herself? raving lunatic or a woman who loved life and saw a chance at greatness, an impulsive, swirling woman whose thoughts proliferated so fast she could barely believe they were her own. Did not believe they were her own, and inscribed them from above because she wasnt going to burn in public if they were from below. Is that my choice? Become patient, demeaned, sick, hospitalized, contained, or became hidden, suppressed, suffer secretly and never publically admit or show that i have mania. depression. mania. depression. i go from obsession to obsession. my children go from house to house. back and forth. split life mirrors split nature. am i strong enough to fight for them in court? will i win or will i lose? am i stable enough to care for them full time? i worry about my daughter. my son.

i worry I'm a bad mother. my mother says i am. notes how i become distracted with them, fly off into another thought zone. I'm dreamy sometimes. its great for a professor, not so great as a mother i guess. mothers are perfect.

And I hunt.

WORKS CITED

These are incomplete. See author's explanation.

Cixous, Helene. *The Laugh of the Medusa,* p. 170.

Coleman, Lerita M. and Bella M. DePaulo. "Uncovering the Human Spirit: Moving Beyond Disability and 'Missed' Communications". *'Miscommunication' and Problematic Talk.* Edited by Nikolas Coupland, Howard Giles and John M. Wiemann pp.61-84. Print.

Davis, 1977

Frank, 88; Goffman, 1963b; Levitin, 1975; Voysey, 1972

Irigaray

Leyser and Abrahams study, 1982

Safilios-Rothschild, 1970

9.

Disabling Mothers

Constructing a Postpartum Depression

LYNDA R. ROSS

In addition to challenges, expectations, and perhaps normal apprehensions of anticipating childbirth, women bring into their pregnancies, and ultimately into new motherhood, all of the social, cultural, economic, political, psychological, and relational complexities permeating their lives before becoming pregnant. In short, women's lives are complicated, not simplified, by the prospect and reality of motherhood. The wonders of birth and the joys of motherhood are ideals celebrated in contemporary Western societies. Not all women are able to approach and experience motherhood with such positive feelings. At the same time as motherhood is being glorified, these unique events in a woman's life are also being used as the basis for further "disabling" women. Although not exclusively, psychiatric and biomedical discourses tend to capitalize on these spaces in a woman's life through pathologizing pregnancy and the period following birth. From this perspective these life events are being treated as "risk" elements, capable of triggering or exacerbating major depressive episodes. In reality it is the deprivation and hardship women are forced to live with as they enter into motherhood that is responsible for precipitating their grief.

Women have historically been the targets for mental disabling for a variety of well documented reasons. During the 1950s and 1960s, for example, clinicians "were still being taught that women suffer from penis envy, are morally inferior to men, and are innately masochistic, dependent, passive, heterosexual, and monogamous ...it was mothers – not fathers, genetic predisposition, accidents, and/or poverty – who caused neurosis and psychosis" (Chesler 1). The "disorder" paradigm in which women are situated serves to undermine the need for economic, social and political reform while at the same time privileging socially (psychiatrically) constructed notions of normalcy. In earlier times, where women's biology was blamed for their disordered minds; more recently, socially and culturally constructed gender roles have been identified as root causes contributing to women's mental disabilities (e.g., Appignanesi; Chesler)[1]. The number of adults in Western societies currently disabled by mental illness is staggering and has risen at a rapid rate over the past 60 years. Whitaker, for example, reports that in 2007, one in 76 adults in the United States is debilitated by mental illness – a figure double the rate seen in 1987 and six times that in 1955 (7). Depression, a disorder affecting disproportionately more women than men – by a ratio of 2:1 (Stewart, Cucciardi, and Grace 2) – has been described by the World Health Organization as the leading cause of "disease burden" for women worldwide (46). In addition to an unprecedented growth in the number of individuals diagnosed with some form of mental disease, the past 60 years have seen an explosion of drug therapies designed to treat or cure mental disability.

Depression during pregnancy and the postpartum period are not described as disorders distinct from other affective disorders. However, the most recent published version of the *Diagnostic and Statistical Manual of Mental Disorders* (American Psychiatric Association "5th Edition") does allow for an additional "specifier" for the diagnosis of a Major Depressive disorder "With Peripartum Onset" that can be applied "if onset of mood symptoms occurs during pregnancy or in the 4 weeks following delivery" (186). Although the previous version of the DSM (4th Edition, Text Revision) did not identify the number of women who might be affected by this disorder, it did note the importance of distinguishing "postpartum mood episodes from the 'baby blues,' which affect up to 70% of women during the 10 days postpartum" (423). Reference to the frequency of the 'baby blues' has been removed from the DSM-5 and incidence statistics have been added indicating that "between 3% and 6% of women will experience the onset of a major depressive episode during pregnancy or the weeks or months following delivery. Fifty percent of 'postpartum' major depressive episodes actually begin prior to delivery. Thus the episodes are referred to collectively as peripartum episodes" (186). As well, the 'baby blues' have been incorporated into the 'disorder' paradigm with the DSM-5's proclamation that "mood and anxiety symptoms during pregnancy, as well as the 'baby blues,' increase the risk for a postpartum depressive episode" (187). In addition to the DSM highlighting both the ante- and post-natal periods as providing special circumstances for the onset of a major depressive episode, a vast extant scientific literature gives further credence to the notion that these are unique times in a woman's life for the onset of depression.

INSANITY IN THE POSTPARTUM PERIOD: LEARNING FROM THE PAST

Diagnosing mental illness in the postpartum (postnatal) period has had a relatively long history. Gooch, an obstetric physician, wrote the first English language treatise on puerperal insanity in 1819. In his manuscript, published posthumously in 1831, Gooch explained the risks of childbirth to women:

> During the long process, or rather succession of processes, in which the sexual organs of the human female are employed in forming, lodging, expelling, and lastly feeding the offspring, there is no time at which the mind may not become disordered: but there are two periods at which this is chiefly liable to occur, the one soon after delivery, when the body is sustaining the effects of labour, the other several months afterwards, when the body is sustaining the effects of nursing. (54)

Clearly, Gooch's analysis relied on ideas of the time that saw women as fragile beings whose body's natural functions exerted control over their minds. The idea that women were especially susceptible to disordered minds was further elaborated by Gooch in considering the causes of puerperal insanity. He found that

> a large proportion [of cases] have occurred in patients in whose families disordered minds have already appeared. The patients too were of susceptible dispositions, nervous, remarkable for an unusual degree of that peculiarity of nerve and of mind, which distinguishes the female from the male constitution. (63)

Of "lying-in" or nursing as a precipitating factor for insanity, Gooch proposed

> ...the sexual system in women is a set of organs which are in action only during half the natural life of the individual, and even during this half they are in action only at intervals. During these intervals of action they diffuse an unusual excitement throughout the nervous system; witness the hysteric affections of puberty, the nervous susceptibility which occurs during every menstrual period, the nervous affections of breeding, and the nervous susceptibility of lying-in women ...these states are liable to produce these conditions of the nervous system. (64)

Ironically, while women's biology was used to explain their predisposition to insanity generally, and puerperal disease specifically, in reality the disorder afflicted a very small percentage of women following birth. Being locked into explanations for insanity that were so tied to women's biology left little room for physicians to explore other factors that might have contributed to women's disease during and following pregnancy. This explanation, however, did little to explain why the vast majority of women did not succumb to the disorder.

By the mid-1800s, others began speculating about causes that were somewhat removed from women's biology. They focused more on physical and contextual issues that might contribute to the disorder. In 1851, MacKenzie, a physician to the Paddington Free Dispensary for the Diseases of Women and Children, wrote about the "difficulty in arriving at correct views respecting the nature of this disease" given the contradictions that abounded in the medical literature (504). Not satisfied with the causes proposed, although agreeing that "[h]ereditary tendencies and [a] highly nervous temperament" (504) were perhaps amongst the most important precipitating factors, MacKenzie provided compelling evidence that showed how in "... the majority of cases in which puerperal insanity occurs, it is mainly dependent upon the existence of anaemia antecedently to labour" (505). Although MacKenzie did not claim that all cases of puerperal insanity could be attributed to anaemia, he did maintain that for many women "anaemia constitutes an important pathological element" (521).

In the early 1900s, Robert Jones, medical superintendent of the London County Asylum in Claybury noted how, for most women, pregnancy and childbirth protected them from bouts of insanity, but that for some "the dynamical changes in the nervous currents are so great that insanity does actually occur about once in every 700 confinements" ("Puerperal Insanity

[Part 1]" 579). This figure translates to approximately 1/10th of a percent of women who would receive an insanity diagnosis. Some fifty years earlier, this estimate was corroborated by MacKenzie when he noted "the disease in question is admitted to be comparatively rare" (504). Although an uncommon disease, in reviewing available statistics related to puerperal insanity, Jones ("Puerperal Insanity [Part 1]") found the actual proportion of women admitted into asylums with some form of the disease was relatively high in comparison to their overall admissions. For some asylums, the proportion of women admitted with puerperal insanity was as low as 5% and for others, as high as 20% (Louden 77). Thus, while the disease was indeed considered rare, there were in fact large numbers of women suffering from puerperal insanity admitted to the asylums. In trying to make sense of the diagnosis today, these asylum incidence rates are significant for a number of reasons. The concentration of women admitted to asylums undoubtedly allowed for a closer study of the disorder and encouraged, based on the observation of multiple patients, a more careful description of the course and consequences of the disease. Jones ("Puerperal Insanity [Part 1]") described the symptoms and etiology of the disorder as follows:

> The almost universal symptom of insanity in puerperal cases is loss of sleep. The progress of the case is described by those who have the care of the patient as first sleeplessness, then feverish and anxious restlessness, a busy concern about trivial details, distrust, a suspiciousness, loss of appetite, and a readiness to take offence when none was meant, an exacting irritability and ready reaction to outward stimulus, culminating in wild delirious excitement and mania...(582)

To our contemporary sensibilities the symptoms described would seem excessively broad and would serve to capture any number of ailments. Presumably, articulating symptoms also encouraged a search for effective treatments. Jones ("Puerperal Insanity [Part 2]") also pointed out that "[t]his form of insanity is considered by all authorities to be the most recoverable" (646) with some physicians suggesting recovery rates as high as 80% (White 306). White noted how treatment in the asylums often included a combination of "extreme quietude of surroundings...careful skilled supervision of patient...[a] diet [that] should be liberal and sustaining" (306). Additionally, opium or sedatives, wine or brandy, iron supplements, hot baths, and medicines to re-establish menstruation, fresh air, as well as the clearing of the bowels, were all strategies used to treat the women suffering from puerperal insanity (Jones, "Puerperal Insanity [Part 2]" 651; Rigden 1255 -1256). Guarding patients "against all excitement" (White 306) was stressed by many of the asylum physicians as a critical intervention to ensure women's recovery. While some of the methods used in the asylums, by today's standards, would appear brutal and perhaps excessive, treatment appeared to be, by and large, driven by an ethic of care derived from physicians' understandings of the appalling conditions that many women were living in prior to their admission into the asylums.

Hilary Marland, a contemporary scholar of puerperal insanity, in analyzing the detailed notes written by asylum doctors about their patients, suggests that the physicians "were often highly sympathetic to women's plight..." (306). The case notes "reveal[ed] a more complex diagnosis" (307) of the disease, one that went beyond heredity or biology for its explanation, describing women admitted to the asylums as frustrated, worn out, and sad (307). Physicians often highlighted women's economic situation as a primary factor contributing to their insanity, with alienists (the psychiatrists of the day) frequently grounding "their explanations in terms of the strains of women living in poverty" (Marland 301). As described earlier by physicians in their academic papers, case notes also highlighted the "[m]any women [who] were admitted in appalling physical health, often made worse by breast-feeding for months on end when they were not fit to do so" (Marland 311), as well as specifically remarking on the "'half-starved' condition of many women" admitted to asylums (Marland 311). These notes provide evidence that physicians were sensitive to the traumas women faced, their disappointments in marriage and in life, to the grief they felt, and sometimes to the fears they shared in relation to childbirth – fears that were particularly poignant amongst unmarried mothers. In addition to a focus on the economic hardships women faced, Marland found references to abusive, violent husbands that were identified as a primary cause contributing to some women's insanity. Overall, in diagnosing puerperal insanity, many doctors appeared to recognize "that motherhood, in association with [other hardships], could be disruptive, over-demanding and disappointing" (Marland 318). Although not a desirable outcome, for many women puerperal insanity was considered as a predictable response to the physical, emotional, and economic hardships they faced during their childbearing years. Treatment it seems was primarily designed in direct response to these understandings.

CONTEMPORARY MOTHERS AND MENTAL DISABILITY

By 1935, puerperal insanity, as a diagnosis, had all but disappeared; attributing mental illness to women during pregnancy and during the postpartum period has not. In fact, more women are now diagnosed with a mental illness during their childbearing years than has been seen in any other period of history. Puerperal insanity should not be equated with the ante- and post-natal depression diagnoses of today. However, these periods in a woman's life continue to be identified as "two periods of increased vulnerability to depression" (Le Strat, Dubertret, and Le Foll 128). Statements such as this, often seen in the scientific literature, reflect what now seems to be almost common knowledge: pregnancy and new motherhood are two periods in a woman's life fraught with risk for mental disability. Such statements set the agenda for contemporary studies focused not only on prevalence rates, but also on the predictors, correlates, and treatments of major depressive episodes during and following pregnancy. Though recent years have seen an increase in feminist analysis sympathetic to the impact of context in affecting women's mental health (e.g., McMullen and Stoppard; Stoppard), much of the depression literature continues to rely on psychiatric-biomedical discourses with their overwhelming focus on individual risk factors to explain mental disability (Lloyd and Hawe 1783-1795). This approach assumes first and foremost that "depression" following pregnancy is a medical problem, representing an "abnormal" state of mind. From this perspective, while an ethic of care undoubtedly still guides diagnosis and treatment, the underlying cultural, social, economic, political, and relational factors contributing to women's responses to pregnancy and new motherhood are largely ignored. Where the treatment of puerperal insanity over a century ago recognized the hardships faced by many women in their transition to motherhood, contemporary analysis has turned hardships into "risk factors." In doing so, the social, economic, and personal factors that profoundly affect women's mental health are less likely to be acknowledged as those that are primarily responsible for women's suffering.

NO JOY IN PREGNANCY?

In relation to the childbearing years, interest in women and depression has historically been focused on the postpartum period. However, the past two decades has seen an increase in research related to depression during pregnancy. This relatively recent attention to the antenatal period may be a consequence of a recognition that, at least in some cases, there would be a benefit to conceptualizing postpartum depression (PPD) as part of a continuum, where depression may be present during (or even prior to) pregnancy.[2] In acknowledging the possible continuous nature of depression, research in antenatal depression could serve a number of useful purposes particularly if attention were focused on the social and economic factors underlying the disorder. Though, antithetically, this new trend has brought with it the beginnings of discussions about costs and benefits of using drug therapy to treat depression during pregnancy (e.g., Bryant; Campagne; Coverdale, McCullough, and Chervenak; Dubnov-Raz et al.; Gentile and Galbally; Grzeskowiak, Gilbert, and Morrison).[3]

As with studies exploring PPD, those looking at depression during pregnancy tend to use conventional methods of measuring the construct and to a large extent draw conclusions supporting the same conventional understandings about treatment needs (e.g., use of specific therapies and/or drugs). Like PPD studies, it is also not unusual for research articles about depression during the antenatal period to begin with statements reflecting its frequency, severity, and the consequences of the disorder to both mother and child. When studies begin with the premise that antenatal depression occurs frequently and impairs function, the next logical step in a positivist approach is to look for risk factors that contribute to the problem. Though methodological problems plague these studies, from several dozen reviewed here, the percentage of pregnant women who would be considered at high risk for a major depressive episode ranged from a reported low of just under 6% (Söderquist, Wijma, and Wijma 136) to a high of 70% (Lindgren 210). An important factor accounting for the dramatic differences between these studies in the proportions of women reported as meeting criteria for depressive symptomology appears to be sample characteristics. In other words, the majority of variation can be accounted for by simply looking at the sample of women used in each of the studies. Notably, some of the lowest proportions were found in studies conducted in countries like Sweden (5.9%: Söderquist, Wijma, and Wijma 136; 8%: Rubertsson, Waldenström, and Wickberg 116), Finland (7.7%: Pajulo et al. 12), and to a lesser extent, the Netherlands (16.7%: van de Pol et al. 1411). Lower proportions of women identified with depressive symptomology were also reported by researchers who studied antenatal depression in samples of women from higher socioeconomic and advantaged status groups (11.5%: Hoffman and Hatch 538; 11.3%: Rich-Edwards et al. 378) and in groups of women whose social networks provided them with high levels of social support (7.3%: Elsenbruch et al. 873).

Conversely, researchers studying samples of women whose circumstances were largely defined by economic, social, and personal hardships generally reported much higher proportions of women meeting criteria for depressive symptomology. For example, studies looking at low income minority African American women, Latinas, inner city women, disadvantaged teenagers and low socioeconomic groups of women living in the USA, reported incidence rates of depressive symptomology ranging from a low of 22% to a high of almost 70% (Bennett et al. n.p..; Canady et al. 295; Cheng and Pickler 218; Holzman et al.133; Rich-Edwards et al. 378; Ritter et al. 579; Séquin et al. 586, Westdahl et al. 137; Zayas, Jankowski, and McKee 377). Similarly in Canada, incidence rates were high for Aboriginal (Bowen and Muhajarine 494) and unemployed immigrant women (Zelkowitz et al. 457). As well, women whose social networks provide them with little support (Elsenbruch et al. 873), unmarried women (Lindgren 210), women reporting mistimed or unwanted pregnancies (Leathers and Kelley 527), women experiencing a previous perinatal loss (Armstrong 768) and women with a history of being subjected to interpersonal violence (Rodriguez et al. 48) were all identified as populations with elevated levels of depressive symptomology ranging from a low of almost 31% to a high of 70%.

Some studies of antenatal depression do not provide the percentages of women in their samples with elevated depressive symptomology scores, but they do summarize data in other ways that provide further insight into the hardships women face in their pregnancies. For example, a study of HIV-positive women, many of whom are young, not well educated, living on limited income, and taking medication (zidovudine prophylaxis) were found to be predisposed to depressive symptomology (Blaney et al. 408-411). Elevated depressive symptomology scores were also evidenced in a group of disadvantaged African American women facing unwanted pregnancies (Orr and Miller 41-42) and in groups of married Caucasian women who were victims of physical or sexual violence (Records and Rice 236-237; Richard-Edwards et al. 378).

From these studies, itemizing percentages of depressed women or providing discussions of elevated depression symptoms explain very little about women's experiences, or about the real challenges they face during pregnancy, but they do provide a hint as to the social, economic, and personal hardships that can contribute to depression during pregnancy. For those studies, notably ones conducted in Sweden, it seems no small coincidence that fewer women would experience depressive symptomology in a country that is acknowledged to have less poverty, higher levels of social support, and greater gender equality than any other industrialized nation. In summary, many of the research studies, either directly through discussions of low income, low education and/or low socioeconomic status, or indirectly through the practice of using historically disadvantaged minority populations to study antenatal depression, clearly implicate poverty and the oppression that results from economic disadvantage as a primary factor contributing to the hostile environments in which women experience their pregnancies and consequently their depressive symptomology.

BRINGING THE BABY HOME

Although there are many affective disorders (e.g., post traumatic stress, anxiety, psychosis) identified as plaguing women in the postpartum period (e.g., Dennis, Parant, and Callahan; Grigoriadis et al.), depression is by far the most frequently researched and diagnosed "disorder" for women in their childbearing years.[4] Published studies focused on depression and motherhood often open with broad statements that reflect competing ideologies. Moore and Ayers, for example, note how "[f]or many women and their families, birth is a time of excitement and great joy" (443). These authors then go on to say how it is "unfortunate" that "some new mothers suffer beyond the typical concerns of parenthood and experience varying degrees of postnatal mental health problems" (443). To add weight to the authors' concerns for women in the postpartum period, such general statements are often followed by discussions of the high prevalence rates associated with depression following childbirth. Like the studies that look at depression in the antenatal period, postpartum studies also report different proportions of women in the population who suffer from depressive symptomology. O'Hara's much cited study published in 1987 noted prevalence rates for PPD ranging from 10 to 15% (205).[5] This proportion was corroborated by O'Hara and Swain in a study published almost a decade later (37). Reported in a slightly different way, O'Hara's numbers suggest that 1 to 1.5 women out of 10 will suffer from a major depressive episode during the postpartum period. This is not a trivial number but rather an alarming caution about the possible perils of having a baby.

The literature on "causes"—predictors and correlates—provides mixed evidence about factors contributing to PPD. Socio-demographic variables, biological factors, gynecological and obstetric factors, stressful life events, interpersonal relationships, previous psychopathology, and personality factors have all been studied as possible causes of PPD. In reviewing 57 recent articles on post-partum depression, Wylie and her colleagues isolated a number of critical factors associated with the disorder. As was seen in regards to depression rates during pregnancy, at the top of the list of factors predicting postpartum depression were those related to the social and economic conditions which govern the context of women's lives. Low social class and a woman's or her partner's unemployment were strongly associated with postpartum depression (Wylie et al. 50). Not surprisingly, negative events specifically associated with the women's pregnancy, including life stressors, complicated pregnancy and birthing experiences, unplanned pregnancies or ambivalent feelings about becoming a parent, were also associated with postpartum depression. Post-pregnancy factors including chronic stressors, difficult infant temperament, difficult or violent relationships with spouses or partners, and lack of support from family and friends were predictive of postpartum depression (Wylie et al. 50). Women's history of sexual abuse, poor relationships with their own mothers, and a prior history of psychopathology were also related to PPD (Wylie et al. 50). In short, almost all of the of factors identified in the literature as major contributors to PPD reflect the oppressive circumstances framing the contexts in which many women live and in which they are then asked to bear and care for their infants. It is little wonder that these exacting environments result in a state of despair.

Understandings about the causes and consequences of PPD derive largely from research conducted in high-income countries. By comparison, very little work has addressed women's mental health concerns in low- and lower-middle-income countries worldwide (Fisher et al. 140). Prior to the year 2000, Patel and colleagues were able to find only five separate studies looking at four low- to middle-income countries (Zimbabwe, Goa India, Brazil, and Chile) assessing associations between gender, poverty and common mental disorders (CMD). These authors noted how in all five studies they reviewed, "female gender, low education and poverty were strongly associated with CMD" (1462). They concluded that "[w]omen's mental health cannot be considered in isolation from social, political, and economic issues" (1446). Further they noted how "it is clear that there are sufficient causes in current social arrangements to account for the surfeit of depression and anxiety experienced by women" (1466). More recently, Fisher et al. identified 47 studies assessing prevalence rates associated with ante- and post-natal depression in low- to middle-income countries (141). Differences in methodologies used to gather information make comparisons between low- and lower-middle-income and high-income countries difficult.[6] Notwithstanding methodological concerns, Fisher and colleagues concluded from their review that prevalence rates surrounding common perinatal mental disorders (CPMD) are "highest among the most socially and economically disadvantaged women" (146).

TELLING IT LIKE IT IS: POVERTY AS THE PRIMARY SOCIAL CAUSE OF DEPRESSION

Poverty is a multifaceted construct. It takes into consideration not only issues related to nutrition, education, living standards, and income inequality, but also acknowledges the cumulative and exponential effects on well-being that result from multiple and overlapping hardships (United Nations 7-8). The USA measures poverty on the basis of income alone. Using this indicator, just over 15% of persons living in the USA in 2010 were identified as living in poverty, with poverty rates for Blacks and Hispanics in this same year identified as 27.4% and 26.6%, respectively, compared to 9.9% for non-Hispanic whites and 12.1% for Asians (National Poverty Centre n.p.). Further, poverty rates are at their highest for families headed by single women (31.6%). Still higher rates of poverty are seen when families are single-headed by Black or Latina women (Cawthorne n.p.). In Canada, while 12% of men and 11% of women live in poverty, specific groups of women are disproportionately represented with 51.6% of lone parent families headed by women, 44% of Aboriginal women living off reserve and 47% of women living on-reserve, living in poverty (Women's Legal and Education Action Fund n.p.).

The Canadian Research Institute for the Advancement of Women (Morris and Gonsalves) states: "Being poor erodes the spirit just as malnutrition erodes the body" (n.p.) That poverty has a profound negative effect on mental health has been well established in studies looking at these issues in high income countries. The clear relationship between poverty and mental health points further towards a "social causation" hypothesis as a powerful way to understand depression (Lund et al.). In reviewing 115 different studies, Lund et al. found that "[m]ost studies reported positive associations between a range of poverty indicators and [common mental disorders] CMD" (520). Adding to the existing burden of the poor, economic inequality takes a further toll on individuals who live in countries where income inequities prevail. "Most scholars agree that wealth inequality in the United States is at historic highs, with some estimates suggesting that the top 1% of Americans hold nearly 50% of the wealth, topping even the levels seen just before the Great Depression in the 1920s" (Norton and Ariely 9). For those higher income countries that enjoy greater wealth equality, overall rates of mental illness tend to be lower. Wilkinson and Pickett correlated differences in the proportion of people suffering from mental illness – ranging from 8 percent to 26 percent – with a nations' level of income equality. Countries rated with the highest level of wealth equality (e.g., Germany, Italy, Japan, and Spain) also reported fewer than 1 in 10 people who had been mentally ill within the previous 12 months; whereas countries with poorer levels of wealth equality (e.g., Australia, Canada, New Zealand, and the UK) saw mentally ill rates closer to 1 in 5 people (63-72). The USA, rated as the country with the highest level of income inequality of the nations compared, showed more than 1 in 4 people with a mental illness in the previous 12 months (Wilkinson and Pickett 67).

In light of the hardships endured by many women who live in poverty, it is also likely that many of these same women will not receive the physical and emotional care needed to sustain healthy mental states. One of anthropology's most important contributions to understanding human behaviour is "[t]he demonstration that biological and cultural systems are interdependent" (Stern and Kruckman 1027). Although childbirth is a universal biological event, it is not an event that is independent of its social and cultural context. Childbirth "is differentially patterned and organized according to [a society's] specific values, attitudes, and beliefs" (1027). In 1983, anthropologists Stern and Kruckman noted that in contemporary western societies "[l]ittle consideration has been given to the impact of the cultural patterning of the post-partum period" (1028). Further, these authors contended the need to acknowledge PPD, not as a disease or mental disorder, but instead as a "culture-bound syndrome of the West resulting in part from modern birth practices" (1028). Descriptions of postpartum rituals and caring activities taken from non-Western societies, cultures where PPD was less frequent or nonexistent, provides some insight into the specific ideologies and communities of care which can be used to cushion or prevent the experience of postpartum depression. These include, for example, the formalizing and structuring of a distinct period of time postpartum; protecting new mothers from the stresses and strains of "normal" life through mandated rest periods, social seclusion, assistance from relatives and/or midwives for extended periods following childbirth; rituals honouring mother's new position including gifts and celebratory meals to celebrate a mother's new social status (Stern and Kruckman 1039).

Some thirty years ago, O'Hara, Rehm, and Campbell identified caesarean section as the most stressful method of giving birth, and yet in assessing the impact of stressful deliveries on postpartum depressive symptomology found that women undergoing caesarean sections reported the
lowest levels of depressive symptomology. These authors concluded that
this "counterintuitive finding" could be explained by the fact that women
who undergo caesarean sections receive higher levels of social and physical
support postpartum, factors which tend to ameliorate the possible effects of
the stressful obstetric event on precipitating postpartum depression (460).
Evidence suggests that new mothers would greatly benefit from formalized
structures designed to honour mother's role and acknowledge the physical
and emotional challenges that face women as they transition into motherhood.

CONCLUSION: STOP BLAMING MOM

There is no doubt that depression causes real suffering for women, for their
infants, for their families, and is a burden to society. In the past we saw social
and economic explanations for puerperal insanity that not only privileged
understandings of how untenable social and economic circumstances could
lead new mothers into states of despair, but we also saw how these understandings were used to guide the physical and emotional care of women.
Today, though antenatal and postnatal depressions are diseases largely as-
cribed to individuals, they are, not unlike understandings of earlier mental
disorders, afflictions that have their origins, not in unhealthy women, but
in unhealthy societies. These disorders would barely exist but for the untenable social, economic, and political climates in which women are forced to
live their lives. Though birth is clearly celebrated in Western cultures, as evidenced by rituals surrounding birth announcements, baby "showers" and
gifts for the newborn, less attention is paid to the impact of childbirth on
women's physical and mental health. Sustained maternal care can be sorely
neglected for many women living in contemporary western societies. As it
currently stands, psychiatry and the pharmaceutical industry have been able
to capitalize on women's pained responses to pregnancy and to the postpartum period through pathologizing moods, feelings, and behaviours that
might otherwise be seen as appropriate ways to react to the experience of
motherhood under extremely difficult circumstances. Individual therapy
might offer some women some relief from the depressive symptomology.
Drug therapy is less likely to be effective and also carries with it the risk of

exacerbating symptoms associated with mental disability. Both approaches assume the problems belong to individuals. It is time we stopped disabling women in their childbearing years and instead place the burden of responsibility for the causes of women's mental disability where it belongs. Only when there is a dramatic shift in the focus of ante- and postnatal depression away from the individual toward society will spaces be opened up for a re-imagining of how mothers and their infants can be cared for in ways that will promote, rather than disable, healthy mental states.

NOTES

[1] In North America definitions of what constitutes mental "disorder" largely rely on information drawn from the various versions of the Diagnostic and Statistical Manual of Mental Disorders (DSM; American Psychiatric Association "2nd Edition"; "3rd Edition"; "4th Edition"; "4th Edition, Text Revision"; "5th Edition"). Though the current DSM does, in some instances, take into account context as a factor that might contribute to a "disordered" diagnosis, largely it focuses attention on individuals and their behavioural and emotional deficits."

[2] See for example the DSM-5's conceptualization of 'peripartum' specifier of a major depressive episode which includes onset in both the ante- and post-natal periods.

[3] There has been great deal of evidence showing the damaging effects of both non-prescription drugs (e.g., alcohol, tobacco related toxins, heroin) and some prescription drugs (e.g., thalidomide) on foetal development. Given these findings it is not surprising that pregnant women have been previously excluded from drug trials designed to assess the efficacy of antidepressants. This exclusion has led to a paucity of empirical evidence that would either support or preclude drug treatment of any sort during pregnancy. However, the past few years have seen an interest in reversing this trend even though evidence from non-clinical trials, gathered from small samples of women taking antidepressants during pregnancy, suggest the negative effects of antidepressant use during pregnancy on foetal development. Antidepressant use during pregnancy has been linked to increased risk of abortion, lower infant birth weights, increased risk of early term births, and increased risk of infant heart defects. As well, infants born to mothers on antidepressant medication suffered withdrawal from the drugs following birth.

[4]Over 6,000 articles focused on postpartum depression currently appear in the Social Sciences Citation Index, dating from 1950 to the present. Approximately 80% of these articles have been published since the year 2000.
[5]Variations in reported rates range from a low of 5.5% to a high of 33.1% (Le Strat, Dubertret, and Le Foll 128).
[6]Fisher and colleagues note difficulties in making comparison between studies because "[t]he settings, recruitment strategies, inclusion and exclusion criteria, representative adequacy of the samples and assessment measures used in the studies varied widely" (145).

WORKS CITED

American Psychiatric Association. *Diagnostic and Statistical Manual of Mental Disorders.* 2nd ed. Washington: American Psychiatric Association, 1980. Print.

—. *Diagnostic and Statistical Manual of Mental Disorders.* 3rd ed., Revised. Washington: American Psychiatric Association, 1987. Print.

—. *Diagnostic and Statistical Manual of Mental Disorders.* 4th ed. Washington: American Psychiatric Association, 1994. Print.

—. *Diagnostic and Statistical Manual of Mental Disorders.* 4th edition, text revision. Washington: American Psychiatric Association, 2000. Print.

—. *Diagnostic and Statistical Manual of Mental Disorders.* 5th ed. Washington: American Psychiatric Association, 2013. Print.

Appignanesi, Lisa. *Sad, Mad and Bad: Women and the Mind-doctors From 1800.* Toronto: McArthur & Company, 2007. Print.

Armstrong, Deborah S. "Impact of Prior Perinatal Loss on Subsequent Pregnancies." *Journal of Obstetric, Gynecologic, & Neonatal Nursing* 33.6 (2004): 765-773. Print.

Bennett, Heather A., Heather S. Boon, Sarah E. Romans, and Paul Grootendorst. "Becoming the Best Mom that I Can: Women's Experiences of Managing Depression during Pregnancy – A Qualitative Study." *BMC Women's Health* 7.13 (2007): n. pag. Web. 13 Feb. 2012.

Blaney, Nancy T., Isabel M. Fernandez, Kathleen A. Ethier, Tracey E. Wilson, Emmanuel Walter, and Linda J. Koenig. "Psychosocial and Behavioral Correlates of Depression among HIV-Infected Pregnant Women." *AIDS Patient Care and STDs* 18.7 (2004): 405-415. Print.

Bowen, Angela, and Nazeem Muhajarine. "Prevalence of Antenatal Depression in Women Enrolled in an Outreach Program in Canada." *Journal of Obstetric, Gynecologic and Neonatal Nursing* 35.4 (2006): 491-498. Print.

Bryant, Allison. (2012). Antidepressants and fetal risk: a new look at SSRIs during pregnancy. *Journal Watch Women's Health* (Jan 19). Expanded Academic ASAP. Web. 13 Feb. 2012.

Campagne, Daniel M. "Fact:Antidepressants and Anxiolytics are Not Safe during Pregnancy." *European Journal of Obstetrics & Gynecology and Reproductive Biology* 135.2 (2007): 145-148. Print.

Canady, Renée B., Bertha L. Bullen, Claudia Holzman, Clifford Broman, and Yan Tian. "Discrimination and Symptoms of Depression in Pregnancy among African American and White Women." *Women's Health Issues* 18.4 (2008): 292-300. Print.

Cawthorne, Alexandra. "The Straight Facts on Women in Poverty." *Centre for American Progress.* Issues, 2008. Web. 28 Mar. 2013.

Cheng, Ching-Yu, and Rita H. Pickler. "Maternal Psychological Well-Being and Salivary Cortisol in Late Pregnancy and Early Post-Partum." *Stress and Health* 26.3 (2010): 215-224. Print.

Chesler, Phyllis. *Women and Madness.* New York: Palgrave MacMillan, 2005. Print.

Coverdale, John H., Laurence B. McCullough, and Frank A. Chervenak. "The Ethics of Randomized Placebo-Controlled Trials of Antidepressants with Pregnant Women: A Systematic Review." *Obstetrics & Gynecology* 112.6 (2008): 1361-1368. Print.

Dennis, Anne, Oliver Parant, and Stacey Callahan. "Post-Traumatic Stress Disorder Related to Birth: A Prospective Longitudinal Study in a French Population." *Journal of Reproductive and Infant Psychology* 29.2 (2011): 125-135. Print.

Dubnov-Raz, Gal, Harri Hemilä, Yael Vurembrand, Jacob Kuint, and Ayala Maayan-Metzger. "Maternal Use of Selective Serotonin Reuptake Inhibitors during Pregnancy and Neonatal Bone Density." *Early Human Development* 88.3 (2012): 191-194. Print.

Elsenbruch, S., Benson, S., Rücke, M., Rose, M., Dudenhausen, J., Pincus-Knackstedt, M., Klapp, B. and Arck, P. "Social Support During Pregnancy: Effects of Maternal Depressive Symptoms, Smoking and Pregnancy Outcome." *Human Reproduction* 22.3 (2007): 869-877. Print.

Fisher, Jane, Meena Cabral de Mello, Vikram Patel, Atif Rahman, Thach Tran, Sara Holton and Wendy Holmes. "Prevalence and Determinants of Common Perinatal Mental Disorders in Women in Low- and Lower-Middle-Income Countries: A Systematic Review." *Bulletin of the World Health Organization* 90.2 (2012): 139-149. Print. (149a-149g – Appendix).

Gentile, Salvatore, and Megan Galbally. "Prenatal Exposure to Antidepressant Medications and Neurodevelopmental Outcomes: A Systematic Review." *Journal of Affective Disorders* 128.1-2 (2011): 1-9. Print.

Gooch, Robert. *On Some of the Most Important Diseases Peculiar to Women; With Other Papers.* London: The New Sydenham Society, 1831. Print.

Grigoriadis, Sophie, Diane de Camps Meschino, Elaine Barrons, Lana Bradley, Allison Eady, Alicja Fishell, Lana Mamisachvili, Greer Slyfield Cook,
Maura O'Keefe, Sarah Romans, and Lori E. Ross. "Mood and Anxiety Disorders in a Sample of Canadian Perinatal Women Referred for Psychiatric Care." *Archives of Women's Mental Health* 14.5 (2011): 325-333. Print.

Grzeskowiak, Luke, Andrew L. Gilbert, and Janna L. Morrison. "Long Term Impact of Prenatal Exposure to SSRIs on Growth and Body Weight in Childhood: Evidence from Animal and Human Studies." *Reproductive Toxicology* 34.1 (2012): 101-109. Print.

Hoffman, Susie, and Maureen Hatch. "Depressive Symptomology during Pregnancy: Evidence for an Association with Decreased Fetal Growth in Pregnancies of Lower Social Class Women." *Health Psychology* 19.6 (2000): 535-543. Print.

Holzman, Claudia, Janet Eyster, Linda Tiedje, Lee Roman, Elizabeth Seagull, and Mohammad Rahbar. "A Life Course Perspective on Depressive Symptoms in Mid-Pregnancy." *Maternal and Child Health Journal* 10.2 (2006): 127-138. Print.

Jones, Robert. "Puerperal Insanity [Part 1]." *The British Medical Journal* 1.2149 (1902a): 579-586. Print.

—. "Puerperal Insanity [Part 2]." *The British Medical Journal* 1.2150 (1902b): 646-651. Print.

Kirsch, Irving. *The Emperor's New Drugs: Exploding the Antidepressant Myth.* New York: Basic Books, 2010. Print.

Leathers, Sonya J., and Michelle A. Kelley. "Unintended Pregnancy and Depressive Symptoms among First-Time Mothers and Fathers." *American Journal of Orthopsychiatry* 70.4 (2000): 523-531. Print.

Le Strat, Yan, Caroline Dubertret, and Bernard Le Foll. "Prevalence and Correlates of Major Depressive Episode in Pregnant and Postpartum Women in the United States." *Journal of Affective Disorders* 135.1-3 (2011): 128-138. Print.

Lindgren, Kelly. "Relationships among Maternal-Fetal Attachment, Prenatal Depression, and Health Practices in Pregnancy." *Research in Nursing & Health* 24.3 (2001): 203-217. Print.

Lloyd, Beverley and Penelope Hawe. "Solutions Forgone? How Health Professionals Frame the Problem of Postnatal Depression." *Social Science & Medicine* 57.10 (2003): 1783-1795. Print.

Louden, I. "Puerperal Insanity in the 19th Century." *Journal of the Royal Society of Medicine* 81.1 (1987): 76-79. Print.

Lund, Crick, Alison Breen, Alan J. Fisher, Ritsuko Kakuma, Joanne Corrigall, John A. Joska, Leslie Swartz, and Vikram Patel. "Poverty and Common Mental Disorders in Low and Middle Income Countries: A Systematic Review." *Social Sciences & Medicine* 71.3 (2010): 517-528. Print.

MacKenzie, F.W. "On the Pathology and Treatment of Puerperal Insanity: Especially in Reference to its Relation to Anaemia." *London Journal of Medicine* 3.30 (1851): 504-521. Print.

Marland, Hilary. "Disappointment and Desolation: Women, Doctors and Interpretations of Puerperal Insanity in the Nineteenth Century." *History of Psychiatry* 14.3 (2003): 303-320. Print.

McMullen, Linda M., and Janet M. Stoppard. "Women and Depression: A Case Study of the Influence of Feminism in Canadian Psychology." *Feminism & Psychology* 16.3 (2006): 273-278. Print.

Moore, Donna, and Susan Ayers. "A Review of Postnatal Mental Health Websites: Help for Healthcare Professionals and Patients." *Archives of Women's Mental Health* 14.6 (2011): 443-452. Print.

Morris, Marika, and Tahira Gonsalves. "Women and Poverty – Third Edition." *Canadian Research Institute for the Advancement of Women (CRIAW)*. Publications, 2005. Web. 28 Mar. 2013.

National Poverty Center. "Poverty in the United States." *National Poverty Center*. Poverty Facts, 2012. Web. 29 Mar. 2013.

Norton, Michael I., and Dan Ariely. "Building a Better America—One Wealth Quintile at a Time." *Perspectives on Psychological Science* 6.1 (2011): 9-12. Print.

O'Hara, Michael W. "Post-Partum 'Blues,' Depression, and Psychosis: A Review." *Journal of Psychosomatic Obstetrics and Gynaecology* 7.3 (1987): 205-227. Print.

O'Hara, Michael W., Lynn P. Rehm, and Susan B. Campbell. "Predicting Depressive Symptomatology: Cognitive-Behavioral Models and Postpartum Depression." *Journal of Abnormal Psychology* 91.6 (1982): 457-461. Print.

O'Hara, Michael W. and Annette M. Swain. "Rates and Risk of Postpartum Depression—A Meta-Analysis." *International Review of Psychiatry* 8.1 (1996): 37-54. Print.

Orr, Suezanne and C. Arden Miller. "Unintended Pregnancy and the Psychosocial Well-Being of Pregnant Women." *Women's Health Issues* 7.1 (1997): 38-46. Print.

Pajulo, M., Savonlahti, E., Sourander, A., Helenius, H., and Piha, J. "Antenatal Depression, Substance Dependency and Social Support." *Journal of Affective Disorders* 65.1 (2001): 9-17. Print.

Patel, Vikram, Ricardo Araya, Mauricio de Lima, Ana Ludermir, and Charles Todd. "Women, Poverty and Common Mental Disorders in Four Restructuring Societies." *Social Sciences & Medicine* 49.11 (1999): 1461-1471. Print.

Records, Kathie, and Michael Rice. "Psychosocial Correlates of Depression Symptoms during the Third Trimester of Pregnancy." *Journal of Obstetric, Gynecologic and Neonatal Nursing* 36.3 (2007): 231-242. Print.

Rich-Edwards, Janet W., Tamarra James-Todd, Anshu Mohllajee, Ken Kleinman, Anne Burke, Matthew W. Gillman, and Rosalind J. Wright. "Lifetime maternal experiences of abuse and risk of pre-natal depression in two demographically distinct populations in Boston." *International Journal of Epidemiology* 40.2 (2011): 375-384. Print.

Rigden, Alan. "The Insanity of Childbirth." *The British Medical Journal* 2.2393 (1906): 1253-1257. Print.

Ritter, Christian, Steven E. Hobfoll, Justin Lavin, Rebecca P. Cameron, and Michael R. Hulsizer. "Stress, Psychosocial Resources, Depressive Symptomology during Pregnancy in Low-Income, Inner-City Women." *Health Psychology* 19.6 (2000): 576-585. Print.

Rodriguez, Michael A., MarySue V. Heilemann, Eve Fielder, Alfonso Ang, Faustina Nevarez, and Carol M. Mangione. "Intimate Partner Violence, Depression, and PTSD among Pregnant Latina Women." *Annals of Family Medicine* 6.1 (2008): 44-52. Print.

Rubertsson, Christine, Ulla Waldenström, and Brigitta Wickberg. "Depressive Mood in Early Pregnancy: Prevalence and Women at Risk in a National Swedish Sample." *Journal of Reproductive and Infant Psychology* 21.2 (2003): 113-123. Print.

Séguin, Louise, Louise Potvin, Michele St.-Denis, and Jacinthe Loisell. "Chronic Stressors, Social Support, and Depression during Pregnancy. *Obstetrics & Gynecology* 85.4 (1995): 583-589. Print.

Söderquist, Johan, Klaas Wijma, and Barbo Wijma. "Traumatic stress in late pregnancy." *Anxiety Disorders* 18.2 (2004): 127-142. Print.

Stern, Gwen, and Laurence Kruckman. "Multi-Disciplinary Perspectives on Post-Partum Depression: An Anthropological Critique." *Social Science & Medicine* 17.15 (1983): 1027-1041. Print.

Stewart, Donna, Enza Gucciardi and Sherry Grace. (2004). Depression. *BMC Women's Health,* 4 (Supplement 1):S19. Retrieved 13 February 2012 at http://www.biomedcentral.com/1472-6874/4/S1/S19

Stoppard, Janet M. "Moving towards an Understanding of Women's Depression." *Feminism & Psychology* 20.2 (2010): 267-271. Print.

United Nations Development Programme. *Human Development Report 2010, 20th Anniversary Edition—The Real Wealth of Nations: Pathways to Human Development.* New York: Palgrave Macmillan, 2010. Print.

United Nations Development Programme. *Human Development Report 2010 – Sustainability and Equity: A Better Future for All.* New York: Palgrave Macmillan, 2010. Print.

van de Pol, G., van Brummen, H., Bruinse, H., Heintz, A., & van der Vaart, C. "Is There an Association Between Depressive and Urinary Symptoms During and After Pregnancy?" *International Urogynecology Journal* 18.12 (2007): 1409-1415. Print.

Westdahl, Claire, Stephanie Milan, Urania Magriples, Trace S. Kershaw, Sharon Schindler Rising, and Jeanette R. Ickovics. (2007). "Social Support and Social Conflicts as Predictors of Prenatal Depression." *Obstetrics & Gynecology* 110.1 (2007): 134-140. Print.

Whitaker, Robert. *Anatomy of an Epidemic: Magic Bullets, Psychiatric Drugs, and the Astonishing Rise of Mental Illness in America.* New York:

Broadway Paperbacks, 2010. Print.

White, Earnest W. "A Note on the Treatment of Puerperal Insanity." *The British Medical Journal* 1.2197 (1903): 306-306. Print.

Wilkinson, Richard, and Kate Pickett. *The Spirit Level: Why Greater Equality Makes Societies Stronger.* New York: Bloomsbury Press, 2010. Print.

Women's Legal Education and Action Fund. "Women and Poverty." *Women's Legal Education and Action Fund.* n.p., 2009. Web. 29 Mar. 2013.

World Health Organization. "The Global Burden of Disease: 2004 Update." *World Health Organization.* n.p., 2008. Web. 29 Mar. 2013.

Wylie, L., Hollins Martin, C., Marland, G., Martin, C., & Rankin, J. "The Enigma of Post-Natal Depression: An Update." *Journal of Psychiatric and Mental Health Nursing* 18.1 (2011): 48-58. Print.

Zayas, Luis H., Katherine R.B. Jankowski, and Melissa D. McKee. "Prenatal and Postpartum Depression among Low-Income Dominican and Puerto Rican Women." *Hispanic Journal of Behavioral Sciences* 25.3 (2003): 370-385. Print.

Zelkowitz, Phyllis, Joy Schinazi, Lilly Katofsky, Jean François Saucier, Marta Valenzuela, Ruta Westreich, and Joelle Dayan. "Factors Associated with Depression in Pregnant Immigrant Women." *Transcultural Psychiatry* 41.4 (2004): 445-464. Print.

10.

My Daughter, My Selves?

Motherhood, Multiplicity, and the Creation of Meaning

KRISTINA PASSMAN NIELSON

All the events of my life swim in and out between each other. Without chronology...there is no linear sense. Language is a metaphor for experience. It is as arbitrary as the mass of chaotic images we call memory—but we can put it into lines to narrativize over fear.

—Lidia Yuknavitch, *The Chronology of Water: A Memoir* (28)

Disability's clarification of the body's corporeal truths also suggests that the body/self materializes...not so much through discourse but through history. The self materializes in response to an embodied engagement with its environment, both social and concrete.

—Rosemarie Garland-Thomson (33)

In this paper, I intend to present my experience of mothering with a mental disability—mental illness. Upon giving birth to my daughter I developed a new identity as a biological mother. My experience is particular to me and to my mental illness, Dissociative Identity Disorder, a complex collection of symptoms created through trauma;[1] there may be aspects of my story universal to all mothers who struggle with such disabilities. I hope to use my experience to shed light on mothers and mothering with a mental or emotional disability. My method is to write an autoethnography of motherhood from my multiple perspectives, reflect upon these experiences, and provide an analysis combining feminist theory, feminist disability studies, object-relations theory, recent views of the self from developmental neuropsychology, and theories of narrative.[2] In the text, you will encounter multiple voices of my multiple selves. My Self was severely fragmented in earliest childhood, and has continued to fragment throughout my life. But where, in the past, I could not call up my separate Selves (they would simply appear, and I would "be" that Self), I have learned to invite them to be present when it is necessary for therapeutic or health reasons. I have invited these Selves to speak in their own voices for this paper. This may cause some confusion, and I have used footnotes, to indicate my chronological and emotional age for each section of what follows.

I lie on my side on the carpeted floor, teddy bear clutched to me. I sleep on the floor, in a corner of the living room. Grannie has my bedroom, the room I share with my sister. My sister stays in the bedroom with Grannie. I don't know why I don't have a place to sleep. I don't know why I am sleeping on the floor. My teddy bear hugs my belly. My belly has a secret baby in it. Nobody knows. Nobody can know. I rock back and forth, rocking me, rocking us, rocking baby.

I am sweeping the floor in our flat. That's what married women do. It is my first day in my new home, a 3 bedroom flat with a gas and gas heater. January snow is blowing outside. My hair is in braids and I am wearing my sister's old sundress; it fits my swollen belly. It is sleeveless and light cotton. We have no radio or television, and I sing the songs I would like to listen to. Someone knocks at the door, and I want to hide, but I open it. A woman tells me she is my downstairs neighbor. She looks at me with hard eyes, says in her Massachusetts accent, "I'm Connie. I work the night shift at the old folks' home." I introduce myself, but don't know what else to say. She looks around. I offer her some Red Rose tea. She shakes her head. "Gotta go. Kids'll be home soon." She pauses, "I always have leftovers and nobody eats them at my place. I throw them away. I'll bring you some." She asks me no questions.

The pains have been going on all day. I have been alone all day. My husband is sleeping. He spent the day in jail. The students were protesting the shootings at Kent State. They wouldn't let me go because I am so pregnant. I have been sad because I did not want to be alone when I went into labor. He promised not to get arrested, but now we have a radio and on the underground station I heard that they were arresting protesters and no one was leaving. Someone from the American Civil Liberties Union told me I could call them if I needed transport to the hospital. I said I would call to get them off the phone. When he was released, I told him I was in labor, and he went giddy – it was hunger, he said. They only gave them boloney sandwiches in jail. I made some dinner. He went to bed. Told me to wake him up when I wanted to go to the hospital. I boil myself an egg for strength. I try to read P. G. Wodehouse. I am lonely, I think. It isn't the pain, it is the silence. I can't stand it, and wake him up. Better to be alone in the hospital, where there are people around.

I am in labor forever, but I do not make a sound. The other women in the delivery room are screaming, and the nurse tells one woman that this is what she gets for fooling around. I am very frightened of the nurses. After a long time, a nurse checks on me. She is kind and tells me I can cry or scream if I want to. I smile and am very polite. She asks me if my mother is in the hospital, that she could let her come and be with me. I shake my head. I tell her proudly that my husband is in the waiting room. She looks sad. Husbands aren't allowed.

I am in labor forever but I am not there. Sometimes I surface when the nurse comes to check me. I can tell she is worried because I make no sound, but I cannot figure out how to reassure her. There is no pain. There is no fear. I am no one. They cannot hurt me.

They pull her out of me. They place her on my chest. I look into her eyes and she looks into mine. Grey-blue, wise eyes from a place I cannot fathom, from inner space. I look into her eyes and she looks into mine. I never want to stop looking. I never want to let her go. We never want to let her go.

The nurses don't like mothers who are breastfeeding, but we do not give in. I read a used book from the La Leche League. We know that good mothers breastfeed their babies. The nurses only bring her to me at scheduled feeding intervals. They tell me she is hungry all the time and they are giving her sugar water. They tell me she is crying all the time. We hate them and want to go home. I do not feel well, but I want to take my baby home. I can take care of her best. Finally, even though I have a fever, they send me home.

The ones who called me a whore and told me I ruined their lives are waiting when I get home. I just want to hold my baby forever and love her. They talk and talk. They look down on my apartment, the home I have made. They look at the pictures of great art I cut out, and at the cardboard frames I made, spray-painted gold or silver to make them fancy. They laugh at the cardboard box beside the bed. I decorated it with paper flowers and made it cozy for my baby. I don't care. I know I can be brave always now with her to hold and protect. Something happens in my stomach and I feel very bad. I put the baby in the box beside the bed, where I can touch her and see her. I go to bed and the bleeding starts. They give me ice cream and will not call the doctor. In my mind, although I do not want it to be true, I know they are letting me die, and I cannot do anything about it. I tell my husband to give me the baby so I can say goodbye. I have been a mother for four days.

We say goodbye to her and are sad we are dying. We wanted to be a mommy. We wanted to be alive for her. Now the terrible people will get my daughter, and they will hurt her. Now the lights lighting my body are going out. Now they are taking me in a stretcher down the stairs. My drunk neighbor says he didn't do it. The medics are angry that someone let this little girl die. I wonder who they are talking about. Then I know. They are saying I am dead at the hospital. But we can hear them talking, and we try and try to make them know we are alive.

I wake up in the hospital and I am alive. I am weak and sick. They bind my breasts and it hurts. They are trying to make my milk go away. I go home. My mother has been taking care of my daughter and does not want to let me hold her. She tells me I am lazy. She will not let me rest. The doctor told me not to sweep or do housework, but she makes me clean my house. She tells me I am a bad mother, and that my daughter cried all the time because I would not feed her from a bottle. She says she has changed that. I hold my baby and we look into each other's eyes. She makes me a mother again and I make her my baby and we are never going to let each other go.

My mother wants to take my baby. My mother loves babies. My mother says my baby is hers. My father orders me to give the baby to my mother, saying she will have a much better life than I can give her. My father offers money. I am too weak to stop them. My husband does not believe that my parents will take our baby. I am desperate and then he sees my mother beginning to take the baby out the door to the waiting cab. I tell him in my bravest voice to stop my mother. He tells her that our daughter is *his* baby. He makes her his, not mine, and they cannot argue with that. They go away angry.

I know my breast milk will come again, because I read the book. I try and try, and pain does not matter. I will feed my baby. I am a mommy. I kept my secret. I got away safely. I am alive and they cannot take her from me. I do not have to be afraid. We do not have to be afraid any longer.

It is May. I will be twenty in July.

REFLECTION[3]

The birth of my daughter created me. It was the physicality of the act of pregnancy and birth that allowed me to create a self that was continuous, fairly stable, and coherent. It is important to note that, as I reflect back on this phenomenon, it is only the "mothering" self, including areas vital to the well-being of my child that exhibited these qualities. I could remember doctor's appointments for her, for example, but not for me. In the analysis section below, I shall discuss how recent work on the connection between embodied consciousness and the creation of identity is probably essential to understanding this. Before the birth of my child, I had no identity that was continuous, although there was a sketchy and unstable presenting self that I cobbled together each day in an awkward way that often failed. I was unpredictably amnesiac, except where mothering was concerned. I have very few connected memories of this time.

In this next part of this essay, I discuss how my primitive and chaotic selves came together to create a "good enough mother" through the challenges of raising my daughter.[4] I lived with terrible fears all those years she was growing up, the fears all mothers with mental illness live with. *Someone will take our children from us.* We try hard to pass as normal, as good mothers, as stable human beings. In moments of clarity we live with sorrow and the guilt: what are we doing to our children because we are (labeled) mentally ill, are often parenting while heavily medicated, often embarrass and frighten our children by our oddness, and constantly fear for their future.

As my sense of self became more mature, my language became clearer, and my understanding of the world improved.

MAGIC MOMMY[5]

I am a magical mommy.[6] I am whatever age my child is, and enter her worlds at each age and stage of her development. I can be her best friend and her mommy, slipping easily from one role to another.

I make a hippy wife self. I like her better than the 1950s wife I had been trained to be.

I make another self who is a student and I go to college.

I make a radical feminist self that I like very much. This radical feminist self understands the world in terms of power and control. This self explains to us all about patriarchy and oppression. This self thinks about Lesbianism and wonders.

As my child develops, I am changing. By being able to BE the ages of my daughter, and, at the same time, by being able to mother her, I am healing myself. By standing, fierce and protective, against any violence or violation—emotional or physical danger—I am becoming stronger and more defined.

I am secure, I am safe, I am loved and I love back. My husband. My daughter. It is simple. I am happy.

REFLECTION[7]

The world is simple to the child suffering violation and trauma. Desperate to make rules and find the consistency in life, and the love in life, we watch for cues to the hidden mechanisms of the world. In the world I inhabited, absolute belief and obedience to the Word of the Father came first, then, later, to whomever took the place of the Father, that is, whoever held my body in his hands, held my obedience and my heart.

The Word of my Father, and then the Word of my Husband was the only Word there was. When my husband became distant and erratic in his behavior, no matter what I did and how hard I tried, I tried harder. I tried to become whatever he needed. Confused and desperate, I sheltered my child as best I could, drawing a magic circle around her. I believed I could keep the darkness from her, and as I replicated more selves the dissociative episodes became greater and greater.

He changed, as he had to. I could not change. A normal relationship evolves through intersubjectivity, as my relationship with my daughter was capable of evolving. I was not capable of the kind of change a mature and committed relationship required. Because emotionally I was very young, I brought a limited understanding to the needs of a complex and developing adult relationship.

Finally, my husband told me that he was leaving, because he could not abide my terrible childishness and dependency.[8]

CRAZY MOMMY[9]

I am a crazy mother with a grieving child. I am isolated and must find a way to make money. I am completing my dissertation. I am teaching 4 courses per quarter at University. I am applying for jobs and borrowing money to travel to conferences for interviews. I spend money I don't have for a few outfits to have the right kind of clothing. I am bright and professional.

I am a crazy mother who fears losing her child, and my relatives frighten me. I fear they will see the depths of my insanity, of my lost time, of my terrible games with death. I have moved far away from anyone who knows me. I keep having breakdowns and they are terrible, but I must hide them so I can keep my job. I am medicated with Mellaril and Tofranil. I am told I have clinical depression. I am told I will always be on these medications. I am encouraged to check myself into a hospital.

I must work. I must be a mom. I must publish so I can get a permanent job. I must keep giving papers, building a reputation, being a perfect teacher. I must make sure my girl takes music lessons, has friends, goes to parties, and is safe. I must never let anyone know my constant fear, my terror of losing time, myself, my daughter. I must never let anyone know the shame I feel at being diagnosed as clinically depressed, suicidal, at being divorced, a failure, of not knowing who I am, where I am, what age I am.

In the middle of the night I find some comfort. I drink, ignoring all the warnings about pills and alcohol, figuring it can't get any worse. I gain respite. I sit outside, under the kind night sky, bottle in hand, rocking, rocking.

REFLECTION[10]

When I understood that to be a good mother, I also had to be a good provider, I was impelled to follow the only path I understood, since I came to consciousness in a college environment—that of being an academic and a teacher.[11] I was able to see the connection between creating security for my child and competent mothering. My professional self was radically different from my mothering self, but I managed to negotiate this as I imitated and tried to mirror the academics around me.

As a mother with a chaotic, episodic identity, engendered by a chaotic, episodic self, I tried to give my daughter the semblance of normalcy. She needed to feel she belonged, even though her mother was a bit strange. I often was the "wrong" age to assist my daughter with a problem. I made certain she saw other families, I wanted her to see other models, others ways, since I could not know whether I was giving her the tools she needed to have a good life.

I knew that something was very wrong with me emotionally; the global anxiety and terror I felt constantly, the voices I heard, and the suicidal urges sent me to psychiatrists wherever I lived, but I carefully kept my symptom list edited. I accepted whatever diagnosis I was given.[12] Trying to teach under heavy, thorazine-based medication was hellish. The world continued to be unpredictable and chaotic in my experience of it. I could see that the way things worked clearly made sense to everyone else, but not to me. For other people, the world turned, they made plans for the future, time passed. They understood the mysterious inner logic of a normal life. I watched them carefully and imitated them. I tried to feel I had succeeded in fooling them into thinking I was one of them.

ANALYSIS[13]

Initial thoughts

When my daughter arrived and they placed her on my chest, we gazed into each other's eyes. In *Of Woman Born,* Rich states that:

> The child gains her first sense of her own existence from the mother's responsive gestures and expressions. It is as if, in the mother's eyes, her smile, her stroking touch, the child first reads the message: You are there! And the mother, too, is discovering her own existence newly. She is connected with this other being, by the most mundane and invisible strands, in a way she can be connected with no one else except in the deep past of her infant connection with her own mother. (36)

For me, in that moment when I gazed upon the new-old eyes of my newborn daughter, a new self, literally, came into being. This self had one purpose–to love, protect and nurture this infant. Although I had never experienced the continuity of a whole and integrated self-identity, recreating myself from day to day and most probably from hour to hour, what was born in me in that moment was a self that would never dissociate from the needs and wellbeing of this child. My naïveté and defective understanding of the world would test that bond, which was created from no history I had.[14]

To be a "good enough mother," I had to learn to separate from the enchantment of being the same age as my daughter, and grow into an adult, and hope that adult would cohere.

I was fortunate in that I did not know the diagnosis of Multiple Personality/Dissociative Identity Disorder. I, like so many women of my generation, already struggling and with almost no ego-strength, would have surely succumbed to the authority of the psychiatric community, would surely have lost everything, including my child. In line with the protocols of the time, I would have been medicated beyond any hope of having a life to call my own.[15]

Self, Identity and Autobiography

According to Eakins and Damasio, we make our lives as we narrate our lives. There seems to be a close connection between the stream of consciousness or the movie-in-the-mind that each person experiences, and the creation of autobiographical identity.[16] Damasio's research in neuroscience suggests that we have a pre-linguistic self, a core or proto self, the purpose of which is to monitor bodily systems and preserve homeostasis. Out of this self develops two further selves—an extended self, experiencing continuity backwards and forwards through time, and an autobiographical self, enabled through the large memory capacity of human beings. This autobiographical memory permits a constantly revised and updated record of who we are and who we have been, both physically and behaviorally. It also allows us to have a sense of who we can be in the future.[17]

Eakins contends that in the ongoing mental narrative, we create our selves and our identities: our concept of who we are. The stories we tell ourselves and other people become our identities.[18] Most people—but not all—experience their identities as continuous and unchanging. Conventional truth holds that "normal" people have an invariable identity with a stable and reliable memory. In fact, recent studies of memory have established fairly clearly that what seems to be solid memory actually changes over time and circumstance, but we are shielded from perceiving the revision. Damasio, an evolutionary neurobiologist, describes the link between the actions of the autobiographical self and the core self; just as the core self maintains the stability of the systems of the body, the autobiographical self maintains the stability of the systems of consciousness, of which memory is one.[19]

Most psychologists and neuroscientists today go so far as to agree that identity is experienced both as continuous (I am who I was yesterday, last week, last month, and last year) and episodic (I am new each day, and the memories I have belong to someone that I used to be). In both cases, however, there is a feeling of truth about the narrative of the past (memory), present (autobiographical identity), and an ability to extend into the future. All humans probably experience both identity-states, and are, regardless, considered reliable narrators, informants, and witnesses.[20]

Feminism and Mothering Theory

Because my memory is unreliable, I am an unreliable narrator.[21] The stigma of mental illness makes me doubt my reliability. The internalized assumptions of patriarchy make me question my right to claim my life, my story. The slipperiness of identity, which I have struggled with all my life, makes me wonder who is speaking when I say "I." The fear I have that you will doubt every word I say as a woman who has been told she has Multiple Personality Disorder[22] makes me hesitate to even try to describe what it was like to mother my daughter. The Others who dwell within me speak or sing or cry or shout or scream that we cannot, must not do this. Must not break the silence. There is terror that I will lose everything by telling the truth of my experience. And I may.[23]

At the same time, I have the perspective of age and years of therapy with feminist (and not so feminist) providers. Although there will always be many voices in my head, I have made peace with most of them, and have worked toward healing. And, I was fortunate to come of age in the 1970s, to learn to question the received truths of our culture and to actively participate in the second wave of feminism.

This allowed me to see myself. I am not saying, "see myself differently," because I had never thought to be self-reflective. Participating in formal and informal feminist groups gave me permission to try on different modes of being. For a while, I understood that some part of me was a victim. Some part of me was traumatized and lived in what I called the trauma-world, where the rules for avoiding danger and abuse were the rules needed for survival. (I still live there at times.) Next, I learned that I had choices in the ways I viewed my world and myself. I created a competent, empowered, transgressive self, and took great joy in being this woman.

This was the woman I ultimately chose to be in my mothering of my daughter as she became older. I had internalized patriarchal wifehood, but was fortunate to experience custodial, post-war mothering, bordering, in my case, on neglect. As mentioned above, my mother was distant. As a hippy and alternative mother, I practiced the kind of intensive mothering Andrea O'Reilly describes as growing out of post-war mothering in the west.[24]

Alternating between guilt about my unstable mental status, and pride in being an empowered, transgressive, and feminist mother, I knew I had to embrace the most positive way of being a mother and mothering my daughter. The patriarchal motherhood model was simply impossible to attain, and definitely undesirable. The circle of women in whom I found my strength and solidarity were strong and marginalized women, and I found acceptance and even a feeling of comfort. They, too, were striving to raise children in a different and positive way.[25]

If my daughter was going to be disadvantaged in patriarchal society by having a mother who was deemed crazy by the society in which we lived, then it was incumbent upon her mother to give her some other tools, some other examples. These would set her apart, but she was already going to be different.

So, we chose agency.

> The theory and practice of empowered mothering recognizes that both mothers and children benefit when the mother lives her life and practices mothering from a position of agency, authority, authenticity, and autonomy. ... [T]his new perspective, in emphasizing maternal authority and ascribing agency to mothers and value to motherwork, defines motherhood as a political site wherein the mother can effect social change. She can do this by challenging traditional patterns of gender acculturation through feminist childrearing, and by challenging the world at large through political-social activism. (O'Reilly, 12-13)

Feminist Disability Studies have supplied an important missing piece, for feminist theory alone could not account for my experience of disability.

Patriarchy was disabling, and had disabled me. It had created severe tensions between my intuitive sense of what I needed to do in mothering my daughter: the ongoing obstacles I faced in my desire to breastfeed my daughter, the poverty, fear, and humiliation I faced in being a single mother, and the ongoing scrutiny and rush to judgment if I stumbled as a single mother who refused a relationship with a man. But my disability, the result of experiences of abuse and terror that effectively caused the massive dissociation (and related amnesias), PTSD, psychosis, and depression with which I have lived, could not be addressed completely by feminism. Feminist disability theory addresses the lived experience of disability. Further, feminist disability theory treats disability, like gender, as culturally determined and defined; definitions and attitudes towards disability are seen as fluid across time and culture, as reflections of human variation.[26]

CONCLUSION

Life teaches us that the answer to any question involving human beings is never simple. My question for this work was how to write about motherhood and disability from a variety of perspectives, because only a variety of perspectives can do the quest justice. Using autoethnographic methodology (autobiographical narrative, refection, and analysis), I have tried to depict and explain my experience as a mother with a mental disability. What emerged is a complex and evolving portrait of the interconnection of consciousness, identity and self through the embodied experience of pregnancy and birth, and how that experience radiated out and became an organizing principle for aspects of my own growth and development.

One of the framing quotes at the start of this essay is Garland-Thomson's statement about the manner in which the study of disability as an existential category clarifies the emergence of the body/self through engagement with its environment, "both social and concrete."[27]

This notion, in conjunction with Rich's description of how the initial and subsequent mother-child gaze creates maternal identity and the child's identity, forms the theoretical center of this work. When my daughter emerged from my body, and we shared that initial gaze, my identity as a mother materialized. This is not the cliché of the creation of motherhood, but the lived reality of a survivor of trauma and how I was able to build from this experience to create an encapsulated mothering experience for my daughter and myself. We developed and matured in tandem, and I adapted to circumstance and environment. It is essential to note that the environment was not only physical, but also ideological. Immersed in the patriarchal institutions of wifehood and motherhood, I had to find a way to develop myself and mother my child outside of the paradigm, because according to the paradigm, I must fail as a mother. Mothering with mental illness was difficult, but other "outlaw mothers" assisted me. These mothers had exited from patriarchy and, in befriending me, shared alternative ways of mothering that addressed issues of poverty and fear, and affirmed me as a "good enough" mother. Lived feminism gave me strength and showed me the way to become an empowered mother, giving me the tools to show my daughter alternative ways through childhood that, I hope, benefited her.

It is in the process of writing this piece that I have come to appreciate feminist disability theory, disability theory in general, and the contributions of neuropsychology and theories of autobiographical narrative. They allowed me to reflect upon my experience as a mother with a mental disability, providing perspectives I could inhabit as someone with a severe dissociative disability.

Neuropsychology, evolutionary and developmental psychology, and theories of autobiographical narrative provide much on the subject of the formation of the self and have much to say about memory. When applied to a person with labile selves and intermittent and variable memory, these theories can provide insight into non-normal selves, which may lead to greater insight for those who experience the world in a radically different fashion from others. Many of us who experience the world in this way become mothers. We have to accept society's view that we are deficient, and live with the terror of losing our children. Sometimes we find ways to empower ourselves as transgressive mothers. If and when disability is seen as an example of human variation, of human diversity, then a more inclusive view of mothering and a more humane definition of motherhood may emerge.

NOTES

[1] 1. Dissociative Identity Disorder (formerly Multiple Personality Disorder):
A. The presence of two or more distinct identities or personality states (each with its own relatively enduring pattern of perceiving, relating to, and thinking about the environment and self).
B. At least two of these identities or personality states recurrently take control of the person's behavior.

C. Inability to recall important personal information that is too extensive to be explained by ordinary forgetfulness.
D. The disturbance is not due to the direct physiological effects of a substance (e.g., blackouts or chaotic behavior during Alcohol Intoxication) or a general medical condition (e.g., complex partial seizures). Note: In children, the symptoms are not attributable to imaginary playmates or other fantasy play. DSM IV. 2000. See also van der Hart, Nijenhuis, and Steele, 7, 92-95, 101.

[2]Rich (1986, 1976); hooks (1994, 2000); Hall (2011); Garland-Thomson (2011); Eakins (2006); Ellis (2004, 2011); Winnicott (1953,1960); Damasio (1999, 2012).

[3]My chronological age in this section is 60, as is my emotional age.

[4]"The good-enough mother ... starts off with an almost complete adaptation to her infant's needs, and as time proceeds she adapts less and less completely, gradually, according to the infant's growing ability to deal with her failure" Winnicott, 1953, 2.

[5]In this section, I am my 25 year old Self chronologically, and both a young child Self to play with my daughter, and a 25 year old when I must be responsible for her well-being. My Wife Self at this time is emotionally about 16. You are hearing the voice of my 25 year old Self.

[6]I do not use language of multiplicity. I am not a clinician, and I have never experienced my identities in the way they are described in the literature. I am narrating how I understand my life looking back over the years."

[7]My chronological age in this section is 60, as is my emotional age.

[8]We sheltered in each other for 10 years, then, barely 30, went our separate ways. I will always be grateful for the friendship and support he gave me in that early, crucial period.

[9]My chronological age is 29. During this time, my predominant Selves are about 25, 16, 12, and the age of my original traumas, when my Self fragmented over and over, around 2. The voice you are hearing is my 25 year old Self.

[10]My chronological age in this section is 60, as is my emotional age.

[11]My daughter was born when my husband was an undergraduate in college, so that was the world I was born into.

[12]I was able to repress my symptoms and so used to passing that I was never institutionalized, although perhaps I would have benefited from it. The diagnosis of Multiple Personality Disorder, psychosis and depression came much later, in my 40s, and precipitated a period of even greater chaos.

[13] For the rest of this article, including the endnotes and reference material, you are hearing the voice of who I am now. I am living side by side with the others, and we talk often. I am grateful to them for lending their voices to this article. My chronological age in this section is early 60s, as is my emotional age.

[14] I was adopted 5 days after my birth in a private adoption, common in the late 1940s and early 1950s. I was meant to be a "cure" for my adoptive mother, deeply depressed, and sometimes suicidal. The idea of child as solution was repeated four more times in the family; each successive child was a solution. My sister was adopted as a companion to me, my brother because we didn't have a boy. My youngest brothers were adopted because babies made my mother feel young. My mother liked motherhood in those days, but left mothering to others. In that sense, she was a transgressive mother in 1950s suburban America, working outside the home as soon as she could. She gifted me with this element of transgression, and it served me well. The trauma and abuse I experienced at a very early age, however, combined with my mother's inability to actually mother me, resulted in the development of a very sketchy consciousness on my part, and my being-in-the-world was built around survival and reactivity to my environments, rather than a sense of continuity. I call upon Winnicott again, "With the care that it receives from its mother each infant is able to have a personal existence, and so begins to build up what might be called a continuity of being. On the basis of this continuity of being the inherited potential gradually develops into an individual infant. If maternal care is not good enough then the infant does not really come into existence, since there is no continuity of being; instead the personality becomes built on the basis of reactions to environmental impingement."

[15] I had a friend who lost custody "temporarily" upon voluntary institutionalization, and had to fight to get her child out of the foster system and away from the very relatives who perpetrated or abused them. A talented poet who willingly underwent electroshock therapy, hoping to appease the system and keep her child, she committed suicide when she realized she was still depressed and had lost the ability to write poetry. She was awarded temporary custody on the day she killed herself, and was informed that her parents, who had destroyed her life as a child, would be designated by the state as her guardians due to her mental instability.

[16] Eakins, 2-4. Damasio (1999), 222-225.

[17] Damasio (1999), 195-202.

[18] Eakins, 22-31.

[19]See Damasio (1999) p.224-225; (2010) p. 191-3, 223-226.

[20]Both Eakins and Damasio address the "normal" human being, pointing out extreme pathologies, such as Korsakov's Syndrome and Alzheimer's, to prove their points.

[21]Eakins on the connection between memory and reliability, from a societal standpoint, 46-51.

[22]People with Multiple Personality Disorder pretty much ignore the DSM change of name for the disorder – Dissociative Identity Disorder. But no one asked us.

[23]Early on in my diagnosis, I found this passage by Frank Putnam, one of the pioneers in the treatment of MPD: Having MPD does not preclude the ability to perform effectively in demanding occupations, but it is a handicap. The thought of a multiple being a peer or a professional is often greeted with horror or derisive humor by other professionals. In fact, many of the MPD professionals that I know perform at above-average levels in their field. Unfortunately, many of these people are afraid to be in treatment, lest their multiplicity be revealed and cost them their jobs. We may hope that increasing...awareness...will allow these people to be viewed for who they are – survivors of extreme childhood trauma. (101).

[24]O'Reilly, 7

[25]O'Reilly, 59-73.

[26]"Disability as diversity," a description I first heard from Lu Zeph in the 1990s, is finally being discussed in Disability Studies programs throughout the world. The term is closely connected to social justice and civil rights movements in its implications for awareness, inclusion, and dignity.

[27]See Garland-Thomson, 33.

WORKS CITED

American Psychiatric Association. *Diagnostic and Statistical Manual of Mental Disorders,* Fourth Edition, Text Revision. 2000. Web.

Damasio, Antonio. *The Feeling of What Happens: Body and Emotion in the Making of Consciousness.* Orlando: Harcourt, Inc. 1999. Print.

—, Self Comes to Mind: Constructing the Conscious Brain. New York: Random House. 2010. Print.

Eakins, Paul J. *Living Autobiographically: How We Create Identity in Narrative.* Ithaca: Cornell University Press. 2008. Print.

Ellis, Carolyn. *The Ethnographic I: A Methodological Novel about Autoethnography.* Walnut Creek, CA: AltaMira Press. 2004. Print.

Garland-Thomson, Rosemarie. "Integrating Disability, Transforming Feminist Theory." *Feminist Disability Studies.* Ed. Kim Q. Hall. Bloomington, Indiana University Press, 13-47. 2011. Print.

Hall, Kim D. (ed.) *Feminist Disability Studies.* Bloomington: Indiana University Press. 2011. Print.

hooks, bell, *Teaching to Transgress: Education as the Practice of Freedom.* New York: Routledge, 1994. Print.

— *Feminism is for Everybody: Passionate Politics.* Cambridge, MA: South End Press, 2000. Print.

O'Reilly, Andrea (ed.) *Mother Outlaws: Theories and Practices of Empowered Mothering.* Toronto: Women's Press. 2004. Print.

Putnam, Frank W. *Diagnosis and Treatment of Multiple Personality Disorder.* New York: The Guilford Press. 1989. Print.

Rich, Adrienne. *Of Woman Born: Motherhood as Experience and Institution. Tenth Anniversary Edition.* New York: W. W. Norton & Company. 1986, 1976. Print.

van der Hart, Onno, Ellert R.S. Nijenhuis, Kathy Steele. *The Haunted Self: Structural Dissociation and the Treatment of Chronic Traumatization.* New York: W.W Norton and Company. 2006. Print.

Winnicott, D. "Transitional Objects and Transitional Phenomena." *International Journal of Psychoanalysis,* 34 (1953): 89-97. Print.

Yuknavitch, Lidia. *The Chronology of Water: A Memoir.* Portland, OR: Hawthorne Books and Literary Arts. 2010. Print.

11.

Ideal Motherhood and Surveillance

Young Mothers with Intellectual Disabilities Share Their Stories

AMANDA MALONE

INTRODUCTION

This essay discusses the findings of a graduate research project that explored the lived experiences of young mothers with intellectual disabilities and their experiences with both formal and informal support providers. The topic is of particular importance to social workers and the social work profession given the frequency with which parents with intellectual disabilities are involved with various services, including child protection. Knowing what these parents deem as effective supports is highly relevant for establishing trusting relationships and enhancing the profession's ability to respond to the unique needs of this group.

Despite the large number of research studies which focus on the topics of teen pregnancy, and disability and parenting, there are very few studies which address the unique experiences of being a young mother (or a young parent) with an intellectual disability. Thus the first section of the literature review focuses on teen pregnancy and parenting while the second focuses on mothers with intellectual disabilities.

TEEN PREGNANCY AND PARENTING

Within contemporary society, the issue of teenage pregnancy and parenting has received a lot of attention, with prevention programs and supports for young mothers appearing in even the smallest of communities. Much of the literature on teen pregnancy and parenting focuses on prevention and risks for both the child and the parent. While attitudes surrounding teen pregnancy have changed over time to reflect the changing values of society, there is a general consensus that having a child while one is young is not ideal. Bissell explains that much of the literature on this topic (and, it can be argued, many social policy and program responses) are based on the assumption that having a child while a teenager is unintended and untimely (200). There is a considerable amount of literature that focuses on the developmental vulnerability of young mothers (e.g., Cassidy, Zoccollio & Hughes; Furstenberg, Brooks-Gunn & Levine; Flanagan, McGrath, Mayer and Garcia-Coll; Farber; Shapiro). Without a doubt, young mothers with disabilities experience the same developmental vulnerability along with those that arise more specifically from their disability.

DISABILITY AND PARENTING

Echoing some of the literature about teen pregnancy and parenting, a common theme in the research about disability and parenting is the assumption of inadequacy to parent. As Case & Gang note, "historically, people with developmental disabilities have not had the supports necessary to form and maintain their own families" (709). Many of the families that have been studied to date have grown up in the era of segregated residential facilities for those with intellectual disabilities. Booth & Booth indicate that, "evidence shows that parenting by people with learning difficulties is not a new phenomenon and probably was more widespread in the past than has ever been officially recognized or acknowledged" (461). In more recent years, a decline in segregated services and more community supports have enabled more people with intellectual disabilities to seek the highly valued and respected social role of parent. Budd & Greenspan explain that this change has brought with it a shift from concerns about specialized supports to child welfare and child protection (qtd. in Booth & Booth *Parenting with Learning Difficulties* 462). Budd & Greenspan share that the response to the increase of parents with intellectual disabilities has simply been a shift in concerns about specialized supports for families to child welfare and child protection.

As early as the 1980s some authors were advocating that many mothers with intellectual disabilities could parent effectively when provided with appropriate supports. (Wengler- Thomson; Budd & Greenspan; Tymchuk & Andron; Feldman et al. *Parent Education Project III,* Whitman et al.). More recently, others have indicated that despite the risks, with appropriate support many mothers with intellectual disabilities not only have the potential for growth in their parenting but are adequately able to parent over the long term (Booth & Booth, McGaw, Scully & Pritchard; Case & Gang; McConnell, Llewellyn, Traustadottir, & Bjorg Sigurjonsdottir).

SOCIAL ROLES AND IDEAL MOTHERHOOD

Condor et al. discuss that, within our society, starting a family and becoming a parent is a highly valued social role regardless of age or socio-economic status. Many young people who become parents have a wish for stability, independence and a desire to be treated as an adult (Kaufman). Young women with intellectual disabilities are not exempt from the desire to attain this very valued social role. The role of being a parent is closely related to assumptions about sexuality and identity. From a feminist standpoint, these identities that women take on are important to consider. As Garland-Thomson explains,

> Many parallels exist between the social meanings attributed to female bodies and those assigned to disabled bodies. Both are cast as deviant and inferior; both are excluded from full participation in public as well as economic life; both are defined in opposition to a norm that is assumed to possess natural physical superiority. (7)

While Garland-Thompson is discussing women with physical disabilities, the same dynamic also applies to those with intellectual disabilities. Coupled with contemporary and historical assumptions about intellectual disability and sexuality, pregnancy and parenting also challenge the notions of identities attached to disability and to motherhood. In Western society, there has been much discussion amongst feminist scholars about ideal motherhood. However, according to Mayes & Bjorg Sigurjonsdottir, within these debates, women with intellectual disabilities have been absent (28).

Yet, despite the lack of examination, these women are still judged based on the notions of an ideal mother. Choi et al. describes an ideal mother as someone "who mothers naturally, who is always and immediately present to care for her baby and who does this mothering selflessly and seamlessly" (qtd. in Malacrida 100). These are difficult expectations to say the least for any mother regardless of age or physical or intellectual ability. Women with intellectual disabilities face the same set of oppressive expectations as other women when it comes to mothering, while at the same time often having fewer resources or appropriate formal or informal supports available. One could presume that a young mother with an intellectual disability would experience even greater difficulty meeting these often impossible standards of being an ideal mother.

RESEARCH DESIGN AND THEORETICAL FRAMEWORK

This research project is informed by critical feminism and the social model of disability in its design, analysis and evaluation. Critical feminism is one of the theoretical foundations of this research project because of its focus on difference, its emphasis on social justice, and its ability to critique existing social relations (Brown & Strega 9). Standpoint feminism is also used in this research project because young mothers are best able to speak to their own realities and experiences of oppression as well as the realities and experiences of those who have more power (such as service providers or social workers). Feminist standpoint theory is the notion that the less powerful in society experience a different reality than those with more power because of the oppression that they experience. Because of their experience, not only do the less powerful interpret reality better, but they are also better able to have a complete view of the social reality of a situation because they are able to experience the dominant group's experience of society at the same time as they are experiencing their own (Harding 54; Swigonski 173). Using feminist standpoint theory to inform this research project allows for a broader examination of the issue.

The social model of disability rejects the traditional medical model which centers disability as an individual problem of personal deficits. The social model understands disability to be an experience that is socially constructed; therefore the "problem" is not situated within the individual or due to personal deficits, but rests within the structures of society. In the instance of young mothers with intellectual disabilities, a common theme in the literature was that children of parents with intellectual disabilities are at a greater risk for abuse or neglect because parents with intellectual disabilities are not able to adequately care for their children. With a social model analysis of disability, the problem is that there is not enough support for young mothers with intellectual disabilities or enough funding to provide the intensive family support or education that these young mothers require. By examining disability within a social context, it becomes a political and structural issue.

It is important to note that one of the major criticisms of the social model has been that it is exclusionary of individuals with intellectual disabilities, for example Chappell 1998. Some would argue that because this project discussed the experience of young mothers with intellectual disabilities in terms of obtaining the valued social role of mother, that Social Role Valorization (SRV) would be a more suitable theoretical approach. However, the decision to examine the experiences of the mothers in this research project from a social model was deliberate. One of the differences between the two approaches lies in their level of focus. As described earlier, the social model takes a more macro level of focus while SRV focuses more on a micro level. The hope of this project was to learn what the mothers deemed as effective supports—thus examining their experiences in relationship to broader social level supports and services. Race, Boxall and Carson discuss the differences, but more importantly, the commonalities between the social model and SRV. The authors explain that both models can be considered as a matter of a "difference in application rather than a difference in substance" (517) and suggest that there is room for both approaches to work together within disability studies.

A qualitative phenomenological research design is used to explore the lived experience of young mothers with an intellectual disability. A qualitative method of inquiry is in alignment with the chosen theoretical frameworks of critical feminism and the social model of disability. A phenomenological research design emphasizes an examination of the lived experience of a person or persons experiencing a common phenomenon. Creswell posits that phenomenology provides a deep understanding of a phenomenon experienced by several individuals and seeks to find the essence (or common experience) of the phenomenon. Given the nature and scope of this research, a phenomenological research design is appropriate.

PARTICIPANT DESCRIPTION

A total of five mothers participated in this research project—Emily, Selena, Beth, Jennifer and Rachel. A group description and pseudonyms are used to protect the anonymity of the mothers and all of the mothers provided informed consent before participating in this research project. The number of children in each family ranged from one to four. The mothers' ages at the time of the research project ranged from 20 to 33 years old; their ages at the birth of their first child ranged from 16 to 25 years old. At the time of the interviews, all five women lived in Toronto, Ontario and were referred to this research project by an agency which supports adults with intellectual disabilities. While the name of the agency was not included in this paper in order to protect the privacy of the mothers, it is important to note that the agency's mission is to provide supports and services to individuals with intellectual disabilities. All five women were involved with a variety of support providers and had had various contacts with Child Protective Services. The parenting arrangements within each family varied with some women mothering alone, others with a partner, and others with family members or foster families sharing the parenting responsibilities. The interviews were semi structured, approximately one hour in length and occurred in the mother's home, in the community or at the agency. Ten open-ended questions were presented to the mothers, asking them to share their experiences, both positive and negative, of being a young mother, their experiences with various supports and what it means to be a "good" mother.

RESULTS

Two overarching, mutually reinforcing themes were evident throughout the stories and experiences shared by the women. The first of these, experienced by all of the mothers, had to do with ideal motherhood: its expectations, rewards, challenges and performance. The second overarching theme, of surveillance, was so intertwined within the notion of ideal motherhood that it was hard to separate the two. Both themes reflect the high value placed on mothering as a social role as well as the tremendous pressure that women are under to be the selfless, ever present, infinitely patient nurturer and caregiver and "super-mom" for their children. Surveillance for the mothers who participated in this study was experienced in a compounded manner and took on many forms. Smaller themes were also identified as the experiences of becoming and being a mother, performing mothering, and the women's experiences with their formal and informal support systems.

IDEAL MOTHERHOOD

Becoming a Mother: Ideas about Motherhood

Like any group of women, the journey towards and experience of becoming a mother was varied and complex. All the women came from varied backgrounds and familial structures and their individual journeys to learning about and becoming a mother also varied. One of the discussion topics during the interviews was how the women learned how to mother and what it meant to be a good mother. In all instances, the women had learned what it meant to be a good mother from informal supports such as family and friends. For those who had siblings or younger cousins, their parenting skills came from caring for their younger family members and using those skills to mother their own children. Given that all the women became pregnant or had at least one child during their adolescence, friends and peers also played an important part in learning what it meant to be a good mother.

There was also a role in learning about mothering from formal resources such as support workers or parenting classes. All the women shared that they had attended parenting classes at one point or another and shared that they all enjoyed the classes and found them to be helpful. Selena shared, "So I take the classes to say ok. How do I discipline this child when they do something? How do I handle them when they misbehaving? What is some of the things I should do and should not do? So I learn a lot of those parenting classes."

All the women shared that an additional source of teachings about parenting and mothering came from television. All but one woman shared that they had watched reality television shows about labour and delivery, parenting and caring for infants and children and explained that they used these television shows to learn about mothering or what to expect during labour.

For women with intellectual disabilities, there are concerns by service providers about the ability to learn to mother safely and effectively. Coupled with the experience of becoming a mother at what Western society considers to be a young age, the women experienced a variety of reactions from themselves and from others when they discovered that they were going to be mothers for the first time or subsequent times. Overall, the women who participated in this study shared that becoming a mother was both scary and exciting. When asked to describe how they felt when they found out they were going to become mothers, Emily and Jennifer shared that they were fearful of the experience of labour and of telling their parents about their pregnancy.

The fear of disclosure did not just apply to parents, but also to support providers and friends. All the women shared that they had experienced previous or current involvement with Child Protective Services. The women who had children in care worried about whether their family and service providers thought that they were "ready" to have children and whether they would be able to keep their children.

Despite their fears and concerns, all the women expressed excitement when they learned that they were going to have a baby. For example, Selena shared her excitement, saying "I call and make an appointment. I come in, they did the test. They say- oh you pregnant. Pregnant?! I said. I said are you mad? But I was excited. I would say ohh thank you…thank you…thank you Jesus…thank you!"

Being a Mother

While all of the women and their experiences were unique, there were a few similarities amongst the women. These include the experience of being a young mother with a disability, and the strengths and challenges that they bring to mothering based on their age and life experience. Generally the mothers who participated in this study identified themselves simply as a young mother. They did not define their identity in terms of being a young mother with an intellectual disability. When asked to describe specifically how their disability impacted their ability to parent, three women indicated that their disability did not have any impact on their parenting abilities. When their disability posed a challenge for them, the women shared that they developed strategies for accommodating for their limitations. For example Jennifer shared that her disability had an impact on her parenting ability because she had to find a way to work around her perceived limitations and to stand up for herself.

> I just told people the truth. I was scared of the truth. I don't like to hurt people's feelings. But now I just tell people how it is. I was tired of people using me. Like ever since I was young

like people just step on me. So like, you take my kindness for weakness and stuff.

While three of the women did not explicitly state that their disability impacts them in a major way, Jennifer's comments echoed some of the challenges that the other women identified with when they spoke of the difficult aspects of being a mother.

Challenges and Positive Experiences of Motherhood

Many of the challenges that are shared by the mothers in this study are similar to challenges faced by all parents. These challenges include the difficulty experienced when children do not listen, getting out of the house on time each morning, and not being able to give children everything that you wish you could when you have a limited financial budget. Many of the positive experiences of parenting the women described included seeing your children smiling and laughing, having your children tell you they love you, and shopping/providing for children. Despite the literature on risks, concerns about safety and the abilities for abstract reasoning and problem solving, overall the mothers in this study were clear that they wanted to instill certain lessons in their children. Rachel wanted to ensure that her child could read for school. She shared that she had difficulty with reading herself, so had been shopping around for electronic books that would read aloud to her daughter and which would help Rachel with some of the more difficult words.

SURVEILLANCE

Performing Motherhood

Alongside the benefits and challenges of being a mother, the experience of performing motherhood was explored. Motherhood is considered a performance because it goes hand in hand with femininity. Butler helps to understand some of the invisible pressures that are associated with these performances and explains that performativity and the ways that we perform gender are not voluntary but are shaped by discourse and social structures which inform masculinity/femininity and our conceptualizations of gender. In the context of mothering and this study, performing ideal motherhood goes hand in hand with the expectations around femininity and what it means to be female.

In addition to the societal pressures and expectations of performing ideal motherhood, these women also had service providers conducting various forms and amounts of surveillance on them to ensure that they were performing motherhood and meeting all of the expectations associated with this performance effectively.

> Every time they say oh you don't take care. You don't know what's going to happen with (your child). If you don't do this you don't know what is going to happen with (your child) we are going to take him away- you don't care properly. You can't do this, you can't do that. So I feel like, you know, they're always in my life. Like they are always bothering me. (Emily)

Experience with Support

All the women who participated in this study had a support network consisting of both informal supports from family and/or friends, and formal supports such as agency staff. All five women had the ongoing support of an adult protective service worker from an agency that serves individuals with intellectual disabilities and all the women had experienced previous or current involvement with Child Protective Services. The role of support workers in the lives of the women included case management supports around basic needs, services, and providing referrals to community resources such as childcare, affordable housing, parenting supports, etc. The role of the Child Protective Services workers was to ensure the safety and care needs of the children were being met and to work with other service providers to provide advocacy and wraparound supports.

Formal and Informal Supports

Overall the mothers who participated in this study did not have positive experiences with formal support received from Child Protective Services. All shared that it was difficult to reach out and ask for help. They reported that their support workers were not hearing what their needs were. Selena said: "You leave an abusive life, you run. You go to get help. But when that help you get fails you- what do you do then? I didn't know this is how the people listen there."

Many of the women also shared that they felt there was a lack of positive feedback and encouragement from the other support workers. Specifically, these mothers perceived that the Child Protective Service workers would often express their doubts about the women's ability to care for their children instead of talking about the strengths that the women felt that they had and could bring to their parenting,

> Umm one time I had a CAS worker, and I forget her name, but um, she just told me oh I don't think you can handle three kids and stuff. She's like I can't even handle three kids- like trying to bring me down and stuff. So I just kept fighting it. Like I don't really like to listen to anybody so I was just like whatever, I'll just work harder. (Jennifer)

Many of the positive comments about experiences of supports were in relation to family and friends and to the women's Adult Protective Service Workers. These women reported that one of the most important supports provided by their Adult Protective Service Workers was assisting them to take control of their own lives, families and abilities in order to be the best parents possible. Jennifer shared "I started going to women's group and stuff and I started building my confidence and he didn't like that you know? He wanted to run me and stuff but I said no this is my life."

Worries about Supports

All of the women shared that, while they had positive experiences with support providers, it was difficult to negotiate all of the support. Sometimes the messages from different support providers were contradictory and sometimes they didn't know how long or how much of that support was going to be available. All of the women shared that they felt as though they were "stuck" with unwanted supports from Child Protective Services and felt unable to express this to anyone. Emily shared, "It's like they never gonna leave you alone. It's like when they stuck with you. They stuck with you until how long? You never know!" As a result of these experiences, many of the women worried about the reaction and action of their support providers.

ANALYSIS

As mentioned previously, the overarching themes of ideal motherhood and surveillance were echoed throughout the discussions with the women and were evident within the smaller themes of becoming a mother, being a mother and the experience of support.

Meeting Expectations

The pressure and expectations around ideal motherhood and its perfor-mance are very high. As Malacrida outlines, when mothers fit into cate-gories that are deemed high risk by social policy, child protection, health-care systems, etc., they are not only judged on their actions, but on their personal, emotional and psychological traits. As a result, they are likely to experience mother-blame that comes with intense scrutiny, judgment and intervention (101). It was evident from the stories of these women that they were all experiencing scrutiny, judgment and intervention from fam-ily, friends and various support providers. While the women found that help was needed and useful, there were certain forms of support that were more invasive than others. The pressure to perform ideal motherhood and the surveillance to ensure that the women were meeting all of the expecta-tions around ideal motherhood took on many forms. There were obvious forms of surveillance to ensure appropriate performances of motherhood such as supervised access visits with children, along with more subtle forms of surveillance. Many of the mothers observed that cleaning and having a clean home (despite, in many instances, having young children) meant that they were being a "good" mom.

Our construction of ideal motherhood, risk and adequacy to parent regarding young mothers with intellectual disabilities is problematic. Bas-ing parental adequacy on ability (whether that is cognitive, developmental or age related) is problematic because it focuses on risk alone, personalizes larger structural issues and examines the challenges associated with parent-ing without examining larger contexts such as poverty, access to healthcare, employment, education, parenting supports in a community, housing, etc. In addition, this process of ignoring contextual issues and focusing on ade-quacy to parent essentializes the experiences of all the mothers and creates a higher risk for inadequate supports.

The standards and expectations that we as a society–and as service providers–have adopted, set people up to fail. Yet despite these unfair ex-pectations, the women in this research project are finding ways to mother that they feel are good. By performing mothering in a variety of ways, these women are challenging our traditional understandings of ideal motherhood. The process of challenging traditional understandings helps to support a new way of constructing motherhood and paves the way for examining motherhood from a "difference-centered" perspective. As Moosa-Mitha states, "...theorizing in this way interrogates normative assumptions and practices that exist both in marginalized as well as privileged spaces, resulting from the social exclusion of people on the basis of their difference from an assumed norm" (63). Thinking about mothering from a difference-centered perspective reflects the dynamic and changing needs of families and of mothers and creates a space for valuing and honouring the variety of mothering arrangements and abilities that exist not only amongst the women in this research project but for other women who are mothering in a variety of parenting arrangements.

CONCEPTUALIZING IDENTITY

In addition to being young mothers with intellectual disabilities and all of the other identities that they embodied (such as adolescent, friend, daughter, etc.), all of the women interviewed for this project were also racialized mothers. The Canadian Race Relations Foundation describes racialization as "the process through which groups come to be socially constructed as races, based on characteristics such as race, ethnicity, language, economics, religion, culture, politics, etc. That is, treated outside the norm and receiving unequal treatment based upon phenotypical features." While the purpose of this research project was to examine the lived experience of young women with intellectual disabilities, it is important to create a space for discussing the intersectionality of the various identities that the women held and aligned or did not align with. Being a racialized woman did not seem to be considered as a part of four of the mothers' self-described identity. Only one mother discussed what it meant for her to be a racialized mother.

When asked to speak about their experiences as young women with intellectual disabilities, the women did not readily identify as being disabled women. Instead, each identified first as being a young mother. While there are a number of reasons for identifying a certain way, one explanation could be that it reflected the ongoing difficulty that society and support providers have with conceptualizing an identity that includes an intellectual disability–particularly when it has to do with sexuality and parenting. It also speaks to the hierarchy that exists amongst disabilities and the ways that our society has adapted to accommodate and understand some disabilities yet ignore others. One potential reason for not identifying as a mother with an intellectual disability or as a racialized woman with an intellectual disability could be credited to the experience of internalized oppression, wherein the women have internalized the invisibility that society has granted to persons with intellectual disabilities. While the women did not deny that their disability impacted them in certain situations, it was not a defining factor for determining how well they were able to mother. For the most part the women did not identify the challenges they experienced as parents as a direct result of their intellectual abilities. So why should that define who they are?

This inability to address or align with an intellectual disability in one of our society's most valued social roles could suggest that the women in this research project have found their own ways to redefine what it means to be an ideal mother while living within multiple sets of expectations of service providers, friends and family. As service providers, thinking about these women as either a young mother or as a woman with an intellectual disability is problematic because it continues to construct their identities in terms of risk and limitations. These constructions continue to focus on deficits and to situate difficulties or challenges as individual issues, unrelated to larger structural issues.

While living within the social constructions of what it means to be an ideal mother, what it means to be a racialized mother, what it means to be a young person and what it means to have an intellectual disability, these women have found ways to resist dominant constructions and to mother in ways that work for them. Although there is a long way to go in terms of providing appropriate support, programs and services to individuals with an intellectual disability particularly in the area of parenting, the findings of this study suggest that there is hope for re-conceptualising motherhood and its expectations to allow for a larger variety of parenting arrangements.

WHAT DOESN'T WORK

All of the women identified that when support providers only focused on their weaknesses or risks associated with their age and disability, not only were they perpetuating the unreasonable standards around ideal mother-hood and its performativity, but mothers did not identify that support as being particularly helpful. In addition, only focusing on the needs of the children and failing to accommodate or address the learning needs of the mothers was also a challenge for the women in this study. Providing sup-ports which encompass the learning needs of the mothers as well as the health and social needs of the children is essential to providing effective sup-ports and creating a relationship where the women feel comfortable asking for help. Encompassing learning needs could be done by providing verbal instead of written instructions, or writing instructions in plain language. As

Malacrida outlines, "Social constructions of disability as synonymous with incompetence keep disabled women from accessing equal educational and occupational opportunities" (100). In short, maintaining these constructions of incompetence and failing to create a space for the support needs of the mother in addition to the children does not foster appropriate or effective support.

WHAT *DOES* WORK

All the women involved in this project had the support of an Adult Protective Service Worker (APSW) from an agency which provided a range of supports to persons with intellectual disabilities. Adult Protective Service Workers provide case management services to men and women with intellectual disabilities. All of the women identified their relationship and the type of support that they received from their APSWs as being very useful and appropriate for their needs. Based on the literature and the lack of research and interventions around the social model of disability and intellectual disabilities, it can be argued that there are unique and often unnoticed challenges experienced by mothers with intellectual disabilities. For example, because the barriers these women experience are often invisible ones, such as difficulties with reading or processing information, the need for supports around these challenges is not obvious and requires more attention and exploration from service providers. Based on the positive things that the mothers had to say about their relationships with, and the support received from, their APSWs, it was clear that these support providers were able to take the time to provide flexible supports to the women that addressed their specific needs.

Providing support to these women based on the philosophy of the social model of disability is an effective approach. Race indicates in his work *Social Role Valorization* and *Learning Disability- A Social Approach* that,

> A Social Model analysis also prompts us to consider disability in the widest possible terms; rather than focusing exclusively on localized barriers, it prompts us to highlight and challenge disabling policies, practices and assumptions beyond the concerns of the individual, and work towards dismantling the barriers of a disabling society. If people with 'severe' or 'profound' learning difficulties are supported to achieve valued social roles ... they too—by challenging prevailing assumptions

and attitudes about the roles which people with learning difficulties can fulfill – play a part in transforming their society.
(qtd. in Race et al., *Towards a Dialogue* 516)

By providing support that encouraged and supported the mothers to
parent in ways that would both reflect and encourage their strengths and
abilities, the APSWs were approaching mothering from a difference-
centered approach and providing accessible services that could be coordi-
nated and geared towards the needs of the women.

CONCLUSION—WHERE DO WE GO FROM HERE?

The stories shared by the five mothers in this research project serve to highlight the lived experience of young mothers with intellectual disabilities. In
sharing their stories and experiences, the women demonstrated other ways
of conceptualizing motherhood. The stories also indicated that there is still
much work to be done in terms of constructing motherhood within a set
of attainable standards versus an oppressive set of unattainable standards.
There is much work to be done around our conceptualizations of intellectual disabilities and the limits that we have constructed around the identities of women who experience this particular type of disability. Information and supports around healthy and safe relationships, sexuality and parenting are needed in forms that are meaningful for these women. We also
need to examine and challenge the larger structures within our society that
continue to perpetuate the inaccurate messages around sexuality, parenting and disability. Despite the needed changes, these women have found
ways to unsettle and challenge the ways of conceptualizing disability and
parenting, to find meaning in the support that they receive and to mother
their children in spite of the challenges they face. As support providers, we
should be humbled by their strength and resilience.

WORKS CITED

Beth. Personal Interview. 15 Mar. 2011.
Bissel, Mary. "Socio-economic Outcomes of Teen Pregnancy and Parent-
hood: A Review of the Literature." *The Canadian Journal of Human
Sexuality* 9 (2000): 191-204. Print.

Booth, Tim and Wendy Booth. "Parenting with Learning Difficulties: Lessons for Practitioners." *The British Journal of Social Work* 23.5 (1993): 459-480. Print

Brown, Leslie and Susan Strega. "Transgressive Possibilities." *Research as Resistance.* Eds. Leslie Brown and Susan Strega. Toronto: Canadian Scholars' Press, 2005. 1-18. Print.

Budd, Karen, and Stanley Greenspan. "Parameters of Successful and Unsuccessful Interventions with Parents who are Mentally Retarded." *Mental Retardation* 23 (1985): 269-273. Print.

Butler, Judith. *Gender Trouble: Feminism and the Subversion of Identity.* New York: Routledge, 1990. Print.

Case, Laurie and B. Gang. "People with Developmental Disabilities as Parents." *Developmental Disabilities in Ontario.* Eds. Ivan Brown and Maire Percy. Toronto: Ontario Association on Developmental Disabilities, 2003. 709-715. Print

Cassidy, Beverley, Mark Zoccollio, and Susan Hughes. "Psychopathology in Adolescent Mothers and its Effects on Mother-Infant Interactions: A Pilot Study." *Canadian Journal of Psychiatry* 41 (1996): 379-384. Print.

Chappell, Anne Louise. "Still out in the Cold: People with Learning Difficulties and the Social Model of Disability." *The Disability Reader.* Ed. Tom Shakespeare. New York: Continuum, 1998. 211-220. Print.

Choi, P, S. Baker, and J. Tree. "Supermum, Superwife, Supereverything: Performing Femininity in the Transition to Motherhood." *Journal of Reproductive Infant Psychology* 23 (2005): 167-180. Print.

Condor, Jennifer, Brigit Mirfin-Veitch, Jackie Sanders, and Robyn Munford. "Planned Pregnancy, Planned Parenting: Enabling Choice for Adults with a Learning Disability." *British Journal of Learning Disabilities* 38 (2010): 1-8. Print.

Creswell John. "Five Qualitative Approaches to Inquiry." *Qualitative Inquiry & Research Design.* Ed. John Creswell. Thousand Oaks: Sage Publications, 2007. 53-83. Print.

Emily. Personal Interview. 22 Mar. 2011.

Farber, Naomi. *Adolescent Pregnancy: Policy and Prevention Services.* New York: Springer, 2009. Print.

Feldman, Maurice, et al. "Parent Education Project III: Increasing Affection and Responsivity in Developmentally Handicapped Mothers." *Journal of Applied Behavioural Analysis* 22 (1989): 111-222. Print.

Flanagan, Patricia, et al. "Adolescent Development and Transitions to Motherhood." *Pediatrics* 96 (1995): 273-277. Print.

Furstenberg, Frank, Jeanne Brooks-Gunn, and James Levine. "The Children of Teenage Mothers: Patterns of Early Childbearing in two Generations." *Family Planning Perspectives* 55 (1990): 54-61. Print.

Garland-Thomson, Rosemarie, comp. Centre for Women Policy Studies. *Re-shaping, Re-thinking, Re-defining: Feminist Disability Studies.* Washington: Centre for Women Policy Studies, 2001. Print.

Harding, Sandra. "Rethinking Standpoint Epistemology: What is Strong Objectivity?" *Feminist Epistemologies.* Eds. Linda Alcoff and Elizabeth Potter. New York: Routledge, 1993. 49-82. Print.

Jennifer. Personal Interview. 21 Mar. 2011.

Kaufman, Miriam. "Day to Day Ethical Issues in the Care of Young Parents and their Children." *Teen Pregnancy and Parenting: Social and Ethical Issues.* Eds. James Wong and David Checkland. Toronto: University of Toronto Press. 1999. 25-37. Print.

Malacrida, Claudia. "Performing Motherhood in a Disablist World: Dilemmas of Motherhood, Femininity and Disability." *International Journal of Qualitative Studies in Education* (QSE) 22.1 (2009): 99-117. Print.

Mayes, Rachel and Hanna Bjorg Sigurjonsdottir. "Becoming a Mother- Becoming a Father." *Parents with Intellectual Disabilities.* Eds. Gwynnyth Llewellyn et al. Malden: Wiley Blackwell. 2010. 17-32. Print.

McConnell, David, et al. "Conclusion: Taking Stock and Looking into the Future." *Parents with Intellectual Disabilities.* Eds. Gwynnyth Llewellyn et al. Malden: Wiley Blackwell. 2010. 241-262. Print.

McGaw, Sue, Tamara Scully, and Colin Pritchard. "Predicting the Unpredictable? Identifying High Risk versus Low Risk Parents with Intellectual Disabilities." *Child Abuse & Neglect* 34 (2009): 699-710. Print.

Moosa-Mitha, Mehmoona. "Situating Anti-Oppressive Theories within Critical and Difference- Centered Perspectives." *Research as Resistance.* Eds. Leslie Brown and Susan Strega. Toronto: Canadian Scholars' Press. 2005. 127-152. Print.

Race, David, Kathy Boxall, and Iain Carson. "Towards a Dialogue for Practice: Reconciling Social Role Valorization and the Social Model of Disability." *Disability & Society* 20.5 (2005): 507-521. Print.

—. *Social Role Valorization and the English Experience.* London: Whiting & Birch Ltd., 1999. Print.

—. *Learning Disability- A Social Approach.* London: Routledge, 2002. Print.

Rachel. Personal Interview. 15 Mar. 2011.

"Racialization Glossary." *Canadian Race Relations Foundation,* n.d. Web. 29 April. 2013.

Selena. Personal Interview. 21 Mar. 2011.

Shapiro, Janet, and Sarah Mangelsdorf. "The Determinants of Parenting Competence in Adolescent Mothers." *Journal of Youth and Adolescence* 23 (1994): 621-641. Print.

Swigonski, Mary. "Feminist Standpoint Theory and the Questions of Social Work Research." *Affilia* 8.2 (1993): 171-183. Print.

Tymchuk, Alexander, and Linda Andron. "Clinic and Home Parent Training of a Mother with Mental Handicap Caring for Three Children with Developmental Delay." *Mental Handicap Research* 1 (1986): 24-38. Print.

Wengler-Thompson, Ann. *The Assessment and Remediation through Play Therapy of Parenting Competencies of Mentally Retarded Mothers.* Ohio: Ohio State University, 1984. Print.

Whitman, Barbara, Betty Graves, and, Pasquale Accardo. "Training in Parenting Skills for Adults with Mental Retardation." *Social Work* 34 (1989): 431-434. Print.

Mothers with Multiple Social "Stigmas"

12.

Centering the Broken, Brown Body

Reflections on Disability, Race and Motherhoods

SEEMA BAHL

INTRODUCTION

This essay examines mothering at the intersection of disability and race. I explore certain meanings attached to female embodiment and mothering. The shift of the female body from so-called "object-of-desire" to nurturer and protector of young life is profoundly complicated when one considers the effects of racism and ableism[1] on the disabled woman of color. Drawing from Rosemarie Garland-Thomson's characterization of the disabled female body as unfit for motherhood in the eyes of ableist society, I take a deeper look at the impact of racialization on disabled women of color as they navigate the shifting terrain of new motherhood.

I draw primarily upon my own experience as a disabled mother and second generation South Asian living in the United States. Growing up struggling to come to terms with a social environment that rendered me both invisible and racially "othered," my disability, acquired in my early 30s, cast a new layer of complexity onto this challenging journey on the margins of female embodiment. Still, partly to fight my "broken" body, I chose motherhood. In so doing, I gave my body a new function and new value, thus claiming space for my centrality as female form. This article explores my body's nontraditional journey across the landscape of new motherhood as a disabled woman of color whose body continually seeks honor, dignity and visibility.

PERSPECTIVES ON FEMALE RACIAL EMBODIMENT: SOUTH ASIAN AND BLACK IDENTITIES

South Asian American analyses of gender, race and identity tend to look at specific socio-cultural and familial struggles of the South Asian Diaspora. Somewhat less common are analyses of the experiences of South Asian second-generation females in terms of racial devaluation and oppression in the genre of Black feminist analyses. There may be passing references to discrimination in schools and longing for whiteness, but these themes are generally not taken up as issues that would unify the second-generation South Asian experience with the African American experience of discrimination in America. Rather, these are secondary topics to more "pressing" immigrant issues such as cultural preservation versus assimilation, South Asian patriarchy and gender dynamics, the problem of categorizing "South Asians" as "Asian-Americans," and "model minority" issues.

This said, brilliant mavericks such as Vijay Prashad have called upon South Asians to band together with African American and Latino liberation movements to recognize the commonality of experience as racially oppressed groups operating within the capitalist white hegemonic construct that has defined the U.S.

> There can be no radical politics of South Asian America that does not deny the model minority stereotype and that does not ally itself with elements of the black and Latino Liberation Movement ... To craft a solidarity is to negotiate across historically produced divides to combat congealed centers of power that benefit from political disunity. (121, 122)

It is in this spirit that I draw from both the sage works of Black feminists and newer South Asian American writing on female embodiment in the Diaspora in order to make claims about both the challenges and political triumphs of disabled mothers of color.

EMBODIMENT

Gender and Race

> [Black women's silence was] the silence of the oppressed—
> that profound silence engendered by resignation and accep-
> tance of one's lot. Contemporary Black women could not join
> together to fight for women's rights because we did not see
> "womanhood" as an important aspect of our identity. Racist,
> sexist socialization had conditioned us to devalue our female-
> ness and to regard race as the only relevant label of identifica-
> tion. (hooks 1)

As a second-generation South Asian American that grew up in the '70s, my early struggles would not have perfectly mirrored hook's experience as a prominent Black feminist scholar and activist. However, the sentiment applies; my femaleness was devalued as a girl child as I navigated the harsh landscape of white suburban life as a racialized other. At first targeted due to my dark brown hue and later ignored as the invisible apparition in the classroom, I sat silent in school for years. Taunts, ridicule and menacing threats were met with resignation and social isolation, as I tried to make sense of a world that I still believed in as a child of hopeful immigrants who moved to the US from a privileged, educated class of South Asians.

This disillusionment, of course, is not a unique story in the second-generation immigrant world. Strength in the realization of that common experience of ethnic alienation often comes only in adulthood, when one can be schooled on the violent effects of racism and seek out anti-racist reme-dies. Santayani and Shamita Das Dasgupta articulate this dynamic in a South Asian second generation context:

> While growing up, daughters of Asian-Indian immigrants are
> surrounded by television and advertising images of blonde,
> blue eyed beauty, a standard against which they can only come
> up short. Indian-American women, like most women of color,
> often admit to seeing themselves as "ugly" in their youth, em-
> phasizing a preoccupation with their darker skin color. (121)

Like many girls and young women of color in the United States, devalu-ation starts very young, when media images deliberately fail to represent the diversity of society at large. Children are bombarded by messages that render brown skin invisible. The normative standard of female beauty, as powerfully conveyed in Toni Morrison's *The Bluest Eye,* has always been white, thin, heterosexual and able-bodied, and to me that meant an obsession, early on, with nursery-rhyme icons, fairy-tale heroines, and Barbie dolls that were invariably the blonde, blue-eyed princesses to which the Dasguptas refer. Many of these standardized emblems of beauty were represented in my virtually all-white, middle class classrooms and schoolyards of the 1970s Seattle suburbs, and I could only respond to this burden of invisibility by seeking approval, friendship, and romantic relations with the white world. This propelled me into an existential crisis in my 20s that would soon be graced by an unwelcome introduction to the world of chronic illness and disability.

Disability

The seemingly catastrophic catapult into bodily disarray left me gasping for air as I was in the midst of reconciling my racialized past and claiming power as a woman of color. Graduate school gave me the opportunity to develop a rigorous analysis around my personal experience of alienation and racialization, which, combined with a solid community of academics and activists of color, was tremendously healing. However, as stated above, the prospect of disability threw a so-called "monkey wrench" into that process of racial healing and liberation. I again was forced to contend with a "crisis of embodiment" as I faced, head-on, the challenge of a Multiple Sclerosis diagnosis.

My sudden bodily shift to an altered set of capacities introduced me to a grieving process common to those with chronic illness and disability. All of a sudden, the physical and psychic empowerment that I was feeling with regards to my racial identity was acutely complicated by my rapidly morphing (or so it seemed) bodily reality so as to halt liberation in its tracks, as it were. How was I to feel that my body was valuable, productive and meaningful in any way as the disease was wreaking havoc on it in the forms of unimaginable neuropathic pain and sensory discomfort, weakness and cognitive impairment? How was I to make peace with my past exclusion and move forward with confidence and dignity in the world as another mark of stigma, to use Erving Goffman's term,[2] was thrust upon me? All of a sudden, I embodied Ayesha Vernon's characterization of the "multiple Other" (389) who would undergo "simultaneous oppressions" (394). I was now situated at the intersection of race, gender and disability and could not figure out where I should go or what I should do.

The few scholars that have laudably written about this "intersectionality" posit that a crisis ensues when one has to navigate among competing marginal subjectivities (Erevelles; Vernon; Bell). One can experience ableism within communities of color and racism within disabled white communities (Vernon). All the while, mainstream society never ceases to exclude, isolate, and oppress individuals that fall into any category of Other, and this is intensified immensely when one becomes a "multiple Other." Vernon explains:

> Multiple oppression refers to the fact that the effects of being attributed several stigmatized identities are often multiplied (exacerbated) and they can be experienced simultaneously and singularly depending on the context. (395)

Scholars have also contributed to the disability studies canon a rigorous analysis of the ways in which people of color, queer and transgendered individuals, and women have been derogated and even vilified by society using the language of disability and how disability is often conflated variously with race, gender, or sexuality (Baynton; Garland-Thomson; Erevelles). According to Erevelles, this conflation is not incidental; capitalism demands that the stark reality of social inequality have a biological rationale. The argument that the "biological inferiority" or "natural deficiency" of certain groups underpins this inequality is clean and easy. Erevelles argues:

> The 'ideology of disability' is essential to the capitalist enterprise because it is able to regulate and control the unequal distribution of surplus through invoking biological difference as the natural cause of all inequality, thereby successfully justifying the social and economic inequality that maintains social hierarchies... [Disability] is the organizing grounding principle in the construction of the categories of gender, race, class, and sexual orientation. (qtd in Erevelles and Minear 133)

MOTHERHOOD

Choice, value and empowerment

As a newly self-defined "multiple Other," I began a spiritual search for reconciliation and equanimity, yet the engine of life churned on and I soon found myself married and deciding upon whether to have children. I was at a juncture: my internalized ableism was paying due allegiance to the medical model of disability[3] by attempting to dissuade me from having children. Concurrently, an indignant, self-possessed commitment to pursuing all that I wanted and deserved (read: being a mother) regardless of disability surged forth. Hesitation was minimal, and I resolutely chose motherhood. I refused to deny myself the opportunity to fulfill my desire and right to bear and raise a child.

With regards to Black motherhood, bell hooks writes:

> Systematic devaluation of Black womanhood led to a downgrading of any activity Black women did. Many Black women attempted to shift the focus of attention away from sexuality by emphasizing their commitment to motherhood. (70)

Here, hooks is referring to the consistent devaluation, subordination, and violence cast upon Black women since the days of slavery in the areas of work, marriage, sexual freedom, and autonomy. Pathologized as both sexually deviant and abject, Black women chose motherhood as a path to respect, value, regard, and entitlement from an otherwise hostile society. Patricia Hill Collins also notes:

> The controlling images of the mammy, the matriarch, and the welfare mother and the practices they justify are designed to oppress … In contrast, motherhood can serve as a site where Black women express and learn the power of self-definition, the importance of valuing and respecting ourselves, the necessity of self-reliance and independence, and a belief in Black women's empowerment. (176)

Although their analysis is astute, hooks and Collins did not consider the impact of disability on this potential dynamic, and I wonder how my own journey in choosing motherhood as a disabled woman had been bound up in this nasty system of gender and race oppression. In other words, how did disability compound my already compromised sense of self-worth as a woman of color and lead me on a mission to seek value in and for my body via motherhood? Although I did not actively navigate the waters of post-slavery trauma, the experience of society's devaluation of my body was real. Add to this a profound crisis as chronic illness and disability wreaked havoc on my entire being, and the choice that I made to mother in order to save the integrity of my broken female body, in the spirit of Black motherhood that hooks describes, was extremely compelling.

In addition to "adding value back" to my body via motherhood, I argue that my choice has been an act of resistance. Garland-Thomson characterizes ableist notions of the disabled female body as both asexual and unfit for motherhood in society:

> Whereas motherhood is often seen as compulsory for women, disabled women are often denied or discouraged from the reproductive role that some feminist thinkers find oppressive. (26)

In this vein, choosing to be a mother as a disabled woman is a radical act. It is an act that defies even feminist notions of reproductive justice that call for the right to abort fetuses that may show signs of "deformity" or "defect." The act sends a message to ableist society that reproductive justice can also mean a "defective" adult woman's right to procreate. Choosing to be a disabled mother tells the world that we demand equal opportunities and that we are not less than nondisabled mothers, though we may face different and unique challenges. These challenges can actually invite our children to be more empathetic, enlightened, compassionate and whole individuals that understand the diversity of human experience and the right to universal human dignity. Disabled mothering spits in the face of our nation and world's shameful history (and arguably, continued practice) of forced sterilization of disabled women, women of color, and poor women. Hooks and Collins remark on motherhood as both an empowering and a political site of hope and creativity for Black women. Similarly, the choice to be a disabled mother calls upon our deepest commitment to our identities as simultaneous nurturers and warriors.

According to Heather Hewett, third wave feminists and "revolutionary mamas"[4] call upon feminism and mothers' movements to honor the diversity of "mama" identities and experiences, including those of mothers of color, poor and working class mothers, immigrant, queer, and transgendered mothers. Specific attention to disabled mothering is unfortunately lacking in this call, and I invite these movements to honor and celebrate the complexity that would emerge from engaging in a movement for and of disabled mothers, who are caregivers but also in need of care. For these mothers, the trade-off wouldn't necessarily be that of professional and economic self-determination versus the demands and rewards of raising children in the home. Nor would it be limited to the current lament of the injustice of the "supermom" ideal[5] imposed upon mothers by media and patriarchal systems of dominance. Ultimately, disabled mothers would intensify this lament by decrying their constant, agonizing negotiation of self-care versus any small demand upon their body, be it childcare, employment, housework or basic activities of daily living.

From a more mainstream societal perspective, mothering can confer a productive value upon the disabled woman who otherwise may be seen as a "burden" to society. Bearing and raising children has been the oldest of all jobs, and most would argue that it has been placed almost entirely upon women's shoulders. The disabled mother of young children who is "fortunate" enough to be able to "pass"[6] as nondisabled may be able to circumvent unwelcome curiosity, judgment and reproach for not "doing anything productive." Of course, visibly disabled mothers may be criticized as "unfit" (to re-invoke Rosemarie Garland-Thomson's observation), and may consequently not have the privilege of public acceptance, admiration, and support as a new mother. If the mother is single, without family support, and/or unable to work due to her disability, she may also face severe financial and practical roadblocks in her mothering journey. The "social model of disability"[7] would call this dynamic out as a clear failure on the part of society to make parenting accessible to the disabled. Emi Barkus, a dear friend and fellow disabled mother, conveyed this in no uncertain terms:

> Because of being disabled from the age of 14, I live on SSI and food stamps, on less than half of poverty level income. I have my daughter about 60% of the time during the school year (more during the summer) and receive no child support. My parents help me pay for a car for transportation (otherwise I'd be home-bound), which is a huge privilege I am endlessly grateful for. I have a very wealthy sister with a drastically different value system who doesn't believe in helping me at all financially. All that is just to say that, if I weren't sick all the time, I could have some kind of job which would support me

and my child financially better than the $621/mo I get from SSI.

The Challenges of Motherhood

Disabled motherhood demands that we proceed as warriors on several fronts as we embark upon this lifetime journey. During the first years of my son's life, I was undergoing IV treatment for my disease, a monthly ritual to which my son became accustomed. The "sick mom" paraphernalia that gave me nightmares was routine, familiar and commonplace to him: IVs, needles, nurses, pumps and the ghastly medical adhesives that would refuse to come off the skin. It was "normal" for him to see a tired mother, a depressed mother, and a mother in pain. This would upset me tremendously and invoke guilt, fear, and shame as I would sink into the abyss of self-blame typical of disabled people that contend with societal judgment, oppression, and the persistence of the "medical model" framework. However, he would always respond with incredible empathy, paying attention not only to me, but to many of those around him that may on occasion display signs of duress, either physical or mental. And although he registered that I had limitations that he did not see in other mothers (simply translating to, "Mommy, you're slow"), he was always very sensitive and attuned to the variability in human embodiment and the need for creative forms of adaptation when tasks needed to be accomplished and conditions were limiting. This, I am sure, will be a great benefit to him as he grows and faces life in all of its uncertainty and challenge.

The task of navigating the demands of an infant or toddler when one's body is challenged is herculean. I wake up every morning knowing that I will be juggling very limited resources, and that I have to plan accordingly by allocating my energy very carefully throughout the day to complete the tasks necessary to be a mother, spouse, cook, and person who maintains a house. The boundless energy of my 5-year old son must be channeled and nurtured, as does his curiosity and academic eagerness. Healthy food must be put on the table, and my own paranoia around environmental toxins and their link to disease and mortality must be checked for my own mental health. I must be prepared for the unpredictability of my bodily functionality during the day, making space for bouts of pain, sensory attacks, exhaustion, or weakness. These episodes will invariably be accompanied by emotional swings that must be managed in order to retain salience and dependability as a mother and spouse.

These challenges are well known among disabled mothers, who face each exhausting minute of the day with courage and resilience:

> Being chronically ill for me isn't a part of my identity that I can swap into and out of public and private spheres at will. I have no control over the vicissitudes of when I'll be too sick to attend a school field trip, play a board game, clean the house. I have no control over when I need to use my walker or my cane, but even in my most "invisible" years I have been limited in my abilities as a parent, and that has been experienced starkly by my child (and my once partner). My child sees, even when no one else in the world does, the ins and outs of my disability. (Emi Barkus)

Notwithstanding such everyday struggles and mini victories, our bodily experiences and emotions will always vanish in the face of any threat or concern around our children, be it health related, bullying issues, developmental concerns, or their personal fulfillment. It is that inexplicable bond between mother and child that continues to astound me as I experience my "broken" body's own intuition and genius as I forge through the unknown and sometimes terrifying land of parenting. No maps, no compass, no instruction book, yet society expects us all to "do it right." To be sure, disabled mothers are deeply enmeshed in the powerful, wrought values and exigencies represented in newer mothering movements such as "intensive mothering,"[8] but with the added burden of managing their disabling limitations.

Public vs. Private Mothering Contexts: Walking the tightrope between disability and race

Patricia Hill Collins eloquently writes about Black motherhood in a middle class context as a distinct experience from the working class and poor mothering contexts that have been pathologized by white society. Regarding middle class racialized motherhood, she writes,

> U.S. middle class family life is based on privatization—buying a big house so that one need not cooperate with one's neighbors, or even see them. American middle-class families participate in the privatization of everything, from schools and health care, to for-fee health clubs and private automobiles. (182)

She continues to compare this privatization of mothering and family life with the traditional mothering networks of poor and working class Black culture ("othermothers," neighbors, friends, and relatives sharing childrearing duties, particularly when the mother is single or head of household). So although establishment in the middle class has been considered a commendable achievement for historically oppressed people of color, this privatization has also served to isolate the Black mother from her extended family and community. For the disabled Black mother in the middle class white neighborhood with a house and a picket fence, this could become a very alienating and arduous experience.

One could compare this dynamic with the nuclear family dynamic among middle class South Asian families of the Diaspora. Whereas both the privileged and the poor in India could often rely either on extended family networks or hired help (privileged classes and castes only), South Asian families that have immigrated and established themselves in this country are often faced with the rude awakening of shifting class and race dynamics that essentially shrink their social networks and often force them to rely exclusively on their nuclear family and private services for support. Manisha Roy comments on the impact of this cultural dislocation:

> When the parents immigrate to the United States, their reasons are clear... to avoid joint family responsibility (mostly for the newlywed wife), to enhance educational skills, to improve economic conditions, and to offer better educational opportunities to their children... (but later) parts of them wish they could go back to the old existence in India, with its security of joint family and relaxed lifestyle. (103, 104)

This situation becomes incredibly challenging when a disability is involved in the family. South Asian scholars have noted that professional families of the South Asian Diaspora are pressured to conform to the expectations placed upon them not only as "model minorities" in the U.S., but also to the traditional, gendered household expectations that men will be successful outside of the home and that women will be efficient and gracious mothers, wives, cooks, housekeepers, and possible breadwinners (either professional or working class) as well (Dasgupta; Roy; Shah). I further suggest that when a South Asian wife and/or mother is disabled, the cultural ruptures already impacting the Diaspora are magnified. The disabled mother must negotiate her new identity and range of abilities within the family and community, and pains are often taken to hide the challenges faced in order to maintain an "appropriate" image and social status. This often leads to guilt and shame for the disabled mother and her family and, in combination with the privatized isolation elucidated by Collins, can serve to shut these mothers living at the nexus of various oppressions out of public spaces altogether, both physically and psycho-spiritually.

The tremendous pressure that this isolation places on the disabled mother of color and her family can lead to attempts to re-engage with society (and more importantly, the family's cultural community) as a nondisabled person when possible. I have commonly chosen to "pass" (again, using Goffman's concept) as nondisabled in public spaces for these very reasons, and often do not feel any obligation or reason to disclose my disability to my immediate public. As a mother, my social role has become one of "support": caretaker, cook, chauffeur, educator, and champion of my son. In this position, I recognize the importance of his primacy as a developing child and one who needs my love and guidance at every turn. My disability is relegated to a private space and attended to when necessary, but I often sacrifice my need for self-care when obligations to my son are beckoning (which they always are!). I manage to develop and maintain relationships with his peers' families and take him to the sports and activities that as an educated suburban woman, I know will be "good" for his development. When my illness rears its ugly head, I am in the fortunate position to call upon my partner for support in caring for my child.

Seeking Public Spaces for Disabled Mothers of Color: Forming Community and Disability Justice

As a disabled mother of color, I have had difficulty finding a community of mothers with similar experiences and shared challenges and anxieties around parenting. Mothers of infants and young children routinely come together to form community based on activities, play dates, fitness outings with children, shared politics, etc. Mothers of color may bond with a common goal of maintaining cultural traditions and values, as well as creating spaces of inclusion and racial/cultural empowerment for their children in white society. Disabled mothers may attempt to form community with the goal of supporting one another as they travel the often treacherous path of "child rearing with limitations." These attempts at community formation can be difficult, as community-seeking disabled mothers are often spread apart within a given geographic location and may already be at their limits in terms of time and energy. In this environment, successfully convening often enough to build and maintain strong support networks can be very challenging. In addition, those with intersecting marginalities often feel out of place in monolithic spaces, as there is always tension and compromise when one has to prioritize one marginal identity over the other (Vernon). In other words, for a disabled mother of color, it may be hard to express authenticity around racial/ethnic issues in a white-dominant disabled space for mothers just as it would be difficult to bring up disability challenges in a space designed to empower mothers of color.

Trying to bring political, disabled mothers of color into "disability justice"[9] spaces can pose other obstacles. The disability justice movement calls upon us to understand how different oppressions of race, gender, sexuality, class, and religion enable and reinforce one another and invites us to fight against those oppressions while celebrating and honoring all of our interwoven, marginal identities as powerful forces on earth. Those mothers of color who have acquired a disability in adulthood may shy away from these radical spaces as they may be struggling with the reality of taking on an additional "Othered" identity and unwilling to celebrate the onset of bodily limitations. Having faced oppression and alienation as racialized women all of their lives, they now have to contend with the world as racialized and disabled women, and this can sometimes be too much to handle.

From a practical standpoint, mothering responsibilities can be all-consuming, and disabled mothering can be so overwhelming that choices must be carefully made as to where to invest personal and political resources. Radical disabled mothers, like all mothers, must also choose from a reserve of "ability" on any given day, but often, this will compromise their ability to engage in direct political and social justice action. Nonetheless, we must insist that our prioritization of self-care, child care, and less physical forms of political work such as writing and remote-access organizing is just as legitimate. Furthermore, our effort to inculcate our most powerful sociopolitical commitments into the spirits of the next generation is truly invaluable political work.

CONCLUSION

As I reflect on the solitude that emerges from occupying the unique space at the intersections of both marginality and responsibility, I take solace in the powerful words expressed by others. I feel the warm, healing glow of the words of Aurora Levins Morales:

Within the ever-shifting dynamics of capacity and incapacity, illness and health, vulnerability and strength, each of us holds truths that are partly submerged. I know my survival depends on communicating both my competence and incompetence, my resilience and know-how, and my stark limitations; that I have to hold my own and surrender, accept limits and push against them.

In confronting my new, polymorphous identity, I am constantly traversing the range of embodiments available to me; from "passing" suburban South Asian American mother to valiant rebel mama in search of racial liberation, gender equality, and disability justice. I will never give up on finding a community of mothers that I can claim as my own. They may not reflect all parts of me, but we will fight for a "maternalism" that honors our unique histories of oppression and understands our transmutation from liminality to solid centrality as disabled mothers, mothers of color, or all of the above.

NOTES

[1] Simi Linton cites the Readers Digest Oxford Wordfinder in defining ableism as "discrimination in favor of the able-bodied" (9). She furthers the definition thus, "[ableism claims that] people with disabilities as a group are inferior to nondisabled people" (9).

[2] According to Erving Goffman, stigma refers to "bodily signs designed to expose something unusual and bad about the moral status of the signifier" (1), such as individuals with "physical deformities," blemishes of...character," and "tribal stigma of race, nation or religion" (4).

[3] The medical model of disability regards disability as a personal tragedy and places the entire responsibility of managing the impairment on the affected individual.

[4] For an explanation of "mama" in the third wave context, see Hewett 45.

[5] De Marneffe characterizes the super-mom ideal as the pressure on "mothers to perform excellently on all fronts, in a job, with their children, with their partner, at the gym, and in the kitchen, making those fifteen-minute meals" (qtd in Hallstein 106).

[6] Erving Goffman has described "passing" as the practice of hiding one's stigma in order to avoid awkwardness and condemnation from society.

[7] The social model of disability counters the medical model by insisting that environmental barriers to access and social resources serve to actively "disable" the individual, ultimately asserting that disability is a societal rather than an individual issue.

[8] Hallstein outlines the work of Sharon Hays in defining intensive mothering's threefold framework: first, the mother should be the "single, primary caretaker"; two, "copious amounts of time and energy" should be devoted to the child; and three, mothering is "separate from...paid work" and "outside the scope of market valuation" because children are "priceless" (97).

[9] Disability justice is a recent liberation movement that centers and works to empower those that have been historically marginalized within mainstream disability rights spaces, such as disabled people of color, queer and transgendered disabled individuals, and the disabled poor.

WORKS CITED

Barkus, Emi. Unpublished document. 6 September 2012.

Baynton, Douglas C. "Disability and the Justification of Inequality in American History." *The New Disability History: American Perspectives.* Eds. Paul A. Longmore and Lauri Umansky. New York: New York University Press, 2001. 33-57. Print.

Bell, Chris. "Introduction: Doing Representational Detective Work." *Blackness and Disability: Critical Examinations and Cultural Interventions.* Ed. Chris Bell. East Lansing, Michigan: Michigan State University Press, 2011. 1-7. Print.

Collins, Patricia Hill. *Black Feminist Thought: Knowledge, Consciousness, and the Politics of Empowerment.* 2nd ed. New York: Routledge, 2000. Print.

Dasgupta, Santayani and Shamita Das Dasgupta. "Sex, Lies, and Women's Lives: An Intergenerational Dialogue." *A Patchwork Shawl: Chronicles of South Asian Women in America.* Ed. Shamita Das Dasgupta. New Brunswick, New Jersey: Rutgers University Press, 1998. 111-128. Print.

"Disabled Parents Allowed to Keep Newborn Son." CBC News Toronto. 4 May, 2012. Web. 11 September 2012.

Erevelles, Nirmala and Andrea Minear. "Unspeakable Offenses: Untangling Race and Disability in Discourses of Intersectionality." *Journal of Literary & Cultural Disability Studies* 4.2 (2010): 127-146. Print.

Garland-Thomson, Rosemarie. *Extraordinary Bodies: Figuring Physical Disability in American Culture and Literature.* New York: Columbia University Press, 1997. Print.

Goffman, Erving. *Stigma: Notes on the Management of Spoiled Identity.* New York: Simon & Schuster, Inc., 1963. Print.

Hallstein, D. Lynn O'Brien. "Conceiving Intensive Mothering." *Journal of the Association for Research on Mothering* 8.1,2 (2006): 96-108. Print.

Hewett, Heather. "Talkin' Bout a Revolution: Building a Mothers' Movement in the Third Wave." *Journal of the Association for Research on Mothering* 8.1,2 (2006): 34-54. Print.

hooks, bell. *Ain't I a Woman: Black Women and Feminism.* Boston: South End Press, 1981. Print.

Linton, Simi. *Claiming Disability: Knowledge and Identity.* New York: New York University Press, 1998. 1-33. Print.

Munasinghe, Viranjini. *Callalloo or Tossed Salad? East Indians and the Cultural Politics of Identity in Trinidad.* Ithaca, New York: Cornell University Press, 2001. Print.

Morales, Aurora Levins. "Coming Out Sick." *Aurora Levins Morales.* 7 January 2012. Web. 10 September 2012.

Morrison, Toni. *The Bluest Eye.* New York: Holt, Rinehart and Winston, 1970. Print.

Prashad, Vijay. "Crafting Solidarities." *A Part, Yet Apart: South Asians in Asian America.* Eds. Lavina Dhingra Shankar and Rajini Srikanth. Philadelphia: Temple University Press, 1998. 105-126. Print.

Roy, Manisha. "Mothers and Daughters in Indian-American Families: A Failed Communication?" *A Patchwork Shawl: Chronicles of South Asian Women in America.* Ed. Shamita Das Dasgupta. New Brunswick, New Jersey: Rutgers University Press, 1998. 97-110. Print.

Shah, Sonia. "Three Hot Meals and a Full Day and Work: South Asian Women's Labor in the United States." *A Patchwork Shawl: Chronicles of South Asian Women in America.* Ed. Shamita Das Dasgupta. New Brunswick, New Jersey: Rutgers University Press, 1998. 206-22. Print.

Vernon, Ayesha. "The Dialectics of Multiple Identities and the Disabled People's Movement." *Disability & Society* 14.3 (1999): 385-398. Print.

13.

Motherhood Experiences of Racialized Disabled Women

BAHJA NASSIR

This chapter describes a qualitative study on the motherhood experiences of racialized[1] disabled women. Drawing on in-depth individual interviews, along with telephone conversations and email correspondence, this study examines the motherhood experiences of four racialized disabled women residing in the Greater Toronto Area, Canada. These women reported that they were discouraged by family members, friends, and health care professionals from considering motherhood because they are perceived as undesirable partners and likely to be incompetent mothers. While they encounter people who doubt their ability to parent effectively, they believe that their children have acquired exceptional characteristics due to being raised by disabled parent(s). All identify how interlocking forms of oppression due to race, gender, class, religion, and immigration status shape their motherhood experiences. Finally, they take great joy in their role as mother and perceive motherhood to be a site of power and resistance.

INTRODUCTION

In western culture ideal mothers are positioned as "natural mothers, immediately able to care for their babies, and ultimately fulfilled in this role of selfless carer and nurturer" (Choi, Henshaw, Baker, and Tree 168). Ideal motherhood is considered an essential task of women, as well as a crucial part of their identity (Phoenix, Woollett, and Lloyd 6). Disabled women are perceived as dependent and asexual, and thus not ideal mothers (O'Toole 2-16; Gill 183-185). Prilleltensky argues that while society may pressure non-disabled women to have children, disabled women, as a group, are discouraged from becoming mothers, and thus are often prevented from fulfilling the traditional female role of motherhood ("A Ramp to Motherhood" 22). However, in spite of society's discouragement, many disabled women do become mothers (O'Toole 2-4). A few studies have explored the motherhood experiences of Caucasian disabled women; however, little is known about the motherhood experiences of racialized disabled women.

The literature on disabled mothers mainly accounts for diversity in disabilities but fails to acknowledge diversities among disabled mothers along other social identities. In addition, the majority of studies that explore the experiences of motherhood among disabled women interviewed Caucasian mothers, while the experiences of racialized disabled mothers are rarely mentioned. Some of these studies focus on a narrowly defined subgroup, typically defined by a shared condition such as physical disability or intellectual disability. However, regardless of the category of disability, medical diagnoses, functional limitations, or impairments, many of the same themes, concepts, and issues are repeated throughout the literature.

A number of researchers[2] have documented that the major barriers encountered by disabled mothers are mainly societal, rather than being caused by their actual bodily impairments. These barriers often reflect societal assumptions that these women are incompetent or inadequate mothers and may lead to constant surveillance from social service and health care professionals. Disabled mothers fear being judged as inadequate mothers, and, thus, feel pressured to demonstrate that they are competent and able to perform ideal motherhood.

The most extensive Canadian research that examined the awareness of the demands placed upon disabled women to perform ideal motherhood and the challenges they experienced in doing so, is a study conducted by Malacrida. She interviewed 45 disabled mothers in Alberta, Canada. The study found that disabled mothers have great awareness of social and health care professionals and lay perceptions of them as inadequate mothers, and of their children as not being adequately cared for, which led them to make extra efforts to appear as competent mothers (106). Similarly, some of the mothers in Thomas' study stated that they consistently feared being judged as inadequate mothers and the care they provided to their children would be viewed as insufficient, thus leading to the possibility of losing custody of their children (633-636). Thomas found that this fear pressured disabled mothers to engage in "over-conscious" mothering in order to prove that they were "good enough mothers" (635). Similarly, a study in Norway by Grue and Laerum revealed that disabled mothers work hard, performing like "supermum[s]," in order to represent themselves as normal mothers and show their capacity to mother adequately, because their motherhood roles were constantly monitored by other people (677).

A few studies have explored the relationship between parental disability and their children's well-being. Research that was conducted prior to the 1990s[3] is mostly quantitative, hypothesized and claimed to verify negative outcomes. More recent studies differentiate between the disadvantages experienced by children as a direct consequence of having a disabled mother and those disadvantages that are an effect of society's reaction to disability.[4] Prilleltensky examined the relationship between physically disabled mothers and their children ("My Child Is Not My Carer"). She found that it is not the mothers' bodily impairments that shape this relationship, but rather the context within which the relationship is embedded, such as the lack of formal support services that would facilitate the motherhood roles of such women.

Several studies[5] have identified that the lack of funded services that facilitate the motherhood roles of disabled women to be a major challenge. Khedr interviewed eight racialized disabled parents, including five mothers and three fathers who live in Toronto, Canada. Khedr is a blind mother of four children, who identifies herself as a "Muslim-Pakistani-Canadian" (4). She found that these parents from diverse backgrounds encounter extensive barriers because of their disability, gender, ethno-racial/ethno-cultural backgrounds, faith, financial status, family composition, and the intersectionality of these identities.

A major barrier identified in Khedr's study is the lack of access to formal support services, such as special transportation for themselves and their family, homemaking, and nurturing support (19-20). For example, disabled parents who do not themselves need support for their personal care (e.g. bathing) are not eligible for homemaking services. Similarly, transportation services designed for disabled people have very strict eligibility criteria and restrictions. Children or other non-disabled family members are not permitted to accompany the disabled parent. This meant that disabled parents are restricted from participating in many kinds of family activities since the service does not allow families to travel together. Furthermore, access to alternative transportation, such as a taxi, is not feasible for most of these parents, as it is too expensive for low income families and cannot accommodate large groups.

Khedr notes that strict Canadian immigration sponsorship requirements have further hindered racialized disabled parents from accessing support from their extended family (19). Even when the extended family had immigrated to Canada, the lack of resources to make homes accessible and the inaccessibility of social housing have forced some racialized disabled parents to live apart from their extended family (19). This lack of informal support from their extended family, coupled with the strict eligibility criteria for funded services, has complicated their parenthood experiences.

Despite society's impediment of motherhood roles for disabled women, many studies[6] report that motherhood is satisfying and empowering for disabled women. As Grue and Laerum observe, the bodies of disabled women are "made into something of great value, something capable of producing new life" when they become mothers (676). Also, being able to present themselves as mothers influenced other people to look at them as responsible adults in charge of their own lives and the lives of other people, rather than as dependent disabled women (Grue and Laerum 676). Similarly, one of the participants in Dossa's study, Firouzeh, a physically disabled mother, explained that motherhood has brought enormous happiness to her and she takes great pride in having been able to raise four happy children whilst being in a wheelchair (109). By adapting the *valorized* role of a mother, Firouzeh is also able to subvert the stigmatized identity of a racialized disabled woman (Dossa 120).

Firouzeh's story was drawn from a large study on the everyday lives of Muslim disabled women in Vancouver, Canada. In her book, *Racialized Bodies, Disabling Worlds: Storied Lives of Immigrant Muslim Women,* Dossa critically analyzes the experiences of four Muslim women who suffer disabilities, or who are the main care-givers to disabled children. The book brings forth these women's diverse experiences. It illustrates in detail how they are rendered socially invisible, stigmatized, and struggle to assert their dignity both in their dealings with mainstream Canadian society, and within their own communities.

The first narrative is Mehrun's, a 48-year-old physically disabled woman who came from Uganda at the age of 19 with her parents (31-63). She has primarily struggled with dealing and subverting the perception of disabled people as dependent and passive. Her story is used to illuminate the multi-faceted oppressions experienced by immigrant disabled women in their effort to be independent, integrate within Canadian mainstream society, and become contributing citizens.

The second story is Tamiza's, who immigrated to Canada from Tanzania (64-91). As a mother of two disabled children, Tamiza's story sheds light on her struggles in securing social services for her children and the different ways in which she as well as her children are excluded from social situations. Tamiza's story speaks to the fact that racialized people lack awareness about social service systems and the inaccessibility of formal support services to such group, and how this heightened the burden on parents and extended family members. Thus, her narrative illustrates how racialized people are excluded from full citizenship entitlements in such areas as social services, housing, health, and cultural rights.

The third's narrative is about Firouzeh, a physically disabled mother, who came from Iran at the age of 50 after being sponsored by her husband (92-120). Her experiences exemplify the different ways in which disability plays out in particular contexts, in the western and non-western societies. Firouzeh's story is used to explore how disabled women are excluded and marginalized by the Canadian immigration systems that evaluate people on their productivity and largely favors able-bodied males. Furthermore her narrative highlights the isolation and vulnerability to abuse (both domestic, and from the system itself) experienced by immigrant disabled women in Canada.

The final story is about Sara, who came to Canada as a refugee escaping domestic violence in Iran and became disabled after a car accident in Canada (121-150). Her narrative illuminates the barriers experienced by disabled immigrant women during settlement as well as the effects of poverty and a socially irresponsible welfare policy on the lives of these women. Sara's story also captures the racism experienced by this group when accessing health care and social services.

With the exception of Dossa's and Kedhr's studies, the literature about disabled mothers focuses mainly on the motherhood experiences of Caucasian disabled women. Therefore, little is known about the motherhood experiences of racialized disabled women. In general, there are very few studies about the experiences of racialized disabled people. Dossa attributes this to a lack of funding or interest in the issues and experiences of this population (20). Dossa claims that racialized disabled people are invisible in Canada due to two factors (4). Firstly, Canadian Immigration Policy does not grant admission to racialized disabled men and women, except under special circumstances such as refugee related issues. Secondly, racialized disabled people are invisible because their experiences are barely mentioned in the growing literature on disabilities. Dossa argues that their exclusion is also reinforced by anti-racist and feminist scholars that have given little attention to the lives of racialized disabled women (4-24). Accordingly, Dossa contends, "[w]hile disability studies have begun to recognize gender to some extent; this field has yet to deal with the issue of race. Likewise, antiracist feminism has yet to give adequate space to disability and accommodate it conceptually as a field in its own right, rather than as a subfield within existing bodies of work" (156). Dossa's book is a significant step forward in bridging antiracist feminism and disability studies.

If little has been done to explore the experiences of racialized disabled people, even less has been done to examine the experiences of motherhood among racialized disabled women. This study takes one small step in addressing this gap. Utilizing the analytic frameworks of the social model of disability and anti-racist feminist theory, it builds on previous studies, providing a more in-depth analysis of how race, gender, disability, class, religion, and immigration status, and the intersectionality of these identities shape the experiences of motherhood among racialized disabled women.

THEORETICAL BACKGROUND

This research project is informed by a number of theoretical perspectives. It draws from both the social model of disability and anti-racist feminist theory, with specific focus on Patricia Hill Collins' analysis of Black motherhood. The need to draw from both approaches reflects the multifaceted experiences of racialized disabled women, which cannot be comprehensively examined through the disability lens or the anti-racist lens alone.

The social model of disability[7] makes a clear distinction between impairment and disability. This approach perceives impairment and disability as socially constructed conditions, and defines disability as a social oppression. It refers impairments to the biological characteristics of the body and mind, but disability to environmental and social barriers that do not allow "people with perceived impairments" to participate and integrate as full members of society, and mainly focuses on the societal barriers (Barnes

78). Garland-Thomson explains that the disabled body is commonly devalued, as disabled bodies are socially constructed as abnormal, inferior, and disabled people are seen as incompetent, and overly dependent (5-9). The author notes that such a construction of disabled people affects their access to resources and participation in society. Furthermore such a construction shapes how they make sense of their own experience. While the social model of disability has been criticized for its exclusive focus on societal barriers and for rendering the lived reality of an impaired (different) body invisible,[8] it does help to bring into focus societal barriers disabled people encounter. Drawing on the social model of disability, this chapter explores how motherhood experiences of racialized disabled women have been significantly impacted by social, economic, cultural, and political barriers.

Oliver uses the term "double disadvantage" to account for the oppression experienced by Black disabled people due to their race and disability (73). Rather than this kind of additive approach, an intersectional approach to oppression, extensively articulated by anti-racist feminists, provides a more appropriate analytical tool to conceptualize the experiences of racialized disabled people. Kimberlé Crenshaw's intersectionality approach to oppression demonstrates that marginalized identities and oppression are not cumulative and do not act independently from each other. Based on her analysis of Black women's experiences, Wing argues:

> We, as black women, can no longer afford to think of ourselves as merely the sum of separate parts that can be added together or subtracted from, until a white male or female stands before you. The actuality of our experience is multiplicative. Multiply each of my parts together, 1X1X1X1X1, and you have one indivisible being. If you divide one of these parts from one you still have one. (31)

Anti-racist theory is the "body of knowledge that positions the lives and experiences of women of colour as the starting point for feminist analysis" (Dua and Robertson 9). Anti-racist feminists mainly analyze the way race, gender, and class interact to cause social inequity. They show that the experiences of women of colour are impacted by their multiple and intersectional identities, such as race, class, gender, disability, and sexuality (Mandell 87-104). As Dossa observes, the issues of racialized disabled women remain peripheral in the anti-racist feminist literature (154). Still, this body of feminist knowledge is a key analytical framework in exploring interlocking systems of oppression experienced by racialized disabled mothers.

STUDY DESCRIPTION

Participants

Several Toronto organizations for disabled people agreed to distribute electronically a flyer that described the project and invited potential participants to contact me. Because the response to this was poor, a snowball technique was employed. Each woman who participated in this study identified herself as a racialized disabled person and the mother of one or more children.

Four racialized disabled mothers were interviewed. Three of the mothers (Shya, Sultana, and Angel) have vision impairments while one participant (Zeina) has mobility impairment. All participants were in their 40s and all are highly educated with a post-secondary degree, and one was working on her post-graduate degree. Three were married; two have or had ablebodied husbands, while two had disabled husbands. Although the research did not aim to do so, all participants came to Canada as immigrants. Three of these mothers (Zeina, Shya, and Angel) immigrated to Canada within the last 20 years, as adults; one of the participants (Sultana) came to Canada as a child. These mothers are not culturally and ethnically diverse. Two participants came from Sri Lanka, one from Lebanon, and one from Pakistan. The lack of diversity among participants likely reflects the snowball technique I relied on.

Data Collection and Analysis

Data collection occurred during the spring of 2011. Data was collected through in-depth semi-structured narrative interviews, telephone conversations and email discussions. Through these, participants were encouraged to share their experiences in their own way. All interviews were carried out in the participants' houses. After transcribing all interviews personally, follow-up consultations were conducted over the phone, email, and in person in order to gain some clarification or explanation about certain issues that were said in the interviews. All initial and follow-up interviews and telephone conversations were audio-taped and transcribed, with the written and verbal consent of participants. To ensure confidentiality, participants provided pseudonyms that would appear on the report, and discussions of other identifying information on the report that would jeopardize their anonymity were avoided. Grammatical adjustments were made on some of the direct quotes for clarity.

Analysis of the data occurred throughout the research process, as well as during the more discrete analysis phase at the end of the data collection. After all interviews were transcribed, the transcripts were read and short descriptive headings written in the margins (e.g., ideal motherhood). These headings were then listed on a separate sheet of paper and grouped together to identify major themes. Finally, an outline was developed with these themes, starting from the most to the least often recurring themes. The findings and analysis sections were emailed to the participants for review. This chapter focuses on the most often recurring themes.

FINDINGS

A number of major themes emerged from these interviews. The first of these was society's assumption that disabled women are unsuitable to become or be mothers.

Unsuitable for Motherhood

Participants indicated that they received subtle and not-so-subtle messages from family members and friends that marriage and motherhood were not feasible for them. Sometimes this reflected a belief that no one would want to marry them, a feeling some internalized. Referring to her misshapen eye, one woman explains:

> To begin with, I never thought someone would marry me because of my looks and the culture and the society I came from. The men wouldn't want to … there were times people don't want to look at me also because they are scared. They are scared because, you know? I look different, right? So, until I was 30, I had a lot of friends, but I never had an affair or something like that. (Shya)

In other instances, there was the assumption of parents, friends or health care professionals that the woman would not be able to cope with being pregnant or that it would jeopardize her health.

> Nobody wanted me to be pregnant. Even close people to me; they said I should not get pregnant. [They asked] how am I going to walk? And, how I'm going to deliver? (Zeina)

Since disabled women are not considered as potential wives and mothers, participants reported that many people were surprised when they found that they were married, pregnant, or mothers. The woman who uses a wheelchair explains:

> Obviously they know I have kids. "Were you married before the disability?" I said 'No.' "Were you disabled before you have kids?" Imagine the train of thought and the perception inside ... They wanted to know if I was married before, you know? Assuming that nobody is going to marry me like that. (Zeina)

"Deprived Children"? No!

Participants discussed at great length how many people feel sorry and over-sympathize with their children, based on the assumption that the children are not receiving adequate care, and they must do more chores at home than other children. They said:

> One time, even, somebody gave money to our children, you know? When we were walking ...Some people are like that (Angel). They feel sorry for the kids and try to focus on the kids, how the kids are great, how they help us out and we must be grateful. (Zeina) Lots of people are commenting that "children are helping and they are mostly doing things". Children are children always. We have to do things, but they [other people] think they are the ones who are doing everything. (Angel)

Contrary to society's assumption that children who are raised by disabled parents could not possibly receive adequate care, three of the participants claimed that their children not only did not suffer, but were able to acquire exceptional characteristics from being raised by disabled parents. They stated that their children have exceptional characteristics such as being more independent, determined, and helpful than other children, and being very flexible, cooperative and adaptable. They attributed these characteristics to being raised by disabled parents. They explained:

> The children are very cooperative. Children are very independent, right? They are interdependent too. We help the children, and they help us. The children are so smart because

when they are little, they are trained to manage their own thing. (Angel) I found our kids are much more strong, much, much more determined, much, much more independent and responsible and it comes because we are not there at every little step. (Zeina)

Although all participants defined themselves as competent mothers, they also talked about their feelings of inadequacy when describing their performance in motherhood roles. Angel explained that she sometimes worried that she was not providing perfect care to her children because she was not able to participate in her children's activities that required sight. She described this feeling with a guilty tone as follows:

If I could see, I could [do more] things for the children. Sometimes, I have a feeling, you know? If I was able to see, I would be able to provide better, you know? Help to my children, for example, if I go to the mall or something, I can't give that much help. For example, if they get a shirt or dress, they always ask me "mama, is it good?" But I cannot tell the right thing ... It is kind of little sad ... If I was able to see it, I could be able to help more. (Angel)

Unavailable or Inaccessible Information and Formal Support Services

With the exception of Zeina, participants stated that they mostly depend on informal support from family members and friends. All come from middle-class families, who, with some reservations about their initial plans to pursue motherhood, accepted them and have always been supportive throughout their lives, particularly during early motherhood. As a group, they had/have partners with good careers and were/are supportive. Even Shya, who is a single mother, complimented her ex-husband on still being supportive. Similarly, they all acknowledged that being highly educated, financially well off, having supportive families and partners who have sustainable careers, situated them in a better position compared to low-income racialized disabled mothers who do not have such privileges.

Participants strongly emphasized that a major barrier they have faced was lack of information that would facilitate their motherhood roles. Specifically, Sultana and Zeina explained that they did not have access to any information about reproductive health or motherhood experiences as they relate to disabled women, as well as services that are available to such women.

They also commented that they did not know anyone with a similar disability that they could go to and discuss their experiences.

When it comes to formal support, Angel and Zeina receive services from disability organizations, such as Homemaking Services and Wheel-Trans. Angel mentioned that all these programs greatly facilitate her motherhood roles. However, Zeina explained that she was forced to accept personal care support in order to qualify for other services she required, such as looking after her baby, cooking, and cleaning. She described the personal care support she received from Homemaking Service, such as bathing and dressing, as a degrading experience because it violates her cultural belief regarding the need to protect the privacy of the body. She stated:

> Homemakers help you once in a week to help you shower. It was so degrading. And, I had to take a shower when she comes [pause]. I did it a couple of weeks ... because if you don't need help in the shower, you are not qualified.

Zeina explained that she was forced to endure such embarrassment in order to qualify for services, such as looking after the baby, cooking, and cleaning. After a very lengthy and emotionally draining advocacy, Zeina was able to receive financial support from the Centre of Independent Living's Direct Fund Program, which she uses to pay the care attendants she hires. She explained that this fund makes a great contribution to her family life. Similarly, although Sultana needed help, such as sorting out laundry or walking her young children to school, she noted that she was not qualified for Homemaking Services because she did not need personal care support. As a result, she had to rely on her mother's help and paid support services.

Participants talked at great length about the lack of accessible transportation. For example, Zeina explained that traveling with her three children as a family was her main challenge. That is the case since Wheel-Trans, which is designed to provide accessible transit service for physically disabled people, is not accessible to a large family or to parents who have young children, as there is no car seat for children. As she put it:

> They [Wheel-Trans services] wouldn't take me [because] they don't have a car seat. She [her third child] is a baby ... What do I do? Leave her home and go to the doctor?... Imagine! When I have the third one, look! I'm not allowed three with me, only one in the bus.

Interlocking Forms of Oppression

Participants did not just talk about how their motherhood experiences are impacted by disability, but they also talked about how these experiences are shaped by their multiple and intersectional marginalized identities. As disabled women in Western society, all four discussed that they experience oppression on two fronts, namely, sexism and ableism within their communities, while simultaneously experiencing oppression within mainstream society because of their race, class, religion, and immigration status. Sultana says:

> In your place of origin, you experience sexism and ableism, right? In [Canada], you add racism and faithnessism to that scenario in my case, right? And, you battle it at two fronts. You have the dominant culture and you have the cultural and faith community, right? For example, attitude and barriers, I run into it are different than a White disabled woman, right? I also run into barriers related to my disability within my cultural community, and our cultural communities, you know?

Participants, particularly Zeina and Sultana, said that they deal with discrimination and stereotypes associated with their identities of race, gender, religion, and immigration status. As Muslim women who wear hijabs, Zeina and Sultana explained that they or their children have been discriminated against and treated differently when accessing services, based on stereotypes associated with immigrant Muslim women. In our email discussion, Zeina wrote:

> Some of the hard times I experienced were at the hospital where the nurse was showing me how to breast feed ... mind you this was with my 3rd daughter ... I was physically weak ... and needed more support for my arms to be able to hold the baby onto my breast for 20 minutes ... she kept talking harshly to me ... and asking me to hold the baby tight ... I decided not to go again to that nursing station at the hospital ... and feed my baby while laying down on my hospital bed, because it is easier for me and the baby. The experience above was more intense because I am an immigrant ... So; the assumption was that I do not know any better. (Zeina)

Even though most participants discussed the various types of discrimination they experienced in Canada, collectively, they made it clear that they are better off in Canada than their country of origin. As a group, they explained that their own communities overtly discriminate against disabled people. Shya explains:

> We [came] from Asian world, I mean it is not easy like the culture ... If you are disabled, they look down upon you. As I told you, our society does not let disabled person lead a normal life [pause] because they are not open minded yet because the education about disabled people is very limited back home, right? (Shya)

All participants noted that generally disabled people are treated well in Canada, since there are at least some supports and services available for such people, although they are not all easily accessible for racialized disabled people.

Regarding access to disability specific services, Zeina explained that disability services particularly are less accessible to racialized disabled people, as they are marginalized and lack knowledge about the system. During the interview, Zeina was asked: "As a racialized or ethno-racial woman, how do you think your experiences are like or unlike those of Caucasian disabled mothers?" After commenting that she did not have direct contact with such mothers, Zeina reflected on how her situation as a disabled, racialized, immigrant woman might compare with a non-racialized disabled mother, highlighting her increased sense of vulnerability:

> For example, for their kids, they [Caucasian disabled mothers] would know where to go for things, while we don't. I feel we don't have any reference points ... to go to. Besides [pause] how can I say it? I think you are vulnerable. I think as [a] racial[ized person], you are double vulnerable because you have the feeling that you don't belong, one, because of your background. And, [pause] that feeling that you are disabled that is also one, right? I find they feel empowered. If you feel entitled, you are empowered. You understand what I mean? It is the action you take. It is not the entitlement itself. It is what you are going to do with it? For me, I don't feel entitled as a racial[ized person] because I don't know how the system works. It is lack of knowledge too.

Motherhood as a Site of Power and Resistance

All participants emphasized that giving birth brought them tremendous joy. When describing their reactions to giving birth, they were full of emotion and used phrases like: "I don't need anything else." "I was very happy." "I have achieved the only dream I have," and "I could not believe that I have a baby." All shared these profound feelings of excitement and fulfillment. All participants stated that motherhood brought them a high level of excitement, fulfillment, pride, confidence, self-esteem, and respect from others. They explained that they were able to divert people's attention away from their disabilities toward their motherhood status by introducing themselves as mothers and focusing on their motherhood roles in conversations with others. They said:

> I think motherhood shapes you beyond your wildest dreams [pause]. Being a mother, I think it is the top. I will write it above all everything I have. If you ask me what I am, first I like to say 'I'm a mother'...I think for me because of the disability, [it] is proving that I could do it. That is the one thing because against all stereotypes. I mean if you are disabled woman, getting married is an achievement [laugh]. [Getting married] is like [receiving] an Oscar [laugh], just to find the right man. Having kid is beyond Oscar. (Zeina) I became more confident [when I became a mother]...As I told you, I never thought I would marry and I got married. But, marriage didn't give me confidence, but becoming a mother gave me confidence...I'm proud that I'm a mother...When she [her daughter] was born, I felt that people recognized me as a normal person. Recognition meant they saw beyond my disability. They respected me more. (Shya)

DISCUSSION

"Ideal Mothers"?

Many authors[9] articulate that disabled women are discouraged from considering motherhood because they are viewed as asexual and dependent, and thus, not ideal mothers. In Western societies, ideal mothers are positioned as "ever available, ever nurturing providers of active, involved and expert mothering...[as well as being] always and immediately present to care for their babies]" (Malacrida 99). This means that ideal mothers are expected to be all things, at all times, to their dependent children. It is clear that ideal motherhood does not reflect the fact that no woman can be all things, at all times to her children due to various personal and societal barriers. Accordingly, the concept of an ideal mother sets an impossible standard for all women, since a mother cannot be all things, at all times, to her children. Thus, it creates particular challenges for disabled women whose impairments and societal barriers make being a mother much more challenging. As Segura observes, Western society's construction of ideal motherhood is based on White middle-class able-bodied women "and lacks immediate relevance to less-privileged women," such as women of colour, disabled women, and White working-class women (369).

"Deprived Children"? No!

Although many people assume that disabled women are incompetent mothers and over-sympathize with children who are raised by disabled parents, the mothers in this study asserted that their children were better able to acquire exceptional characteristics due to being raised by disabled parents. Collectively, they proudly explained that their children have outstanding qualities, such as being highly determined, independent, and helpful, when compared to other children. They attributed these qualities as important values acquired by children raised by disabled parents. Similarly, some disabled mothers interviewed in Grue and Laerum's study reported that their children acquired important values, such as being helpful, responsible, and tolerant of differences, due to growing up with disabled mothers (680). Additionally, Malacrida found that those mothers who have disabled children reported that being disabled significantly enhanced their mothering and explained that by experiencing disability themselves they were better able to meet their children's needs (108).

The racialized disabled mothers in the current study also stressed that their children are very flexible, cooperative, and adaptive. Contrary to assumptions that ideal mothers must always and immediately be present for their children, the participants argued that their children have these exceptional characteristics because they were raised by mothers who are not there for them for every little thing. By doing so, they challenge Western society's construction of ideal motherhood and childhood.

Unavailable or Inaccessible Information and Formal Support Services

The racialized disabled mothers explained that information and formal support services are absent or inaccessible. Additionally, even disability specific services, such as Wheel-Trans, are often difficult to utilize due to strict eligibility criteria. Furthermore, they are designed based on mainstream assumptions about disabled women and family composition. As a result, they highly depend on informal support. Several studies[10] also found that disabled mothers mostly receive inconsistent support from families, friends, and neighbours due to lack of funded support services and limited resources that assist such mothers. Many authors[11] explain that the unavailable and inaccessible information on reproductive health regarding disabled women, as well as the lack of funded services that would facilitate their motherhood roles, significantly reflect dominant societal assumptions about disabled women as dependent, asexual, and thus, not ideal mothers. As Dossa and Khedr have demonstrated, unavailable and inaccessible formal support services could be detrimental to racialized immigrant and refugee disabled mothers, who are usually without the social supports they were accustomed to in their country of origin, such as families and friends.

Interlocking Forms of Oppression

The participants' narratives demonstrate that the motherhood experiences of these racialized disabled women are shaped by interlocking forms of oppression. Studies about disabled mothers rarely touched on how these marginalized identities, as well as the intersectionality of these identities and oppressions, play a significant role in the motherhood experiences of disabled women. The studies mainly focused on the impact of disability on these women's motherhood role. The racialized disabled women in the present study explained that their motherhood experiences are not solely shaped by their disabilities, but their race, gender, class, religion, and immigration status also impact their experiences.

As racialized disabled women, they experience oppression on two fronts. They explained that they face sexism and ableism within their communities, while simultaneously experiencing oppression within mainstream society due to their race, religion, and immigration status. Their stories reveal that their marginalized identities are interdependent and simultaneously affect their distinctive motherhood experiences. With the exception of one woman (Angel), who stated that disability has significantly affected her life, the mothers in this study did not create hierarchy among their identities, and argued that one type of identity does not prominently determine their motherhood experiences. Two of the participants, Zeina and Sultana, articulated how every aspect of their identities shape their motherhood experiences. They explained how experiencing interlocking forms of oppression significantly impact their motherhood experiences. Their narratives relate to Collins' observation that motherhood experiences of women of colour reflect interlocking systems of oppression: race, class, and gender ("Shifting the Center" 311). Their stories illustrate that each aspect of their multiple marginalized identities and the intersection among them influence their day-to-day motherhood experiences.

Black Motherhood as a Site of Power and Resistance

All participants explained at great length how motherhood empowered them, brought them tremendous happiness and satisfaction. They emphasized that motherhood was their biggest achievement in life. Motherhood is the source of joy and rewarding experiences for many women, disabled or not. What may be different is that the participants revealed that becoming a mother boosted their self-esteem and changed the way they, as well as others, look at their bodies. Overall motherhood changed their self-image in positive ways. Prior to motherhood their self-image was negative, and they perceived themselves as women who were not able to be mothers. Since being a mother is a role many women aspire to, it is not surprising that these racialized disabled women should also see it as one that is highly desirable. Being a mother increased their status and enabled them to see themselves as a caring and competent person, well able to successfully raise children who display many fine qualities. They explained that they were strategically able to divert others' attention from their marginalized identities towards their valorized motherhood status. They did this by introducing themselves as mothers and focusing on their children and motherhood roles in conversation with others. That way, they were recognized as mothers, rather than primarily or solely as disabled women.

Patricia Hill Collins has extensively written about how motherhood is a site of power and resistance to Black women. Collins defines Black motherhood as social activism, and thus a site of power (*Black Feminist Thought* 192-198). While emphasizing the multiple and intertwined societal barriers and oppression Black mothers experience and the need to challenge oppression, Collins explains that "within African-American communities, women's innovative and practical approaches to mothering under oppressive conditions often bring recognition and foster their empowerment" (195). She also notes that motherhood is a symbol of hope and empowering exercise for many Black women. According to Collins, through motherhood, Black women can develop their sense of empowerment, acquire status in the Black community, and resist oppression (179). Clearly, the narratives of the racialized disabled mothers who participated in this study demonstrate how motherhood can be a site of power and resistance where disabled women are empowered and acquire a valorized status within society.

CONCLUDING REMARKS

Although only four racialized disabled mothers were interviewed in this study, their experiences reflect larger societal structures. Their stories reveal that whereas motherhood experiences of each racialized disabled mother is unique, each woman is connected through her challenges, aspirations, and accomplishments. The participants' narratives also show that their motherhood experiences are similar to those of Caucasian disabled mothers. However, experiencing interlocking forms of oppression renders racialized disabled mothers more vulnerable. In a nutshell, some of the participants' motherhood experiences are similar to non-disabled mothers, but also different in significant ways, as participants encounter extreme social barriers.

ACKNOWLEDGEMENTS

I would like to thank the four racialized disabled mothers who participated in this research. Zeina, Shya, Sultana, and Angel–I thank you all for welcoming me into your homes and sharing your stories with me. This book chapter would not have been possible without the consistent help, support, and encouragement of Dr. Judith Sandys at Ryerson University. From the inception of this study, her advice and unsurpassed knowledge of disability issues within a socio-political context have greatly helped me focus and capture the concept into a concrete proposal.

NOTES

[1]For the purpose of this chapter, "racialized mothers" refer to mothers who are non-Caucasian or of non-European descent.

[2]See, for example Choi et al.; Grue and Laerum; Malacrida; Thomas

[3]See Arnaud; Peters and Esses

[4]See Alexander, Hwang, and Sipski; Conley-Jung and Olkin

[5]See Malacrida; Prilleltensky "A Ramp to Motherhood;" Thomas

[6]See O'Toole et al; Ehlers-Flint; Grue and Laerum; Prilleltensky

[7]See Oliver and Barnes to learn more about the social model of disability.

[8]See Crow and Shakespeare for review of academic and political debates over the social model of disability.

[9]See Choi et al.; Gill; O'Toole

[10]See Khedr; Prilleltensky, "A Ramp to Motherhood;" Thomas

[11]See Olkin, especially chapter 10; O'Toole

WORKS CITED

Arnaud, Sarah. "Some Psychological Characteristics of Children of Multiple Sclerotics." *Psychosomatic Medicine* 21.1 (1959): 8-22. Highwire Press Free. Web. 26 July 2011.

Choi, P., C. Henshaw, S. Baker, and J. Tree. "Supermum, Superwife, Supereverything: Performing Femininity in the Transition to Motherhood." *Journal of Reproductive and Infant Psychology* 23. 2 (2005): 167-80. Scholars Portal. Web. 19 January 2011.

Collins, Patricia Hill. "Shifting the Center: Race, Class, and Feminist Theorizing about Motherhood." *Maternal Theory: Essential Readings.* Ed. Andrea O'Reilly. Toronto: Demeter Press, 2007. 311-30. Print.

—. *Black Feminist Thought: Knowledge, Consciousness, and the Politics of Empowerment.* 2nd ed. Boston: Unwin Hyman, 2000. Print.

Conley-Jung, Connie, and Rhoda Olkin. "Mothers with Visual Impairments Who Are Raising Young Children." *Journal of Visual Impairment and Blindness* 95.1 (2001): 14-29. Academic Search Premier. Web. 21 June 2011.

Crenshaw, Kimberlé. "Mapping the Margins: Intersectionality, Identity Politics, and Violence against Women." *Critical Race Theory: The Key Writings that Formed the Movement.* Ed. Kimberlé Crenshaw, Neil

Gotanda, Gary Peller, and Kendall Thomas. New York: New Press, 1995. 357-83. Print.

Crow, Liz. "Including All of Our Lives: Renewing the Social Model of Disability." *Equality, Participation and Inclusion 1: Diverse Perspectives.* Ed. Jonathan Rix, Melanie Nind, Kieron Sheehy, and Christopher Walsh. New York: Routledge, 2010. 124-139. Print.

Dossa, Parin. *Racialized Bodies, Disabling Worlds: Storied Lives of Immigrant Muslim Women.* Toronto Buffalo London: University of Toronto Press, 2006. Print.

Dua, Enakshi, and Angela Roberts, eds. *Scratching the Surface: Canadian Anti-Racist Feminist Thought.* Toronto: Women's Press, 1999. Print.

Ehlers-Flint, M.L. "Parenting Perceptions and Social Supports of Mothers with Cognitive Disabilities." *Sexuality and Disability* 20.1 (2002): 29-51. Scholars Portal. Web. 11 July 2011.

Garland-Thomson, Rosemarie. "Integrating Disability, Transforming Feminist Theory." *Feminist Formations* 14.3. (2002): 1-32. ProQuest. Web. 23 January 2011.

Gill, Carol J. "Dating and Relationship Issues." *Sexuality and Disability* 14.3 (1996): 183-90. Scholars Portal. Web. 11 July 2011.

Grueb, Lars, and Kristin Tafjord Laerum. "'Doing Motherhood': Some Experiences of Mothers with Physical Disabilities." *Disability and Society* 17.6 (2002): 671-83. Scholars Portal. Web. 12 October 2010.

Khedr, Rabia. "Parenting with a Disability: Diversity, Barriers & Requirements." *Diversityworx*, Oct. 31, 2005. Web. Jan. 19, 2011.

Malacrida, Claudia. "Performing Motherhood in a Disablist World: Dilemmas of Motherhood. Femininity and Disability." *International Journal of Qualitative Studies in Education* 22. 1 (2009): 99-117. Scholars Portal. Web. 16 February 2011.

Mandell, Nancy. *Feminist Issues: Race, Class, and Sexuality.* 5th ed. Toronto, Ontario: Prentice Canada, 2010. Print.

Oliver, Michael. *The Politics of Disablement: A Sociological Approach.* New York: St. Martin's Press, 1990. Print.

Olkin, Rhoda. *What Therapists Should Know about Disability.* New York: The Guilford Press, 1999. Print.

O'Toole, Corbett Joan. "Sex, Disability, and Motherhood: Access to Sexuality for Disabled Mothers." *Disability Studies Quarterly* 22.4 (2002): 81-101. DOAJ Directory of Open Access Journals. Web. 16 February 2011.

Peters, Lois C., and Lillian M. Esses. "Family Environment as Perceived by Children with a Chronically Ill Parent." *Journal of Chronic Diseases* 38.4 (1985): 301-8. Elsevier SD Backfiles. Web. 28 August 2011.

Phoenix, Ann, Anne Woollett, and Eva Lloyd, eds. *Motherhood: Meanings, Practices, and Ideologies.* London: Sage Publications, 1991. Print.

Prilleltensky, Ora. "My Child is Not My Carer: Mothers with Physical Disabilities and the Well-Being of Children." *Disability and Society* 19.3(2004): 209-23. Scholars Portal. Web. 16 February 2011.

—."A Ramp to Motherhood: the Experience of Mothers with Physical Disabilities." *Sexuality and Disability* 12.1 (2003): 21-47. Scholars Portal. Web. 16 February 2011.

Segura, Denise A. "Working at Motherhood: Chicana and Mexican Immigrant Mothers and Employment." *Women and Migration in the U.S.-Mexico Borderlands: A Reader.* Ed. Denise A. Segura and Patricia Zavella. United States of America: Duke University Press, 2007. 368-87. Print.

Shakespeare, Tom. "Cultural Representations of Disabled People: Dustbins of Disavowal?" *Disability and Society* 9.3 (1994): 283-99. Scholars Portal. Web. 17 March 2011.

Thomas, Carol. "The Baby and the Bath Water: Disabled Women and Motherhood in Social Context." *Sociology of Health & Illness* 19.5 (1997): 622-43. Blackwell Synergy Free. Web. 12 October 2010.

Wing, Adrien Katherine. "Brief Reflections toward a Multiplicative Theory and Praxis of Being." *Critical Race Feminism: A Reader.* Ed. Adrien Katherine Wing. New York: NYU Press, 2003. 27-34. Print.

14.

Non-existent & Struggling for Identity

VICKY D'AOUST

WE DO NOT EXIST

We aren't in the news. We aren't on TV. We certainly are not mentioned at school or in the community. Mainstream/malestream media do not acknowledge us, and very few alternative publications include articles about us.

Why? Because we do not exist.

Who are we? We are women who have disabilities and are lesbian mothers.

Our multiple minority status is difficult to understand unless one looks at the various contributing factors: women exist as persons only by the legal statute of the Persons Act; lesbians have primary status as women, and secondary status as women who love women. This latter affiliation has a negative stigma which sometimes overrules any positive status acquired by virtue of being female: Lesbians are not seen to be "real" women. We are told that "real" women have children (and, usually, husbands). We are told that lesbians do not have children. So lesbian mothers form another category of women who are relegated to a marginal position that is not enviable in the least.

Lesbians who have children (either by becoming pregnant through various means or by adoption/co-parenting) are not discussed in public. We do not exist in the public consciousness.

Describing lesbian mothers, Ellen Lewin writes:

> They understand that homosexuality is generally disapproved of, and want to protect their children from being stigmatized in the way they feel themselves to be. Some of them also understand that motherhood tends to be perceived as contradictory to lesbianism, so that the mere fact of being mothers can protect them from being identified as gay. As Valerie Thompson, the mother of a twelve-year-old daughter, said: "Of course I have the mask. I have a child. I'm accepted (as heterosexual) because I have a child and that's a kind of protection. (110)

Finally, add to this mixture the status of women with disabilities. We form another group that is marginalized because, as everyone knows, disabilities are "bad," even if it is politically correct to support charities by sending (guilt) money. Disability is feared like death and taxes because it is just as inevitable. The roles assigned to disabled people – the roles of the sick, the passive and the grateful—are not in the least desirable:

> The models of disability which most commonly inform the role of people with disabilities are the 'personal tragedy' and medical models of disability. Those who subscribe, consciously or unconsciously, to these models view disabled people as individuals whose experience is determined by their medical or physical condition. (Morris 180)

Some people even think women with disabilities would be better off dead, or perhaps just having never been born. Yet, some of us women with disabilities were born without disabilities and acquired them through accidents or violence, while still others became disabled through illness or are becoming progressively disabled as we continue to live.

And, yes, some of us happen to be lesbians. But lesbians with disabilities do not exist: "The general public, disabled people and even non-disabled lesbians assume that disabled lesbians do not exist, rendering us effectively invisible. The invisibility protects us and, at the same time, isolates us (Doucette 61). We are usually not visible in community events or public relations campaigns. We may not be visibly "out" in the disability community and may not even participate in the organizations or activities of people with disabilities.

Some of us lesbians with disabilities (who may or may not have partners) have children. Some lesbians with disabilities are mothers, by choice or chance. But, wait: Lesbian mothers with disabilities do not exist. We are not part of the community of mothers or the community of lesbians or the community of people with disabilities. Once again, we do not exist.

Even a very brief review of support material available to gay and lesbian parents will show that information on disabled lesbian parents is not available, although information on adopting disabled children is sometimes presented. Similarly, a list of resources for disabled parents—both mothers and fathers—yields information on technical assistance, support groups and literature, but nothing about parents with disabilities who are gay or lesbian.

So, women with disabilities who are mothers and lesbians are effectively and actually invisible. We go about our lives trying to avoid as many barriers as possible and, in the meantime, we recreate our invisibilities. I know, because I do it. My life as a woman with disabilities who is a lesbian mother is full of identity management. It is a part of my everyday life to determine how best to present my "selves" to the world, to my daughter and to my inner self. This practicality of living is not exclusive to lesbian mothers with disabilities, but it is particularly problematic for us.

Now that I have described the interlocking puzzle of my status, I will attempt to describe some of these problems. In the paragraphs that follow, I will alternate between describing myself and others as lesbians with disabilities who are mothers, mothers with disabilities who are lesbians, and lesbians who are mothers and women with disabilities, to demonstrate our identity dilemma.

MULTIPLE MINORITY STATUS

A multiple minority[1] group, then, is any group of people who are singled out from others in the society in which they live for differential and unequal treatment because they are defined as members of more than one minority group and who therefore regard themselves as objects of this combination of collective discrimination. (Deegan)

Women with disabilities who are lesbian mothers are faced with multiple barriers and levels of discrimination, which are not merely the sum of our oppressions. In an article exploring the experiences of disabled lesbians, Joanne Doucette quoted one woman as saying: "It is commonly assumed that disabled women are asexual, and hence cannot be mothers or lovers. Some people think there's no such thing as disabled lesbian mothers. It's not true. I'm the proof of that" (62). There may only be a small number of us, but we do exist, despite stereotypes about sexuality, disability and motherhood. As a small minority in terms of numbers, we have less access to support, less solidarity within our group and, because of barriers in the existing minority communities, less opportunity for participations outside the group than other minorities. Mothers who are lesbians with disabilities must find common ground and support among a diversity of groups: other mothers, others lesbians and other people with disabilities.

Women as a group continue to struggle for equality in society, in the workplace and at home. We struggle to be free from violence and stereotyping. Lesbians, as a sub-group of women, also have to fight against stereotypes and violence in a more particular way. Lesbians must fight against society's expectations of heterosexuality as much as they fight against sexism and inequality in general. For most women, gender is difficult to hide, but lesbians often have a choice (if it can even be called that) to be "out" or identified as a lesbian. It could be said that every day when a lesbian goes out into the world, she must choose whether or not to come out all over again. She must make this choice for each new face, because identity is so elusive. It is not an easy choice because, in some circumstances, the stigma attached to lesbianism can be permanent and damaging.

"Coming out" is also an issue for those of us who have visible (and invisible) disabilities. But being disabled does not preclude being homophobic and being a lesbian does not guarantee awareness and being female certainly does not a feminist make. The lesbian mother with disabilities has to face multiple levels of oppression based on different levels of identity. One lesbian mother I talked to found that "most mothers were more open to my disability than to my lesbianism, but most lesbians had more trouble with me being disabled than me being a mother." The mix of oppressions might not always be the same, but lesbian mothers with disabilities always risk facing more than one barrier. Joanne Doucette quotes a lesbian with disabilities making this astute observation:

I do not think that lesbian feminists have quite the fixed stereotypes that the general public has, perhaps because there is a
higher level of awareness of us within this segment of the population. I do find, however, that like the general public, they
often do not see accessibility as a human right but as a privilege and so they can get affronted when we are not grateful for
something they have done. Then they see us as demanding...
Most lesbians are just as uneducated and prejudiced as the rest
of the population. (68)

Women with disabilities are considered to be "deviant" and "defective."
Our "coming out" is to ask for help. Every time we ask for a door to be
opened, a call to be made on our behalf or for physical assistance, we are
seen again as disabled. The preconception of us as helpless, sick, inferior or
even evil, makes our needs, our dependence, even more difficult. Regardless
of our physical disabilities or lack thereof, regardless of our mental health
or mental illness, our identities are managed by how much of ourselves we
need to show, reveal and expose in order to cope.

Women with disabilities try as much as possible to minimize the "hand-
icapping effects" of having a disability. The social construction theory of
disability demonstrates that our physical or mental disabilities are not in
and of themselves problematic. Instead, environmental inaccessibility, structural inequality and systemic attitudinal discrimination create handicaps.
Theoretically, this is a very good way to explain how disabilities can become
handicaps. But, on a daily basis, women who have disabilities do have to
"cope" with the physical and/or mental limitations imposed on them by
the disability itself, in addition to those imposed by society. This means
making your disability less distracting in daily life. Some researchers have
considered this a form of denial or "passing," which implies that women
with disabilities who do this are not acknowledging reality. For me, this
is similar to being closeted or passing for straight when, in reality, one is a
lesbian. However, I do not agree that this is denial or even that it is a false
reality. It is part of *our* lives that we live as lesbians, as disabled women and
mothers, regardless of how we are perceived by others. Our management
of our identities is essential to our survival—whether that identity is about
our sexual orientation or our disabilities.

Some women with physical disabilities just get used to not doing some
things, because places are inaccessible. Women who are deaf know that
most TV shows aren't captioned and that most public services have no TTY

device that can be called directly. Women using wheelchairs know which buses won't take them and which restaurants are not accessible. So we avoid the barriers and make our lives as little trouble to others (and ourselves) as possible.

Doucette suggests that, while coming out as lesbians can be a form of resistance for disabled lesbians, "coming out is a two-edged sword. It can result in more isolation, public violence, rejection by friends and families, loss of jobs, ejection from nursing homes and other institutions and denial of services (69). Furthermore, lesbians with disabilities find that even some parts of the lesbian community are inaccessible, including women's clubs, bars, camps and festivals[2], lesbian community centres, lesbian phone lines, lesbian newsletters and books, erotic bookstores and even language itself. The community of lesbians is often constructed on a minimal budget and the needs of disabled women are costed out and weighed against other needs. Most lesbians who have disabilities are significantly restricted in how they can participate in the lesbian community.

Mothers with disabilities, too, are restricted in their activities with their children. They are not able to fully take advantage of the same range of options available to other mothers. Instead, most mothers with disabilities are far more isolated and restricted in their choices. The problem is further compounded by the fact that most services in the community are categorized by type of disability and age, and often only children with disabilities are eligible for assistance in home care or education. Parents with disabilities are not considered for these services, and often find the system far more willing to remove children to state care than provide financial support to assist in parenting at home.[3] The result of inadequate support *may* be that children of mothers with disabilities grow up too fast and become more responsible earlier than other children, or they may have disabilities or learning problems too. In some cases, the problems of children of mothers with disabilities are blamed on poor parenting skills and the disabilities of the mother. In reality, the disabilities or difficulties of the child are indeed a social construction—a direct result of inadequate resources and inaccessibility to resources.

Despite the argument that disabilities are central in the lives of women with disabilities, those of us who are mothers also have to live as mothers, not just as disabled women. Like other women with disabilities, mothers with disabilities spend as much time as possible preventing our disabilities from being a problem. We also try to minimize the negative impact of having children. Mothers with disabilities need to have an income, either from state or work sources, which does not create additional barriers to participating as a mother in society. Ensuring adequate child care and homemaking assistance is a priority for most mothers with disabilities. A great deal of effort is put into ensuring that the children are not restricted by the disability of the mother, and that the mother can parent to her best ability "in the best interests of the child."

Lesbians with children may also make attempts to ensure that motherhood doesn't prevent them from participating in community activities. Some lesbians seek out other lesbians with children for support, some try to find any women who are mothers for support (Lewin 120). Lesbian mothers struggle to find a level of safety in bringing their children to events or in talking about their needs as mothers within a community where children are not often present. Although some women choose to "postpone lesbian life" or hide their lesbianism from their children and other parents, others are able to live both as lesbians and mothers in public. These women help create visibility for lesbian mothers. A lesbian of colour, Angela Bowen, made an interesting observation about the difficult decision of being out as a lesbian mother:

> So, for those of us out who've already stuck our faces out the door, rather than retreating into the closet to protect our children, we need to work to develop surroundings conducive to cushioning our children from the hostility of heterosexism by finding competent, loving allies among lesbians, gay men and progressive heterosexuals who will know and honour who we are. By hiding, we are not helping our children. And putting our lesbianism on hold until they're grown is not a solution. We can come up with more creative solutions to mothering than retreating into a closet. (253-54)

Still, whether we are in a closet, in a house, in school, in care or in a wheelchair, we are often invisible as lesbian mothers with disabilities. We may be invisible because we choose to be, or we may be invisible because it is safer, it hurts less, it is easier and less complicated. We may be invisible because society does not want to see us. But, in truth, we are everywhere. Literally. Anywhere you see women, there are lesbians. Anywhere you see women, there are women with disabilities of all kinds. Anywhere you see women, there are mothers. Lesbian mothers with disabilities are everywhere – yet we do not exist. What do we do if we do not exist? We struggle for a sense of self.

VICKY D'AOUST

FINDING A SENSE OF SEL(F)VES

Identity politics are very important to lesbian activists, and feminists in general. People with disabilities, too, hold entire conferences on the issue of "self-identification" of disability. The practical issues faced by mothers with disabilities may not be significantly different for either straight or lesbian women, but sexual orientation is a critical *identity* issue. I recognize that there are other categories besides straight and lesbian—some women identify as either bisexual or transgendered. Because being a mother, in itself, requires an extensive network of people, sexual orientation is important in that it has a dramatic effect on the make-up and strength of an individual's network. Being a bisexual woman, or a woman who had children in a heterosexual marriage, or a woman who enjoys sexual contact with men but identifies as a lesbian, can have a significant impact on how a mother with disabilities finds support in her community or communities.

Imagine applying for a job and having to answer a list of questions about sexual activities. Would we identify ourselves sexually? What if we were offered employment equity measures as a reward for reporting our membership in "categories"? Would we identify ourselves if there was something in it for us? This is one dilemma that lesbians, women with disabilities and mothers face. Most of the benefits of identifying as a lesbian, as disabled, or even as a mother, are outweighed by the possible negative effects of public disclosure. Disclosing gender and race offers different conundrums: if we refuse to identify as female or as women of colour, if that is what we are, who are we fooling? Who are we hurting?

WE—lesbian mothers with disabilities—need to first know who we are, before we can find our own answers to these questions. Who are we? How do we define and identify ourselves? I can only really speak from my own experiences, but other lesbian mothers with disabilities have offered their assistance and I will speak for "us," basing my comments on a plurality of experience.

One woman spoke to me about having no problem with her disability, because it was self-evident and non-intrusive. She was able to parent and work and continue on her own path without her physical disability creating barriers. (Her physical disability affects her spine, although she can walk unaided.) However, she felt, as a *mother,* that raising her daughter in the women's community was difficult. She was not always able to find safe and welcoming places for her child. Her membership in a community and identification with lesbians, she felt, was in conflict with her motherhood.

Women with disabilities who are lesbians and mothers need the support of other lesbians. We shouldn't have to choose between being mothers and being lesbians. A common lesbian refrain is quoted by Dian Day in her article "Lesbian/Mother": "Real lesbians don't have children. This is proclaimed with equal loudness by both straight women (and men) and 'real' lesbians... Real lesbians are not interested in children—especially male children" (36).

A lesbian couple, who both have disabilities and are mothers of their own birth children and co-mothers of each other's children, talked to me about being more able to relate to other mothers than to single women with disabilities. This echoed comments made by lesbian mothers, who found they had more in common with single, straight mothers than with childless single or lesbian women. This couple, each of whom had different physical disabilities, also mentioned that their ability to deal with their own disabilities assisted them in understanding each other's limitations. This brings up a big issue for women with disabilities in general, whether they are straight or lesbian: should their partner be someone with a disability (and if so should it be a similar disability) or someone without a disability? This debate may be akin to the controversies in inter-racial or inter-religious marriages, where there is also concern about compatibility and equality.

Women who have disabilities and are lesbians may find they have a much smaller "pool" of potential partners due to the fact that the lesbian community is indeed much smaller than the heterosexual community, and the community of lesbians with disabilities is smaller still. Some lesbians with disabilities are very comfortable having relationships with any other lesbian, regardless of whether she has a disability. This may cause problems, however. In at least one case that I am aware of, there is a power imbalance. An acquaintance of mine, who has cerebral palsy, has a lover who is not disabled and who does most of the driving and chores. Although the woman with cerebral palsy is the mother of a child, her lesbian lover, who is not disabled, does more of the physical work and in some ways resents this obligation. This situation, however, is also one of dependency: the woman who is "able" can withhold favours and support whenever she wants to. There can be healthy ways to deal with this kind of situation, but some lesbians with disabilities have chosen to avoid the imbalance by seeking out partners who share similar disabilities, or at least share experiences with disability.

One mother I spoke to, who is deaf and a lesbian and is co-parenting her child with a hearing woman, also said that being lesbian is less problematic for her than being deaf. Although she said that being deaf, a mother and a lesbian were all important to her in different ways, she identified first as being deaf, then as a lesbian. She does not feel the same sense of identity in the lesbian community as she does in the deaf community because "most of the lesbian community are hearing, they do not understand deaf[ness], no matter if I am a lesbian." In her family of origin and with her child, being deaf was more of a problem than being a lesbian or being a mother. Her most central role, however, was that of mother, because she is always a mother. Still, every day a different part of her identity emerges, depending on context. At work her central identity is that of being deaf; around her partner, it is being a lesbian. "I feel that I am riding a merry-go-round," she says.

This woman felt that other mothers were both homophobic and supportive. If they were deaf, she could come out to them as a lesbian, but she felt that she could not do so with hearing mothers. The commonality among deaf mothers made her feel safe. As a mother, however, she found the lesbian community to be often "child phobic." Some lesbians even told her they did not like children. "Among the lesbian community, where most of them do not accept children and disability, it is quite tough for me to attend [events] and try to mingle with them. I have to teach them about deafness first, before trying about children."

The most positive thing in this woman's life was meeting and being in a relationship with a woman who understands her deafness. "Being with a wonderful partner who is not disabled and has no child is most rewarding to me. I feel very valuable to be with her and she is working hard to understand my deafness and try better about my mixed race son. It is very rare to have that experience when not many lesbians with [hearing] disabilities who have children have a hearing partner."

Many lesbian mothers with disabilities express a sense of isolation. Without the support of their birth family, and with alienation from some of their past lovers or even husbands, many lesbian mothers felt alone in the world. One of the most satisfying experiences for them was meeting others in the same boat. If women can benefit from the support of other women, and mothers benefit from meeting with other mothers, so lesbian mothers profit from contact with other lesbian mothers. It makes sense, then, that women with disabilities who are lesbian mothers need this contact and peer support even more. It helps us identify ourselves.

It is difficult to avoid comparing ourselves to the "selves" that are portrayed as desirable and normal to the "rest of the world." Being a lesbian is different than being straight, being disabled is different than being non-disabled, being a woman of colour is different than being a white woman. But the liberating part of being a lesbian with disabilities who is also a mother is the impossibility of ever achieving any semblance of the "norm"— and not wanting to. One of the most oppressive assumptions about women (and men) with disabilities is that we want to be other than what we are— that we want to be "normal." Friends, family, educators, rehabilitators, and many of those who offer services are all attempting to make something resembling normal out of the "disabled" person. Many disabled people "pass" as normal and have internalized the idea that normal is better, thus emulating the norm that provides status and success. However, disabled woman Pam Evans clearly has a different view:

> The real liberation is essentially our own. For we are all accomplices to the prejudice in exact proportion to the values and norms of our society that we are prepared to endorse. We are not normal, in the stunted terms the world chooses to define. But we are not obliged to adopt those definitions as standards to which we must aspire—or, indeed, as something worth having in the first place. (qtd. in Morris 38)

OUT & ABOUT (NOT)

As I have indicated, one of the significant issues for me in my experience as a mother is that of identity management. I have always wanted to be private about my sexual contact with individual women, but not about my politics. Being a feminist was never something I felt the need to hide, but being a lesbian was more of a risk for me. I am afraid that children are still not immune to the homophobia expressed to (and about) their parents. Most women with disabilities have a difficult time hiding their disabilities from the public. Even women with invisible disabilities are often labeled by the system that provides services to them. However, being a lesbian can (perhaps sadly) be hidden from the "authorities." As a mother, then, I must make the choice whether or not to be identified as both disabled and a lesbian.

I have experienced clinical depression and hospitalization, and I am very aware of the dangers of having my child removed from my home. I sometimes need support from the child welfare system simply because I am more isolated than some other women, but it is frightening to think that it is possible I might be discriminated against on the basis of disability, mental health or lesbianism. I try to reduce the risk as much as possible, for my sake and for my child. The fact that I have needed assistance in dealing with an identified but invisible disability has made me more vulnerable to being examined for other "weaknesses."

An American disabled woman is quoted by Jenny Morris as saying:

> I pretend to forget how deeply disabled people are hated. I pretend to forget how this is true even within my chosen home, the lesbian and feminist communities. My survival at every level depends on maintaining good relationships with able-bodied people. (Lambērt 72)

It is this dependence on others that makes our identities particularly important to manage. Most women with disabilities have contact at some point with the social services system for rehabilitation, income assistance, medical services or child care. Managing identity—or focusing on disability rather than sexuality—is sometimes a requisite for getting and keeping services (although it shouldn't be). Women with disabilities are consumers of many more systems than most women. We use the medical, social and service systems more regularly. This includes using specialized transportation, interpreters, personal care attendants and caregivers in and outside of the home. The requirement for heavy use of support people often makes it difficult to have a choice of just who those people will be, and this, in turn, makes it difficult to be honest and out with all people. If you are dependent on a transit driver to pick you up, yet afraid of harassment or persecution if the driver knew you were a lesbian, concern for your own safety might outweigh the need to be out. Yet if you are in the company of another lesbian, or people with whom you are out, it can be difficult to maintain privacy during the third party intervention of personal care attendants or interpreters. Here are a couple examples of such difficulties: discussing, through an interpreter, a plan to attend a lesbian festival presumes that the interpreter will not use that information against you; using an attendant to lift you into bed with your lesbian lover also presumes that the attendant will not withdraw other services or tell people about your personal life. It is very difficult to be free and feel safe about lesbianism when disabilities make us already vulnerable to abuse.

Dependency on others goes hand in hand with lack of privacy, which also leads to shame and invisibility for lesbian mothers with disabilities. Hiding any evidence of lesbian interests from my homemakers became a weekly ritual for me until I came out to the home support co-ordinator. I was afraid that I might lose services or that specific workers would stop coming if they knew I was a lesbian. Having your home open to professional people makes it less safe to be who you are in your own home. One autobiography by a lesbian with disabilities, Connie Panzarino, makes a strong statement about the feeling of needing independence and privacy as a lesbian. At the Michigan Womyn's Music Festival, Connie met a lesbian named Judy. "I wished I was able-bodied, just so I could get up quietly, without waking my attendant, get dressed, and figure out some excuse for needing to go over to the cabin to check on the refrigerators or something in case Judy might be up having another meal" (246).

One deaf lesbian friend told me she couldn't count the number of times she wished she could pick up a phone and call a woman without using an operator as a third party. Our disabilities often necessitate the involvement of others, and we thereby lose privacy. Women with disabilities are often heavy consumers of professional and para-professional support. For this reason, lesbians with disabilities and mothers with disabilities have a great deal in common. Non-mothers and lesbians without disabilities have less contact with intrusive agencies and can be relatively sure that their homes are safe places. Having children or having disabilities makes you subject to protection agencies, social workers, homemakers, and doctors.

Indeed, one of the reasons that women who are mothers and also lesbians with disabilities do not exist (publicly) is because so much of our lives is public and so little of our lives is private. Without a private life and without a safe place to be out, we must be invisible in public. This is not always a choice—not all women with disabilities can hide their disabilities and some lesbians cannot hide their orientation and generally motherhood is something that can be disclosed or not depending on the situation. However, for women with children, disclosure of one's identity is dictated by the fact that the children often take priority. Family, social workers and so-called friends are famous for offering advice to women with disabilities, and lesbians, about how to better meet the needs of the child. They offer advice "for the child's sake." In most cases, this advice is based on the assumption that the status quo is *not* meeting the needs of the child. Therefore, suggestions are made to assist the mother—for example, advice to be not so obvious about the lesbian "thing"—in serving the child better. In extreme cases this can mean removing the child from the home. Lesbians have often lost custody to family members, ex-spouses and protection agencies due to a perceived inability to provide for the child:

The overwhelming strategy of the courts (although this is slowly changing) has been to deny lesbians custody of their children, as punishment for lesbianism. The "learned judges" use three main arguments to support this violation of basic human rights. They argue that the child will 1) grow up sexually abused (if a girl) or rejected (if a boy); 2) grow up stigmatized by her/his peers because of the mother's sexuality; and 3) be more likely to grow up gay." (Day in Stone 42)

These are similar arguments to those used to take children away from disabled mothers: the child will be neglected because of the disability of the parent, or be forced to serve as a caregiver inappropriately, or the stigma of having a disabled parent will harm the child, or there will be environmental and institutionalized phobia around disability.

A disabled lesbian mother has a significantly increased risk of losing custody to the state or an ex-partner, or as the Sharon Bottoms case in Virginia has shown, a grandparent:

Lesbian relationships involving children are also subject to legal interference by nonlesbians who are not parents to the child. These third parties can include interested relatives, foster parents, or the state. In these cases the third party must generally prove the mother unfit. (Robson 131)

Women with disabilities face similar discrimination. In many cases, they are not given the opportunity to parent. It is difficult, if not impossible, for most disabled parents to adopt or successfully get access to new reproductive technology. In some situations, being single is enough to prevent women with disabilities access to motherhood, but being a lesbian with disabilities makes it significantly harder to access the traditional and not-so-traditional ways to have and keep children. In one of the most widely read texts on lesbian and gay parenting, April Martin asks the reader to consider his or her own health before deciding to have or adopt children:

Especially if you are planning to make babies biologically, but also if you are just committing yourself to the role of parent, it behooves you to get a thorough medical evaluation. It is worth knowing ahead of time if you have a health condition which might interfere with your ability to parent... Your decision will be your own, but it should be an informed decision, made in the best interests of your child. (29)

Perhaps without intent, the implication of this passage is that having health limitations would do damage to the child and that it would not be in the best interest of a child to be raised by a "sick" parent. However, on just the next page, Martin distinguishes between sickness and disability by suggesting that, "if you have physical limitations or disabilities, you may wonder whether you will be able to provide the physical care a baby or toddler needs, or to continue to work and provide for the family's financial needs" (30). The only other discussion in the book about disability is in reference to adopting or raising disabled children or "special needs" children. The author does not make it clear that disabled lesbians and gay men are equally competent parents as those without disabilities.

It may be that these oversights can be explained by the fact that the author was well informed about the limitations of social economic programs to support women with disabilities. In Canada, for example, there are very few support resources for disabled parents raising children. In her autobiography, Connie Panzarino, who is not a mother, wrote about wanting to be a parent. As a lesbian with disabilities, she was aware of the limitations imposed by lack of support services:

> I knew I had had no choice. I remember reading about several women with disabilities losing their children to foster care or adoption because Medicaid wouldn't pay for personal assistance to help them take care of their children. If I had taken Dawn with me form California, Social Services could have done the same to me and taken her away. After all, she wasn't legally my child, and even if she had been they wouldn't have provided me with attendant services to help me care for her. But I knew that I would have been a better mother for Dawn than her own mother.(252)

As an adoptive mother myself, I do not like to compare myself to my child's birth mother or even compare myself to other mothers that I know. As a lesbian mother, I am very sensitive to criticisms which I feel are unfairly hurled by straight mothers or by lesbians who are not mothers. As a woman with disabilities, I am very aware of my differences and, perhaps, proud of how deviant from the supposed norm I am. However, it is as a mother—especially a mother of a girl who is becoming a young woman—that I am also keenly aware of the difficulties facing young women in achieving a sense of self-confidence and self-love in a world which promotes an unachievable norm.

Because of these difficulties, coming out to a child at any age is always an issue. In the literature I have read about parenting and lesbians, the advice is usually *tell tell tell*. I have rarely read that it is wise to hide the sexuality of a parent. But these advice books are decontextualized and, sometimes, psychologized. Common sense tells us that honesty is better than deceit. However, context is very important. A single lesbian mother with a five-year-old may not have as much need to discuss her sexuality as do a lesbian couple with teenage children.

As well, we are not always in relationships. It is much harder to conceal one's lesbianism when one has a woman lover in the house. How can you be a lesbian if you are single? My daughter once told me she preferred me when I was straight. I asked her what she meant by "straight," and she replied "without a woman friend (lover)." I asked again if she meant without anyone, just alone, and she said, "yes." She wanted me to be single, not straight. Straight, to her, was the way I was when I had no partner and had much more time with her—she saw it as single parenting.

My daughter had to get used to many things: new disabilities which I acquired after adopting her; my sexuality; and, because of a racial difference, we dealt with an ethnicity issue. I think that children are more able to deal with difference if they experience it early on. My daughter had many more problems adjusting to my "new" disabilities than she did to the ones she knew about when we met. When I had adopted her, as a five-year-old, she had not been aware of my sexuality and I did not have the disabilities I now have. Her adjustments to my new disabilities and my lesbianism were significant and similar, and occurred over time.

Race, sexuality, disability, ethnicity, class and numerous other "categories" are part of our lives as lesbian mothers with disabilities. But the categories that define our realities are not the same as our realities. In fact, quite the opposite. Our lives exceed and overlap all categories, and we cannot be constrained by other people's perceptions. As women, we already fight against male-defined values, goals and standards, but as women with disabilities who are lesbian mothers, we must find our own place to be. Our identities cannot be homogeneous because we are not homogeneous, and our relationships to our communities will be different.

There are some similarities among all women, however, that can help us understand each other. Women may not identify as being disabled but might actually have experiences that are similar to those of women who do identify as disabled. Lesbian mothers, for example, might be adult survivors of sexual abuse, recovering addicts or alcoholics, students (this should be at least a temporary disability), consumers of mental health services or many other less obvious "handicaps." All of these contribute to commonalities among lesbians that transcend the limits of disability. Straight mothers with disabilities claim that their biggest problems have to do with finances and accessibility. This includes not being able to afford specialized help or technical aids and not being able to access traditional services. All of these problems exist for lesbians with disabilities as well, yet seem to be less a priority than issues of sexuality, identity and parenting.

BECOMING VISIBLE: LESBIAN MOTHERS WITH DISABILITIES

For some of us, choosing to identify with one or more of our "roles" may not be difficult; in my experience, however, the opposite is true: lesbian mothers with disabilities are constantly challenging the assumptions about their motherhood, disability and sexuality, and have to swing between roles to keep up. I think this movement from being "mother" to "lesbian" to "woman with disabilities" has some advantages because it reduces our rigidity. However, on a personal level, it is just plain tiring. How useful it would be if we had one word to describe "us" and our experience.

First, we must recognize that we do experience multiple minority status and that our lives are complicated by the exponential nature of this status. Our plurality is not only significant in our individual lives; among women with various disabilities there is incredible diversity. Blind women who are lesbian mothers may (or may not) have much in common with lesbian mothers who are deaf and lesbian mothers who use wheelchairs. Women with psychiatric disabilities who are lesbian mothers; lesbian mothers with learning disabilities or invisible disabilities—all are struggling for a sense of self. Our lives are filled with challenges—challenges from the outside about our right to mother, to love and to live; and challenges from the inside about giving ourselves and our children as much as we possibly can. We need as much support as we can get in order to survive and emerge as visible in our communities.

This support will come first from within, from our own connections with other lesbian mothers with disabilities. Support will also come from our allies: lesbian mothers without disabilities, or straight mothers with disabilities. We will also require the support of all lesbians, all mothers, all people with disabilities, because we are all part of larger communities, not just the lesbian or disability communities. Our children, whether or not they are themselves disabled, are part of the larger community and need access to the entire range of opportunities as much as we do.

We must de-categorize service and deconstruct disability, so that all women, all mothers, all people with disabilities have access to services, regardless of sexuality, disability or maternal status. We must ensure that our visibility is not only seen, but really noticed by those who have the power and ability to make a difference.

We do exist. We are everywhere.

AUTHOR'S NOTE

Permission to reprint this chapter has been granted by Katherine Arnup. "Non-existent & Struggling for Identity" appeared first in the 1995 Gynergy Press book titled *Lesbian Parenting: Living with Pride & Prejudice,* Editor, Katherine Arnup.

NOTES

[1]Maria Barile's 1986 sociology paper, "Dis-Abled Women as Deviant," (written as part of a Masters in Social Work at McGill University) was of particular help to me in understanding the issues of intersection/action.
[2]It appears that Michigan deserves special mention for its efforts to make the camp and festival accessible and accommodating for women with disabilities of all kinds
[3]For a good description of how exclusion from policy of women with disabilities has an adverse impact, see Blackford.

WORKS CITED

Blackford, Karen, "Erasing Mothers with Disabilities Through Canadian Family-Related Policy," *Disability, Handicap and Society,* 8(3): 1990. Print.

Bowen, Angela. *Another View of Lesbians Choosing Children. Lesbian Parenting: Living with Pride & Prejudice.* Ed. Katherine Arnup. Charlottetown: Gynergy Press, 1995. Print.

Day, Dian. *Lesbian/Mother. Lesbians in Canada.* Ed. Sharon Dale Stone. Toronto: Between the Lines, 1990. Print.

Deegan, M. J. *Multiple Minority Groups: A Case of Physically Disabled Women.* University of Nebraska, 1982. Print.

Doucette, Joanne. *Redefining Difference: Disabled Lesbians Resist. Lesbians in Canada.* Ed. Sharon Dale Stone. Toronto: Between the Lines, 1990. Print.

Lambert, Sandra. *Disability and Violence.* Sinister Wisdom 39 (1989). Print.

Lewin, Ellen. *Lesbian Mothers: Accounts of Gender in American Culture.* Ithaca: Cornell UP, 1993. Print.

Martin, April. *The Lesbian and Gay Parenting Handbook.* New York: Harper Perennial, 1993. Print.

Morris, Jenny. *Pride Against Prejudice: Transforming Attitudes to Disability.* London: The Women's Press, 1991. Print.

Panzarino, Connie. *The Me in the Mirror.* Seattle: Seal Press, 1994. Print.

Robson, Ruthann. *Lesbian (OUT) Law: Survival Under the Rule of Law.* Ithaca, NY: Firebrand Books, 1992. Print.

Disabled Mothers and the Judicial System

15.

Disabled Mothers

Misadventures & Motherhood in the American Courts

ELLA CALLOW

INTRODUCTION

*It is 9:45 on June the 18th and I'm worried you can't hear me;
my disability has taken away my voice...*

So begins my first voicemail of the day. It's Jaycee, a mother with multiple
sclerosis. Her rich purring drawl is a whisper today. She is right. It is hard
to hear her. But the phrase she utters so encapsulates a sentiment disabled
mothers continually express to me that I hit the replay button once, twice,
and take the time to write it down. The voices of disabled mothers in the
American custody court system are largely silenced. Jaycee lost custody of
her ten-year-old son Adam two years ago. Her disability was used against
her during the case. She calls all the time, looking for some way to change
the outcome and break the silence.

    The National Institute for Disability Research and Rehabilitation fun-
ds me to provide technical assistance—legal information and advocacy—to
disabled mothers and fathers nationally. I direct the legal program of The
National Center for Parents with Disabilities and their Families at Through
the Looking Glass in Berkeley, California, a clinical and research agency that

has worked with disabled parents and children for thirty years. The parents who contact me stand to lose or have already lost custody of their children and roughly half of these parents are involved in dependency courts. If they lose their cases to the state's child welfare system, their legal relationship to their children is severed and the children are given to foster or adoptive families.

There are abusive and neglectful parents among any population, including disabled mothers. Child welfare performs an important function in protecting children from actual harm. But children suffer needlessly when disability discrimination drives child welfare interventions and terminations of parent-child relationships.

And disability discrimination is driving many of these cases. Having worked on hundreds of cases involving disabled parents it is apparent to me that despite thirty years of disability activism, society, represented by the legislature and judiciary in dependency cases, remains highly threatened by disabled motherhood. Unable to prevent it, society seeks to undo it. I recently completed a study involving disabled parents in mainly the family law and dependency systems. Below I will briefly describe the study and cohort. I will then analyze three themes that ran though the dependency cases: pathologized existence, resistance, and disenfranchised grief.

THE STUDY: THE PERSPECTIVES AND DEMOGRAPHICS OF PARENTS WITH DISABILITIES IN CHILD CUSTODY LITIGATION

There are an estimated 6.6 million children under age 18 in the United States, and 2.3 million disabled mothers (Kaye 1). Yet little is known of their custody court experience. During an 18-month period between 2008 and 2011, I provided technical support to 102 disabled parents involved in custody litigation in America.[1] Sixty-four of the disabled mothers agreed to participate in an exploratory study concerning disabled parents in custody litigation.[2] This involved an interviewing process that secured extensive quantitative and qualitative data on their experience and demographics.

Court Systems

Thirty-one of the mothers were involved in dependency cases. These are cases where the state is removing your child because you are found to be unfit to parent. The worst case scenario is you will have your parental rights legally terminated and be a stranger to your child by law. Thirty were involved in family court cases. Three were involved in probate court cases, which adjudicate adoptions and guardianships of children.

Education

Of the mothers, educational background was well distributed. Eight had graduate degrees, 8 had college degrees and 23 had 'some college.' Sixteen had graduated from high school or dropped out but later secured equivalent general education degrees. Seven had dropped out of high school and never secured an equivalent degree.

Race & Ethnicity

They were racially and ethnically diverse. Twelve were African American, 31 were European American, 11 were biracial, three reported other, one reported Hispanic/Latino and one reported Native American. Ten participants listed their ethnicity as Hispanic, Latino, or Spanish origin. Those reporting biracial were most often Hispanic/Latino or Native American and another race.

Marital Status & Children

Family size and style varied widely. Thirty-seven of the mothers had one child. Seventeen had two children, eight had three children, one mother had four children, one mother had more than four children. Twenty-three were divorced moms, 11 were separated but not yet divorced. Eleven were still married and 19 had never been married at all.

Disability

There was a range of disability and many had multiple disabilities. Four of the mothers were blind or visually impaired, the same number that were deaf or hard of hearing. Eight had a physical disability and 26 had a chronic health condition such as multiple sclerosis. Thirty-nine had a psychiatric disability and two had traumatic brain injury. Twelve had an intellectual disability and 17 had a learning disability. Four of them were autistic (an increasing population in our ranks as the first identified generation of autistic people has aged into adulthood).

Class

Despite this range in race, family size and style, disability and education, almost all of the disabled mothers lived at or below the poverty line. Half of the mothers had less than $15,000 a year in income, and 46 of them had less than $25,000 a year in income. Seven were between $25,000 and $75,000 and four made more than that. Six didn't know their income and one withheld the data.

DISABILITY FRAMEWORK

People identified as 'disabled' have traditionally been deemed abnormal and denied the basic right to live, denied the right to live in society, and certainly denied the right to occupy cherished social roles (Kanter 427).

Thus, disabled motherhood is a loaded proposition. Motherhood has historically been societally strictured—narrowed and regulated. "Good mothers are situated in traditional medical and professional discourse as heterosexual, married, able-bodied, Caucasian, middle-class, stay-at-home caregivers...this both is punitive to women and serves gendered, classed, ableist, and racialized normative orders" (Malacrida 368). It is a defiling of motherhood for disabled women to occupy this role, the role "that has dominated all cultural concepts of women—eclipsing even of beauty, softness and ever-present sexuality...." (Asch and Fine 248). Disabled mothers threaten the hegemony of normalcy.

Society responds to this perceived threat through the mechanisms of law and policy. From a Foucauldian perspective, disability ultimately has become a category of social policy and the definition of disability applied to people is really subjection–a labeling of who will be subjected to the social policy (Davis 30, 31). Law both expresses and drives social policy. In the words of disability studies scholar Arlene Kanter, "...to the extent that law is generally viewed as a system of rules that shape politics, power, and society, it becomes the vehicle with which the status quo and existing power relationships are maintained" (Kanter, 445).

During most of the 20th century American disability policy *preemptively* struck at disabled motherhood. Widespread sterilization and institutionalization prevented disabled women from becoming mothers (Silver 864). This policy was justified as being in the best interest of society (Lombardo 1, 3). When Eugenics fell from favor, society still censured and condemned disabled motherhood.

The courts currently remove children of disabled mothers at shockingly high rates—40-80% in some disability communities (Lightfoot & LaLiberte 2). In dependency cases, the law separates children from parents identified as legally "unfit" (Callow, Buckland and Jones 11). Disability is variously equated to unfitness by law in 37 American states and is, therefore, justified as being in the best interest of the child (Callow, Buckland and Jones 11). Both the preemptive and reactive strategies represent a pattern of structural violence (United Nations 8) aimed at creating a legal fiction that no disabled woman was, in fact, ever a mother at all.

EXISTENCE

Disabled mothers affront society simply by moving, sounding, appearing, thinking, acting and/or interacting differently. In the study, 61.29% of disabled mothers in dependency cases were accused of being unable to care for the child due to their own disability. Yet, there is often no evidence of a nexus between the disability and well-being of the child. While theoretically the power of the state may only be leveled against disabled mothers where there exists a nexus between the disability and harm to the child, this requirement is malleable at best. Furthermore, many disabled mothers in my study were reported to child welfare solely for existing: they frequently lose custody of their child at birth based only on their medical diagnosis and speculation that they cannot adequately parent (National Council on Disability).

Sara[3] has cerebral palsy and an intellectual disability. Someone reported her while she was pregnant. Child welfare required her to prove she could parent while still pregnant by parenting a Reality Baby: a computerized doll with an internal monitor that tracks caretaking tasks performed for the doll. Sara failed the test and they removed her daughter Naomi at birth:

> [*Sara*][4] 2 hours after she was born cps and the cops show up. They said that they had to put Naomi in foster care. She couldn't even be in my room at the hospital; they made her go to the hospital nursery…Lawyer told me I had two choices give her up with Conditions…or no Conditions. Conditions are I only get to see my Daughter Naomi once a year for 2 hours only…I can only write her cards only on Christmas and her Birthday but gotta sign it Sara and not mom. Which is wrong…She is excited when she is with me. And it breaks my

heart every day when I think about her. How is a two year old going to remember me as her Real Mothe…She is my life and I miss her so much and I just would like her home and today was the last visit. And it broke my heart.

I am currently working to help Sara challenge the relinquishment agreement in which she signed away her parenting rights for the chance at two hours a year with Naomi.

Child welfare workers often remove children at birth after a call from 'concerned' hospital staff. Most hospital staff is provided no special training regarding disabled mothers and often see maternal disability as endangering the child. Alexis has post-traumatic stress syndrome. When I interviewed her, she was articulate in describing her experience at the hospital and analyzing the motivations of those who facilitated the removal of her daughter Leila:

> [*Alexis*] When the social workers came to the hospital I ask—
> 'what specifically are you concerned about?' The social worker
> says 'you have a medical record showing mental health prob-
> lems.' I ask, 'what acts do you think I can't do?' 'Not getting
> up early enough in the morning.…' They go overboard. They
> don't realize it is drastic. Maybe they don't realize that taking
> away the child is traumatic. They just don't have the empathy.
> [It's] not until the appellate court level that law is dealt with.
> At trial court they do their own thing; they are not conserva-
> tive about the law. They come with the idea that the parent
> can be treated differently.

Alexis won a case overturning the termination of her parenting rights to Leila. The higher court ordered the matter back to the trial court with instructions. The lower court balked. Alexis is returning to the higher court for remedy. She has been fighting for Leila for five years.

A speculation-based removal can act as substantive support for later removals. Pamela and Leroy, a husband and wife with intellectual disabilities, never presented with abuse or neglect, addiction, criminal behavior/history, substandard housing or any other risk factor. Their first child was taken based solely on parental IQ and correlated "functioning level." This removal bolstered the next two state removals of their children. This is disturbing as IQ has been widely disproven as a predictor of parental capacity (Llewellyn, Traustadottir, McConnell & Sigurjonsdottir 246).

[Dependency Petition Text] The Department received a referral from a public health nurse that the mother was pregnant with her first child and that both parents have significant developmental delays... the mother has cerebral palsy and mental retardation... and functions at the level of an eight to eleven year old and the father has the functional level of a twelve to fifteen year old. The paternal grandmother stated to this social worker that she does not see any risk to the parents having the newborn in their care. She also stated that she herself received special education in high school. This social worker is concerned that she does not understand the risks to the newborn...

Pamela and Leroy are now divorced. They have no children.

Mother-blame

Feminist scholars have endeavored to deconstruct the mother-blame that holds mothers responsible for all child outcomes. But as discussed by researcher Linda Blum "... the concept has 'extraordinary elasticity,' with 'bad mothers' blamed for everything from the Communist menace to crime, delinquency, and schizophrenia" (Ladd-Taylor & Umansky 18). And "while all mothers are potentially unfit, mothers raising children with disabilities pose an important "deviant" case (Blum 203).

This dynamic disparately impacted disabled mothers in our study: 40.6% of those in dependency cases had disabled children. When child welfare is establishing unfitness maternal disability is often identified as the locus of both alleged current and future child harm and neglect. This is especially true where the children are delayed or disabled.

Heidi, who has an organic speech delay, was blamed both for her four-year-old son Marcos' current and potential future delays:

[Judge's Memorandum of Decision] The child had developmental speech delays because of the mother's own receptive language disability and inability to model appropriate speech for her son ... During the course of the dependency, it was determined that the mother had neurological deficits, resulting in extreme difficulty understanding spoken words, especially idioms and figurative speech. She was only able to process simple, concrete speech. Because the mother's language deficits

are organic, there is little likelihood that sufficient improvement could be made ... so that the mother could ever provide the child with age-appropriate communication once he starts school ... Mother will not be able to communicate with him or model more advanced speech for him once he is in school.

Even though Marcos was in foster care, Heidi's disability was accepted by the judge as the locus of the speech delay.

Keri and Ming are blind partners and mothers to Alexander. Keri reported that "CPS first became a part of my life six hours after the birth of my baby boy, Alexander ... I had been afraid they would get involved and take him out of my arms before he was even conceived ... afraid we would wake to CPS like so many blind adults had done before us." After the case was opened, blindness became the locus of all Alexander's alleged current and potential delays/vulnerabilities:

> [*Keri*] I was told to have a bonding screening done, as well as a developmental screening...Alexander was not developing well enough to meet their standards because he was not focusing on the testing people; we worked with him daily on the things they told us to do. We were to go in front of him and smile, and stick our tongues at him, and then since we were blind to feel his chin to see if he'd stick his tongue back at us...I got sick with fever that lasted six days. In that time my milk dried up and Alexander had to transition to formula...[a home health nurse] said I was mixing the formula wrong... he'd lost over a pound. We switched formula and he was gaining weight. [Then one of the workers] said that Alexander had been enrolled in Early Head Start...Alexander was to stay in there for five hours a day, five days a week...[he] told me that it was so that Alexander could be socialized and so that he could have other eyes and ears watching him. What if I'd missed the first time he crawled, or the first step he took? I was told in no uncertain terms to just deal with it, so I did for fear that I'd lose Alexander ...

At this point Keri was told by a CPS intern that her case was only being held open because Keri and Ming were blind. We provided Keri with strategies and resources that would hopefully address child welfare's concerns. When last we spoke Keri and Ming were still in custody of Alexander.

At a conference during the period of the study I was stopped by a woman named Judith who is bipolar. She told me her own story, which highlights how invisible disability, once exposed, can become the locus of harm. Judith and her partner are raising Judith's birth child Maribelle together. Maribelle is also bipolar. At 13 she had a very difficult year, including acting out in school and home, truancy and running away. For the first time the family had contact with child welfare. Judith reported that the social workers looked at the family constellation and assumed the lesbian couple had adopted a high needs child. They were repeatedly commended for adopting Maribelle. However, once Judith clarified that Maribelle was her birth child and that Judith herself was also bipolar, their attitudes inevitably changed:

> [*Judith*] You could see that they didn't think I was so great anymore! I know they feel like I'm irresponsible to have a child with my disability and that I gave it to her, that this is all my fault. But, you know what- she sees me and I'm a success. I'm in law school and we have a lot of friends that live with bipolar, too. And I'll tell you something, when she is having a hard time and I tell her "Honey, I know how you feel…" Man, I REALLY know how she feels!

Despite identifying the mother's disability as the locus of current and future child harm, child welfare and the courts rarely provide disabled mothers with services designed to address the concerns of the state or accommodated in light of the disability so that they are actually useful to the mother.

"Treasonable Services"

Typically, "unfit" parents cannot have their parental rights terminated unless the state shows child welfare has provided 'reasonable services' to reunite the family (Callow, Buckland and Jones 12). Disabled mothers require services accommodated to their disability. Few mothers in the study reported receiving such services despite the significant number of cases in the study wherein disability was identified as the locus of harm.

Iris has a diabetes-related physical disability and an intellectual disability. Child welfare took her son Deshawn because Iris was homeless and considered unfit due to her disabilities. They provided no services to reunify the family. Her attorney filed an Extraordinary Writiv, requesting more time and services:

[*Writ*] Petitioner was provided no services to assist her in learning to care for herself in regards to her diabetes [and she had had no medical insurance since aging out of state-sponsored care at 21]... Although it was known to the child welfare worker that petitioner suffered from depression, largely due to her inability to regain custody of her son, she was provided no referrals to psychological services. Nothing in the original reunification plan... addressed the fact that the appellant was learning disabled and developmentally delayed. The child welfare worker did not follow through on referrals to a supported living situation... The court acknowledged "that the services that mother received in this case have not been perfect... [but we] are all aware the law does not burden the agency with providing perfect or ideal services, merely the provision of treasonable services."

Whether a typographical error or a Freudian slip, the attorney's phrase "treasonable services" is an accurate description of what Iris received.

One very common service is an evaluation of parenting capacity. Evaluations shape services and outcomes in dependency cases. They are also highly problematic; often conducted using inappropriate psychological measures, administered improperly, by persons unfamiliar with disability (National Council on Disability Ch. 8).

Sylvia, mother to 2-year-old Annie, is deaf. When Annie was sick Sylvia took her to the hospital. A social worker interviewed Sylvia without an interpreter. A linguistic misunderstanding made the social worker think Sylvia was an unfit parent. Though cleared up later through an interpreter, child welfare required Sylvia to undergo psychological evaluation prior to being reunited with Annie. Sylvia was found to be psychotic with borderline psychological functioning. Sylvia then obtained a second opinion from Dr. Dessler, an ASL fluent doctor experienced with deafness/Deaf culture:

[*Dessler Evaluation Report*] She has been assessed by a Psychology Assistant who seems to have had no training or experience in assessing Deaf individuals, at least as judged by the election of the Stanford Binet as an assessment tool, which is inappropriate for these individuals. The report did not mention the presence of an interpreter and it appears none were there. Deaf individuals are "somewhat suspicious" of hearing professionals who have no experience with their community. They are right to be suspicious as work in their area requires specialized training and experience. (One pilot study in Cincinnati re-evaluated 6 hospitalized Deaf patients and found that all 6 had been misdiagnosed and placed on the wrong medication).

Dr. Dessler found Sylvia was not psychotic and was in the average range of intelligence. Nonetheless, child welfare closed their case with orders of custody to Annie's paternal grandparents even though residing with them is Annie's father who committed domestic violence against Sylvia. A private firm has taken her family law case pro bono. I've provided to them all the documentation we generated during the child welfare case to assist them if they choose to appeal or file a federal civil rights case.

Disabled mothers are typically represented by overwhelmed public defenders. Few of them appeal decisions that turn on poor services or the lack of services. Seventy percent of disabled mothers in the study were told their attorney would not appeal poor outcomes. Public defenders are also at a disadvantage as most have no special training in disability. Sadly, of the 17 study mothers who requested representation from Protection and Advocacy—the federally funded legal services specifically for disabled people in the U.S.—all were rejected.

RESISTANCE

Feminist legal theory has critiqued the oppression of women in the courts, including those in dependency court (Flynn 333, 340). For disabled mothers, there are additional barriers to accessing and meaningfully participating in their own defense (Kirshbaum and Taube 27-39). Nonetheless, the study was rife with examples of disabled mothers resisting.

Lucy has Asperger's syndrome and is the mother of a grown daughter and two tweens, Celeste and Celene (12 and 13). Both tweens are autistic. Overwhelmed trying to care for her two daughters alone, Lucy temporarily placed them with child welfare in order to get services, but her daughters' were never returned to her:

> [*Lucy*] I have not held, touched, kissed my girls in so long...I raised one daughter a adult of 28 years ALONE after my divorce just as I was raising my two younger girls...I was informed by [my attorney] she is new to juvenile court and that

scares me. I need advocacy as I am hugely being discriminated against and I am going to lose my girls forever if I don't have "real" help here. Because I am poor I am only offered what they seemed to have available even my attorney stated she didn't understand autism and aspergers. I am going to be one of these lost in the system like my kids....

Lucy photographed her daughter Celeste to document the neglect and abuse she was suffering after months in foster-care and sent the photos to me and the child welfare department. In the photos Celeste is dirty, her nails were long, jagged and filthy, her teeth were coated and clumped with a yellow substance and her gums swollen and inflamed. She had sores on her face and hands. The only result of Lucy sending the photos was that her visitation with Celeste was reduced. Lucy undertook a one-woman protest in front of the Court. She wore a placard with her story and carried pictures of her three girls. She undertook and sustained a hunger strike for a short period.

Despite connecting child welfare to proper services for Lucy, she was eventually bypassed. Bypass is a practice in several states under which disabled parents may be denied all services if they are assessed and their diagnosis is deemed by medical professionals to imply they are too intellectually or psychiatrically disabled to benefit from services.[5]

Some disabled mothers resist by reframing disability. Valencia was born with reversed extremity joints, and developing arthritis and diabetes as a young person. Valencia fondly recalled her own beloved disabled mother, for whom she helped care. Valencia and her cognitively impaired husband Luke's daughter Autumn experienced complications during birth. This resulted in Autumn's diagnosis of mild cerebral palsy, head injury and hypertonicity. Many mothers of medically fragile infants experience grief; Valencia did not. She told me that Autumn reminded her of her mother and that Valencia's own experience of disability would make her a better mother to Autumn. Valuing and caring for disabled people was part of her family culture.

Sadly, others did not share this view. Her attorney refused to request services and adaptive parenting equipment that could have created a path home for Autumn. The parents' rights were terminated.

Disabled mothers resist by contacting our agency. Kathy has an intellectual disability. Her husband Dan has Asperger's syndrome. After a year of fighting for their son Paul they contacted me. Together we filed a complaint with the Office of Civil Rights and secured an accommodated evaluation with service recommendations to facilitate Paul's safe return home. The court and child welfare fought it:

> [*Dan's Grandfather/Family Advocate*] The court has denied Kathy's request for expenses for Dr. Anderson to come to "the trial" to be a witness for Kathy; actually, Dr. Anderson was to be here to explain and answer questions about the Family Reunification program that she developed. I guess [child welfare] just did not like, or is afraid of, what she might have to say.

Dan's grandfather was barred from the courtroom, but the report was eventually accepted into evidence. I continued to work with the family, their wonderful supporters and lawyer and this summer the child welfare agency was found to have failed to provide appropriate services. Termination was not granted.

GRIEF

As we have seen, disabled mothers are constructed as other. Heart-wrenchingly, their grief is therefore not assigned the same legitimacy as non-disabled mothers who lose their children. "The grief that persons experience when they incur a loss that is not or cannot be openly acknowledged, publicly mourned or socially supported" is termed "disenfranchised grief" (Crenshaw 293). "Disenfranchised grief can apply to unrecognized... grievers" which includes "those who are mentally disabled, to the extent that society sees these people as being either incapable of grief or simply not needing to grieve" (Crenshaw 293). This creates an underclass of grievers whose needs are not addressed (Doka 13). I would suggest that not only "mentally disabled" but *all* disabled mothers are disenfranchised as grievers in dependency cases, where their underclass status is more explicit because they have been judged failed mothers. "Motherhood has traditionally been constructed as a natural way for women to be: to fail at motherhood bears a particular burden in that it also means failing as a woman (Malacrida 372).

Marisol has cerebral palsy and seizures. Her son Austin was born premature and "medically fragile." Marisol wasn't allowed to take him home because child welfare felt she could not care for a medically fragile child. To regain custody of Austin she moved to a city with supportive services:

adapted housing, transportation and personal attendants. Child welfare by law must concurrently work at reunifying parents and children and adopting the child out, creating a contest between non-disabled and disabled mothers. Child welfare eventually recommended adoption for Austin. In protest, Marisol wrote a letter to the judge. It read in part:

> [*Marisol*] For the first time my disability is my curse. The fact of the matter is that I'm involved with child welfare due to my seizures and lack of supervision and services. My seizures are no longer constant as they were while I was pregnant they are controlled thru medicine as my doctors have confirmed to this court…When [child welfare] came into my life and took my son away I went thru deep depression…I have always loved my son…It's funny, [they've] stated numerous times that I have no proper bond with my son, but yet, my son knows my voice as his mom. Your Honor, I want to appeal to this court's compassion…I will do anything it takes to keep my son he is all I have Please…I want my son back…This is not the usual case of an abused child, I never hurt my son…I want my son as any other mother wants her child.

She and Austin's relationship was terminated. She was appealing when we last spoke.

The following is from an email sent to me by Timmony. She is bipolar, lost rights to her son Wesley in dependency court and wanted to challenge the order:

> [*Timmony*] The bottom line that the judge gave me for denying me my son back was: "The state of California does not like to take children away from their parents. I am not taking him from you because you are Bipolar, but I am doing it anyways."…In the meantime I sit in classes with parents that lost their children due to ACTUAL PROVEN abuse and neglect knowing that they have a better chance of getting their kids back. It's unjust and I am so sad. I've called every attorney in the area…and was treated badly. Mostly their secretaries just said "We don't do pro bono" and hung up….

Many mothers saw the poor treatment they received, as compared to that received by abusive parents, as proof of discrimination by the judicial system as embodied by their judges. Of the disabled mothers responding to a survey question asking if a judge discriminated against them, 59.6% responded in the affirmative.

Mickey's case was especially hard because it seemed so arbitrary. Given loco parentis [in place of parent] status when she took her newborn nephew from foster care, Mickey was optimistic she would get "Moshie" (her nephew Moses) back. Moshie had lived with her for over a year when she experienced complications post-surgery, placed him with her neighbor/babysitter and went to the hospital. They found bleeding in her brain, and it was clear she would not be released that afternoon. She told the babysitter her situation and provided Moshie's location to the social worker (he was still formally a ward of the court). They removed Moshie; Mickey hadn't had permission to leave him with a third party. The neighbor/sitter was a wheelchair user.

I called the day the court ruled on whether "Moshie" would be returned. She had lost the case and was in agony, wailing and sobbing. I wrote down some of her words: *[Mickey]: Oh God, why didn't they just kill me?!! Why?!! It would be better if they'd just killed me...."* Suicidal thoughts are not uncommon after losing a child, yet, to my knowledge, there is no policy of providing counseling to this vulnerable population of mothers.

CONCLUSION

This study provides qualitative and quantitative evidence that every day in America disabled mothers exist, resist and grieve in silence, unsupported in their battle to keep their children. There are two key limitations to the study. It is a convenience sample; these are parents who chose to call us. Thus, we may be hearing from parents with clearer episodes of discrimination and parents who are higher functioning overall. However, it actually bolsters the case for how pervasive discrimination is against disabled mothers if the highest functioning and least offending parents are experiencing such pathological treatment. Also, a limitation may be that in many cases we are relying on their version of events. However, this is often supported by the primary source documents like those cited in this chapter—legal briefs, evaluation reports and written judicial decisions. Even if it were not, we must question why it is that we assume the disabled mother's narrative is less plausible than that of the state, whose narrative is that she was unfit to parent in our society.

Despite the disastrous state of affairs for disabled mothers in dependency cases, I see reason to be hopeful. In 2012 I was contacted by more attorneys requesting technical assistance in appeals of dependency cases involving disabled parents, and related federal civil rights cases, than in the prior seven years combined. In October 2012 the National Council on Disability invited our agency to contribute extensively to the first national policy report on this issue: *Rocking the Cradle: Ensuring the Rights of Parents with Disabilities and their Families.* Inspired by the experiences of mothers like Jaycee, Keri and Sara, I contributed constitutional analysis, model state and federal legislation, and developed a blueprint for a national support system of clinical and legal resources based on existing local and international models. In the last 10 years several states have worked with our agency, other agencies, or alone to amend their child welfare and family law codes and remove or refine how disability can be considered in custody cases. And more than ever I am seeing this issue integrated into discussions of human and civil rights, prompted in large part by the increasing influence of disability studies programs and the United Nations Convention on the Rights of Persons with Disabilities' Article 23: The Right to Home and Family.

Changing American social policy regarding disabled mothers will require collaboration across fields, across levels of government and between government, non-profit/advocacy organizations and academia. It will require national policy advocacy like the NCD report, and case by case advocacy, but it will also require *that the disability community acknowledge the ongoing subjection of disabled mothers by the legal system.* The community must *prioritize* the protection of its mothers and their children and ensure that disabled mothers do not exist, resist and grieve in *silence* any longer.

NOTES

[1]This figure does not include the many other parents for whom I provided technical assistance directly to the parent's attorney (because the client couldn't or wouldn't participate) or social worker, child's counsel, appellate counsel, support persons, etc.

[2]This research project is one of several national projects at Through the Looking Glass and its National Center on Parents with Disabilities, funded by the National Institute on Disability and Rehabilitation Research, U.S. Department of Education. The study of Perspectives and Demographics

of Parents with Disabilities in Child Custody Litigation spans two separate grants: H133A080034 (2009-2011) and H133A110009 (2012-2016).
[3] All names and locations have been changed to protect the anonymity of research subjects and their families.
[4] Extraordinary Writs allow a higher court to review a judge's decision or ruling before a final order is issued when a typical appeal process will not address the problem
[5] California Welfare & Institutions Code §361.5.

WORKS CITED

Asch, Adrienne, and Michelle Fine. "Nurturance, Sexuality and Women with Disabilities: The Example of Women and Literature." *The Disability Studies Reader.* Ed. Lennard Davis. New York. Rutledge, 1997. 241-256. Print.

Blum, Linda M. "Mother-Blame in the Prozac Nation: Raising Kids with Invisible Disabilities." *Gender and Society* 21.2 (2007): 202-226. Print.

Callow, Ella R. et al. "Parents with Disabilities in the United States: Prevalence, Perspectives & a Proposal for Legislative Change to Protect the Right to Family in the Disability Community." *Texas Journal on Civil Liberties and Civil Rights* 17.1 (2011): 9-41. Print.

Crenshaw, David A. "The Disenfranchised Grief of Children." *Disenfranchised Grief: New Directions, Challenges and Strategies for Practice.* Ed. Kenneth J. Doka. Champaign: Research Press, 2002. 293-306. Print.

Davis, Lennard. *Bending Over Backwards: Disability, Dismodernism and other Difficult Positions.* New York: New York University Press, 2002. Print.

Doka, Kenneth J. *Disenfranchised Grief: Recognizing Hidden Sorrow.* Landam: Lexington Books, 1989. Print.

Flynn, Colene. "In Search of Greater Procedural Justice: Rethinking Lassiter v. Department of Social Services." *Wisconsin Women's Law Journal* 11 (1996): 327-350. Print.

Foucault, Michel. *Madness and Civilization: A History of Insanity in the Age of Reason.* New York: Random House, Inc., 1965. Print.

Kanter, Arlene. "The Law: What's Disability Studies Got to do with It or an Introduction to Disability Legal Studies." *Columbia Human Rights Law Review* 42 (2011): 403-479. Print.

Kaye, H. Steven. "National Estimate of the Prevalence and Demographic Characteristics of Parents with Disabilities and their Families." Berkeley, CA: Through the Looking Glass, 2012. Print.

Kirshbaum, Megan, Daniel Taube and Rosalinda Lasian Baer. "Parents with Disabilities: Problems in Family Court Practice." *Journal of the Center for Families, Children and the Courts* 4 (2003): 27-48. Print.

Ladd-Taylor, Molly, and Lauri Umansky, eds. *"Bad" Mothers: The Politics of Blame in 20th Century America.* New York: New York University Press, 1998. Print.

Llewellyn, Gwynnyth, Rannveig Traustadottir, David McConnell and Hanna Bjorg Sigurjonsdottir. "Conclusion: Taking Stock and Looking to the Future." *Parents with Intellectual Disabilities: Past, Present and Future.* Eds. Gwynnyth Llew-ellyn, et al. West Sussex: Wiley-Blackwell, 2010. 241-262. Print.

Lombardo, Paul A. "Medicine, Eugenics and the Supreme Court: From Coercive Sterilization to Reproductive Freedom." *Contemporary Health and Policy* 13 (1996): 1-25.

Malcrida, Claudia. "Alternative Therapies and Attention Deficit Disorder: Discourses of Maternal Responsibility and Risk." *Gender and Society* 16.3 (2002): 366-385. Print.

Silver, Michael G. "Eugenics and Compulsory Sterilization Laws: Providing Redress for the Victims of a Shameful Era in United States History." *George Washington Law Review* 72 (2004): 862-890. Print.

United Nations. Human Rights Council. *Report of the Special Rapporteur on Violence Against Women, its Causes and Consequences,* 2 May. 2011. Web. 22 Oct. 2012.

United States. National Council on Disability. *Rocking the Cradle: Ensuring the Rights of Parents with Disabilities and their Children.* 27 Sep. 2012. Web. 22 Oct. 2012.

16.

Unruly Mothers or Unruly Practices? Disabled Mothers Surviving Oppressive State Practices in Australia

CAROLYN FROHMADER, HELEN MEEKOSHA AND KAREN
SOLDATIC

INTRODUCTION

Motherhood is political; being a mother gives women a particular place in communities and nations. Feminists have tried to capture its central role within the nation, where the privileging of some forms of motherhood is constructed as maternal citizenship – to delineate the ways in which the state prioritizes those feminized bodies that are relied upon to reproduce the nation (Lake 26). Others, such as Yuval-Davis (27), have critically distilled the ways in which motherhood is central to shoring up the boundaries of the nation state, where the site of motherhood symbolizes national collective belonging through the purity of blood and biology that arrives with birth.

Globally, mothers have realized the power of this unique status and have come together to form political movements, demanding justice for their missing children. The collective power of these mothers, such as Mothers of the Plaza de Mayo in Argentina who for over three decades fought to gain access to their disappeared children, reveals the ways in which 'motherhood' maintains a particular moral power within the nation. Whether this is to contest the nation state asserting their moral authority as mothers of the nation, or to reproduce the myth of mothers as the nation, motherhood is typically revered, esteemed and respected.

Yet, the place of motherhood within the nation is uneven and differentiated. Motherhood as a site of citizenship is a contested space—where a set of hierarchical feminized relations is established that grants privileges and rights to some, while removing the right to be a mother for others (Frohmader and Meekosha 289-293). Within the western media and public discourse, the role of working mothers versus 'stay-at-home' traditional mothers is an ideological battleground. While these debates are embodied with race and class, disabled mothers are not represented, given they are not even 'presentable'. Some mothers are seen as unfit to parent biologically and culturally – that is, to be biological reproducers of the nation or as responsible for the cultural reproduction of the nation (Yuval-Davis). These mothers are imbued with both biological and/or cultural meanings that are delegitimized, stigmatized and marginalized (Soldatic and Meekosha, "The Place of Disgust" 139-156). Feminists, such as Tyler (17-34), have identified the ways in which working-class mothers are particularly targeted under new moral discourses of mothering with the advent of neoliberalism.

Gillies clearly articulates the positioning of working-class mothers in neoliberal policy as abhorrent to the cultural respectability of middle-class mothers, who socially embody the feminized space of national cultural belonging. While working-class mothers are singled out by their lack of cultural status, black, ethnic minority and Indigenous mothers bear the markings of a scientific racism (Bashford, 281). There are many such instances. A clear example of this is the 'Stolen Generation' in Australia, which refers to the children who were forcibly removed from their Aboriginal mothers with the onset of the new nation in the early 1900s, a policy which remained in place until the 1970s (Human Rights and Equal Opportunity Commission). After years of campaigning, Aboriginal communities were given an official apology from Prime Minister Kevin Rudd on 13 February 2008. These mothers had a lifetime of grieving and the removal had a devastating impact on the children.

The history of disabled women who have had their children removed at birth or soon after is less well known. Lewiecki-Wilson and Cellio argue that as both disability and motherhood are liminal states, the blurring of the categories can reveal an abject othering of both identities (7). The stories of disabled mothers are yet to be told and the impact of child removal on both the mothers themselves and their children is yet to be adequately researched. The Australian nation state has long removed the children of disabled women. A current inquiry in the State of Queensland has heard that it is disabled mothers that have been particularly targeted under the state's child protection regime (Community Living Association).

This chapter seeks to set motherhood and disability in Australia within the context of the moral discourses of disabled mothers as 'unruly' and the practice of denial of motherhood as consistent with authoritarian neoliberal policies of welfare and motherhood. We will draw upon a recent case study which reveals the continuance of the historical legacy of eugenics in policing, controlling and placing under surveillance disabled women's reproduction and mothering. The right to 'found a family' and to 'reproductive freedom' is clearly articulated in a number of international human rights instruments to which Australia is a signatory. Furthermore, the UN Convention on the Rights of Persons with Disabilities (UNCRPD) in article 23 states that signatories "shall take effective and appropriate measures to eliminate discrimination against persons with disabilities in all matters relating to marriage, family, parenthood and relationships." However, for many disabled women in Australia, such fundamental human rights have yet to be realized. As we shall describe in Julie's case, around which this chapter is written, disabled women are still having their babies removed. A linked area is lack of access to reproductive technologies for disabled women, which will be discussed later in the chapter.

Most research focusing on parenting and maternity experiences of disabled women comes from North America and the United Kingdom, with limited research from the global South and across different cultures. In Australia, research conducted primarily by Llewellyn and McConnell has focused almost exclusively on parents with intellectual disabilities. Their research has focused on issues such as the over-representation of parents with intellectual disability in care and protection proceedings; the threat of child removal; parenting capacity; parent training programs; support networks; and the contextual factors that influence the success or otherwise of intervention programs (see for example Llewellyn and McConnell; Llewellyn, McConnell, and Ferronato; Llewellyn, Mayes, and McConnell;

Mayes, Llewellyn, and McConnell; Wade, Llewellyn, and Matthews). That women with mental health issues, cognitive impairments and physical and sensory impairments are also denied the right to parenthood is less well known. However, it is the experience of Women With Disabilities Australia (WWDA) that removal or threat of removal of babies/children is also an issue for women with other disabilities, and in particular for women with mental health issues.

Julie's Story[1]

*"Please help me. I just want my daughter back, no one is giving me a chance."
(Julie, a woman with mental health and mild developmental impairments.)*

Julie's mother: Given the opportunity my daughter would have made a great mother. But she was never offered the chance.

Earlier this year [2012] my daughter Julie gave birth to a healthy baby girl, Susie. Five days later, Child Services forcibly removed my grandchild. They gave us no advice of any impending removal. I arrived at the hospital to find my daughter's room blocked by two security guards. I could hear her sobbing inside. It turned out my beautiful granddaughter had already been taken.

It was more than three weeks after Susie was taken that we were told of the reasons for the removal. Child Services believed that my daughter had demonstrated poor parenting skills and was not capable of taking care of Susie. You see Julie has had mental health issues in the past and both she and her partner have mild intellectual disabilities. Amongst the allegations from Child Services were that Julie was starving her child. In fact she was having severe difficulties with breast-feeding. I was with her every day as she repeatedly pleaded for help, only to be ignored or told to 'persist with it'. Despite these allegations, Susie left the hospital at a healthy weight as confirmed by the Child Services paperwork.

Detailed support plans were put in place before Susie was born. Julie saw perinatal services, met regularly with her case worker, had arranged for daily support visits after the birth, had the support of family and has recently moved into a new home. Sadly, these support plans were then used against her to suggest she was not a capable parent. This was in spite of evidence by her psychiatrist that Julie would be a fit mother.

When everything first happened, I engaged a lawyer who felt that this was a clear case of disability discrimination and that the allegations could easily be proven as false. Despite this, they warned it could take up to a year for the case to be resolved. Four months later, my daughter and her husband are still only able to see Susie twice a week for an hour at a time. We have been in constant contact with Child Services and are doing everything right but still there has been no progress. Meetings are cancelled, calls not returned, hearings moved, previous arrangements suspended without warning or reasons given. We are told the caseworkers are 'sick', 'unavailable', 'on leave' and that no one can help us. Requests for promised documentation are ignored.

Another Child Services case officer who recently became involved recommended Julie enter a mothers and babies residential support program. If she 'behaves' then they will consider returning full custody. Despite being initially promised a place, we are now on a wait list. It could take months, even upwards of a year to get a place. While we wait, my daughter continues to miss out on all of her first times with her child that she can never get back.

Our family has no history with Child Services. I have raised my children well. They have never been in jail or had any problems with alcohol or drugs. I have written to everyone I can think of pleading for help. Most have said there is nothing they can do. Child Services is seen to have all the power.

We are being treated like criminals but have done nothing wrong. I cannot help but think of my grandmother who was part of the Stolen Generation. I have come here to WWDA to ask for help, to ask for justice for my daughter and for my grandchild. Please help us.

Julie's case highlights a number of processes that operate to deny disabled women the experience of motherhood. Gendered inequalities have a greater impact on disabled women. Seen as unfit to reproduce the nation, they remain a target for disciplinary regimes of the state. Furthermore, the state acts in a dual but contradictory role as providing support services, while at the same time enforcing control of disabled women as inappropriate and incompetent mothers (Malacrida 392). Using a political economy approach to disability, it can be argued that disabled women who are parents, or are seeking to become parents, are subject to interlinking economic and social dynamics. Poverty, un/underemployment, inaccessible housing, social isolation, and heightened vulnerability to violence and abuse all feed in to the discourses of the 'unruly disabled mother' and her 'natural' unsuitability for motherhood. Meanwhile, welfare reforms in Australia are targeting single parents for employment planning when their baby is six months old. Mothers who fail to comply will have their payments removed (Cox). Many single mothers who previously met eligibility criteria for the Disability Support Pension are now being moved to single parent payments, a lower income payment with lower entitlements. This constitutes the neoliberal government's ideological shift from supporting motherhood to punishing mothers on the margins. Moreover, at a sociocultural level all these factors are part of an ableist culture, where disabled women are still not seen as worthy citizens.

In Australia, parenting remains an attitudinal minefield for disabled women and an area in which they are likely to encounter significant prejudice and discrimination. As exemplified by Julie's case, those considering having and/or raising a child are often subjected to the skeptical beliefs of family members, health and medical practitioners, social workers and even complete strangers, regarding their ability to care for a child. Surveillance by child welfare officers can make them feel they have to work harder in order to be accepted as competent. In fear of being judged 'inadequate' as a parent (and of the consequences this might bring), they go to extraordinary lengths to present themselves and their children as managing and competent – often at significant personal cost in terms of comfort, and emotional and physical well-being.

STOLEN CHILDREN

Parents with intellectual disabilities are more likely than any other group of parents to have their children permanently removed by child welfare authorities to placements at considerable distance from the parents' home (Booth et al.; IASSID; Llewellyn and McConnell). In many cases, child re-

moval is ordered without evidence of abuse, neglect and/or parental incapacity, and occurs at the time, or within days, of a child's birth (McConnell
and Llewellyn 33-6). Reports to WWDA from mothers with intellectual
disabilities and/or their advocates suggest that this remains a current practice in Australia. The Disability Discrimination Legal Service in Australia
has identified the removal of babies and children from women with intellectual disabilities as one of the key legal issues facing such women in
Australia today (WWDA "Parenting Issues for Women with Disabilities
in Australia").

Negative stereotypes about women with intellectual disabilities clearly
still affect and influence the decision-making process in the legal system,
overriding any imperative for family preservation. As well as being over-
represented in care proceedings, termination of parenting rights is often
based on the misconception that the women's intellectual disabilities auto-
matically make them incapable of adequately raising children, and that they
lack the potential to learn. Women with intellectual disabilities who are parents are scrutinized very closely and held to higher standards than those that
are applied to non-disabled women who are parents (Aunos and Feldman;
McConnell, Llewellyn, and Ferronato). The evidence used to judge potential for parental inadequacy may be based on unfair and invalid assessment
procedures (Aunos and Feldman 285-9), which are often carried out in un-
supportive environments (Burgen 54-61).

The removal of babies/children from women with intellectual disabilities is often based on two prejudicial and invalid assumptions. Firstly, a diagnosis or label of intellectual disability *per se* is mistakenly taken for *prima
facie* evidence of parental incapacity or risk of harm to the child (IASSID).
Secondly, such incapacity is deemed to be an irremediable deficiency in the
parent such that it cannot be overcome or corrected. According to IAS-
SID, in this situation, the state 'naturally' holds little hope of improving
the child's situation, resulting in the permanent placement of the child away
from their family home. Both assumptions are incorrect and invalid (IAS-
SID; McConnell, Llewellyn and Ferronato.). Naïve, prejudicial and discriminatory attitudes and practices lead to premature termination of the
parenting rights of women with intellectual disabilities. This is contrary to
family legislation that almost universally requires that such action should
be a last resort and that the state has an obligation to make efforts to keep
families together (Aunos and Feldman 291).

DISCOURSES OF DEPENDENCY

In Julie's case we can see the embedded discourses of gender and ableism in the division between dependence and independence, between those who 'care' and those who are 'cared for'. This division has contributed to the depiction of disabled women as exclusively on the receiving end of care and support. Disabled women who are parents are stereotyped as people in need of personal assistance, and rarely as parents who provide it (McKeever et al.; Radcliffe). The dichotomy between the 'carer' and the 'cared for' is reflected in legislation, policies and programs which provide services to individuals on the basis that they are either a 'disabled person' or a 'carer'.

A number of studies on children of disabled parents conclude that they are at-risk for 'parentification': assuming adult roles before they are emotionally or developmentally ready; they are "born into caring" (Smyth, Cass, and Hill). The assumption that children of disabled parents will be parentified remains pervasive and continues to persist in research as well as legal and custody proceedings (Smyth, Cass, and Hill). Olkin suggests that there are four problems with the assumption that children of parents with disabilities are parentified: 1) it is based on prejudice; 2) it is presumptuous; 3) it ignores cultural and socio-economic differences in the expectations for children's helping behaviours; and 4) it is not supported by recent research (1-3). In fact, recent studies have found that: women with disabilities who are parents frequently take on increased responsibilities and risks rather than ask their children for assistance (Grue and Laerum; Mazur; Radcliffe); adolescents of disabled parents perform the same number of household tasks as adolescents of non-disabled parents (Olkin); some responsibilities are appropriate and perfectly reasonable (Grue and Laerum; McKeever et al.; Olsen and Clark); and the availability of resources is an important mitigating factor in the degree and type of assistance required within the family (McKeever et al.; Preston; Radcliffe).

A significant barrier for women with disabilities who are in a parenting role and require service support, is the often inflexible boundaries of elements of the service system, such as those services available to assist adults, and those available to assist children. Children's services tend to focus exclusively on assessing children's needs and welfare, including child protection issues; whereas adult services tend to focus only on the provision of personal services to disabled adults. Disabled women who are in a parenting role and require attendant/personal care have reported frustration that restrictive policies do not permit the attendant/carer to assist the disabled woman in performing child care duties.

Policy makers, service providers and the broader community have limited understandings of accessibility, believing it requires only a ramp or an accessible toilet (WWDA "More Than Just a Ramp"). In fact 'accessibility' has much wider meaning, including being able to receive all service and program information in an accessible format. Experience of Australian community support services suggests that access of this kind is very limited both in terms of appropriate content (i.e., that reflects the experiences of disabled women) and format of information available (such as Braille, audio, Easy English and the use of telephone access relay services and sign interpreters) (WWDA "More Than Just a Ramp").

Another dimension of access includes being able to understand and meaningfully participate in the services and programs available. Again, experience suggests that the women themselves generally have had limited input into the development of services and programs, including information and education resources (WWDA "Women and Children with Disabilities"). The lack of appropriate, accessible information on all aspects of childbearing and childrearing is an area where women with disabilities who are parents, or seeking to become parents, experience significant barriers (Radcliffe).

POLICY BORDERLANDS: ACCESS TO ASSISTED REPRODUCTIVE TECHNOLOGIES

As we have suggested in the previous section, disabled women also occupy the "policy borderlands" (Cassiman 289) of disability and motherhood. But as we have argued, they remain unable to cross borders into terrains, where they have no legitimacy. For disabled women, who are more likely to find themselves without a male partner, access to reproductive technologies remains an important route to motherhood. Yet, according to Petersen in Australia, some women have traditionally been denied access to assisted reproductive technology (ART) – typically single heterosexual women, lesbians, poor women, and those whose ability to rear children is questioned, particularly disabled women or women or who are older.

The predominance of white, middle-class, able-bodied women living in heterosexual couples is evident across private IVF clientele. This is, in part, due to the costs to the client associated with the procedure (Petersen 280-285). In Australia, Medicare[2] covers the treatment of IVF for medical infertility, but for women who are deemed not to be 'medically infertile' (such as single women and lesbian couples), then no Medicare rebate is available. This fact alone would prevent many disabled women (particularly those who are single or who are in a lesbian relationship) from accessing ARTs.

In Australia, the eight state and territory governments have responsibility for assisted reproduction services, rather than the federal government. Some have enacted legislation to control the procedures involved, while others have traditionally adhered to the National Health and Medical Research Council (NHMRC)[3] guidelines.

The Council's *Ethical Guidelines on the Use of Assisted Reproductive Technology in Clinical Practice and Research,* revised in 2007, effectively ignore access and eligibility issues for disabled women by failing to address them. Instead, the guidelines recommend that each assisted reproduction clinic should develop a 'protocol' around access to, and eligibility for, treatment (NHMRC 21). While some individual clinics specify that assisted reproductive treatment procedures are not denied to women on the basis of marital status or sexual orientation, none mention disability. The decision for eligibility for assisted reproductive services therefore rests with the individual clinics/fertility consultants.

> Many assisted reproductive technology medical professionals feel entitled to exercise power over the reproductive autonomy of their referred potential clients, denying some women freedom of procreative choice by electing to reinforce entrenched ideologies about the family unit and sexuality." (Petersen 282)

In 2007, the Victorian Law Reform Commission (VLRC) released its final report on ART and adoption. The VLRC had been commissioned by the Victorian Government to enquire into and report on the desirability and feasibility of changes to the *Infertility Treatment Act 1995* [Vic] and the *Adoption Act 1984* [Vic] to expand eligibility criteria in respect of all or any forms of assisted reproduction and adoption (VLRC). In relation to access to assisted reproductive technology, the VLRC decided:

> … not to include impairment or disability as one of the grounds on which discrimination in relation to access to ART should be prohibited. This is because in some cases there is a nexus between disability and risk of harm to a child (for example, some forms of severe mental illness). Such a nexus does

not exist in relation to marital status or sexual orientation. This does not mean that people with a disability or impairment should be refused treatment, but that in some cases a different approach is justified. Such an approach should involve making enquiries about any potential risk to the health and wellbeing of a prospective child. (VLRC 60)

The resulting amended legislation, renamed the Assisted Reproductive Treatment Bill 2008, omits disability from its non-discrimination clause: "… persons seeking to undergo treatment procedures must not be discriminated against on the basis of their sexual orientation, marital status, race or religion" (Part 1, 5, p.8). This omission appears to be in breach of the Victorian Government's *Charter of Human Rights and Responsibilities Act 2006*.

HIDDEN FROM HISTORY

A major obstacle in estimating the number of disabled women who are parents, as well as their demographic characteristics, is the lack of data (Blackford; Kirshbaum; Morris and Wates; Olkin; Preston). The acute lack of available gender and disability specific data in Australia—at all levels of government and for any issue—has been consistently highlighted by WWDA for more than a decade, and identified by the United Nations as an area of concern (CEDAW).

An absence of research examining the broader social and structural issues that are important for disabled women who are parents, or seeking to become parents, remains critical. The impact of poverty, poor or inadequate housing, un/underemployment, access to education, heightened vulnerability to violence and abuse, social isolation, inadequate health care, multiple forms of discrimination, poor access to services, and denial of citizenship impact on their right to motherhood. Importantly, there is a dearth of research around the experiences of all aspects of parenting from the perspective of women with disabilities themselves, and little work that addresses the positive aspects of parenting for women with disabilities. One example is from Nancy Mairs, in her now classic account of living with a degenerative disease, *Waist-High in the World,* where she explores her sense of guilt in not being a "normal" mother, but in hindsight reflects how she was nevertheless an "adequate mother" (34-6).

Data, research and information about women with disabilities who are parents, or seeking to become parents, is necessary to guide and inform policy, direct funding, and inform service development (Morris and Wates; Olkin; Preston). It also enables the monitoring of equality of opportunity and progress towards the achievement of economic, social, political and cultural rights for women with disabilities. The lack of data, research and information results in invisibility and marginalization in society, invariably leading to a critical lack of resources for women with disabilities (Kirshbaum 19).

Comprehensive research and data collection encompasses both quantitative and qualitative methodologies and in the Australian context, includes national, state/territory, regional, local and service levels. Of paramount importance is the need for all aspects of research about parenting to include disabled women. This entails the funding and empowerment of groups and organizations of women with disabilities, to undertake their own research in order to put forward their own experiences of issues, and their recommended strategies to address these issues (Calderbank; DAA; WWDA "The Role of Advocacy in Advancing the Human Rights of Women with Disabilities in Australia").

Indeed, women with disabilities have made it clear that one of the best ways to challenge oppressive practices, cultures and structures is to join with other women with disabilities – to share experiences, to gain strength from one another and to work together on issues that affect them – describing, researching and recording their issues and experiences, developing programs to address these issues, and working to influence legislative, policy, and service development (see for example Corinne Manning's history of disability and activism at Kew Cottages in Australia). This coming together promotes the development of personal identities, where women with disabilities are able to recognize the need for personal autonomy, and importantly, develop a sense of self-worth. At the broader level, it enables the formation of a collective identity, where women with disabilities are able to speak out about their experiences and take action to collectively improve their lives (Duncan and Berman-Bieler; WWDA "The Role of Advocacy in Advancing the Human Rights of Women with Disabilities in Australia").

CONCLUSION

The right to found a family and to reproductive freedom is clearly articulated in a number of international human rights treaties to which Australia is a signatory. Yet, as we have seen in Julie's case, for many women with disabilities in Australia these fundamental human rights are not achievable.

Instead, disabled women experience a range of restrictions to realizing their rights to full reproductive freedoms, particularly their right to found and raise a family. These economic, social and environmental barriers and restrictions are many, varied, and entrenched – yet remain largely ignored in Australian family-related research.

Disabled women are the subject of discriminatory attitudes and widely held prejudicial assumptions, which question their ability and, indeed, their right to experience parenthood. They battle against political and ideological agendas as well as media reports, which cast their children as 'young carers' at risk of parentification and themselves as burdens of care. This simplistic debate conveniently diverts attention away from the significant ways in which the economic, social and physical environments, together with a lack of services, amenities and resources, devalue women with disabilities who are parents, and simultaneously stigmatizes both parent and child.

Women with disabilities bear and parent their babies in spite of the fact that they remain invisible and ignored in maternity, obstetric and related health-care policies, programs and services. They face overt discrimination and inequitable access to assisted reproductive technologies. They have their babies and children removed by child welfare authorities without evidence of abuse, neglect and/or parental incapacity – indeed, simply because they are women with disabilities. They lose their children in custody disputes on the same grounds. The lack of data, research and information about women with disabilities who are parents, or seeking to become parents, contribute to their invisibility and marginalization in society.

Motherhood is thus not always granted the revered status of a national political embodiment of love, care and nurture. And despite the hard-won gains of feminist collective movements to reposition mothering, as recent scholars have argued, mothering and the reproductive sphere remains a central site of struggle. With the intensification of neoliberalism and fiscal austerity measures across the globe, mothers have been particularly targeted (Soldatic and Meekosha "Disability and Neoliberal State Formations" 282). New discourses of dependency are emerging to re-stratify the social relations of mothering (see Hemerijck as an example), where competing discourses of mothering, gender and social welfare exist in the hinter-zones of nation state and supra-state (e.g., the European Union).

Yet we must recognize that the work of advocacy groups such as Women With Disabilities Australia and the 'everyday resistance' of women like Julie and her mother, who are rewriting the experience of disabled mothers and exploding the myths that surround them, constitute both activism for social justice and a politics of belonging.

> In a just society, women with disabilities can mother because there is adequate emotional and material support to them to do so, and given the context of support and approval to reproduce, they can also choose not to bear children. In a just society mothers of children with disability can mother, and they, their children, and other needed caregivers will be adequately supported. In order to bring about such a just society, we need to start having conversations about disability and mothering. (Lewiecki-Wilson and Cellio 15)

ACKNOWLEDGEMENTS

We wish to acknowledge and thank all the women who have been involved with Women with Disabilities Australia, especially all those who have suffered discrimination and the devastating impact of having their infant or child removed from them. We would also like to thank Rebecca Eckert and Kelly Somers for their exemplary assistance in the preparation of this paper.

NOTES

[1] This case has been compiled from confidential written correspondence between Women With Disabilities Australia (WWDA) and the grandmother of a child removed from her daughter and her daughter's partner. The daughter was involved in the correspondence. Names and details have been changed for the purposes of confidentiality.

[2] Medicare is Australia's universal health-care system introduced in 1984 to provide eligible Australian residents with affordable, accessible and high-quality health care. Medicare was established based on the understanding that all Australians should contribute to the cost of health care according to their ability to pay. It is financed through progressive income tax and an income-related Medicare levy. See: www.medicare.gov.au

[3] The National Health and Medical Research Council (NHMRC) is Australia's peak body for supporting health and medical research; for developing health advice for the Australian community, health professionals and governments; and for providing advice on ethical behaviour in health care and in the conduct of health and medical research. See: www.nhmrc.gov.au

WORKS CITED

Aunos, Marjorie, and Maurice Feldman "Attitudes towards Sexuality, Sterilization and Parenting Rights of Persons with Intellectual Disabilities." *Journal of Applied Research in Intellectual Disabilities* 15 (2002): 285-96. Print.

Bashford, Alison. *Imperial Hygiene: A Critical History of Colonialism, Nationalism and Public Health.* London: Palgrave, 2004. Print.

Blackford, Karen. "Erasing Mothers with Disabilities through Canadian Family-related Policy." *Disability, Handicap & Society* 8.3 (1993): 281-94. Print.

Booth, Tim, Wendy Booth, and David McConnell. "The Prevalence and Outcomes of Care Proceedings Involving Parents with Learning Difficulties in the Family Courts." *Journal of Applied Research in Intellectual Disabilities* 18.1 (2005): 7-17. Print.

Burgen, Brenda. "Still Not Accepted: When Women with Intellectual Disabilities Choose to Become Mothers." *Women against Violence* 19 (2007): 54-61. Print.

Calderbank, Rosemary. "Abuse and Disabled People: Vulnerability or Social Indifference?" *Disability & Society* 15.3 (2000): 521-34. Print.

Cassiman, Shawn. "Mothering, Disability, and Poverty: Straddling Borders, Shifting Boundaries and Everyday Resistance." *Disability and Mothering: Liminal Spaces of Embodied Knowledge.* Eds. Cynthia Lewiecki-Wilson and Jen Cellio. Syracuse, N.Y.: Syracuse University Press, 2011. 289-301. Print.

Committee on the Elimination of All forms of Discrimination Against Women (CEDAW). *CEDAW Concluding Comments on the Australian Government's Report 'Women in Australia' (the combined Fourth and Fifth Reports on Implementing the United Nations Convention on the Elimination of All forms of Discrimination Against Women (CEDAW).* CEDAW/C/AUL/CO/5, 2006. New York: United Nations, 2006. Print.

Community Living Association. *Submission to the Queensland Child Protection Inquiry,* O'Connor Moree, 2012. Web. 1 Nov. 2012.

Cox, Eva. "This is Not Tough Love but Rampant Populism." *The Age* 5 May 2011. Web.

Disability Awareness in Action (DAA). *Disabled Women Resource Kit No. 6.* London: Disability Awareness in Action, 1997. Print.

Duncan, Barbara, and Rosangela Berman-Bieler, eds. *International Leadership Forum for Women with Disabilities: Final Report.* New York: Rehabilitation International, 1998. Print.

Frohmader, Carolyn, and Helen Meekosha. "Recognition, Respect and Rights: Women with Disabilities in a Globalised World." *Disability and Social Theory: New Developments.* Eds. Dan Goodley, Bill Hughes, and Lennard Davis. London: Palgrave, 2012. 287-307. Print.

Gillies, Val. *Marginalised Mothers: Exploring Working Class Experiences of Parenting.* London: Routledge, 2007. Print.

Grue, Lars, and Kristan Laerum. "'Doing Motherhood': Some Experiences of Mothers with Physical Disabilities." *Disability & Society* 17.6 (2002): 671-83. Print.

Hemerijck, Anton. "Retrenchment, Redistribution, Capacitating Welfare Provision, and Institutional Coherence after the Eurozone's Austerity Reflex." *Sociologica* 1 (2012): n. pag. Web. 1 Nov. 2012.

Human Rights and Equal Opportunity Commission. *Bringing Them Home: Report of the National Inquiry into the Separation of Aboriginal and Torres Strait Islander Children from Their Families.* Canberra: Commonwealth of Australia, 1997. Print.

International Association for the Scientific Study of Intellectual Disabilities (IASSID) "Parents Labelled with Intellectual Disability: Position of the IASSID Special Interest Research Group (SIRG) on Parents and Parenting with Intellectual Disabilities." *Journal of Applied Research in Intellectual Disabilities* 21 (2008): 296-307. Print.

Kirshbaum, Megan. "A Disability Culture Perspective on Early Intervention with Parents with Physical or Cognitive Disabilities and their Infants." *Infants and Young Children* 13.2 (2000): 9-20. Print.

Lake, Marilyn. "Personality, Individuality, Nationality: Feminist Conceptions of Citizenship 1902-1940." *Australian Feminist Studies* 19 (1994): 25-38. Print.

Lewiecki-Wilson, Cynthia, and Jen Cellio., eds. *Disability and Mothering: Liminal Spaces of Embodied Knowledge.* Syracuse: Syracuse University Press, 2011. Print.

Llewellyn, Gwynnyth, and David McConnell. "Mothers with Learning Difficulties and Their Support Networks." *Journal of Intellectual Dis-*

ability Research 46.1 (2002): 17-34. Print.

—. "You Have to Prove Yourself All the Time: People with Learning Disabilities as Parents." *Learning Disability: A Life Cycle Approach to Valuing People.* Eds. Gordon Grant et al. Berkshire: Open University Press, 2005. 441-67. Print.

Llewellyn, Gwynnyth, David McConnell, and Luisa Ferronato. "Prevalence and Outcomes for Parents with Disabilities and Their Children in an Australian Court Sample." *Child Abuse and Neglect* 27 (2003): 235-51. Print.

Llewellyn, Gwynnyth, Rachel Mayes, and David McConnell. "Towards Acceptance and Inclusion of People with Intellectual Disability as Parents." *Journal of Applied Research in Intellectual Disability* 21.4 (2008): 293-5. Print.

Mairs, Nancy. *Waist-High in the World: A Life among the Nondisabled.* Massachusetts: Beacon Press Books, 1996. Print.

Malacrida, Claudia. "Understanding Disabled Families: Replacing Tales of Burden with Ties of Interdependency." *The Routledge Companion to Disability Studies.* Eds. Nick Watson, Carol Thomas, and Alan Roulstone. London: Routledge, 2012. 402-13. Print.

Manning, Corinne. "From Surrender to Activism: The Transformation of Disability and Mothering at Kew Cottages, Australia." *Disability and Mothering: Liminal Spaces of Embodied Knowledge.* Eds. Cynthia Lewiecki-Wilson and Jen Cellio. Syracuse, N.Y.: Syracuse University Press, 2011. 183-202. Print.

Mayes, Rachel, Gwynnyth Llewellyn, and David McConnell. "Misconception: The Experience of Pregnancy for Women with Intellectual Disabilities." *Scandinavian Journal of Disability Research* 8.2 & 3 (2006): 120-31. Print.

—. "Active Negotiation: Mothers with Intellectual Disabilities Creating Their Social Support Networks." *Journal of Applied Research in Intellectual Disabilities* 21 (2008): 341-50. Print.

Mazur, Elizabeth. "Positive and Negative Events Experienced by Parents with Acquired Physical Disabilities and Their Adolescent Children." *Families, Systems & Health* 24.2 (2006): 160-78. Print.

McConnell, David, and Gwynnyth Llewellyn. "Parental Disability and the Threat of Child Removal." *Family Matters* 51 (1998): 33-6. Print.

McConnell, David, Gwynnyth Llewellyn, and Luisa Ferronato. *Parents with a Disability and the NSW Children's Court.* Sydney: The Family Support & Services Project, University of Sydney, 2000. Print.

—. "Context Contingent Decision-Making in Child Protection Practice." *International Journal of Social Welfare* 15 (2006): 230-9. Print.

McKeever, Patricia, et al. "It's More of a Production: Accomplishing Mothering Using a Mobility Device." *Disability & Society* 18.2 (2003): 179-97. Print.

Morris, Jenny, and Michele Wates. "Supporting Disabled Parents and Parents with Additional Support Needs." *Adults' Services Knowledge Review* 11. London: Social Care Institute for Excellence, 2006. Print.

National Health and Medical Research Council (NHMRC). *Ethical Guidelines on the Use of Assisted Reproductive Technology in Clinical Practice and Research.* Canberra: NHMRC, 2007. Print.

Olkin, Rhoda. "Are Children of Disabled Parents at Risk for Parentification?" *Parenting with a Disability* 8.2 (2000): 1-3. Print.

Olkin, Rhoda, et al. "Comparison of Parents With and Without Disabilities Raising Teens: Information from the NHIS and Two National Surveys." *Rehabilitation Psychology* 51.1 (2006): 43-9. Print.

Olsen, Richard, and Harriet Clarke. *Parenting and Disability: Disabled Parents' Experiences of Raising Children.* Bristol: Policy Press, 2003. Print.

Petersen, Madelyn. "Assisted Reproductive Technologies and Equity of Access Issues." *Journal of Medical Ethics* 31 (2005): 280-5. Print.

Preston, Paul. "Parents with Disabilities". *National Center for Parents with Disabilities: Through the Looking Glass,* 2009. Web. 20 Mar. 2009.

Radcliffe, Victoria. *Being Brave: Disabled Women and Motherhood.* Diss. The University of Leeds, 2008. Print.

Smyth, Ciara, Bettina Cass, and Trish Hill. "Children and Young people as Active Agents in Care-Giving: Agency and Constraint." *Children and Youth Services Review* 33.4 (2011): 509-14. Print.

Soldatic, Karen, and Helen Meekosha. "Disability and Neoliberal State Formations." *Routledge Handbook of Disability Studies.* Eds. Nick Watson, Carol Thomas, and Alan Roulstone. London: Routledge, 2012. 195-210. Print.

—. "The Place of Disgust: Negotiating Disability, Class and Gender in Spaces of Workfare." *Societies* 3.2 (2012): 139-56. Print.

Tyler, Imogen. "Chav Mum Chav Scum" *Feminist Media Studies* 8.1 (2008): 17-34. Print.

Victorian Government. *Charter of Human Rights and Responsibilities Act 2006. Act No. 43/2006, 2006.* Web. 15 Oct. 2012.

Victorian Law Reform Commission (VLRC). *Assisted Reproductive Technology & Adoption:* Final Report. Melbourne: Victorian Law Reform Commission, 2007. Print.

Wade, Catherine, Gwynnyth Llewellyn, and Jan Matthews. "Review of Parent Training Interventions for Parents with Intellectual Disability." *Journal of Applied Research in Intellectual Disabilities* 21.4 (2008): 351-66. Print.

Women With Disabilities Australia (WWDA) *More Than Just a Ramp – A Guide for Women's Refuges to Develop Disability Discrimination Act Action Plans.* Prepared for Women With Disabilities Australia (WWDA) by Fiona Strahan. Hobart: WWDA, 1997, revised 2007. Print.

—. "Women and Children with Disabilities". *Access & Equity Manual.* Ed. NSW Women's Refuge Movement. Sydney: NSW Women's Refuge Resource Centre, 1999. Print.

—. "Email correspondence to WWDA from members regarding parenting support for women with disabilities in Australia." Message to WWDA. 2007. E-mail.

—. *WWDA Policy Paper: The Role of Advocacy in Advancing the Human Rights of Women with Disabilities in Australia.* Hobart: WWDA, 2008. Print.

—. *Parenting Issues for Women with Disabilities in Australia.* A Policy Paper. Hobart: WWDA, 2009. Print.

Yuval-Davis, Nira. *Gender and Nation.* London: Sage, 1997. Print.

The Child's Perspective

17.

Disabled Mothers

Perspectives of Their Young Adult Children

PAUL PRESTON AND JEAN JACOB

INTRODUCTION

> Growing up, it didn't occur to me that my mother needed ex-
> tra assistance. To me, she was mommy, and she was perfect. As
> I grew older, however, I began to become more aware of her
> limitations. Visiting friends' houses and watching their moth-
> ers playing in the yard with them, chasing them and picking
> them up, made me long for a mother that could do the same.
> I could tell that she longed for this as well, and tried to keep
> any feelings I had hidden.

This quote is taken from essays written by young adults 17-21 who have disabled parents and who are part of a national study being conducted in the
United States (U.S.).[1] Although the study concerns young adults who have
a mother or a father with a disability (or both), this chapter focuses on those
who have a disabled mother. Since the study is still in progress (through
2016), data and results reported here are preliminary and only from the
project's first three years (2009-2011).

Analyses from the 2008-2009 American Community Survey estimate
that there are 6.6 million children under age 18 raised by a disabled parent in the U.S.; 2.3 million of these parents are disabled mothers (Kaye,

2012). What happens to the children of disabled mothers as they mature into adulthood? How does their upbringing impact their development, maturation and eventual matriculation into the larger society? It is common for judicial decisions in custody cases to be influenced by negative speculations about how parental disability will affect children as they mature, even in the absence of supporting evidence of problems in the present (Callow, Buckland & Jones; 2011; Kirshbaum, Taube & Baer, 2003). In her essay, a daughter of two blind parents writes: "When I was born, my parents were forced to face hushed comments such as 'How can they raise a child?' and 'No one will let them keep her.'" Conley-Jung (1996) observes that children of parents with disabilities are frequently seen as victims, with "implicit and explicit criticism of disabled parents, their values, their choices and even their right to have children at all (23)." Unfortunately, many research studies offer little evidence to contradict societal concerns over the long-term consequences of being raised by a disabled parent—leaving unsubstantiated numerous conjectures and generalizations of poor outcomes for children of disabled parents. These speculations are encouraged by investigators who hypothesize that children will grow into less-than-competent adults because their parents were unable to meet their emotional, physical or developmental needs (see Wong et al. 53; Barkmann et al. 477).

Significant methodological flaws, however, call such research findings into question: not distinguishing the types or degrees of parental disability, blurring the age distinctions of children, conflating parental disability and parental illness, over-generalizing from single case studies, and exclusive use of clinical populations (Preston, "Parents with Disabilities"; Olkin 126; Preston "Children of Disabled"; Olsen and Wates 16).

There has been no large scale study of young adult children of parents with disabilities that covers diverse parental disabilities or that gives primacy to the perspectives of these young women and men.

A NATIONAL SCHOLARSHIP PROGRAM

Beginning in 2005, each year Through the Looking Glass' National Center has facilitated awarding college scholarships to U.S. high school seniors and college students who have at least one parent with a disability.[2] This is the first national scholarship program for young adults whose parents have diverse disabilities, recognizing the overlooked and significant financial need of disabled parents and their families.[3] As part of the scholarship application process, students are asked to write an essay about the experience of having a disabled parent.

In the first three years of this program (2005-2008), Through the Looking Glass (TLG) received over 700 scholarship applications from young women and men from all 50 states who have parents with diverse disabilities and chronic medical conditions.[4] Student essays describe routine, remarkable and sometimes difficult stories of parents with disabilities and their children.

> My mother was paralyzed before I was born, so the chair has never seemed out of the ordinary for me. Ever since I can remember, my hugs and kisses came on wheels. All of my friends, however, found it either fascinating or distressing. To this day I am thrown off by my friends' reactions when they meet my mom for the first time. But no matter how strange my peers thought she was I was confident in the fact that she was the coolest mom ever. In my eyes, my mom could do so many things that others couldn't. Nobody else's mom could let them ride on her feet when they got tired, or teach them how to pop a wheelie in a wheelchair, or drive a car with only her hands. For me, these were super powers that only served as building blocks for my world of fantasy.

Essays were not universally positive, and scholarship reviewers frequently noted students' candor in expressing a range of positive and negative perspectives:

> I want to explain the truth about how having a disabled parent has affected my life and yes, it has affected my life positively, but it has also had its negative effects. My mom's disability and lack of independence has put a strain on our relationship. I get frustrated with her and the negative affect her disability has had on our family, both emotionally and financially. I am almost 19 years old, and I struggle with the feelings that my mom is more dependent on me than I am on her.

These scholarships have given voice and visibility to these young adults and their families. Many students began their essays by saying that this was the first time anyone had ever asked them what it was like to have a disabled parent. Several students mentioned not knowing anyone else who had a disabled parent and, as this student describes, feeling alone in their struggles:

> Now, at the age of seventeen, I now know that I was the true source of my own fear, low self-esteem and self isolation. Being so young and impressionable, I did not know how to ignore or worry about what other people said about me; I did not know how to stand up for myself if I was confronted as being the child of a disabled parent. I also did not know how to explain what I was going through. No one explained it to me, so I felt like I was alone when dealing with my mother's situation.

A NEW NATIONAL STUDY

Building upon this scholarship program, in 2009, TLG initiated a systematic research project exploring the experience and impact of being raised by a disabled parent with a multi-year (2009-2016) mixed methods study.[5] To complement the qualitative data from the scholarship essays they submitted as part of their scholarship application, these young women and men could voluntarily take an optional online survey that would provide extensive quantitative data on the demographics and impact of having a parent with a disability.

Our study is guided by an overall ethnographic emphasis–that is, understanding the family experiences of these adult children primarily through their words, recollections and interpretations (Miles and Huberman 172). Particularly in light of the invisibility and lack of data on this population, an ethnographic approach minimizes imposed definitions or predetermined outcomes (Newfield et al. 30).

Methods

The study utilizes concurrent quantitative and qualitative methods to investigate adult children's perspectives on the impact of parental disability. We examine individual, dyadic and family mediators as well as contextual variables to better understand the impact of parental disability (Pederson and Revenson 406).

Specifically, we analyze the impact of parental disability and the young adult child's (1) self-esteem, (2) stigma, and (3) self-perception of how positive the overall experience of having a disabled parent is. We consider whether certain intra-family factors positively or negatively affect these variables (e.g., characteristics of a parent's disability such as type of disability, age of onset, stability; whether the adult child also has a disability; and the gender of the parent and child). We also hypothesize that certain factors are more likely to predict negative experiences for these young adults: low income, little family interaction with others, negative perception of disability within the community, and the lack of family resources. Our hypotheses are derived from informal analyses of the first three years of scholarship essays, from the literature, and from TLG's more than 30 years of clinical work with disabled parents and their children. Using grounded theory (Glaser and Strauss 113), student essays provide opportunities to amplify, modify or reject these hypotheses.

Sample population

The study targets young adults ages 17-21 who are college bound or current college students who were raised by at least one parent with a significant disability – that is, whose parents have a physical, intellectual, visual, hearing, cognitive or psychiatric disability, or medical condition.

This chapter focuses on the 551 study participants who had a disabled mother (29.3% also had another disabled parent).[6] Of the 551 participants, 72.8% were female, 27.2% male. Students identified their race as: African American (21.8%); Asian American (2.5%); Pacific Islander (0.2%); American Indian (0.8%); White (68.6%); and Biracial (6.0%). Additionally, 11.4% of participants identified themselves as of Hispanic, Latino, or Spanish origin. Maternal disabilities included more than 100 different physical, intellectual, hearing, vision, and cognitive conditions that were stable, progressive or unpredictable. The mother's primary disability was assigned into one of six broad categories using the specific disability and functional limitations identified by the student: Deaf (7.8%); Blind (5.8%); Physical (13.7%); Chronic Health (45.9%); Psychiatric (11.3%); Cognitive or Intellectual (2.6%); and those who identified both Physical and Cognitive components as the primary disability (12.9%). Of these mothers, 50.1% had other disabilities in addition to their primary disability (multiple physical disabilities, multiple cognitive disabilities, or both physical and cognitive disabilities), and we are investigating how multiple disabilities impact these young adults compared to those whose mothers have only one disability.

DATA SOURCES

Cross-sectional Survey

The study included a 55-item online survey that obtained: (1) detailed demographic information; (2) parental disability history including diagnosis, age of onset, progression, functional impact of the parent's disability, and any assistive technology used; (3) the family's socialization with others with disabilities, involvement level of parent (home, work, and community activities), amount of personal care provided by the adult child, and amount/adequacy of supports and resources for the family; (4) Rosenberg's Self-Esteem Measure; and, (5) two Scales that were developed specifically for this study – one on Perceived Stigma, and one on Disclosure of the parent's disability.

Essay

Open-ended essays submitted as part of the scholarship program were examined for common themes using qualitative text analyses. Students were asked to write a 2-3 page essay that describes their experience or the impact of growing up with a parent with a disability.

RESULTS

Overall perception

The majority of participants rated their overall experience of having a disabled mother as follows: 59.7% positive to very positive; 33.4% mixed; and 5.8% negative to very negative. The overall positivity of their experiences was also reflected by the fact that while a majority of participants only endorsed 2 of 9 possible challenges associated with having a disabled parent, they endorsed 6 of 9 advantages. Additional findings from the survey are incorporated into discussion below of the themes that emerged from the qualitative analyses of the essays.

Self-Esteem

Students' mean Self-Esteem score was 33.81 (SD= 5.11), reflecting high esteem. This compares with a mean of 32.21 in a U.S. college student and community sample (Schmitt and Allik 631) and 32.1 in a sample of Princeton undergraduates (Kwan, Kuang, and Hui 185).

Narratives

Text analysis of the essays is ongoing, but analyses thus far provide several avenues of insight and exploration. Five principal themes have been identified, reflecting both challenges and strengths of being raised by a disabled mother. Triangulating the qualitative and quantitative data, we are exploring intra- and inter-family variables (family constellation, parental disability and contextual information) for interpreting themes.

THEME 1: STIGMA AND ATTITUDES TOWARDS DIFFERENCE.

As with many other minority groups, disabled mothers may overtly be stigmatized, discriminated against and socially excluded as this one young adult child describes:

> My mother has told me numerous stories of the cruelty and rejection she felt from children and adults alike when she was young. She was so ostracized by her handicap that even the parents of other children her age would not let their children speak to her or be near her.

Their children, too, may share in what Goffman (30) calls "courtesy stigma" – the tendency for stigma to spread from the stigmatized individual to family and friends as this student describes:

> Disability of any nature comes with its own sense of seriousness, challenges and stigmas. However, my mother's disability comes with its own unique set of problems. It is not a disability that I can openly share with others, or talk about with friends and family. Ignorance breeds stigmas. Unfortunately, the stigma associated with HIV often limits children of positive parents, in various opportunities to openly receive the support and fellowship they need. Clearly this has been the case for me. At times I felt I needed, and wanted to share my thoughts and fears with someone outside of my family. However, due to the stigma and prejudices that often come with living as or with a HIV positive person in a rural southern community, I was unable to do so.

From survey data, students' mean perceived stigma was low (27.22, SD=8.08). This compares with the mean stigma found by Gershon et al.

(6) (34.21) among her sample of adolescents with lesbian mothers. The degree of stigma was higher for certain groups of students: those students who also had a disability; those students who reported their families spent no time with others with disabilities compared with those who spent very little or occasional time; and, those students who reported their families were viewed negatively within their communities compared with those viewed more positively.

Most of these adult children consistently distinguished between their internal family norms and functioning (which often considered the parent's disability as normal) and persistent stigma and social exclusion directed at the family from outsiders. These young adults frequently describe a similar pattern of how their sense of difference and stigma evolved. As young children, they were often unaware of their mothers' difference from other mothers.

> As a child, I quickly learned that my mom wasn't normal to everybody else. Anywhere we went, people would stare at her crutches and legs. Back then I would get upset and wonder why they thought staring was a good thing, or why they had to act like she was so different. To me, she was just like everyone else, the only difference was that she had four legs to walk with, and to a little kid, four legs is definitely better than two.

As they grew older, however, the difference became more apparent and negatively perceived–leading some to be embarrassed, while others became angry and defensive:

> When I was younger, more toward my middle school days, I was embarrassed that she was in a wheelchair. I would never want my family to go to back to school night or any school event because my peers would discover her condition. I did not want people to know because of what they would think, what they would say. It was always the same routine when people found out, "Oh, I'm so sorry for you." I hate that phrase. There is nothing wrong with me so do not feel sorry for me.

As they became young adults, many of these men and women's embarrassment and sense of stigma resolved:

> When I was younger, the fact that my mother was different angered me, I just wanted my family to be like my friends'

and the ones I saw on TV. After the anger, I went through an embarrassment stage where I was embarrassed about her disease and what it did to her. I would get embarrassed about going to stores with her for fear that I would see someone I know and they would judge me for having a sick mother. I was even embarrassed by her bad handwriting because her disability prevents her from gripping the pen correctly. Once I began to better understand what was going on with my mother, I stopped being angry and began feeling guilty for my immaturity.

The impact of being different varies, and two possible outcomes are suggested: a) an enhanced valuing of family relationships along with valuing uniqueness and difference in others or b) shame or internalized stigma about the self and/or family. Stigma appears tempered by the support of family and community, but most notably by how the mother herself responded to negative perceptions by others.

THEME 2: LIFE SKILLS: INDEPENDENCE, COPING AND PROBLEM SOLVING.

Depending on the quality of family relationships and resources, children raised by a disabled mother may be more resilient and find creative solutions to problems – or they may be easily defeated and overwhelmed by difficulties. On the survey, participants reported distinct advantages of having a parent with a disability compared to their friends and peers who did not, including: independence (75.9%), better life skills (75.3%), compassion (70.1%), tolerance and respect for differences (71.0%), having a wider range of experiences (63.7%), becoming more aware of what is fair and just (59.7%), and becoming more resourceful (57.9%).

These advantages are comparably reflected in the essays. Most of these young adults described positive outcomes of being raised by disabled mothers: greater social awareness, better problem-solving skills, increased comfort with and acceptance of difference, increased adaptability, and generally having better life skills and being more worldly.

Living with my mother hasn't just been a sob story, though. It has also made me a better person. I learned a lot of things at a young age that other kids my age still haven't learned. I learned responsibility and courage. I learned how to budget money for food and necessary household items, how to cook and clean properly, and how to care for others who can't care for themselves. I am tougher, better able to deal with problems, and definitely wiser about the world around me.

Some students were aware of and challenged outsider perceptions that children of disabled parents needed to be their mother's caretaker:

I never had to handle important matters for my parents as a child. I was a normal kid, all I had to worry about was school, sports, and friends. My parents are clearly independent and I rely on them for everything.

Less than half of these young women and men (43.9%) felt they had too many responsibilities at home. Still, the specter of "parentification" (see Winton 183) looms in the background of several essays:

Growing up, I had to help give my mom a shower, change her clothes, push her around in her wheelchair, and even cook dinner for our family after my parents got divorced. Soon, it felt like I had a child of my own. It was really hard for me, because I was taking care of my mother and it was supposed to be the other way around. I did not think it was fair.

Although it is clear from their essays that some participants felt they had to take on adult responsibilities, Olkin and colleagues' 2006 U.S. national study of adolescents of disabled parents had two findings which bear on whether overall young adults are over-burdened with responsibilities: teens of disabled and non-disabled parents did the same amount of household chores, and both sets of teens thought they did more chores than their parents thought they did. Olkin ("Parentification" 2) criticizes the automatic presumption that children of disabled parents are parentified without considering the specific task and whether it is developmentally appropriate. The presumption also ignores the distinction between parentification, responsibility and interdependence. This is especially problematic considering we know little of the norms within families with disabilities, and they may have different ways of functioning compared to those without disabilities. However, rather than discount the chores or caretaking responsibilities of these young adults, by listening to how they interpret their experiences, we hear that most see positive benefits to what others may consider burdensome:

> Although my mother has a physical disability she has always tried to make my life as normal as any other kid, but I wouldn't want it any other way. My mother having a disability hasn't just taught me to do my chores around the house. It has taught me responsibility, motivation, endless determination, teamwork and given me miles and miles of heart.

THEME 3: ATTITUDES ABOUT DISABILITY.

Young adults may grow up with increased comfort or increased negativity towards disability. Most of these young adults remained protective of their parents, identifying numerous social and environmental barriers as far more problematic than their parent's disability. These perspectives echo an increasing number of disability scholars who describe the social construction of disability – that is, systemic barriers, negative attitudes and social exclusion that create disability rather than the individual's particular functional limitation (Titchkosky 6; Charlton 38).

> Growing up with a physically-handicapped mother, for me, was probably not what a person with a "normal" mother might expect. The first thing they might not understand is, despite her disability, she is a complete mother. She has always put her family first, including her two children, whom she was told by so-called experts she would never be able to have. She was also told by experts that she would never be able to go to college. Today she has two bachelor's degrees and is a thesis short of her master's. She's done community volunteer work for years. She is driven in everything she does, inspiring me to overcome any challenges that I might face - which pale in comparison to hers. She constantly shows me what we're all capable of achieving if we don't create handicaps for ourselves.

In their essays, many of these young women and men distinguished their mother's disability or medical condition from their mother as a person:

> There are many times where I wish I did not have to unload a wheelchair or drive to a doctor's appointment, but I love my

mother for who she is and all of the responsibility that comes along with that. Her disability does not define her and so I should not let it define how I feel about her.

Many students discussed broader perspectives on those with disabilities:

When I was in preschool, I never realized that my family was different. It took until middle school for me to realize that there are people in the world who have never had contact with a disabled person. Since my mother's disability was a part of my daily life, I never stopped to think that others might not know anyone with a disability.

Yet, maternal disability did have real life consequences. Second only to financial hardship, on the survey students reported biggest challenge of maternal disability was activity limitation (68.6%). Physical limitation was also described in many essays:

I would sometimes cry because I couldn't have the same mom as everyone else; a mom that could go places with their kids and do the same activities that their kids did. Instead I was forced to sit out things because of her disabilities.

Some students described how mothers compensated for not being able do as much physically, and did not feel their own activities were limited:

It would have been nice if she'd been able to be more physically active, like bike riding or hiking; but she made sure I still had options. On church ski trips she would guard the gear and snacks in the Community Room. Other times for different activities, she would bring a book while I participated with friends. She might wait in the car for some things; but she made sure I didn't miss out.

Several students described certain advantages to the physical constraints of their mother's disability: notably spending more quality time with their mothers, and even pointing out certain perks: "We received a pass at water parks and amusement parks to go to the front of the lines and not have to wait."

Many students wrote about who knew or who they told about their mother's disability. Several described intentionally hiding their mother's disability—especially during adolescence. Others actively disclosed their mother's disability—whether as a matter of pride, or seeking sympathy or support such as with our scholarships. For some, their mother's highly visible or apparent disability left little option to conceal the disability: "Everyone, just everyone, knows my mom has a disability! There's absolutely no way to hide it. Why would she? Why would I?" Some students avoided situations in which their mother's disability would become known, especially if it was obvious:

> I used to hate going anywhere with my mom. I would hate the fact that she couldn't walk and had to use a wheel chair. There were times I even begged her to "suck it up" and walk like a normal person. I was embarrassed that my mom wasn't like other people's moms and I never had friends over at my house. I didn't want them to see my mom struggle to walk around the house.

For some students, it was the mother herself who avoided visibility and disclosure:

> My mom was really embarrassed about her disabilities and didn't want people over. She didn't want me talking about any of the problems that she had either. She hated it when people looked at her funny and asked a lot of questions about her injuries.

THEME 4: FINANCIAL IMPACT OF MATERNAL DISABILITY.

Financial hardship was the most frequently identified challenge of maternal disability that students reported on the survey (71.5%). Over 20% of students (22.47%) reported annual household incomes of less than $15,000, and 55.06% had annual family incomes of less than $40,000. Text analyses of the essays reinforces this finding: financial hardship was the predominant negative impact of maternal disability in terms of the numbers of essays touching upon this topic (44%) and the cumulative of text (18%) devoted to this issue.

Students consistently offered real-life examples of financial impact of maternal disability that mirror findings from other studies (Kaye 1; Toms-Barker and Maralani 3-17), providing a more detailed and complex picture:

unemployment, loss of employment, underemployment due to the mother's disability; significant medical or equipment expenses related to the disability; loss of or inability to get insurance to cover such expenses; lack of available health care; limitations of social security disability benefits; and other family members needing to take additional jobs to cover disability-related expenses or compensate for the mother's previous income:

> As a result of the serious injury to my mom's spine, our family lost most of our income, our retirement and college savings, our health insurance, and eventually our home ... it seemed each day became more emotionally and financially insecure. I had to decline invitations to my friends' birthday parties because we did not have money to purchase food, much less gifts. To help with paying our bills, I sold our furniture from our house and I picked oranges from our trees.

Several students decided not to attend college away from home in order to keep costs down or reduced their college load so they could work in order to offset their family's financial hardship. Yet, despite limited finances, many students described putting things into perspective:

> Children often find it difficult to deal with a situation that makes them feel different from their peers. Growing up I didn't always understand why we couldn't go on major family vacations, spend money on things, and not do certain activities all the time. I remember seeing and hearing kids get to do all kinds of things like going on vacations far away and getting the new cool thing that was out at the time. I wasn't able to because my mom couldn't go out of state or go too far away because of her situation, or I also didn't always get the new cool toy or clothes at the time because we had to pay for other things such as my mom's medications or doctor bills. Growing up with these disadvantages has made me appreciate what I do have. I didn't always understand why I couldn't get these things, but it definitely made me make the most of what I did do.

THEME 5: MOTHER-CHILD RELATIONSHIP

Finally, and most significantly, adult children underscored the most pivotal issue regarding the impact of their mothers' disabilities: the quality of the relationship they had with her.

> Although my mother is disabled, I grew up with a normal life of having all the things that are needed to take care of me such as there was always food, and always a clean house and mother was always there for me no matter how bad she felt at that time. She is a very open woman, who spoke things out and made sure I understood the situation and was not frightened, she explained her medical ailments to me so I would understand and know what was going on. Mother never asked me for help, she was great and I lived a normal childhood which included family as well as friends, I have participated in sports, and if I needed assistance with school work or had any question or problem she always was there for me to lend a hand or give advice when I needed it.

A parent's disability impacts the entire family system. Some students describe how their families fragmented and dissolved into chaos as a result of their mother's disability, while others saw their families pull together as these two essays illustrate:

> From this tragic event has sprung a family who is stronger than ever. Medical bills and medication costs continue to be astronomical and uncovered by insurance. The financial and emotional toll on my family has been difficult, however it takes these life experiences to make you strong and define who you are. My mom has taught me that you can sit around and wonder why or continue through life the best you can. I feel that this experience with my mom has made me a stronger person and I truly believe that with strong determination and support you can get through anything.

> While I would love to say that Mom's accident brought my family closer together and made us stronger, in reality, it broke what was already a strained marriage and set up my two sisters

and me for a childhood of crying and fighting and scary hospital visits. My family is made up of scarred survivors, seemingly breezing through life but each with their own invisible cord ruthlessly pulling them back to the thing that ties us all together while simultaneously tearing us apart.

DISCUSSION

In their 2005 national report "Young Caregivers in the U.S." the authors call for more studies "to fill in the picture to understand which characteristics of children, their families, and their environment potentially lead to problems and which support a positive outcome" (Naiditch et al. 9). The current study is an attempt to address this gap, guided by the perceptions of these young women and men.

Within our study, comparisons between these young adults need to be considered with a healthy dose of skepticism. Although we continue to investigate consistent themes and numerous factors which may enhance or impede good outcomes, ultimately these are individual stories that cannot simply be reduced to tidy patterns or formulaic predictions. We are reminded that our overall goal is to hear from these young women and men and let them tell us their experiences and what they mean. Ironically, what many are telling us is that their lives are more ordinary than outsiders may think – and it is only when we call attention to their parents' disabilities that we somehow set them apart.

Despite wide variation in parental disability and demographic features among study participants, most talked about the normalcy of growing up with a disabled mother, and the resilience and strength of their families despite social and financial obstacles. Yet, for some, growing up with a disabled mother was frightening, unpredictable and stressful. Many stories are incredibly uplifting, while a few stories tell of young adults overwhelmed and vulnerable. In all those latter cases, significant risk factors were present in the household: substance abuse, violence, extreme poverty, and a complete lack of resources and support. Additionally, the most negative essays generally concerned those whose mothers had severe psychiatric or cognitive disabilities, those whose mothers were seriously ill, and those whose mothers' physical and emotional health were wildly unpredictable. These negative factors and types of parental disability are similarly reported in other studies to predict poor outcomes for youth who have a parent with a disability (see Ireland and Pakenham 632). Survey results also found that students who had mothers with psychiatric, cognitive/intellectual, or combined physical/cognitive disabilities reported a more negative overall experience of having a disabled mother.

Thus far, both quantitative and qualitative analyses suggest stability of the parent's disability has considerable impact on the family and on the student. Specifically, poorer outcomes resulted for those whose parent's disability was not stable – even compared to those whose parent's disability was steadily deteriorating. This finding is supported in other studies on young people whose parent has a specific disability (Korneluk and Lee 179; Pakenham et al. 113; Pederson and Revson 406), but our study documents this across disabilities. These adult children also identified similar factors which contributed to more positive life outcomes: parent's positive self-esteem, availability of extended family support and community resources, presence and support of other adults in addition to their parents, and positive perception of their family by the community.

One limitation of this study should be considered. Our sample population is skewed because it pulls for high-achieving young adults who are soliciting college scholarships. However, we believe there are advantages to using this sample at this time. Based upon many previous studies, disabled parents and their children are extremely reluctant to participate in research due to persistent social criticism, ostracism and discrimination. Considering the high rate of participation thus far among young women and men whose parents have diverse disabilities, the extensive data and findings from this study can provide an important window into the lives of the target population that has largely remained outside research parameters. Many previous studies are individual case studies, while even the larger scale studies have a sample of 30 or less and generally are limited to one type of disability. Future studies can expand upon the knowledge gained from these students to consider a broader range of young adults who have disabled parents. This group of young adults is articulate and candid, and their essays provide insightful perspectives about families of parents with disabilities.

In addition to outright discrimination and pathological assumptions, many of these young adults confirm a more insidious problem for disabled parents and their families. These families are often isolated from each other, surrounded by a society and engulfed by media representations that do not include their families. Such isolation and absence of positive role models frequently leave each such family to figure it out on their own, vulnerable to pathological speculation by outsiders who have little or no familiarity with routine and positive experiences associated with disability. The lack of visibility, available data or perspectives on adult children of disabled parents reflect a broader social problem: the lack of disability norms for families with disabled parents. Documenting the experiences of those who were raised by disabled parents is crucial in developing a more complete picture of the relationships, roles and norms within these families.

NOTES

[1] All quotes from young adults used in this article are taken from essays submitted from young adult children of parents with disabilities as part of TLG's annual Scholarship Program. All students must sign consent forms that their essays can be used in TLG publications as long as no identifying information is included. All scholarship procedures as well as the national study of young adults have been reviewed and approved by an Institutional Review Board (FWA 00012648).

[2] Annually between 2005-2011, TLG has awarded ten $1000 scholarships for high school seniors and current college students of disabled parents. Selection criteria include academic performance, community activities and service, letters of recommendation and an essay describing the experience of growing up with a disabled parent. Beginning in 2012, the number of annual awards has been increased to fifteen.

[3] Analysis of data from the 2008-2009 American Community Survey shows that median family income for parents with disabilities in the U.S. is $35,000, compared to $65,000 for parents without disabilities (Kaye, 2012). There are only a few national college scholarships devoted to students whose parents have specific types of disabilities or medical conditions, notably scholarships offered by the National Multiple Sclerosis Society, National Spinal Cord Injury Association and Children of Deaf Adults.

[4] The application states the criteria for parental disability: "These scholarships are open to anyone who has a parent with a disability or medical condition. The specific type of disability or condition includes a wide range of physical, mental, hearing, learning, vision, systemic or intellectual conditions, or combinations of these. The disability or medical condition should be more than a brief or temporary situation (i.e., not a broken leg that lasts a few weeks)."

[5] This research project is one of several national projects at Through the Looking Glass and its National Center on Parents with Disabilities, funded by the National Institute on Disability and Rehabilitation Research (NI-

DRR), U.S. Department of Education. The study of Young Adult Children of Parents with Disabilities spans two separate grants: H133A080034 (2009-2011) and H133A110009 (2012-2016).

[6]"Disabled mothers" includes biological mothers, adoptive mothers, stepmothers and grandmothers whom the student identified as their "primary parent with a disability." If the student had a second disabled parent (male or female), data was also collected on that parent. However the results reported here only concern those students who identified a disabled mother as their "primary parent with a disability."

WORKS CITED

Alexander, Craig, Karen Hwang, and Marcalee Sipski. "Mothers with Spinal Cord Injuries: Impact on Marital, Family, and Children's Adjustment." *Archives of Physical Medicine and Rehabilitation* 83 (2002): 24-30. Print.

Armsden, Guy, and Russell Lewis. "The Child's Adaptation to Parental Medical Illness: Theory and Clinical Implications." *Patient Education and Counseling* 22 (1993): 153-165. Print.

Barkmann, Claus et al. "Parental Physical Illness as a Risk for Psychosocial Maladjustment in Children and Adolescents: Epidemiological Finding from a National Survey in Germany." *Psychosomatics* 48.6 (2007): 476-481. Print.

Booth, Tim, and Wendy Booth. "Making Connections: A Narrative Study of Adult Children of Parents with Learning Difficulties." *Doing Disability Research*. Eds. Colin Barnes and Geof Mercer. Leeds: The Disability Press, 1997. 123-140. Print.

Bretherton, Inge. "The Origins of Attachment Theory: John Bowlby and Mary Ainsworth." *Developmental Psychology* 28.5 (1992): 759-775. Print.

Buck, Frances, and George Hohmann. "Personality, Behavior, Values, and Family Relations of Children of Fathers with Spinal Cord Injury." *Archives of Physical Medicine and Rehabilitation* 62 (1981): 432-438. Print.

Callow, Ella, Kelly Buckland, and Shannon Jones. "Parents with Disabilities in the United States: Prevalence, Perspectives, and a Proposal for Legislative Change to Protect the Right to Family in the Disability Community." *Texas Journal on Civil Liberties & Civil Rights* 17 (2011): 9-41. Print.

Callow, Ella, and Daniel Taube. Summaries of Legal Precedents and Law

Review Articles Concerning Parents with Disabilities. Berkeley, CA: Through the Looking Glass, 2005. Print.

Charlton, James. *Nothing About Us Without Us: Disability Oppression and Empowerment.* Berkeley, CA: University of California Press, 2000. Print.

Conley-Jung, Connie. The Early Parenting Experiences of Mothers with Visual Impairments and Blindness (NIDRR, Rehabilitation Research and Training Center Grant No. H133B30076). Diss., California School of Professional Psychology, 1996. Print.

Conley-Jung, Connie and Rhoda Olkin. "Mothers with Visual Impairments Who Are Raising Young Children." *Journal of Visual Impairment & Blindness* 96.1 (2001): 14-29. Print.

Dillman, Don, Jolene Smyth, and Leah Christian. *Internet, Mail, and Mixed-Mode Surveys: The Tailored Design Method.* New York: Wiley and Sons, 2008. Print.

Duvdevany, Ilana, Victor Moin, and Rivka Yahav. "The Social Life and Emotional State of Adolescent Children of Parents Who Are Blind and Sighted: A Pilot Study." *Journal of Visual Impairment & Blindness* 101.3 (2007): 160-171. Print.

Gershon, Tamar, Jean Tschann, and John Jemerin. "Stigmatization, Self-Esteem, and Coping among the Adolescent Children of Lesbian Mothers." *Journal of Adolescent Health* 24 (1999): 437-445. Print.

Glaser, Barney, and Anselm Strauss. *The Discovery of Grounded Theory: Strategies for Qualitative Research.* Chicago: Aldine, 1967. Print.

Goffman, Erving. *Stigma: Notes on the Management of Spoiled Identity.* Englewood Cliffs, NJ: Prentice Hall, 1963. Print.

Gullotta, Thomas et al. *Children's Health Care: Issues for the Year 2000 and Beyond.* Thousand Oaks, CA: Sage Publications, 1999. Print.

Ireland, Michael, and Kenneth Pakenham. "Youth Adjustment to Parental Illness or Disability: The Role of Illness Characteristics, Caregiving and Attachment." *Psychology, Health & Medicine* 15.6 (2010): 632-645. Print.

Kaye, H. Steven. "National Estimate of the Prevalence and Demographic Characteristics of Parents with Disabilities and their Families." Berkeley, CA: Through the Looking Glass, 2012. Print.

Kirshbaum, Megan, and Rhoda Olkin. "Parents with Physical, Systemic or Visual Disabilities." *Sexuality and Disability* 20.1 (2002): 65-80. Print.

Kirshbaum, Megan, Daniel Taube, and Linda Baer. "Parents with Disabilities: Problems in Family Court Practice." *Center for Children and the Courts Journal* 4 (2003): 27-48. Print.

Korneluk, Yolanda, and Catherine Lee. "Children's Adjustment to Parental Physical Illness." *Clinical Child and Family Psychology Review* 1.3 (1998): 179-193. Print.

Kristensen, Petter, Tor Bjerkedal, and John Brevik. "Long Term Effects of Parental Disability: A Register Based Life Course Follow-up of Norwegians Born in 1967-1976." *Norsk Epidemiologi* 14.1 (2004): 97-105. Print.

Kwan, Virginia, Lu Lu Kuang, and Natalie Hui. "Identifying the Sources of Self-Esteem: The Mixed Medley of Benevolence, Merit, and Bias." *Self and Identity* 8 (2009): 176-195. Print.

Mazur, Elizabeth. "Negative and Positive Disability-Related Events and Adjustment of Parents with Acquired Physical Disabilities and of their Adolescent Children." *Journal of Child and Family Studies* 17 (2008): 517-537. Print.

Miles, Matthew, and Michael Huberman. *Qualitative Data Analysis.* Thousand Oaks, CA: Sage, 1994. Print.

Naiditch, Linda, Carol Levine, and Gail Hunt. *Young Caregivers in the U.S.: Findings from a National Survey.* Bethesda, MD: National Alliance for Caregiving, 2005. Print.

Newfield, Neal et al. "Ethnographic Research Methods: Creating a Clinical Science of the Humanities." *Research Methods in Family Therapy.* Eds. Douglas H. Sprenkle and Sydney M. Moon. New York: Guilford, 1996. 25-63. Print.

Newman, Tony. "Parents, disability and illness: the impact on children." *Disabled Parents and Their Children: Building a Better Future—A Discussion Document.* Eds. Tony Newman and Michele Wates. Ilford, England, 2005: Barnardo Press. 2005. Print.

Olkin, Rhoda. *What Psychotherapists Should Know about Disability.* New York: Guilford Publications, 1999. Print.

Olkin, Rhoda et al. "Comparison of Parents with and Without Disabilities Raising Teens: Information from the NHIS and Two National Surveys." *Rehabilitation Psychology,* 51.1 (2006): 43-49. Print.

Olsen, Richard, and Michelle Wates. *Disabled Parents: Examining Research Assumptions.* Dartington, England: Research in Practice Press, 2003. Print.

Pakenham, Kenneth et al. "The Psychosocial Impact of Caregiving on

Young People Who Have a Parent with an Illness or Disability: Comparisons between Young Caregivers and Noncaregivers." *Rehabilitation Psychology* 51.2 (2009): 113-126. Print.

Pedersen, Sara, and Tracey Revenson. "Parental Illness, Family Functioning, and Adolescent Well-being: A family Ecology Framework to Guide Research." *Journal of Family Psychology* 19 (2005): 404-419. Print.

Preston, Paul. "Children of Disabled Parents." *Encyclopedia on Disability.* Ed. Gary L. Albrecht. Sage Publications. 2005. Print.

—. *Mother Father Deaf: Living Between Sound and Silence.* Cambridge, MA: Harvard University Press, 1994. Print.

—. "Parents with Disabilities." *International Encyclopedia of Rehabilitation*, 1. Web.

Rolland, John. *Families, Illness and Disability: An Integrative Treatment Model.* New York: Basic Books, 1994. Print.

Rosenberg, Morris. *Society and the Adolescent Self-Image.* Princeton University Press, 1965. Print.

Schmitt, David, and Juri Allik. "Simultaneous Administration of the Rosenberg Self-Esteem Scale in 53 Nations: Exploring the Universal and Culture-Specific Features of Global Self-Esteem." *Journal of Personality and Social Psychology* 89.4 (2005): 623-632. Print.

Titchkosky, Tanya. *Disability, Self, and Society.* Toronto: University of Toronto Press, 2003. Print.

Toms Barker, Linda and Vida Maralani. Challenges and Strategies of Disabled Parents: Findings from a National Survey of Parents with Disabilities. Final Report (NIDRR, Rehabilitation Research and Training Grant No. H133B30076). Oakland, CA: Berkeley Planning Associates, 1997. Print.

Winton, Chester. *Children as Caregivers: Parental and Parentified Children.* Boston: Allyn and Bacon Press, 2003. Print.

Wong, Melisa et al. "Posttraumatic Growth and Adverse Long-term Effect of Parental Cancer in Children." *Families, Systems, & Health* 27.1 (2009): 53-63. Print.

18.

Learning How to Swim

Finding Meaning in Disability from a Daughter's Perspective

GINA BLANKENSHIP

I recently moved across the country for grad school. As I was leaving, before getting into my car, a friend and mentor gave me a strong hug and told me again that I was brave. I returned the hug, saying thank you, even though I didn't feel especially brave. The move no longer felt like a big deal since I had already processed what I imagined to be the bulk of my nerves and fears a couple of weeks before. Sure it was Yale, a place that holds a certain power and mystique in the collective psyche (or maybe repulsion depending on who you are and how you think); and yes, being the first person in my family to go to college makes the experience that much more surreal and charged. However, this wasn't the first time I had moved across the country alone. I did that at age 19 after dropping out of college. I packed up my life from the Wisconsin town along the Mississippi river where I had been born and raised, and took the train west for new adventures in Oregon. A week later I found myself living in the attic of a fancy house in a quiet Northeast Portland neighborhood with a spunky woman in her 70s and her 100-year-old mother. Everything felt so magical then, full of possibility. I was free to be whoever I wanted, free from expectations, wide-eyed and open to the world and to the people in it; soon I fell in love with the neighbor boy and we ran off to work on organic farms and hitchhike across British Columbia together.

At age 21 I traveled alone to Mexico, down the coast of the Baja Peninsula on a bus, camping and staying in cheap *posadas* along the way. I spent Christmas Day sleeping alone under the stars on an isolated island of sand dunes and mangrove swamps; each day brand new and wide open, I roamed freely with nothing more on my schedule than the basics: food and a place to stay. My twenties were a mixture of these kinds of adventures: solo journeys roaming the countryside in rural Nicaragua, volunteering at a shelter in Guatemala, 10 day silent meditation retreats, and long, isolated days working in the woods as a forester in Northern Wisconsin, winters spent trekking on snowshoes across frozen lakes, surrounded by vast wild space, stillness and wolf tracks.

Yet, in spite of this habit of heading off in new directions, I think it is good that my friend reminded me that this movement toward the unknown, away from that which is familiar and comfortable, is a risk that does require a certain bravery–a willingness to be open to new experiences, to stay soft, to become vulnerable—both physically and emotionally—to my surroundings. Perhaps there is something in this desire to encounter wilderness, in the action of wandering and exploring mysterious places, new people and realities, new depths, that allows a person to find out who she is, what she is made of, as she is constantly confronted by and reacting to the unpredictable. For me, these years of exploration have taught me much about who I am and what I care about, but they have also become an act of searching for something outside of myself; a search for insight, for clues—an unending process of trying to understand and make sense of this nonsensical, broken, often painful, and somehow, simultaneously beautiful world.

My need to understand the world, to have it make sense, to have my life make sense, goes back to childhood. It goes back to being young and seeing my mother slowly losing her ability to walk due to multiple sclerosis. It comes from a realization early in life, in my developing mind, that there are no "rules" in this world, no guarantees, no formula in life that will ensure happiness, security, wholeness. It comes from trying to make sense of what happened to my mother, to my family, to see if there is a deeper meaning to the suffering we endured, to understand how things could have been different, if they could have been different in this world, in this lifetime. At the heart, I imagine all of my wandering, my searching, what I have called adventure, is really about finding out what this world is made of—to touch the soul of this collective life, to tap into the love that I suspect to be at the core of all things and to discover how deep and how far it goes, to see if it truly touches the darkest places, has the power to heal all wounds, to make things whole again, to fix what feels broken.

Through my small travels and work experiences, in conversations with strangers and friends, through the collective wisdom found in books and through the insight of other seekers, I do not yet have an answer to the biggest of questions. I am still unsettled, still seeking, still searching for a greater meaning. However, I am hopeful that the next leg of my journey will be more about looking for answers through action—about coming together with others and working to see what can be done. I think it will be much less about me—about trying to learn from the pain of my past, less about trying to make sense of my life–and more about joining myself to the web of the whole. Yet, in spite of my optimism and the sense that I am moving forward, that I am growing spiritually, intellectually and emotionally in preparation for work to come, there is also the heavy presence of fear that is difficult to ignore.

I am now 32 years old, the same age my mother was when she was diagnosed with M.S. in 1982. At that time, I was two years old, my brother was four and my parents were still together. My dad was a factory worker at the local brewery and my mother worked in various clerical and secretary positions. The way the disease affected my mom was slow and progressive. I can't remember when or how my parents told me about it or exactly how my young mind understood what was happening. Certainly there was an awareness that something serious was going on. I'm sure there was an underlying stress that I felt in the environment, that I sensed from my parents; yet aside from a rare night spent in a hotel with my family during a trip to see a doctor in Minneapolis, and a little ceramic bear bank and koala bear poster that my mom brought back for me when she traveled alone to see a specialist in D.C., the earliest memories and awareness of the situation are vague.

The vivid memories didn't come until later after my parents divorced when I was ten and my mother continued to raise my brother and me full time. I remember my mom's avid trips to the gym; her power walks in the neighborhood, her love of exercise and obsession with health. As a little girl I was mesmerized by all the neon and sequence-spattered spandex leotards she wore to lift weights, and I would often try to coordinate her outfits and convince her to wear one of my creations, which she often did. I remember she spent long hours sitting alone at the kitchen table pouring over nutrition books and looking for clues, a natural remedy to bring her body back into balance, to disrupt and reverse the terrifying and unpredictable path it was taking her down. I remember her regular trips to Minneapolis to work with various natural health doctors who were supposed to be healing her through electronic impulse patches and magnetic bracelets. I remember when she started shopping at the health food store and buying expensive jars of organic almond butter in bulk and supplements that were supposed to rebuild the myelin sheath around her nerves. I also remember when she started walking with a cane, when her limbs became heavy and disobedient, when she had to manually lift her foot onto the clutch when shifting gears in the car, when she had to stop driving, and then when she had to succumb, reluctantly, to a wheelchair. At some point the memories began to change and I became the one doing the grocery shopping, sorting the mail, writing checks to pay bills and doing the laundry for the family. In addition to the lifestyle changes that accompanied my mother's physical deterioration, my adolescence is remembered in images and sounds of violence, of screaming, of crying out in complete anguish over the state of my family life, the unbearable weight of it all, feeling completely alone and overwhelmed.

However, my own anguish during that difficult time paled in comparison to the suffering of my mother, of which I have born intimate witness to both during childhood and the subsequent years. In addition to the most visible suffering that she has had to endure while becoming like a prisoner in her own disfigured, defiant body, I believe there has also been a much deeper, more profound suffering of the soul. It is one thing to have an accident, to fall on the bathroom floor while trying to transfer yourself from your wheelchair to the toilet and while falling, to have your arm get caught in the grab rail, and to then have no way to press the lifeline button you wear around your wrist, and so there you lie, helpless. And, it is quite another thing to find yourself in a vulnerable position where you can't afford the help you need and so you take risks, risks that you know you shouldn't take, but for which you see no other option, and so you fall while trying to transfer yourself, and when your arm gets caught, and your body lands on the floor, there is no one around to find you because you live alone, isolated, alienated, hidden from the world. You scream for help to deaf walls, vacant rooms, you cry and scream out for help, you scream and cry out for 8 hours, but nobody is listening. Eventually, your cries turn to curses as you have nothing else to look at but an empty, indifferent hallway, and the helpless, half-naked, useless body you are trapped in, alone, left to fend for yourself in a world concerned only with itself, with its own security, money, power, things.

This part of society, the part that has driven us all to such an extreme form of individualism and competition for security is perhaps at the very heart of this story, the most painful and confusing lesson I have had to absorb as the daughter of a disabled mother. As a child and then an adolescent growing up, the message that became implicit to me–based on the isolation of my mother from the rest of society–was that the world, at its core, is a cruel and lonely place for those who are visibly weak and vulnerable, and that disability (like poverty) is to be hidden and dealt with privately because nobody wants to see it or think about it or have to slow down or change their lives to adjust for it.

I don't think my mom really wanted to be isolated from the rest of society; she is an extrovert by nature: curious and warm, kind and thoughtful toward others, she has a great sense of humor, she is playful and loves to converse, to ask people about their lives and to listen intently to their answers. I believe that my mother's obsessive quest to heal herself, her search for the miracle cure that began 30 years ago, has been less about denying the reality of her situation, and more about not wanting to feel like a burden on others. To me, her determination to heal her body is two-fold. It is one part trying to become "normal" in order to feel comfortable to participate fully in society again, to be welcomed as an equal and treated with dignity and value. And secondly, it is a self-protective creation: her healing regimen and the strict daily schedule she allows it to impose on her life has always provided her with a ready excuse for not participating in the outside world. To participate would require her to be completely dependent on the mercy of others; it would require feeling wanted, loved, valued enough to ceaselessly ask others for help and to trust that they would say yes, that they would want to take the time and energy to help her, to support her in achieving her goals, to be with her. In a society that is so competitive, oriented around productivity, individual success and achievement, where any kind of real and sustained mutual aid rarely extends beyond the nuclear family, I can see very clearly why my mother chose the path that she did, why she felt like she had to do everything herself. Having limited financial resources and living on the fringe of society forced her into a place of extreme vulnerability and isolation.

I am old enough now to understand that suffering is a part of life. Everyone suffers. Even without my painful childhood, I would not have been spared from the sorrow of heartbreak, from disappointment, from failure, from anxiety and sadness, from the anguish of hurting others and seeing others suffer, from self-doubt and self-hatred. Yet, my experiences growing up with a disabled mother, growing up with limited resources and limited community support bring up a key question: when is suffering inevitable and when is it unnecessary? And perhaps even more important: as a society, as individuals, do we even care? Or do we only care when it is too late, when we are the ones who are vulnerable and made to feel worthless, fallen to the bottom rung of the ladder, visibly dependent and therefore, burdensome?

And so this brings me back to the heavy presence of fear that I mentioned before. My life right now feels like a delicate balancing act. There is a part of me that strives to stay positive, to adopt the face of perpetual optimism and enthusiasm that I see in so many of my peers—especially at a school like Yale where many of the students see the world as their own personal oyster, a place full of limitless possibility and opportunity for success and achievement. And then there is another part of me that feels as if I am swimming as hard as I can to keep my head above the water; that I am still striving to figure out how to stay light and buoyant and full of hope while simultaneously having to carry the weight of so much sadness and pain and fear. It is the act of holding within multiple realities at the same time: it is being able to tap into the wide-eyed and open energy of the 19-year-old in me who took the train alone cross country filled with a sense of freedom and possibility, while simultaneously holding the pain of the 24-year-old woman in me who had to take time off college to come home and care for her mother's daily needs: to get her meals ready, to get her out of bed into her wheelchair, to wash her, to dress her, to do physical therapy with her stiff and resistant body, to brush her teeth, wipe her butt, help with wound management, meet with social workers and attorneys to talk about future care options, to hire home health care aides and trust that they were going to take good care of her, and then to return home again a couple years later to see her through an accident in the home which resulted in several months on life support in the hospital before a permanent transition into a nursing home at age 56.

I have not yet figured out how to carry gracefully both pain and hope. Mostly I find myself vacillating between the two—certainly I have periods of time where I am able to transcend the sadness and despair and enter into places of joy, optimism and peace. However, there is always a certain seriousness, a solemnity that never fully goes away. I am aware that many of my peers do not seem to have this same challenge. They seem to move with greater ease through the world, they carry less fear, less sadness, and more confidence. While many choose to volunteer with or work on behalf of the poor, few know what it feels like to live with the compound effects of things like disability, drug abuse, poverty, and violence. For them, there is always the option to escape the most depressing and gloomy parts of life and re-enter a more comfortable, nurturing and joyful existence.

Although the nursing home life leaves much to be desired, it has, in a certain way, given me the gift of my mother back. While I no longer have a family home to return to on holidays, my mother's home, a place where we can relax together in comfort and ease, I also no longer have to worry as much about her safety and question whether I should be sacrificing my own goals to care for her full time. We have been able to regain some of the former mother-daughter balance in our relationship that was harder to achieve when I had to carry so much of the weight of caretaking and household responsibility. However, the collective fear and repulsion we experience on an individual and societal level when the thought of ending up in a nursing home arises, is not without reason.

While my mother's inner beauty, grace and light still shine through, there is a heavy veneer of depression that has settled over her in the past five years at the nursing home. She still tells me specific dates to mark on the calendar—to set aside—because she has a very strong feeling that it might be a special day. What she is referring to is walking again, to leaving the prison of the institution behind, to walking out and never looking back, to getting back the life she has lost, to finally being able to have fun, to celebrate, to serve others, to participate fully in the gift of life, freely and as fully human. When I told her that I was writing a paper on the topic of mothering and disability and gave her a brief synopsis of some of the questions I was exploring, her eyes lit up when I started talking about the question of suffering—when is it inevitable, and when is it unnecessary. She said, "exactly," that aside from the suffering she has undergone due to the disease, there is a separate suffering of the soul, of being locked away in an institution that she describes as a "gossip-house," a place where all-too-frequently the caretakers are immature, selfish, overly preoccupied with their personal lives and consequently she is often degraded, treated as an object, a task to complete before getting back to what really matters: boyfriends, he-said-she-said re-enactments, clothes, things, TV dramas. She said that aside from her physical suffering; it is a sense of dignity, community, and most importantly, joy, which she has been missing.

Disability, especially the kind that hits suddenly, is perhaps one of the most revealing ways to hold up a mirror to our social fabric, to see if it is as strong and healthy as those at the top in positions of leadership and power would have us believe. To acknowledge that the fabric of society is broken would require serious changes to the exact systems that have supported and continue to support the tremendous inequality that allows some to thrive in excess comfort and luxury while the vast majority in the world are left in physical and emotional destitution.

That my mother could be suffering less and enjoying life more, and that there are some specific things that could help her and could help others like her who are vulnerable and in survival mode is certain. There could be more of a safety net—one without such big holes—that could have supported her to live safely in her home for much longer. The costs of the emergency surgeries, life support and expensive nursing home care could have been diverted into maintaining a more dignified life in the home. Even better than living in her house alone would be to find or create a more community-oriented, beautiful, alive and joy-filled home where she could continue to grow, learn and develop her abilities and talents alongside others and to feel like a valued member of the human community instead of being shut away in a depressing and stagnant institution that leaves her feeling like a burden on those around her.

I would be lying if I didn't acknowledge that I have judged my mother and wished for her to be different than how she is. However, it is not the physical disability that I have dwelt critically on, but rather what I have labeled in my own mind as a lack of strength. There is part of me that blames her, that judges her, that has needed her to model for me a fierce defiance, an angry refusal to accept the non-place that society would have her assume. Part of me still wishes that my mother would lash out in rage to those who demean her, to a society that ignores her, to scream out in fury: FUCK YOU! I HAVE RIGHTS IN THIS WORLD TOO, I WILL NOT BE IG-NORED, I WILL NOT HIDE, I WILL NOT GO AWAY QUIETLY, I AM HERE AND I HAVE VALUE. However, the reality is that my mom does not have the luxury to rise up in this kind of defiance. Hers must be a quiet and persistent strength, inwardly focused in order to preserve her limited energy for the daily battles she must endure.

My mother's presence keeps me grounded in important ways. In a world that is frantically reaching and striving to extend itself through innovation, beyond the borders of the commonplace, forcefully pushing forward toward growth, efficiency and development, my mother's sacred presence in this world serves as a potent reminder to slow down, to be still, to be present, to observe, to reflect, to cultivate humility, compassion, gratitude. To be with her is to feel a sense of clarity about what really matters; it is a clarity that comes from peeling away all of the layers we build up around us, that we complicate our lives with. Her presence, like the presence of so many others who live on the margins of society, provides the energetic counterbalance to the limitless growth and expansion that is at the core of so many of the world's problems today. When we ignore and disregard what has become the majority voice—the silent voice of those who are suffering: the poor, the sick, the oppressed–we are actually ignoring the sacred voice of life that is trying to guide and teach us, to show us how to live and how to be in the world.

Resources

Browne, Susan, Debra Connors and Nanci Stern, eds. *With the Power of Each Breath: A Disabled Women's Anthology.* Berkeley: Cleis Press, 1985. Print.

Corbett, C. J. "Sex, Disability and Motherhood: Access to Sexuality for Disabled Mothers." *Disability Studies Quarterly,* 22(4) (Fall 2002): 81-101. Print.

Corbett, Joan O'Toole. "Sex, Disability Studies, Mothering & the 'Unreal' in Children's Fiction." *Disability Studies Quarterly* 24(1) (Winter 2004)

Daugherty, Tanya. *The DisAbled Mom: A Supplemental Guide for Mothers who are Ill, Disabled, or Have a Chronic Condition* [Kindle Edition] 2005.

Delgan, Mary Jo and Nancy A. Brooks, eds. *Women & Disability: The Double Handicap.* New Brunswick: Transaction, 1985. Print.

Dreidger, Diane, ed. *Living the Edges: A Disabled Women's Reader.* Toronto: Inanna Publications, 2010. Print.

Driedger, Diane & Nucgekke Owne, eds. *Dissonant Disabilities: Women with Chronic Illness Explore Their Lives.* Toronto: The Women's Press, 2008. Print.

Dreidger, Diane, Irene Feika and Eileen Giron Batres, eds. *Across Borders: Women with Disabilities Working Together.* Charlottetown: Gynergy Books, 1996. Print.

Fiducia, B. W. and L. R. Wolfe. *Women & Girls with Disabilities: Defining the Issues.* Washington, DC: US Center for Women Policy Studies & Women and Philanthropy.

Fine, Michelle and Asch, Adrienne, eds. *Women with Disabilities: Essays in Psychology, Culture, & Politics.* Philadelphia: Temple University Press, 1985. Print.

Finger, Anne. *Bone Truth.* Minneapolis: Coffee House Press, 1994. Print.

Grimley Mason, Mary, Linda Long-Bellil, eds. *Taking Care: Lessons from Mothers with Disabilities.* Washington: University Press of America, 2012. Print.

Hall, Kim Q., ed. *Feminist Disability Studies.* Bloomington: Indiana University Press, 2011. Print.

Hanna, John and Beth Rogovsky. "Women with Disabilities: Two Handicaps Plus". Ed. Len Barton. *Overcoming Disabling Barriers: 18 Years of Disability and Society.* London: Routledge, 2006. 49-63. Print.

Hannaford, Susan. *Living Outside Inside: A Disabled Woman's Experience.* Berkeley: Canterbury, 1985. Print.

Keith, Lois, ed. *Mustn't Grumble: Writing by Disabled Women.* Toronto: The Women's Press, 1994. Print.

Kidd, Kerry. "The Mother & the Angel: Disability Studies, Mothering & the 'Unreal' in Children's Fiction." *Disabilities Studies Quarterly* 24(1) (2001). Print.

Kuttai, Heather. *Maternity Rolls: Pregnancy, Childbirth & Disability.* Halifax: Fernwood, 2010.

Lewiecki-Wilson, Cynthia & Cellio, Jen, eds. *Disability and Mothering: Liminal Spaces of Embodied Knowledge.* NY: Syracuse University Press. 2011. Print.

Llewellyn, Gwynnyth, Rannveig Traustadottir, David McConnell, Hanna Bjorg Sigurjonsdott, eds. *Parents with Intellectual Disabilities: Past, Present and Futures.* Hoboken: John Wiley & Sons, Ltd., 2010. Print or Ebook.

Lloyd, Margaret. "The Politics of Disability & Feminism: Discord or Synthesis?" *Sociology* 35(3) (2001): 715–728. Print.

Mayes, Rachel. *Becoming Mother: The Experiences of Women with Intellectual Disabilities.* Saarbrücken, Germany: VDM Verlag, 2009. Print.

Morris, Jenny. *Pride Against Prejudice: Transforming against Prejudice.* London, UK: The Women's Press, 1991. Print.

Morris, Jenny, ed. *Alone Together: Voices of Single Mothers.* London, UK: The Women's Press, 1992. Print.

Morris, Jenny, ed. *Encounters with Strangers: Feminism and Disability.* London, UK: The Women's Press, 1996. Print.

Nielsen, Kim. *A Disability History of the United States: (ReVisioning American History).* Boston: Beacon Press, 2011. Print.

Saxton, Marsha and Florence Howe, *With Wings: An Anthology of Literature by and about Women with Disabilities.* New York: The Feminist Press, 1987. Print.

Shaul, Susan, Pamela Dowling and Bernice Laden. "Like Other Women: Perspectives of Mothers with Physical Disabilities". Eds. Mary Jo Delgan and Nancy Brooks. *Women & Disability: The Double Handicap.* New Brunswick: Transaction, 1985. Print.

Thomas, Carol. "The Baby and the Bathwater: Disabled Women and Motherhood in Social Context." *Sociology of Health & Illness* 19(5) (1997): 622-643. Print.

Thomas, Carol. *Female Forms: Experiencing & Understanding Disability.* Maidenhead: Open University Press, 1999. Print.

Titchkosky, Tanya. *Disability, Self, and Society.* Toronto: University of Toronto Press, 2003. Print.

Titchkosky, Tanya. *The Question of Access: Disability, Space, Meaning.* Toronto: University of Toronto Press, 2011. Print.

Wates, Michele and Jade Rowen, *Bigger Than the Sky: Disabled Women on Parenting.* London, UK: Women's Press, 1999. Print.

JOURNALS

Disability Studies Quarterly
Sexuality & Disability

ORGANIZATIONS AND WEB RESOURCES

Disabled Women on the Web
  http://www.disabilityhistory.org/dwa/index.html
DisAbled Women's Network Canada (DAWN-RAFH)
  http://www.dawncanada.net/
Other links to issues on mothering and disabled mothers:
  http://amputeemommy.com/
  http://www.dawncanada.net/?issues=issues
  http://www.disabledparents.net/
  http://www.lookingglass.org/
International Disability Alliance: Women with Disabilities
  http://www.internationaldisabilityalliance.org/en/international-network-
  women-disabilities

RESEARCH

The Centre on Human Policy, Law and Disability
  (Link to issues on motherhood, parenting, reproductive rights)
  http://disabilitystudies.syr.edu/resources/motherhood.aspx

Author Biographies

Seema Bahl received an M.A. in Sociology from New School University and an M.I.A. from Columbia University. She co-founded the Disability Justice Collective in Seattle and will teach Sociology of Disability at Green River Community College. She is passionate about singing flamenco and lives with her husband and son.

Gina Blankenship is a graduate student at Yale University's Forestry and Environmental School where she studies social ecology. She has a B.A. from the Evergreen State College in Olympia, WA.

Dr. Kathryn Boschen holds a Ph.D. in Social Psychology from York University in Toronto, Ontario, Canada. She has been a Research and Program Evaluation Analyst with the Ontario Ministry of Community and Social Services, and was an Associate at what is now the Bloorview Research Institute within the Holland Bloorview Kids Rehab Centre. She spent 12 years as an Assistant Professor in the Department of Occupational Science and Occupational Therapy at the University of Toronto, and she is currently an Associate Professor in the Graduate Department of Rehabilitation Science. In 2001 Dr. Boschen became a Research Scientist at the Lyndhurst Spinal Cord Centre of the Toronto Rehabilitation Institute. She also assisted in the initial development of the Ontario Spinal Cord Injury Research Network across the province which was officially launched in 2012.

Ella Callow, JD, is the Legal Program Director at the National Center for Parents with Disabilities. She's worked with hundreds of disabled parent-litigants. The results of her quantitative study establishing parental disability prevalence in child welfare cases are contained in the *Texas Law Journal of Civil Rights and Civil Liberties* (Winter/2011).

Vicky D'Aoust was the pen name for Tanis Doe. Tanis Doe died in August 2004 and is missed enormously by many in her various and overlapping communities. Doe was a respected Fulbright scholar, mother, gay rights activist and Canadian who identified as having Aboriginal ancestry. Doe worked in both Canada and the United States in the Canadian and American Disability Rights Movement. She worked with the DisAbled Women's Network, Council for Canadians with Disabilities (formally known as the Coalition of Provincial Organizations of the Handicapped), University of California at Berkeley, Gallaudet University, the World Institute on Disability and Ryerson University's School of Disability Studies. Doe's work, grounded in her own lived experience, continues to be influential to disability scholarship and disability activism.

R.A.R. Edwards is an associate professor of history at the Rochester Institute of Technology, in Rochester, New York. She is the author of the book, *Words Made Flesh: Nineteenth-Century Deaf Education and the Growth of Deaf Culture* (NYU Press, 2012).

Gloria Filax, PhD, is an associate professor in the Master of Arts—Integrated Studies, Athabasca University. She teaches in the area of equality and social justice including courses on critical disability studies, gender and sexuality, and equality in context. Her research and written work includes "Queer Youth in the Province of the 'Severely Normal'" and co-editor of "How Canadians Communicate III: The Contexts of Popular Culture" in addition to book chapters and journal articles.

Carolyn Frohmader is the Executive Director of Women With Disabilities Australia (WWDA) and has held this position for more than fifteen years, working at the national and international levels to promote and protect the human rights of women and girls with disabilities. Under Carolyn's leadership, WWDA has received a number of prestigious awards for its groundbreaking work including the National Human Rights Award and a number of national and state violence prevention awards. WWDA has been invited to attend numerous international high level meetings on issues of human rights, gender and disability, playing a key strategic international role in addressing issues of violence against women and girls with disabilities. Carolyn also has an extensive background in women's health, health policy, and community development.

Katharine Hayward, PhD, is the Director of Research and Evaluation for the Tarjan Center, a University Center for Excellence in Disabilities Education, Research and Service, at the University of California, Los Angeles. She designs evaluation methods and instruments to assess the impact of various Center projects that focus on increasing disabled individuals' access to employment, postsecondary education, volunteerism, and psychiatric services. Dr. Hayward also serves as the Project Director for the Statewide Forums on Careers in the Arts for People with Disabilities, a national initiative focused on advancing the careers of disabled artists. Dr. Hayward holds degrees from the University of California, Davis in Psychology and Rhetoric & Communication, and graduate degrees from the University of California, Los Angeles in Public Health.

Jean Jacob, Ph.D. in Psychology, is Research Associate for the National Center for Parents with Disabilities at Through the Looking Glass. She has been working on several studies concerning parents with disabilities and their families including the current national study of young adult children of parents with disabilities.

Anita Kaiser completed a Master of Science degree in Rehabilitation Science through the University of Toronto with a focus on parenting with a spinal cord injury. For the past 12 years Anita has been a Peer Support Volunteer with Spinal Cord Injury Ontario (formerly Canadian Paraplegic Association Ontario) and an injury survivor presenter with Parachute's No Regrets program (formerly Smartrisk). Anita is a board member of the Canadian Spinal Research Organization and Canada International Scientific Exchange Program. Anita also worked as a research assistant with Toronto Rehab, UHN for 6 years before taking a break to start a family. She is now the proud mother of an energetic 5-year-old daughter.

Amanda Malone has a Bachelor of Social Work from King's University College at Western University and a Master of Social Work from Ryerson University. While at Ryerson, her research focused on young mothers with intellectual disabilities. Mandy's experience providing supports to persons with disabilities has included a variety of settings such as basic needs services, social programs and employment counseling. She has recently started a new professional journey as a social worker within a Hepatitis C Care team. Mandy's research and practice interests include community based programming for persons with disabilities; disability and mothering; and disability and addiction.

Helen Meekosha is an Associate Professor in the School of Social Sciences in UNSW, Sydney Australia. Her major research is situated in Critical Disability Studies and broadly covers intersectionality, gender relations, the global South, indigenous experiences of disability and the politics of care. Her work has broken new ground in setting disability in a context of neoliberalism and globalisation, in particular arguing the case for an examination of global North/South relations that affect the incidence and production of disability. She has been active in Women with Disabilities Australia (WDDA) since its inception.

Christina Minaki holds an M.A. in Education, specializing in Disability Studies, and a Masters of Information Studies. She is a published novelist, creative writing teacher, disability rights and social justice educator, public speaker, book reviewer, and former librarian. She is currently writing her second novel. She lives in Toronto.

Bahja Nassir. Originally from Ethiopia, she has resided in Canada since the year 2004, and currently is a Canadian citizen. She holds a Masters of Social Work degree (MSW) from Ryerson University that she completed in October 2011. As a disability rights advocate, she has been previously involved in two Ethno-Racial People with Disabilities Coalition of Ontario's (ERDCO) projects. She was also a research assistant on the "Successful Immigrants with Disabilities" project. This became the inspiration for her own study, undertaken for her MSW degree, which explored the motherhood experiences of racialized disabled women.

Karen Nielsen, PhD and Ann Marie Dewhurst, PhD are feminist therapists who, as part of their clinical practice, work with adolescents and women impacted by Fetal Alcohol Spectrum Disorder. Additionally they are both are active writers, researchers, and teachers. Karen and Ann Marie teach at both Athabasca University and Concordia University in Alberta. Their current research interests are inmate violence and the Good Lives Model of Offender Rehabilitation

Kristina Nielson is an associate professor of Classics at the University of Maine. She works in Disability Studies, Women's Studies, and directs the Peace and Reconciliation Studies Program. She has a biological daughter and a foster son, and lives with her animal companions in Orono, Maine.

Meredith Powell, BA and MA, has research interests in gender studies, digital media theory and design, and post-colonial theory and literature. Her Ph.D. dissertation research embraces all three areas in a study of children and digital technologies.

Paul Preston, Ph.D. Medical Anthropology, is the Co-Director of the National Center for Parents with Disabilities. He has conducted numerous studies concerning families with disabilities, including a national ethnographic study of adult children of deaf parents (Mother Father Deaf, Harvard University Press). He is the adult child of deaf parents.

Dr. Denise Reid is a professor in the Department of Occupational Science and Occupational Therapy and the Graduate Department of Rehabilitation Science, the Institute of Medical Science and the Institute of Biomaterials and Biomedical Engineering at the University of Toronto. She has taught numerous courses in the areas of Pediatrics, Neurology, Assistive Technology, and the Research Project course. She has well over 100 research and clinical publications. She is the director of the Virtual Reality and Rehabilitation Lab where she creates virtual reality programs and has used the IREX Gesture Xtreme™ software for conducting studies in rehabilitation, exploring presence and engagement with disabled children and adults. She is also the coordinator of the Annual Thelma Cardwell Lectureship and student research symposium.

Lynda R. Ross is an associate professor of women's and gender studies in the Centre for Interdisciplinary Studies at Athabasca University, where she also coordinates the Certificate in Counselling Women program. Graduating with a doctoral degree in psychology from the University of New Brunswick in 1998, her research interests include construction of theory, social construction of 'disorder,' and motherhood.

Karen Soldatic is a researcher in the School of Social Sciences, the University of New South Wales, Sydney, Australia. Karen's main area of research traverses critical issues of social categorization and practices of value-oriented identity formation, attempting to capture the structural and agential mechanisms in their ambiguity, fragility and opacity and the ways in which social actors collectively mobilise, to resist, confront and transform these processes and mechanisms. Hence, Karen's research is always concerned with social movement mobilisation, policy dynamism and transformation for a just society.

CONTRIBUTORS

Dena Taylor, M.S.W., is the author of *Red Flower: Rethinking Menstruation*; co-editor of *Women of the 14th Moon: Writings on Menopause; Sexual
Harassment: Women Speak Out; The Time of our Lives: Women Write on
Sex after 40*; and the editor of *Feminist Parenting: Struggles, Triumphs, &
Comic Interludes*. She is retired from Cabrillo College in Aptos, CA, where
she taught Women's Studies, was the coordinator of the Women's Center,
and director of Fast Track To Work, which provided support services to low-
income students. She and her daughter are currently co-writing *Tell Me the
Number before Infinity*, a memoir about growing up with cerebral palsy.

Michelle Tichy is a proud mother of a beautiful little girl. She has lived with
Type 1 (IDDM) Diabetes since she was seven years old, and has worked as
an activist for students with disabilities, especially hidden disabilities, since
she was in high school and continues this work as an adult. Michelle is an
Assistant Professor of Educational Psychology and Foundations at the University of Northern Iowa in Cedar Falls, Iowa.

Samantha Walsh is a disability scholar, activist, and has experience within
the professional service sector. She is currently a Doctoral Candidate at the
University of Toronto-OISE In the department of Humanities, Social Sciences, and Social Justice Education (HSSSJE), formerly Sociology and Equity Studies. Samantha completed a Master's degree in Critical Disability
Studies from York University. She is also the co-host of a blog "East meets
West-Sam and Jo's perspectives: A Canadian perspective on disability issues
in Canada and around the world". http://eastmeetswexx.blogspot.ca/